This collection attempts to set the study of literacy in the ancient world in the wider context of the debates among anthropologists over the impact of writing on society. Was writing a revolutionary innovation, prompting or participating in social change, or a fundamentally repressive and disciplinary technology? The book consists of a series of studies ranging over the whole of the Mediterranean world and much of northern Europe during a period of more than a millennium (*c*. 600 BC – AD 800). The areas examined include Pharaonic and Hellenistic Egypt, Persia and the Near East, Judaea, classical Greece, and the Roman and Byzantine empires. Each of the contributors investigates, in his or her particular area of expertise, the changing roles of writing in history, in particular the extent to which writing played an active role in historical change in antiquity. The book as a whole illustrates and explores the diversity of writing practices and their relations to the construction of power in ancient society, with an awareness of the competing claims of anthropological and historical disciplines.

Ancient and mediaeval historians, anthropologists and anyone interested in the power of the written word will find this book essential reading.

Literacy and power in the ancient world

Literacy and power in the ancient world

Edited by

Alan K. Bowman

*Student of Christ Church and Lecturer in Ancient History
in the University of Oxford*

and

Greg Woolf

Fellow of Brasenose College, University of Oxford

CAMBRIDGE
UNIVERSITY PRESS

Published by the Press Syndicate of the University of Cambridge
The Pitt Building, Trumpington Street, Cambridge CB2 1RP
40 West 20th Street, New York, NY 10011–4211, USA
10 Stamford Road, Oakleigh, Melbourne 3166, Australia

First published 1994
Reprinted 1995
First paperback edition 1996

Printed in Great Britain at the University Press, Cambridge

A catalogue record for this book is available from the British Library

Library of Congress cataloguing in publication data

Literacy and power in the ancient world / edited by Alan K. Bowman and
Greg Woolf.
    p.   cm.
Includes bibliographical references and index.
ISBN 0 521 43369 X (hardback)
1. Literacy – Social aspects – History.   2. History, Ancient.
I. Bowman, Alan K.   II. Woolf, Greg.
LC149.L4958   1994
302.2'244'0901 – dc20   93-5494   CIP

ISBN 0 521 43369 X hardback
ISBN 0 521 58736 0 paperback

Contents

Contents

Illustrations

1 Literacy and power in the ancient world

Alan K. Bowman and Greg Woolf

> Not every society has chosen to use literacy in the same way, but literacy is always connected with power.
>
> R. Pattison, *On Literacy. The Politics of the Word from Homer to the Age of Rock*, p. viii

Why study writing? One possible answer is that the enormous growth, over the past quarter-century, of interest in writing and literacy is simply the latest manifestation of our own society's graphocentrism, our obsession with the written word. We believe that literacy enables us to achieve our full potentials, whether as individuals or as societies, and conversely that illiteracy is a root cause of personal failure and economic and political 'backwardness'. Written documents count for more with us than does speech, whether we are dealing with business contracts or academic publications. Viewed from that perspective, the interdisciplinary maelstrom of literacy studies that has generated not only a huge bibliography but also specialist conferences and seminars, journals and even a monograph series, is the ultimate self-reflexive academic discourse. Like most intellectual tempests, it might be thought to have reached classical studies only when it is almost blown out everywhere else, hence this collection.

Perhaps. But historians have a more pressing and pragmatic need to consider the ways in which texts were produced, circulated and read out in antiquity. Our understanding of the ancient world is overwhelmingly dependent on texts. Our use of these texts, whether they are literary or documentary, depends on the assumptions we make about how they were originally produced, read and understood. Before we use an inscribed decree of the Athenian assembly we need some idea of the reasons for which it was inscribed and set up, and ideally some notion of who could consult it and whether anyone in fact did. When we come across an archive of government documents we need to know whether the record itself or the act of recording was more important in asserting the power of those who wrote over those who were written about. Law-codes and laws can only tell us about society if we know whether they were intended for everyday use, or whether some rulers issued laws in order to show that they were rulers.

1

These examples are all of documentary texts, but the same considerations apply to what are conventionally known as literary works. The differences are easy to exaggerate and several contributors to this collection set the production and circulation of 'literary' texts in similar social contexts to those discussed for documents. Roman officers and Christian leaders used letters in ways that were not dissimilar, and the life of Darius was circulated in literary form among his subjects as well as inscribed in the rock at Behistun for Ahura Mazda to read.

Writing was used in all these contexts to construct power in society. The kinds of power constructed varied widely from empires to groups united by a common set of texts, whether those texts were the Latin or Greek classics or Holy Scriptures. Exploring these relationships between power and literacy is the primary aim of all the papers in this collection. The variety of ways in which writing and power intersect is reflected in the diversity of contributors' approaches to the issue. Because this variety seems real, we do not intend in this introduction to advance some unifying thesis or synthesis, but simply to draw attention to some common themes that emerge from the papers and from the discussions they stimulated in the seminars and conference, held in Oxford in 1992, at which they were first presented.[1]

Each contributor approached the issue of literacy and power from the standpoint of her or his own field of expertise, but most drew in addition for inspiration on work on literacy produced by historians and anthropologists of other periods and places. It is thus fair, as well as useful, to begin by setting these papers in the context of wider debates about literacy and writing. Reviewing recent writing about literacy, however, one has the strong impression that it has done more to dispel fictions than to establish general insights or principles. A number of excellent introductions to the subject now exist,[2] and it would be otiose to recapitulate them here, but the dominant theme of all of them is an account of what *cannot* be held to be generally true about literacy. This negative credo can be briefly summarised. Literacy is not a single phenomenon but a highly variable package of skills in using texts: it may or may not include writing as well as reading and is generally geared only to particular genres of texts, particular registers of language and often to only some of the languages

---

[1] We would like to acknowledge our debt in this chapter to Cyprian Broodbank, Patrick Wormald and all the participants in the seminars and at the conference; also to the participants in a conference on 'Documenting Cultures' organised by Roger Bagnall and Dirk Obbink at Columbia University, New York (October, 1992).

[2] Street (1984) is the best general introduction. Thomas (1992: 1–28) discusses the same issues with particular reference to the ancient world. For similar expressions cf. Larsen (1988), Baumann (1986: 1–22), Finnegan (1988: 1–14).

used within multilingual societies. Moreover, literacy does not operate as an autonomous force in history, whether for change, progress and emancipation or for repression. Literacy does not of itself promote economic growth, rationality or social success. Literates do not necessarily behave or think differently from illiterates, and no Great Divide separates societies with writing from those without it. The invention of writing did not promote a social or intellectual revolution, and reports of the death of orality have been exaggerated.

Positively, many students of literacy have drawn the conclusion that the uses of writing need to be investigated society by society. Quite a number of very successful studies of this kind have now been carried out, both at book length and in collections of essays.[3] Focusing on the uses of documents and writing has shed new light on aspects of social life from law to historical consciousness. We have become especially aware of the extent to which ethnocentric and anachronistic assumptions have been made about the ways writing was used in the past, or is used today in other societies. A number of studies have traced the development of modern and western views of writing, from their origins in the middle ages, and connections have been noted with Protestantism, European expansion, the Enlightenment and the Industrial Revolution.[4]

But if this research has revealed much about both particular historical societies and about modern graphocentrism, it has arguably revealed less about literacy in general. Many studies conclude by noting the damage they have inflicted on generalising models of literacy, but few attempt to establish new ones. Up to a point this insistence on the primacy of carefully nuanced case study over grand theory exemplifies broader trends in the humanities and social sciences. Social anthropologists and historians alike now insist that 'our people do/did things in their own way', while social evolution and world history have become minority interests. Studies of literacy are united not by common doctrines, but by common approaches and common rejection of the most extreme propositions about literacy.[5] The original rejection of those generalisations was certainly justified. Many of the proposed correlations and consequences were empirically falsified as

---

[3] Monographs: Clanchy (1979), Graff (1979), Cressy (1980), Scribner and Cole (1981); Furet and Ozouf (1982), Stock (1983), Thomas (1989), McKitterick (1989). Collections: Goody (1968), Resnick (1983), Baumann (1986), Gledhill, Bender and Larsen (1988: chs. 11–15), Schousboe and Larsen (1989), McKitterick (1990), Humphrey (1991). Numerous journal articles have also appeared on the subject. Graff (1981) is a useful collection of readings from earlier literature.

[4] Graff (1979), Cressy (1980), Clanchy (1983), Thomas (1986) and especially Bloch (1989) and Harbsmeier (1989). Graff (1987) is a not wholly successful attempt to provide a synthesis.

[5] Most commonly rejected are the views of Lévi-Strauss (1958: 347–60), Goody and Watt (1963), Havelock (1982) and Ong (1982). The later work of both Goody (1977, 1986, 1989) and Ong (1986) modifies their earlier positions to some degree.

soon as a wider range of societies was considered, and to some extent the earliest work on literacy was naturally influenced by contemporary graphocentrism. But few continue to hold those positions, and arguably the reaction has gone too far, rejecting not just those strong views that verge on technological determinism, but also weaker versions that characterise writing as an enabling technology or as a necessary but not sufficient precondition for particular developments.[6] Gunpowder, electricity and hypodermic syringes do not have single, predictable or identical impacts on every society, but these technologies are not infinitely malleable and few societies seem to have been able to evade the implications of their invention and wide availability for very long. One does not have to believe in technological determinism, in other words, to believe that some innovations might make a difference or even that the difference made by particular innovations might not be completely unpredictable. Likewise it should be possible to write accounts, and even histories of literacy in general, in which writing neither determines all, nor is wholly determined by, external factors.

But for the moment a better tactic may be to produce studies that bridge the gap between case studies and grand theory.[7] This collection represents an attempt to find such a middle ground. Rather than trying to produce a complete account of literacy within a single society, we chose to concentrate on just one aspect of literacy over a broad geographical, historical and cultural range. Literacy and power seemed a central and important theme, but other choices would have been possible: the relationship of literacy and orality is another major issue which would reward further study,[8] as would the relationship between writing and other symbolic media, particularly when texts are combined with other symbols on epigraphy, coins and monumental architecture. The ancient world seems to us less obviously a unity than some have thought,[9] and it was partly for that reason that so many of the papers were commissioned to deal with its limits, with the confrontation of Greek and Latin literacies with those in other languages, from Iberian and Celtic to Syriac, and with other cultural traditions, from

---

[6] Recent advocates of such a re-evaluation include Larsen (1988), Finnegan (1988: 159), and McKitterick (1990: 5) but a similar formulation was proposed by Gough (1968).

[7] Finnegan (1988: 168) advocates a similar tactic.

[8] Goody (1977, 1989) deals with the issue in general. Clanchy (1979) and Thomas (1989) look at individual societies. The potential of broader studies of the relationship of spoken to written culture in the ancient world is suggested by Desbordes (1990). Bloch (1989) illustrates the diversity of relationships possible.

[9] On ancient literacy in general Harris (1989). On Greece Detienne (1988) and Thomas (1992), both including surveys of earlier bibliographies. On Rome Humphrey (1991) gathers responses to Harris's synthesis. Most of these studies restrict themselves to Greek and Latin literacy.

Judaism to the ancient literate empires of Egypt and the Near East. The range of the studies gathered together here is thus vast; nevertheless a number of common themes do emerge, even if some long-term trends and major areas of difference can be identified.

One crucial determinant of our view of the uses to which writing was put is the archaeological factors which determine the survival of evidence from antiquity. Only a tiny proportion of the total volume of texts ever written has survived: literally less than a handful of individual military pay-records, for example, from a total production of about 225 million in the first three centuries AD.[10] A century ago one would scarcely have guessed how radically the discovery of Greek papyri in Egypt would change the picture. The Vindolanda tablets described in Bowman's chapter provide another example, as do the Vesuvian cities, not just for the graffiti and electoral *programmata* painted on the walls of buildings, but also for finds like the private library of Greek philosophical texts from the Villa of the Papyri, and the Murecine tablets and the archive of Caecilius Iucundus which show the extent to which writing was used in everyday business deals and minor litigation by individuals well outside the civic élites.[11] Our knowledge of all these aspects of ancient literacy depends on a very small number of documentary archives: new evidence will alter the picture, and we do not know how many more unexploded bombs still exist.[12] Yet it perhaps remains legitimate to consider whether this is one case in which more than the usual weight should be given to the *argumentum e silentio* and there is perhaps something to be gained by comparing this issue to the debate over the degree to which the rural world was monetised.[13]

Ancient documents came in a wide variety of formats, genres and languages. Among the texts discussed by contributors to this volume are books, pamphlets, inscriptions, administrative documents and graffiti; yet this list is by no means exhaustive. The interaction between these different genres and literacies seems to have been considerable. The huge range of material discovered on the rubbish tip at Oxyrhynchus shows how a letter about obtaining books might emanate from a cultured circle, but when groups of texts can be related to particular houses or contexts, it is clear that a broad range of written material might exist in a relatively modest milieu. That is a conclusion that would fit the Egyptian picture as a whole and it has been reinforced by the nature of finds at Nag Hammadi, at

[10] Fink (1971: 242).   [11] Franklin (1991) with references to other literature.
[12] For an example from a different period see Franklin (1985).
[13] Howgego (1992). Hopkins (1991) discusses the relationships between the spread of writing, of coin use and of political power.

Vindolanda, at Masada.[14] Thompson and Heather both suggest that less obvious intertextualities also existed, for example between the records of tax-collectors and the literary works through which they were educated, and which were produced as a side effect of state-sponsored education systems. Even if writing was taught to serve mundane purposes, once learnt it might be used to create lead curse tablets to be thrown into the sacred spring, or an amulet with a Christian or pagan religious text. The interplay between these various uses of writing argues against the existence, in much of the ancient world, of segregated specialised literacies. Writing seems to have been a transferable technology and literates seem often to have been competent in creating and using a wide variety of texts.

Our common theme is the relationship between literacy and power. No single, all-sufficient concept of the nature and application of 'power' has been adopted for this collection, and in the treatments of various topics that follow, examples of the political and social, religious and cultural, psychological and physical aspects of power recur, in various combinations and with differing weight of emphasis. Yet at the most general level, two closely interrelated aspects of the relationship between writing and power are worth noting: power over texts and power exercised by means of their use.

Power over texts encompasses restrictions placed on writing, on access to and possession of texts, on the legitimate uses to which the written word might be put and, perhaps most importantly, restrictions on reading texts. In its most fundamental manifestation, this may mean that an élite or restricted group determines both the status of particular kinds of texts and also which people or bodies may use them to legitimise their behaviour. Invocation of such power is often explicit, but it is important to recognise it as implicit even in such apparently neutral and anodyne statements as that of the Canopus Decree that 'a public religious assembly shall be celebrated every year in the temple and throughout the whole country in honour of King Ptolemy and Queen Berenice, the Benefactor Gods, on the day when the star of Isis rises, *which the holy books consider* to be the New Year'.[15]

The most common justification for such manipulation is *religio* (in whatever guise it may appear) but there are other methods of restricting or extending access. We need to consider the effects of straightforward technological change, for example in the writing of reports *transversa*

---

[14] Letter about books: *P. Oxy.* 17.2192. The archaeological records of the excavations at the village of Karanis in the Fayum allow particular groups of papyri and ostraka to be located in individual houses. For samples of the material in the Nag Hammadi Codices see Robinson (1977) and cf. Pagels (1979). Masada: Cotton and Geiger (1989).

[15] *OGIS* 56, translated by Austin (1981: no. 222) (our emphasis).

charta or in the introduction of the codex.[16] Power can be wielded by changing either the way texts are written (both the scripts and formats employed), or the language they are written in. The restrictiveness of hieroglyph can be contrasted with strategies which extend the range of written texts and make them accessible to a wider public by manipulation of the linguistic medium. Political authorities might impose a system of education in a language alien to that of the subject population, or simply make it virtually impossible to manipulate political, social or economic institutions without acquiring literacy in the dominant language.[17] Finally, power can be exercised simply by preventing circulation and availability of undesirable texts, as the Roman emperor Septimius Severus tried to do in Egypt: 'therefore let no man through oracles, *that is by means of written documents* supposedly granted under divine influence, nor by means of the parade of images or suchlike charlatanry, pretend to know things beyond human ken and profess [to know] the obscurity of things to come, neither let any man put himself at the disposal of those who enquire about this or answer it in any way whatsoever'.[18]

When texts are available, the power of authors and exegetes to impose an 'authorised' reading is ranged against the power of readers to generate new interpretations. Conflicts over authority may also result in the creation of competing texts, like the 'propagandist' prophecies known as the Oracle of the Potter and the Oracle of the Lamb, which occur in both pro-Egyptian and pro-Greek versions. Accounts of the past are as susceptible to this sort of manipulation as are prophecies about the future. Contemporary power struggles may be reflected in texts which present themselves as historical, and which may subsequently have an important influence on historiographical traditions.[19] Readers of Homer and Virgil are aware that the poet aims primarily to please his client rather than to document the past. But the literary reworking of the past to justify the present also has consequences for our reading of prose histories, like Livy's account of early Rome.

The generation of new interpretations may be a matter of deliberate strategy. Cameron's discussion of the compilation of *florilegia* to justify a position or as polemic against the opposition is a case in point. The recreation of 'classical Greece' in the context of the Roman empire of the mid-second century AD by the orators of the so-called 'Second Sophistic' is also a reinterpretation, and its perpetrators may well have been well aware of what they were doing.[20] A more elusive development can perhaps be seen

[16] Suetonius, *Iul.* 56.6; the codex, Roberts and Skeat (1983) and the papers collected in Blanchard (1989).
[17] Pattison (1982), quoted at the start of this chapter, argues that literacy should be defined in terms of mastery of and competence in those linguistic skills that empower individuals in this way.   [18] Rea (1977) (our emphasis).   [19] Koenen (1983, 1985).
[20] Bowie (1970) on the use of the past in rhetoric, but Elsner (1992) suggests that some of these

in the so-called Acts of the Alexandrian Martyrs. Here we have a series of fictionalised accounts, based on documentary reports of proceedings, of hearings before Roman emperors in which the Alexandrian patriots were 'tried'. The historical settings range from the reign of Gaius to that of Commodus, and in the earlier accounts anti-semitism predominates while in the later the feeling is anti-Roman. Understanding the purpose and function of these documents may well depend on locating them in the context of the late second or early third century AD,[21] when most of the extant copies seem to have been produced, also the period in which the earliest Christian martyr acts, which resemble them strikingly in form, were set.

The exercise of power through texts makes it essential to regulate their use, but literacy is not easy to control and texts have therefore often been at the heart of struggles for power: rival exegeses, book-burning, conflicts over legislation, censorship and the creation of vernacular literatures have often characterised such struggles. Decisions about what is and what is not acceptable are exemplified just as well by minor philosophical disputes as by the formation of the Canon of the New Testament. Censorship may be exercised overtly by doctoring texts or more insidiously by dictating fashion and taste.[22]

Power exercised *over* texts allows power to be exercised *through* texts. We might distinguish the use of texts to legitimise deeds and spoken words, from the uses to which writing may be put in law, bureaucracy, accountancy, census and population control. The legitimisation of the present through (re)interpretation of an often unknowable past is one aspect of the former (as the examples of the 'Augustan' view of Rome and the Second Sophistic, cited above, illustrate). In different ways the Behistun inscription, the *Monumentum Ancyranum* and the *Lex de imperio Vespasiani* all operated to legitimise the power of the rulers who set them up. Monumental and visible texts are not a *sine qua non* for the exercise of power, of course, just as, alongside the written codification of law, there may legitimately exist the notion of a valid but unwritten law. What the text says may, in any case, not be the whole, or even the primary, point if most people could either not see the writing or could not read it anyway. Monumental texts may exercise power through their location in space and the way they look. A particular layout might be associated with a particular political system, and the practice of *damnatio memoriae*, in which the physical obliteration of the name of a Roman emperor from inscriptions

texts may also have functioned to help Greeks establish an identity for themselves under Roman rule.   [21] Musurillo (1954).
[22] Philosophical disputes: e.g. *P. Oxy.* 42.3008. Censorship: e.g. *P. Oxy.* 47.3331.

was accompanied by the destruction or replacement of statues and other images of him, illustrates how the texts on monuments might be organically associated with iconographic representation.

Power relations sometimes shaped the ways in which writing was used, as is shown by Woolf's study of pre-Roman and Roman Gaul and by Heather's analysis of the emergence of the successor states in Gaul and the rest of the sub-Roman West. But sometimes the uses to which writing was put redefined or helped to redefine those relations, as Lane Fox suggests was the case in the history of early Christianity. We cannot now trace the process by which the tradition about the life and work of Jesus of Nazareth evolved into written form, but the much later compilation of anecdotes and *apophthegmata* which illustrate the lives and deeds of the desert fathers of later antiquity may be analogous in suggesting relationships between the charismatic power generated by deeds and spoken words and its institutionalisation in holy texts, which were easier for religious authorities to control.[23]

Political systems made very varied uses of writing, as is illustrated by the contributions of Thomas, Lewis, Bowman and Kelly. Not all ancient regimes used writing to establish complex bureaucracies, and often the fact that something was written down may have been as important as what it said. Nevertheless, a major preoccupation of modern scholarship has been the relationship between literacy and power in the context of the state and its organisation. There is a clear sense that literacy helps the state to cohere politically but not just because it enables the description of reality or the transmission of information in written form. Nor is it invariably the case that the most powerful and coherent states are those which make more use of literacy and writing. Even when good exemplars are close at hand a state may choose a less literate mode, as Woolf argues may have been the case in Gaul or as Thomas shows happened in Sparta. Alternatively, institutional change may entail changes in the degree of use, prominence or circulation of particular kinds of written material. The fact that we have virtually no imperial letters or edicts on papyrus from Byzantine Egypt at a period when, as Kelly shows, bureaucratic activity at the centre of the eastern empire was at a high level may reflect the nature of authority and the use of certain kinds of documentation (unless it is the product of the randomness of survival). If we think that this can be ascribed to a change of 'need', we must define need in symbolic as well as in functional terms.

Many uses of writing have a degree of symbolism; not simply the obviously monumental, but also the use of different materials for different kinds of texts or to create a psychological effect.[24] Layout and appearance are important in both public and private contexts. Ray shows how greater

[23] Translations by Ward (1975), Ward and Russell (1980).
[24] Materials: Tomlin (1988), Thomas (1992: 82–4). Psychological effect: *Hist. Aug., Hadr.* 7.6.

literacy and a wider use of writing might be promoted, either deliberately or incidentally, by the power-wielding authority, which could introduce or adapt the technological or linguistic tools available. The spread is not necessarily uni-directional from the public into the private sector. Both Thomas and Bowman argue that an increase in the official public use of writing might be stimulated by private practices.

The use of writing by the state as an instrument of organisation requires close attention to the nature of bureaucracy. It consists of more than simply the use of pen and paper. There is a common presumption that bureaucracy develops a mode of its own which can be identified in a variety of features, linguistic style and character of handwriting to name but two. The power of the bureaucracy is easily perceptible and very marked in some periods and we must ask whether and how that power is controlled. Kelly argues that, paradoxically, the overt signs of antipathy between ruler and bureaucrat mask a mutual reinforcement and they remind us of what modern politicians sometimes say about civil servants. But we must also consider the connections between the use of writing and a concern for accountability and redress for those controlled by the bureaucracy, against the role of precedent and the tendency of codification to restrict innovation and reinforce the autonomy of the institution. Put more simply, how effective was the *graphe paranomon* or a petition to a Roman emperor likely to be? Why did an illiterate peasant-farmer think it worth preserving his papers even when he could not read them himself?[25]

The existence of bureaucratic habits creates a bureaucratic élite, and considerable attention is paid by both Lewis and Goodman to the nature of 'scribal classes'. Most historians would now accept that the Roman imperial freedmen of the early principate did not derive their power simply from their bureaucratic functions. In the administrative context of the Greek world and the Roman East, the title and position of *grammateus* often did not simply describe a function but a position with some status and power. In the Achaemenid empire the 'scribal class' consisted of more than just scribes. This will contrast with Judaea where, it is argued, the power of the scribes did derive precisely from what they wrote. The very notion of a 'scribal class' implies a restrictive view of the application of writing and literacy, yet much of what follows tends to suggest that literacy is not a constricting discipline. No simple generalisation will cover all cases but there can be no doubt that, in all of the contexts discussed in the following chapters, we should beware of veering erratically between the view of a literate élite narrowly defined by the limited spread of writing skills and any unrealistic notion of a broad, popular literacy in the ancient world.

[25] Boak and Youtie (1960).

Another issue of major importance is the complex relationship between literacy, language and culture. The notion (or 'myth') of classical civilisation conditions us to approach the subject from the perspective of those who operated in Greek and Latin, a perspective ideally suited to the modern Anglophone. Thus we can observe Greek and Latin coming into contact and conflict with other language groups or cultures and eventually dominating them. The survival of the native, minority languages can then be viewed as a strain of 'resistance' or a manifestation of 'popular' as opposed to 'élite' culture.[26] The survival and importance of languages other than Greek and Latin may be under-represented in modern scholarship because, for instance, the Greek papyri from Ptolemaic Egypt have been very well served by Greek papyrologists whilst the far smaller number of demoticists has not been able to do justice to a corpus of demotic papyri which is very much larger than the published sample would suggest. Even allowing for such bias, the studies which follow alert us above all to the complexity of the linguistic picture and the consequent complexity of the issues involved in the relationship between literacy and power.

A multilingual context in which written communication was required, and clearly took place, is evoked by the studies of Lewis, Ray, Woolf and Brock, but in each case we remain uncertain of the reasons for particular choices made. Bilingual documents, or the rare evidence for translation or the skills of the interpreter are not a complete explanation, for there are many cases in which we have only dockets, endorsements or signatures added in a second language.[27] Once again this suggests some symbolic importance. Nor is the relationship between the written evidence and the language which it represents always easy to interpret, as is strikingly suggested by Ray for demotic, perhaps not Egyptian as spoken but Egyptian as it might have been spoken in a Greekless world. In this particular world, where there is evidence for a very great number of languages in use, we have first the creation of one language and later the privileging of another: the context is political change and one result is some resistance to the culture of the new rulers. The point is neatly emphasised by a letter of the mid-third century BC in which an Egyptian complains that the Greeks 'have treated me with contempt because I am a barbarian' and asks to be paid regularly 'so that I do not die of hunger because I do not know how to ἑλληνίζειν'. It is significant that modern commentators have been uncertain whether to translate the verb as 'to speak Greek' or 'to behave like a Greek', but it is clear that in order to make his point the

---

[26] Cf. Brown (1968), Millar (1968), MacMullen (1990: chs. 4–7).
[27] Examples in Lewis (1989), Boswinkel and Pestman (1978).

Egyptian has to send a letter written in Greek – there would have been no point writing to Zenon in demotic even though the latter could doubtless have found a translator.[28]

The dominance of the Graeco-Roman cultural tradition in our own consciousness inevitably makes us think in terms of those literacies preserving and spreading élite culture. There were other literacies in which this occurred in parallel and in the same context; the role of Greek and Hebrew in Judaea and in the communities of the Diaspora invites attention from this point of view. The spread of an élite culture obviously creates social caste markers and may also reinforce political and cultural coherence, or group identity. Brock's contribution shows how élite status can then be expressed in terms of literacy in a particular language, obliterating the ambiguities posed by issues such as the borderline between orality and literacy and obscuring the extent to which we can differentiate between bilingualism and bi-culturalism. We should not expect a uniform progression towards the complete dominance of literacy in Greek and Latin in this long period and large geographical area, nor should we necessarily expect that the classical language-tradition (if it is one phenomenon rather than two) is self-contained. There is a sub-literary level, relatively poorly represented in our surviving evidence, where the diverse linguistic influences on written (as well as spoken) Latin and Greek can be observed. A century ago it would hardly have been predicted that the areas most productive of evidence for this would turn out to be the edges of the Roman empire, Egypt and Britain, where the handwriting in which Latin texts were written *c.* AD 100 is strikingly comparable.[29]

Yet another kind of relationship between literacy and power is explored by those papers that deal with the centrality of sacred texts to the life and organisation of Jewish and Christian communities. Cameron describes how texts might become both the *foci* of power struggles at the centre of society and the principal weapons used in those struggles, and Goodman shows how the very act of writing a sacred text could bestow status and power on the scribe. Christian texts seem never to have acquired quite the same status, but feelings ran high over the surrendering of scripture to pagan persecutors and, as Lane Fox shows, books entered into the imagination of the early Church. The authority of these texts derived originally from their sacred origin and from their value as guides to the proper way to live, but their use in contests for power, whether between Byzantine scholars or early Christian bishops, must have reinforced their

---

[28] *P. Col. Zen.* 66 translated by Austin (1981) no. 245.
[29] For linguistic studies see Adams (1977, 1992).

status still further. Their interpretation of holy writ was so important to the whole community that rabbis, priests and bishops won authority as expert readers and interpreters, while some exegetical writings acquired a status as secondary authorities. Authoritative exegetes might even attempt to close a canon, to restrict access to texts or to impose an orthodox reading on them. The authority of texts and the expert readers' authority over them thus reinforced each other. Furthermore, the curious blend of symbolic and pragmatic aspects of the written word, already noted in the use of writing by states, recurs in the decoration and thesaurisation of books and in the discipline of the monastic rule. This 'sacral graphocentrism' is distinct from the emphasis placed on the written word in our society, although it is perhaps an ancestor of it.

These Jewish and Christian attitudes to writing contrast markedly with the extensive but very different uses of writing in Greek and Roman religion.[30] Pagans set up painted boards in temples to commemorate vows, and the dedication of votives, altars and temples involved inscriptions. Writing was itself probably a cultic activity in the case of curse tablets and in the cult of the Arval Brethren at Rome.[31] There were even sacred texts, such as the Sibylline books, calendars and inscribed religious laws.[32] Nevertheless, texts never occupied the same position as the Jewish or Christian scriptures. Pagan priests asserted their authority by claiming privileged roles in cult and an expertise that was rarely based on the exegesis of holy writ, while the religious unity of communities centred on common participation in sacrifice rather than on common possession of and by sacred texts.

One manifestation of this possession was communities whose life and identity revolved around reading, writing and living in accordance with particular texts. The term 'textual communities' was coined to describe late mediaeval examples of the phenomenon[33] and several contributors make use of it to show how, within such communities, gradations of literacy created and corresponded to gradations in power. The notion that written texts may be used to unite groups, and to provide a medium for the establishment and entrenchment of relations of dominance, can be applied more widely. Lane Fox's close readers in the desert conform closely to the original conception, but writing also played a central role in uniting groups like the Jewish *soferim* or the scholastic theologians of Byzantium. The work of Roman jurists and Greek physicians too, revolved around common texts, and Heather argues that the late Roman élite were united largely by a common education system based on a canon of 'classics'. Educational canons also lie beneath the rather different unity

[30] Beard (1991), Thomas (1992: 74–88), Veyne (1983).   [31] Beard (1985).
[32] Veyne (1983), Williamson (1987), Day (1989).   [33] Stock (1983).

that could be established via letter-writing, whether by early Roman military personnel or by Symmachus' correspondents.[34] It is true that these groups varied widely in scale and dispersal, as well as in the extent to which texts were revered in themselves, rather than regarded simply as repositories of valued information or as means to acquire particular expertise. The line between groups united by a common culture, in which literacy is valued, and textual communities *sensu stricto* is difficult to draw. Nevertheless, as long as a canon of authoritative texts remains at the centre of a group's collective identity, questions of control and use of the canon, of authority over it and of access to education in its use, are worth asking.

Literacy and power fit together in the ancient world in a bewildering variety of combinations. Two directions suggest themselves for further investigation, the first being to extend, to other periods and cultures, the common themes that have emerged from this collection – literacy and the state, literacy, language and culture, and literacy and religion – the second being to attempt to uncover some unity behind these themes, that might justify our writing of classical literacy and power in more general terms. The first direction is beyond our competence, but the second is appropriately discussed here.

The unity of Graeco-Roman culture is a matter of fierce dispute. Earlier formulations can now be seen to have been created by a whole series of 'classicisations', beginning at least as early as the Roman Republic, but still evident in the privileged role accorded, in general histories and syllabuses, to Greeks and Romans, as opposed to Etruscans, Carthaginians, Semites, Egyptians and others. An authoritative critique and genealogy of the notion of a Classical World, along the lines of Edward Said's *Orientalism*, is still awaited. But the study of writing and its uses has a part to play in deconstructing this myth. Virtually all the writing systems considered in these papers (the exceptions being Egyptian hieroglyphic and hieratic, Hebrew, Old Persian and Syriac) were created within a tradition that stems from earlier West Semitic roots, while the styles of literacy described by Heather and Cameron point the way forward to early mediaeval and Byzantine literacies of which we are ourselves the heirs. If ancient literacy has a unity, it must lie in particular uses of writing and/or attitudes to it, confined to or at least widespread within and characteristic of the Greek and Roman worlds.

We have found it difficult to identify common themes at the requisite level of generality, between the particular uses of individual societies, such

---

[34] Matthews (1974).

as first-century Judaea or early imperial Rome, and features like textual communities or logocentrism that recur frequently enough in history to suggest that they might be considered as general potentials (although not consequences or even implications) of literacy. The general themes that emerge, in other words, seem characteristic of units either much larger than classical antiquity or else contained within it.

Let us take, as an example, an observation that emerged both in the use of writing by states and also in Judaeo-Christian communities, that writing often operates both as a form of symbol, comparable to images like monumental statues or icons, yet also as a form of communication comparable to speech. Debates over the relative importance of the symbolic and pragmatic aspects of texts recur in so many contexts, from law-making to epigraphy, to book-burning and census-taking, that the combination might be thought to be characteristic of the ancient world. Yet as Lewis demonstrates, the combination is already present in Achaemenid Persia, from which it may be traced back via Neo-Babylonian usage to ancient Mesopotamia. Perhaps a better candidate for a classical use of writing would be the high culture of rhetoric, within which written texts were simply used in elementary education or as imperfect records of oral performances. That set of attitudes characterised the élites of both imperial Rome and also classical Athens, and is in marked contrast to the sacral graphocentrisms of Jews and early Christians.[35] Yet in other respects, literacy was articulated with power at Rome, in very different ways than it was at Athens. New uses of writing were a feature of both Roman and Athenian empires. But while the kind of records and accounting systems used at Vindolanda seem to owe something to the way Republican aristocrats used writing to manage the complex finances of their *familiae*, the increased use of writing in the Athenian empire owed more, according to Thomas, to ideologies of accountability than of efficiency, and neither system was comparable with the true bureaucracy described by Kelly for the late empire.

Complex patterns of cultural borrowings and adaption can be traced between the various examples of literacy and power gathered in this volume. The case of rhetorical culture shows how influential these exchanges might be; but that they might also be relatively inconsequential, is exemplified by the tangential contacts between Greek and Syriac literatures, or between classical and barbarian writing in the West. In those instances, contact seems hardly to have affected parallel cultural trajectories. It is difficult to identify a particular classical, ancient or Graeco-Roman style of literacy. The common themes we have identified seem to

---

[35] Cameron (1991) on the complex relationship between rhetorical culture and Christian discourse.

have emerged partly from variation and interaction within a broad west Eurasian tradition, not confined to the 'classical' civilisations but embracing all contemporary writing systems except those of the Far East or of the New World. But they may partly derive from general properties of writing manifested there as well. Our scanty acquaintance with Mayan hieroglyphs and Chinese Mandarin culture suggests that writing is not a completely plastic technology and that its potentials are not limitless. The question of whether or not the general themes that have emerged from these studies of literacy and power have relevance in those contexts too, we leave to others.

2 The Persepolis Tablets: speech, seal and script

D. M. Lewis

There has been some scepticism, which I partly share, about the completeness and accuracy of Herodotus' knowledge of Persian institutions. Nevertheless, I start from a Herodotean story, 3.126–8. If we understand it fully, there is little more to be said about how the Persians exercised power through writing.

During the convulsions of the rule of Smerdis (or Pseudo-Smerdis) and its aftermath of ethnic revolts, Oroites, satrap of Sardis, best known as the murderer of Polycrates of Samos, understandably sat on the fence. There can be no reasonable doubt that he did, as was alleged, take the opportunity of disposing of the satrap of Daskyleion, the other western satrapy, and his son. It is less obvious that the total disappearance of a messenger of Darius, horse and all, could have been firmly pinned on him, but he had certainly offered no help to Darius. Darius, once in power, wanted vengeance and, no doubt, a more reliable satrap in the West. A military campaign was out of the question, since Darius was still not fully established and Oroites had considerable resources, notably a bodyguard of a thousand Persians. Darius called for volunteers to tackle the problem by intelligence rather than by force. There were thirty volunteers and the lot fell on Bagaios.

Bagaios arranged for many papyrus rolls to be written (βυβλία γραψάμενος (middle) πολλά) about many matters and sealed them with Darius' seal, With his load, he went off to Sardis. Admitted to Oroites' presence, he opened the rolls one by one and gave them to the royal secretary to read; all satraps have royal γραμματισταί. His object was to test the possibility of making the bodyguard revolt from Oroites. Seeing that the bodyguard respected the rolls greatly and what was said in them even more, he selected a roll in which was written: 'Persians, King Darius forbids you to guard Oroites.' When they heard this, they dropped their spears. Bagaios, seeing that they obeyed the roll, took courage and handed the secretary the last of the rolls, in which was written: 'King Darius orders the Persians in Sardis to kill Oroites.' When the bodyguard heard that, they drew their daggers and killed him on the spot. You may or may not believe the case I have made elsewhere[1] for supposing that Bagaios was given the hand of the princess Ištin as a reward, but there are certainly few stories which illustrate the power of the Word more conclusively.

In this story, Bagaios does not have to be able to write or read himself, though he does need to be able to communicate instructions to a scribe and to know which roll is which. The Word passes from, say, Susa to Sardis on papyrus. There neither Oroites nor his bodyguard needs to be able to read it, though they do have to be able to recognise Darius' seal (there might be thought to be a difficulty here). The written Word becomes speech again in the mouth of the royal secretary.

All this corresponds exactly to the observed facts. We are dealing with a society in which the top people need not be able to write at all. The Old Persian which they spoke did have an artificial script invented for it a year or so after this, but there is not the slightest reason to suppose that this script was ever used for anything but the display purposes of the King. The ability to write and read it was certainly very confined; after the reign of Xerxes no one ever writes anything in it which has not been written before. The Persians came down illiterate from the hills in the sixth century, and acquired various existing bureaucracies, some of considerable age, which they proceeded to utilise. (Fifteen hundred years later, the Turks would find their bureaucracy among Persians.) Like many mediaeval magnates, they saw no need to write themselves if there was someone to do it for them. The characteristic form of pronouncement by a high Persian official was therefore oral. When reduced to writing, it begins 'Tell X, so-and-so says' and, if the official is high enough, ends with a note of who had actually done the writing and who had communicated the will of the official. At the other end of the transmission, his message again becomes speech in the mouth of a scribe. That the message is his message is authenticated by his seal. He himself need not be concerned about the mechanics of the way in which speech goes in at one end of the process and comes out at the other. Gershevitch[2] has compared the modern business man who does not need to understand electro-magnetism to use his tape recorder.

Several languages carried on the business of the Persian Empire. Bagaios' letters were surely in the most widespread, Aramaic, which, starting from somewhere in Syria, became almost universal, aided by its simple alphabet and the use of a pen; it was normally used on papyrus and parchment, which only survive under favourable climatic conditions. We have one satrapal archive, from Daskyleion in northern Asia Minor, which has totally vanished, leaving a heap of clay sealings.[3] When Aramaic gets

[1] Lewis (1985: 112). Note that ML = R. Meiggs and D. M. Lewis, *Selection of Greek Historical Inscriptions* (rev. edn. Oxford, 1988).   [2] Gershevitch (1971: 3–4).
[3] Balkan (1959); Garrison (1992: 29 n. 121).

on to stone, we have examples of it from Xanthus[4] in southern Asia Minor to Kandahar[5] in the east. At the beginning of this century, the excavations at Elephantine, an island in the Nile near Aswan, produced the papyrus records of a Jewish military colony, including some correspondence with Persian authorities[6] and a copy of Darius' Behistun inscription.[7] Forty years or so later, a clandestine find in Egypt produced the parchment correspondence of Aršam, a Persian governor, a prince of the royal house, now in the Bodleian.[8]

The history of Aramaic writing and its competition with cuneiform is much older than this. From the middle of the eighth century it is used alongside cuneiform in Assyria, where Egyptian and Aramean scribes appear in wine-ration tablets from Calah; pen-men and stylus-men are visible side by side on reliefs of Tiglath-Pileser III.[9] Two reigns on, a letter of the time of Sargon II acknowledges the receipt of papyrus rolls.[10] There is a letter of his urging that letters should be written in Akkadian rather than in Aramaic, but no scholarly agreement as to whether this is motivated by nationalism or a desire for secrecy.[11]

The use of clay tablets in cuneiform went on as it had done for millennia, but, well before the end of the Assyrian Empire, the need to integrate archives and help in information retrieval is attested by scratched Aramaic annotations on cuneiform tablets from Nineveh.[12] That practice continues in Babylonia, almost certainly reinforced by a massive intrusion of Aramaic into everyday speech. Nevertheless, Babylonian cuneiform documentation continues throughout the Persian period and has much to offer the historian of Persian rule, particularly in the records of the great banking house of the Murašu.[13]

The Persian heartland had been silent, and my generation still grew up with a belief that, although bureaucracy may have been all very well for areas which had been used to it, the Persians were more immune to it than the great despotisms which had preceded them. After all, the Greeks had told us that the Persians were principally interested in riding, shooting and telling the truth. Other indications were more or less ignored, the story of Bagaios, the scribes who are twice found writing at Xerxes' side during his

[4] Metzger et al. (1979).   [5] Schlumberger et al. (1958).
[6] Cowley (1923); Porten and Yardeni (1986–).   [7] Greenfield and Porten (1982).
[8] Driver (1957).
[9] Tablets from Calah, Kinnier Wilson (1972: 2 and no. 9); for the date, Dalley and Postgate (1984: 22). Reliefs of Tiglath-Pileser III, plates vol. to *CAH* III[2] pl. 57.
[10] Harper (1892–1914: no. 568).   [11] See *CAH* III[2].2, 185.
[12] For scratched Aramaic annotations on cuneiform tablets from Nineveh, see Millard (1983), Vattioni (1970), Lipiński (1975).
[13] Stolper (1985).

invasion of Greece in 480,[14] and the fact that Theopompus in the next century lists among the stores necessary for equipping a Persian army mountains of papyrus.[15]

Modern treatments of the verbal expression of Persian power have therefore been more or less confined to its use for display, above all in the Behistun inscription which commemorated Darius' rise to power, the tomb-inscriptions of Naqsh-i Rustam, and the building inscriptions of Persepolis and Susa. The Roman copy of a letter of Darius (ML 12) was a rare exception to attract attention.

Darius' Behistun inscription was not only in Persian. It was also in Babylonian and in Elamite; we can now see that it was originally only in Elamite and that the Persian script was invented while the work was going on.[16] Elamite is properly the language of its own locality round Susa. It is a very strange language, neither Indo-European nor Semitic.[17] I used to say that its strangeness could be encapsulated in the fact that it formed its plurals in -p, until I said it once too often at a party and was told firmly that Georgian did so too. That sent me off on an investigation of Georgian vocabulary, so far fruitless. Fortunately, Elamite started to be written in the cuneiform syllabary at a very early date, so we have only very minor problems about sound-values, and the continued use of Sumerian logograms should prevent us from making major mistakes. There used to be a substantial chronological gap, with only one uncertainly dated archive from Susa between texts of 1500 BC or so and its use by Darius, but this is slowly being plugged. Since we knew that Darius could draw on Elamite scribes, it should not have been a great surprise when the excavations of Persepolis in the 1930s started producing Elamite tablets.

These fall into two groups. The smaller, of about 750 with 150 or so usable, was found in a building promptly dubbed the Treasury; its texts record disbursements of silver between 489 and 458 BC. They were published by George Cameron in 1948,[18] with inevitable distortions because of the strangeness of the material and vocabulary, and without making much impression except on linguists; I shall hardly touch on them here.

The second group was a very different matter. They had been discarded, it was thought, and used as filling in the Fortification Wall; there could be

[14] Hdt. 7.100.1–2, 8.90.4.   [15] FGrH 115 F 263.

[16] The major textbooks are bad guides on this, but see Dandamayev and Lukonin (1989: 272–82). The key articles are Trumpelmann (1967), Luschey (1968), Hinz (1968), establishing a position developed, but never published, many years ago by H. T. Wade-Gery.

[17] Grillot-Susini (1987); Hinz and Koch (1987).

[18] Cameron (1948); texts from this volume are cited with the prefix PT. Cameron published further texts in JNES 17 (1958) 161–76, 24 (1965) 167–92, and there was a major revision by Hallock (1960).

doubts about that interpretation now. They emerged in the excavations of
1933–4 and were moved to Chicago for study. There are said to have been
thirty thousand or so, though many are fragmentary or illegible. Cameron
made a start on them, but the main burden fell on Richard Hallock. It
gradually became clear that they were all about foodstuffs and mostly
concerned with transactions in Persian territory, though they go some way
along the road to Susa; so far there is nothing before 509 BC or after 494.[19]
Hallock's *Persepolis Fortification Tablets* of 1969[20] has 2,087 texts, but he
went on copying even after he had sent it to the press. By the time he died in
1980, though he had only published another thirty texts, he had more than
doubled the material. Through the great generosity of his successor
Matthew Stolper, we have copies of his copies in Oxford.[21]

There are two Babylonian tablets from Persepolis,[22] but Elamite is
dominant in the finds. It disappears there after the last dated Treasury
document of 458,[23] whether this be a fact about the excavation, the use of
Persepolis, or an index of a switch to more perishable writing materials in
Aramaic. There is in fact no absolute division between cuneiform on clay
and alphabetic scripts on papyrus and parchment. There are notorious
Aramaic texts on green chert ritual vessels from Persepolis, which have
been published (though not in a way which commanded much assent),[24]
and several hundred on clay Fortification tablets, which have not. Aramaic
annotation on cuneiform tablets occurs here too, and has sometimes been
invaluable. There is one tablet in Phrygian[25] and one in Greek.[26] All one
can say about the first is that it has an Old Persian month-name on it; I have
argued[27] that the latter proves that there was someone out on the
administrative circuit for whom it was natural to write in Greek and who
knew that it would be usable at the centre.

This makes Persepolis administration a complex linguistic phenomenon,
even at the level of script. At the level of speech, to judge by the variety of
ethnics attested for work-groups, the position will have been even worse.
This is a standing problem for an international empire and will have caused

---

[19] The doubts about the terminal date expressed by Vickers (1985: 30 n. 240) are without
foundation; see Root (1988).
[20] Hallock (1969). Texts from this volume are cited with the prefix PF. Hallock (1978) added
additional texts, cited with the prefix PFa.
[21] These unpublished texts, used here with the permission of Professor Stolper and the
Oriental Institute, will be cited with the prefix PF–NN. It must be noted that what I say
about them normally depends, not on the tablets themselves or on drawings, but on
Hallock's hand-written transliterated collations. Good though these are, they are still
subject to checking. In a few important cases, Professor Stolper and Dr C. Jones have
looked at the tablets for me.   [22] PT 85; Stolper (1984).
[23] PT 25, as revised by Hallock (1960) 91.
[24] Bowman (1970). See e.g. Naveh and Shaked (1973), Hinz (1975).
[25] Cameron (1973: 52–3).   [26] Hallock (1969: 2).   [27] Lewis (1977: 12–13).

Fig. 1. A tablet from Persepolis (PF 2070) in Elamite language and modified Akkadian cuneiform: a report to Parnaka about sheep and goats, April 504 BC. (Oriental Institute Chicago. Reproduced by courtesy of Professor M. W. Stolper.)

problems from time to time. Greek literature about the Persian Empire has occasional references to interpreters,[28] though only Darius III, before the battle of Gaugamela, is actually attested as worrying that multilingualism might cause trouble in battle (Diodorus Siculus 17.53.4). That makes him, unless we include Darius I's remarks about the effort needed to publish his Behistun text,[29] the first monarch to be bothered about language since Assurbanipal's interpreters reported their inability to understand the messenger of Gyges.[30]

To match Gershevitch's remarks about tape recorders, we could suggest yet another analogy to reflect the nature of Persepolis record-keeping. We are practically in the position of a future excavator faced with different types of hard and floppy disc and tape, sometimes themselves in different word-processing programs. This was a situation which faced Persepolis scribes and officials every day; no doubt they were better at it.

[28] E.g. Thuc. 8.85.2, Xen. *Hell.* 1.2.17, 5.7, 8.12.
[29] Darius, Behistun Inscription, Old Persian IV 88–92.
[30] Luckenbill (1927: §893) A better text in Piepkorn (1933: 16–17).

Who are we actually talking about? At the top we have Darius himself. No administrative documents of his survive, though his order is occasionally quoted in letters,[31] and many of the travellers drawing rations along the Royal Road drew them on the authority of a document sealed by him.[32] Under him, to confine ourselves to Persepolis, we have two major officials. The first is Parnaka-Pharnakes, almost certainly his uncle.[33] By my present count, we have 36 documents acknowledging receipt of his rations or salary (2 sheep, 90 quarts of wine or beer, 180 quarts of flour a day) and 58 letters in his name; the number of journeys and other payments authorised by him must go into three figures. It looks as if he died in the summer of 497.[34] Alongside him is Ziššawiš, of rather lower status, since his daily ration was $1\frac{1}{2}$ sheep, 30 quarts of wine, 60 quarts of flour. He long survived Parnaka and was still issuing letters at Persepolis in February 467.[35] I have made the hazardous guess[36] that he was a Mede, known to the Greeks as Tithaios son of Datis, one of Xerxes' hipparchs in 480. If we exclude his Xerxes texts, we have 23 ration texts and 51 letters for him; again, I have not yet counted references to disbursements which he is known to have authorised.

I defer discussion of their personal staffs and how they actually did their business, and move on down. One of the more tiresome unsolved problems about the texts is what is meant by saying that work-groups and individuals were 'assigned' by them or 'received their apportionments' from them; the Aramaic texts should throw light on that.[37] These designations are by no means peculiar to Parnaka and Ziššawiš, and there is another group of people for whom they are used. The nature of the responsibilities thus indicated is obscure and was probably flexible. Sometimes it seems to be territorial, sometimes it may be connected with particular commodities. Some of those involved are referred to by titles, though not always the same ones. We can at least now project back far into the reign of Darius the office of Persepolis Treasurer, which had been better known from the Treasury Texts.[38]

Lower still, we have supply-stations, some on the Royal Road, some not,

[31] PF 1620 (and the parallel Fort. 3562), 1856, 1795 (and the parallel Fort. 6764, for which see Hallock (1969) 52).
[32] There are at least eighty of these. See e.g. PF 681–4 for people of high status, but there are many for people of low status as well.   [33] Hallock (1985) 589–92.
[34] The latest dated evidence for Parnaka comes from the 3rd month of the 25th year, June–July 497, for which there are three texts (PF–NN 233, 908, 1752).
[35] PT 33.   [36] Lewis (1985: 114–15).
[37] My feeling is that there is more overlap between the concepts of *damana* (assigning) and *šaramanna* (apportioning) than is generally thought; cf., among published texts, PF 847 with 922–3. But there is an apparently irreducible small number of cases (e.g. PF 1842–3, 1947: 64; also some Treasury texts) where they appear side by side.
[38] The deductions of Koch (1981) and (1990) 235–7 are shown to be correct by the appearance with the designation 'treasurer' of Karkiš in PF–NN 1724 and Šuddayauda in PF–NN 1069, 1411, 2079.

with staffs of varying size and specialisation. At some of them only two people do the job for all commodities; at larger ones grain-supply and wine-supply (generally combined with fruit) fall to different individuals. These stations produce not only records of individual transactions, but, generally a few years in arrear, composite texts listing individual transactions and completed by general statements of their receipts, disbursement and balances and a statement about the auditing procedure.[39] Similar general statements exist for cattle- and bird-farms and fruit depots. Other parts of the royal economy lie outside the scope of the archive. We can, for example, see grain going to horses from grain-suppliers, but we have no statement from a stables about its births and deaths. Clothes and armaments which seem to appear in a pre-Persian archive from Susa[40] do not appear at all.

The documents of the supply-stations give us access to people travelling and people working at a particular site. Travellers described in less or greater detail pass along the Road,[41] carrying the documents, issued by the king or by someone of satrapal status, which describe their entitlements, which vary according to their status. Only one such document survives, a Bodleian parchment; I have written about that.[42] Workers at particular sites get regular monthly rations. Everybody gets a basic ration in corn, which they will have to process; travellers get flour. These rations vary according to status, though not according to sex; women with the same trade-description as men get equal pay.[43] Children are minutely differentiated in ways which were obscure before two unpublished texts turned out to rank them by their size in cubits in a way known from Assyrian texts.[44] Those workers on a certain level for corn get wine regularly as well. Apart from regular rations, there are exceptional bonuses. The only ones we can really understand are those for mothers, twice as large for mothers of boys.[45]

This much detail is necessary for explaining how we come to have data about the scribal class, with which I at last return to our principal subject. Virtually all our quantitative data come from ration documents. It is not always clear where the groups are working, but sometimes detail accumulates. It is now clear for example that the 11 Babylonian scribes assigned by Parnaka in the ninth month of Darius' twenty-third year (from now on, I abbreviate such dates as 23/9) (PF 1807) were at Persepolis, where they are attested earlier in the year (PF–NN 1511, 23/2–4). It is not so clear what the relationship to this group is of the 7 men and 6 boys described as

[39] It is now reasonably clear that Hallock's categories of V-texts (Journals) and W-texts (Accounts) complement one another.

[40] Scheil (1907, 1911); Hinz (1967).   [41] On which see Koch (1986).

[42] Driver (1957: no. VI), with Lewis (1977: 5–6).

[43] For discussion of women in the work-force, see Brosius (1991) 243–84.

[44] PF–NN 1612, 2049, with Stolper, forthcoming.

[45] N-texts, with Hallock (1969: 37–8), Brosius (1991: 283–4).

Babylonian scribes writing on parchment three months later (PF 1810, 23/12). The 11 Persepolis scribes are listed for their wine rations, so they could be closely related to a group still described as assigned by Parnaka eight months after his disappearance from the archive, 13 men, 2 boys, 6 women, 2 girls, 8 servants (PF 1828, 25/10–11), a fairly characteristic example of the almost familial nature of a work-group. This is in fact not quite the largest group of scribes on parchment. It is slightly exceeded by our earliest reference to scribes, at Rakkan, which can almost be described as an industrial centre, where there were 15 in 15/2 (PF–NN 2486), a number which gradually drops off to 14 and 10. By year 21 the Rakkan group, by now explicitly described as Babylonian, may be split between Parnaka and Ziššawiš, with the former having 5 men, 2 boys, 8 women, 3 girls, 8 servants, the latter 3 men and 3 servants (PF 1947, 23–30). Other groups under these headings are smaller in number. Though not all statements are equally explicit, there is nothing against the assumption that all Babylonian scribes write on parchment and all writers on parchment are Babylonians. They will of course be writing Aramaic. The implications of the fact that groups of this size were writing away producing documentation which is totally lost to us are pretty fearsome, but can be invoked to assist our bewilderment on certain matters, notably how the commodities got into the Persepolis system in the first place. There is at least one isolated cross-reference to a parchment document produced at an audit.[46]

That there are grades of scribes and possibly scribes who are a good deal more than scribes emerges from a consideration of the ration-scales. The men in the groups which we have been considering get 1 quart of grain a day, 3 BAR a month, and their wine-rations are minimal, 5 quarts a month; occasionally they get bonuses of fruit. Alongside them we have individuals, generally named, on higher scales, 4 and $4\frac{1}{2}$ BAR a month. One of them,[47] probably called Šaulbaladda, even rises to three times as much grain, 9 BAR a month, and a wine-ration six times the size, 30 quarts a month. He is described as 'scribe in the treasury' and is normally based fairly near Persepolis; his scribal designation sometimes disappears in the simple title 'treasurer'. How unusual he is remains unclear. A few lines down on the account on which his grain-ration appears (PF 1947, 21–2), another pair, described as '– –]battura, a scribe working on parchment at Appištadan and his companion Pu?–ra?–ya?', have been partly read, partly restored, as being on this very high scale. I found this puzzling, since Appištadan is not a major centre, but collation seems to support the reading.[48]

---

[46] PF 1986:31–2. Cf. PFa 27.

[47] PF 1947:17. For the name, cf. PF–NN 544:3. For his wine ration, see PF–NN 1034 (17/4), 2493: 9–11 (19/4–8).

[48] Stolper and Jones (pers. comm. 9.10.1992): 'the number could be any between 4 and 9, that

The groups we have so far considered are by no means the largest in the scribal world. In year 23 we get multiple references over a nine-month period to 29 Persian 'boys' who are copying texts at Pittanan, assigned by Šuddayauda.[49] We should not be misled by *puhu*, 'boys', which merely means they are not *šalup*, 'gentlemen'. Sixteen of them are on the higher $4\frac{1}{2}$ BAR scale, 50 per cent more than most of the Babylonians we have been looking at, and get additional wine-rations as well. Pittanan is no metropolis;[50] activity there is not on a large scale and is more or less confined to this year. There may be something temporary going on in the neighbourhood which requires this large-scale concentration of men without women or children. I have found nothing else like it among the scribes.

What is surprising about this group of 29 is their Persian ethnic, which we would not have expected with this profession. Since we are dealing with one group only which has been locally defined, we can hardly be sure that they are doing something different from those defined elsewhere as writers on parchment, but whatever they are doing it looks likely that it was not part of their cultural heritage; it is something they have been trained to do.

There is in fact more evidence than one might imagine for foreigners acquiring scribal skills. The Babylonian scribal caste is apparently not as closed as I had imagined. We have already seen[51] that there is evidence for Egyptian scribes in eighth-century Assyria, and there is evidently some in Babylonia as well.[52] Since it is at least possible that *sepīru* in Akkadian may be an office with no writing functions (there is a well-known argument about Ezra),[53] I think I have in the past slid over the evidence for an Iranian *sepīru* in the service of Artareme,[54] one of the characters of the convulsion round the throne in 424/3.[55]

I now want to reconsider, which brings me on to the second category of evidence for scribes at Persepolis. As I said earlier, the letters of very high officials like Parnaka and Ziššawiš end with subscripts giving the names of the scribe and those who communicated the word of the high official. In this

---

is, any made out of more than one row of verticals – in spite of which, the traces do look most like 9'.

[49] PF 871, PF–NN 1588; PF–NN 1485, PF 1137.   [50] Koch (1990: 102–5).   [51] See n. 9.

[52] Dandamayev (1967) and (1983: 125, [237]).

[53] Modern discussion of Ezra's title starts with Schaeder (1930); see e.g. Williamson (1985: 100). For general information about scribes in Babylonia, see Dandamayev (1983: 85–96, [236–7]); it looks as if *sepīru* may be office-holders as well as simple scribes, whereas *ţupšarru* only write.

[54] Dandamayev (1983: 75, [236]). The main text is Dar. 394, in Z. N. Strasmeir, *Inschriften von Darius, König von Babylon (521–485 v. Chr.)* (Babylonische Texte 10–12; Leipzig, 1897); cf. BE IX 48:7, in H. V. Hilprecht and A. T. Clay, *Business Documents of the Murashu Sons of Nippur, Dated in the Reign of Artaxerxes I (464–424 BC)* (Philadelphia, 1898).

[55] Lewis (1977: 18 n. 94, 74 n. 162).

evidence we are not talking about any kind of title. The name comes with a verb. I have reviewed these subscripts in the light of the new evidence, which, as far as the scribes go, does change the picture quite a lot. I now have from this type of evidence about 48 named scribes, of whom about 20 are new. Most of them are found with documents of Parnaka. The previous picture by which the great majority of Ziššawiš texts are written by Hintamukka, who had a long career extending well into the period of the Treasury texts, is not much altered. If one lists these scribes, 15, about a third, have obviously Iranian names; I am not claiming that they wrote a third of the texts, though some of them are fairly productive.

It would be possible to suggest that these Iranian names are assumed and disguise an Elamite origin. Some will remember the Assyrian name taken temporarily by Psammetichus I of Egypt[56] and the Babylonian names that Nebuchadnezzar is alleged to have given Daniel and his companions,[57] though I have not yet thought of a Persian parallel. But the Persian boys at Pittanan may give us substantial reason to think that the conquering race did apply itself to acquiring scribal skills.

I add, more or less parenthetically, that the new evidence does not expand the picture of the aides to Parnaka and Ziššawiš to anything like the same extent as it does that of the scribes. There are very few new names, and they are obviously temporary staff drafted in from time to time. The only real excitement is an earlier appearance of a Greek Yaunā, working for Ziššawiš in 15/10 (PF–NN 2566), seven years earlier than the Yaunā who supported Parnaka's last years, of whom I made such a fuss in *Sparta and Persia*.[58] It is quite impossible to say whether they are identical. We do now have much greater precision about terms of office and a bit more evidence about moving from scribe-status to aide-status and back and eventual promotion. I will not discuss again the exact way in which these aides functioned, though Stolper has improved the detail of the interpretation since I wrote.[59]

What is important is the linguistic effect of all this. Aides have to communicate with the scribe, and their attempts at mutual understanding may affect what goes on clay. If we have to allow for scribes in Elamite who are native Persian-speakers, we may have to do more reconsideration. There has always been duplication in the tablets of parallel Persian and Elamite words, which has enabled us to do a good deal (I think, too much) in expanding our Elamite vocabulary.[60] The commonest is the word for sealed document, often a travel-pass, Elamite *halmi*, Persian *miyatukka* (linguistically equivalent to our 'viaticum'). There can be no doubt about that one, but some scholars have been known to tie themselves into knots

[56] Luckenbill (1927: §§ 774, 905).   [57] Daniel 1.7.   [58] Lewis (1977: 12–15).
[59] Lewis (1977: 10–11 with nn.); Stolper (1984: 305 n. 17).
[60] Gershevitch (1969a and b, 1970), Hinz (1973).

before realising that the Elamite word *kapnuškira* does not, in the texts, function differently from the Persian *ganzabara*, i.e. 'treasurer' (that word survives too, but only in Hebrew). Gershevitch[61] has attached great importance to the fact that documents will have to come out in sound in Persian, so that the Elamite scribe may take short cuts. The truth may be more simple than that, if we are dealing with Persian scribes writing Elamite. We can positively expect that there will be different scribal behaviour in different places, and can start looking for more besides the obvious ones; the best-known of these is the increased prevalence of Elamite month-names as against Persian ones the nearer one gets to Susa.[62]

Despite the obvious amount of Aramaic in the area and in the administration, the linguistic barrier between it and Elamite is apparently too strong to produce much intermingling. There is nothing like the tantalising questions about which language is influencing the other which emerge from the Babylonian and Aramaic versions of the Behistun inscription.[63] The point to look at here is the amount of reinforcement which Aramaic gives to the Elamite. The proportion of texts with Aramaic epigraphs is in fact fairly small, about 2 per cent in the published texts. Mostly, the epigraphs are very short, the name of the recipient, the date, or the commodity involved,[64] but there are occasional texts which are almost fully bilingual; this happens particularly with documents concerning Hatarbanuš, the grain-supplier at Memaš.[65]

I do not think I can contribute much to the general questions of the spread of reading and writing skills. My inclination is to doubt that there was all that much literacy around, whether for the noble or for the common man. I once thought I had found circumstances in which the literate might be defrauding the illiterate, but now doubt them.

I have touched occasionally on variations of scribal practice, and could expand on it considerably, even without getting on to what seems to me, but not to assyriologists, the appallingly random nature of Elamite spelling. Apparent variations may represent, not institutional distinctions, but different ways of saying the same thing, even without the Elamite / Old Persian variations. Ziššawiš' scribe Hintamukka tends to have more complex subscripts than other people; does that represent what he thought it necessary to record or a real difference in Ziššawiš' office practice? Sometimes letters give the day of the month and the place where the letter was written; these are a minority.

[61] Gershevitch (1971, 1979).   [62] Hallock (1969: 74–5) and (1978: 111).
[63] Greenfield and Porten (1982: 21). As far as I know, linguistic study of the Babylonian version has been very much neglected, despite its position at the root of Akkadian studies.
[64] Hallock (1969: 82).
[65] PF 855, 857, 858, 1587; PF–NN 293, 486, 717, 742, 743, 1228, 1371, 1837.

This variation becomes more noticeable when one gets on to, say, the travel-documents from different points along the road. Besides their differences about month-names, different stations vary a good deal in the detail which they give about the party which has been supplied and about its route. Some of them have a tendency, irritating for the historian and perhaps even for the auditors, to give the month, but not the year. One of them habitually omits the name of the supplier.

This last omission is only apparent, and I come at last to one of the most important features of the archive, the use of seals. This is a very tricky matter indeed. Hallock himself wrote a very short article[66] about it, which begins:

I have been contemplating the seal-impressions on Persepolis tablets for about thirty-five years. In that time I have made some discoveries about the ways they were used, but I am still confused about many things. It is one of those cases in which if you are not confused you do not understand the problem.

There are unsealed documents in the archive, and I do not understand why, but nevertheless there is an enormous quantity and variety of seals. In this 1977 article, Hallock had distinguished 580 seals with two or more occurrences. Before he died, he had got to 629 and had not tried to count the number of those which appeared once only. We may not know much about the extent of literacy, but we do know something about the spread of seal-usage. Virtually all these seals were made for the purpose, though not necessarily for their present user, but there is the occasional fortunate exception in which coins were used instead. Two tablets are sealed with an Attic owl,[67] two (of which one has not yet got into the literature) with a Type III Persian archer.[68] They have done something to check the gadarene rush to downdate Greek coinage.[69]

Let us start with what may look the easy end. All Parnaka's letters and receipts for rations bear his seal, and so surely did all the authorisations which he gave to travellers and others. In fact, he had two seals, both with Aramaic inscriptions, the first saying just 'Parnaka', the second 'Parnaka son of Arsham'.[70] He changed from one seal to another at a date in May 500, which I cannot narrow to less than a fortnight; this is the most precise date in ancient art. He announced the change in two surviving letters by adding the sentences 'Also the seal which formerly was mine has been replaced. Now that seal is mine which has been applied to this tablet.' One of the tablets has

---

[66] Hallock (1977). Garrison (1992) marks the start of fuller publication on the sealings in the archive, to be conducted by him and Margaret Root.   [67] Starr (1976).

[68] Root (1988: 10–11). There is another on PF–NN 1898 (undated), used by the same recipient, but, apparently, on a different mission.   [69] See n. 19.

[70] See now Garrison (1992: 9 with figs. 9–12). Both are also illustrated in the plates volume to *CAH* IV², nn. 35a and b, together with that of Gobryas father of Mardonius.

the new seal twice, the other once. Just as one might wonder why the Persian bodyguards at Sardis accepted Bagaios' word about the seal of Darius which they can have never seen before (above, p. 18), one could wonder how the recipients of these letters knew that the new seal was genuine and why Parnaka did not take the precaution of putting both the old seal and the new seal on the same tablet to mark the change.[71]

Ziššawiš also has two seals in the Fortification Tablets, though this time there is a gap of a year between their dated appearances. They are very different from Parnaka's and I defer discussion for a moment.

Seals can stand in place of writing. This is most obvious in the case of the single Greek tablet,[72] which simply says '2 marriš of wine for the month Tebet'. It has two seals: one will be for the supplier, one for the recipient. Suppliers' seals normally go on the left edge of the tablet, those of the recipient anywhere else room can be found; there are many exceptions. The way-station which never names itself or a supplier was therefore not anonymous to the auditors or to the central administration; it was punctilious in the use and placing of its seal.[73] I say 'its seal', because there is a good deal of evidence to show that some seals were not personal but could be used by various and succeeding suppliers at the same station.[74]

The fun really starts when we get on to the category of rations for work-groups. Here, although the supplier and the recipient are generally named, there is a whole category of texts which only has one seal-type on it, though it may appear several times. This happens above all with three seals, one of which can be associated with the Treasury and Treasury-workers.[75] The explanation offered is that both supplier and recipient are part of the Treasury or one of the other systems. I still find it a bit puzzling, but it is obviously linked with the equally confusing pattern of the systems of 'those responsible' and 'those apportioning'. There is a fairly serious problem about where these texts were written and sealed, since they cover a wide scatter of places. Was someone moving rapidly around the countryside with the appropriate seal? Hallock thought that could not be so for reasons of the security of the seal, but I do not see that his conclusion that the texts must have been *inscribed* centrally necessarily follows.

Other, even more important, seals were used over a wide area. Three seals record the receipt of commodities for the King. It was not only Bagaios who was allowed the use of the King's seal. At least one of these

[71] Hinz and Koch (1987) 225 translate *pitika* (*pi-ti-qa* for them) as 'lost', which would ease the problems, but makes one wonder how it could have been lost. To explore the usage of the word here would involve a complex treatment of operations with cattle.
[72] See n. 26.
[73] Seal 33, now identified with Seal 88. For an attempt to locate the station, see Hallock (1978: 113 n. 10).   [74] Hallock (1978: passim).
[75] Hallock (1969: 28); Hallock (1978: 129–30); Koch (1981).

(Seal 7) makes its identity obvious with a portrait of the king standing with a spiked crown between strange animals and a trilingual royal inscription of Darius himself, and another (Seal 66) has a seated king with an enigmatic Aramaic legend. These seals are of contemporary manufacture, though of very different styles. But the recipient of cattle for the King had to make do with what Hallock insisted, in the face of considerable scepticism, was an heirloom from the seventh century bearing the legend 'Cyrus the Anshanite, son of Teispes'; it had originally belonged to Cyrus I.[76] The assumption is that, although these are royal seals, they are used in such restricted contexts that misuse is unlikely.

I return to Zissawis. Tidy-minded legalists have always been bothered about how to classify him and Parnaka.[77] Were they satraps of Persis? Very unlikely. Should they be called *Hofmarschallen*? There are considerable problems about that, particularly if you want to find them on Persepolis reliefs. Parnaka is evidently just Parnaka, but there is a little more to say about Zissawis. His original seal (Seal 83) had borne no inscription, though it was no doubt recognisable to many. By February 502 he has acquired his new one (Seal 11), but it is now not personal to him. It bears a picture of the King and a trilingual inscription of Darius. When he returns to Persepolis in 470 or so, he still has no personal seal; he is using one of Xerxes.[78] There are other Darius seals about, however, which are still in use by high officials far into the reign of Xerxes. At least one original agate seal of Darius survives in the British Museum.[79] It is reported to have come from Egypt; we can see that there is no particular reason to assume that Darius used it personally.

My rules allow quotation of the book of Esther provided that it is only used illustratively and not as primary evidence. It may be recalled that the King gives his seal first to Haman (3.10) and then to Mordecai (8.8–10), saying to the latter 'You may write as you please in the name of the king and seal it with the king's ring; for an edict written in the name of the king and sealed with the king's ring may not be revoked.' It is only very rarely that Zissawis and Parnaka actually write in the name of the King, but we cannot doubt that at least Zissawis throughout much of his life stood for him and enjoyed his trust.

And what about those whom he trusted? We have no grounds that I can see for supposing that he was ever literate, ever capable of checking what

[76] These seals are now all treated by Garrison (1992). For Seal 7, see 13–14 with figs. 21–2 ('Court Style'). On Seal 66, now distinguished into two seals, ibid. 10–12 with figs. 15–18 ('Fortification Style'). For the Cyrus seal (Seal 93) ibid. 3–4 with figs. 1–2.

[77] Hinz (1971: 311); Lewis (1977: 7–9); Koch (1990: 224–9), adopting Hinz's 'Hofmarschall', but putting it in quotation marks.

[78] Cameron (1948: 57–8 (Seal 6); Schmidt (1957: 21 no. 6 with pl. 4).

[79] Garrison (1992: 19–20 with fig. 32); also in the plates volume to *CAH* IV[2], pl. 65.

was being written in his name, though no doubt he could have his correspondence read back to him, as Darius had the Behistun inscription read to him before it was sent to the peoples of the empire.[80] Power could exist without literacy, on condition of trusting those who held the seals.

[80] Darius, Behistun Inscription, Old Persian IV 91.

3   Literacy and the city-state in archaic and classical Greece

Rosalind Thomas

Literacy and power often seem to be intimately linked, but both are remarkably slippery concepts. Is literacy an enabling skill, or are its implications largely oppressive? Power for whom, and what kind of power (practical, symbolic, bureaucratic)? Moreover, literacy is a variable, its implications constrained or enhanced by the context in which it is found. One finds conflicting reactions to the written word: it may open up possibilities through education, or serve only to reinforce the dominance of certain social groups. Especially important for the relationship between literacy and power is the distinction between societies in which writing exists (but is perhaps used only by scribes) and societies in which many individuals need to be able to read and/or write for themselves. In many societies the skills of writing and reading, which we group together naturally under the term 'literacy', are quite separable, and it is common to encounter people who can read and not write, but who are not limited by this. Since the written word in Greece was most commonly read aloud (and so accessible even to those who could not read), it seems safer for the purposes of this chapter to concentrate upon the power of writing, rather than that of literacy.

Writing is perhaps most immediately connected with power in relation to the state and its records: one thinks, for example, of state lists of citizens, of their income and whereabouts, or records of taxes, the extensive communication with the population by means of writing. It has indeed been claimed by some anthropologists that a state cannot cohere at all without literacy: that writing is essential for the kind of authoritative communication the state needs, and that an empire or large nation state simply could not hold itself together without the effective long-distance communication that writing provides.[1] Literacy, in this view, is an essential means of control. Lévi-Strauss, in a famous passage, gave a more bitingly

[1] Goody (1986); cf. Larsen (1988). Note that ML = R. Meiggs and D. M. Lewis, *A Selection of Greek Historical Inscriptions* (rev. edn, Oxford, 1988); Tod = M. N. Tod, *Greek Historical Inscriptions* (Oxford, 1946–8); *Syll.* = W. Dittenberger, *Sylloge Inscriptionum Graecarum*[3] (Leipzig, 1915–24).

cynical evaluation of literacy: writing is an essential tool of empire and expansion, it 'seems to have favoured the exploitation of human beings rather than their enlightenment', and 'the primary function of written communication was to facilitate slavery'.[2]

At first glance these suggestions seem only marginally relevant to archaic or classical Greece – indeed they may serve merely to emphasise the gulf between ancient Greece and the modern state's use of literacy. Analysis tends to be studiously vague in these general evaluations, but it seems to be the modern bureaucratic state and a modern Western interpretation of literacy that is assumed.[3] The classical Greek world had nothing resembling bureaucracy: records, if kept at all, tended to be slight, disorganised and in any case largely uncentralised. Even if they were preserved, they were not necessarily used – an important distinction brought home by Clanchy's work on the Middle Ages.[4] In Athens, from which most evidence comes, certain records were destroyed once the transaction was completed (e.g. the records of state debtors), and while there was an archive from at least the late fifth century, it is only in the first half of the fourth that we can trace a greater respect for documentation, writing as proof, written documents as equal in value to oral testimony in court. The idea of the state as an impersonal machine above and beyond the ordinary citizen-body is similarly inappropriate for the *polis*. For its citizens were identified with the *polis*, and, at least in theory, they passed or ratified the laws, decrees and treaties of the state, and, in a democracy, they sat in judgement in the lawcourts. Yet this makes it all the more interesting to consider how the Greek city-states managed with so few written records, what they did choose to record, why or how far state records increase over the classical period, and how far Greek states were aware of the potential power of writing in pursuance of state authority. What seems to emerge is that the Greek city exploited one potential of writing in a manner characteristically Greek: that is, not through bureaucratic records or administration so much as through public display. The power of writing for the Greek city-state lay not so much in its ability to store records and open the way to bureaucracy, as in its potential for publication in its fullest, archaic, sense of open-air public display.

I will start, then, by looking first at writing and control in the archaic and classical *polis* in general, then at the role of inscriptions and the importance of publicity over the same period, then finally turn to the place of inscriptions and the use of non-epigraphic written records by the state in fifth-century Athens.

[2] Lévi-Strauss (1976: 392–3).
[3] As in, for example, Goody (1986).
[4] Clanchy (1979).

Writing and control in the city-state

The role of written records was so far removed from Greek preoccupations, that Greek writers have little to say on writing and its relation to the *polis*; but when they do, their views are almost uniformly idealistic. Writing the laws down, according to Aristotle, encourages justice or fairness, or is an essential basis for democracy (*Pol.* 1286a9–17);[5] 'written laws are the guardians of the just', as Gorgias declared (*Palam.* DK 30, fr. 11a). Aristotle adds, vaguely and briefly, that writing is useful for managing a household, money-making, learning and political life (*Pol.* 1338a15–17). There is no hint, so far as I know, that writing was regarded as an unwelcome tool of the state, of an impersonal bureaucracy, or a tool of propaganda; or even, more neutrally, that it was essential for the business of politics. The contrast with Rome is striking. When Virgil described his idealised image of the countryside, one of its virtues was precisely that it was free of the *populi tabularia*, the public archives (*Georg.* 2.501–2). The image of the urban centre as burdened with records – or even inscriptions – seems peculiarly Roman.

Greek writers, on the other hand, could be and indeed *were* distrustful of writing (written documents could be forged[6]), but the developed and refined criticism of writing is made in the context of education and rhetoric: compare Plato's famous criticism of writing as an inadequate source of knowledge in the *Phaedrus*; or his later reluctance to put his most valuable thoughts into written form, if we can trust the *Seventh Letter* (this may also have been an élitist gesture, if one compares the habits of the Hellenistic philosophical schools); or Alcidamas' entertaining, indeed devastating, critique of the practice of delivering speeches from a written text, entitled (literally) *Against Those Who Write Written Speeches*. In the mid-fourth century, the orator Aeschines had to point out to his Athenian audience the democratic value of the public archives, arguing that the public documents (*demosia grammata*) enabled one to check the lies of one's opponents and therefore strengthen the rule of the demos (2.89; 3.75). Again, writing – when it was considered at all – was generally seen as a positive force for democracy and its rule by written law.

We can see some of the reasons for this (and attitudes for writing in the Greek world are closely bound to its use). The main use of writing for most city-states was to record laws and treaties. Archival documents were a comparatively untapped resource. Public archives were dispersed or uncentralised, or even non-existent in those terms. The central archive in fourth-century Athens, the Metroön, mainly housed decrees of the *boule*

---

[5] Cf. also Aristotle, *Pol.* 1287b5–8, 1270b28; cf. 1272a36–9; Eur. *Suppl.* 433; Solon fr. 36 W = *Ath. Pol.* 12.4.   [6] See Thomas (1989: 41–2).

and assembly. Other public documents lay with the appropriate officials or often in temples. So there was no sole source of documentary authority and to talk of a 'central state archive' is probably to dignify and bureaucratise a more disparate and haphazard system. Even in the Hellenistic period when archives are supposed to have been more complex, archival collections might belong to separate officials, or be kept in temples under divine protection (e.g. the Parian archive, whose organisation has been revealed in a recently published inscription).[7] It has been thought that later Hellenistic practice was to deposit private contracts in the city archive – though this was not uniform even then[8] – in which case one could say that the state archive conferred protection and legitimacy even on private documents. But this was apparently absent earlier. Individuals would deposit copies of contracts with other individuals (sometimes officials), if at all. Even in Hellenistic Delos (pre-166 BC), the contracts for loans from the temple treasuries were left with private persons.[9] The idea that public archives regularly authorised private documents even in the Hellenistic world is much exaggerated.

There is again a contrast with the later Roman world when we look for wholesale attacks on large bodies of written documents. Classical Greek sources seem remarkably unconcerned with the fate of any written documents, even that of Solon's laws, which could well have been damaged by the Persians when they captured the Acropolis: much more alarming was the fate of the temples. True, documents were destroyed in a form of *damnatio memoriae* in the amnesty in Athens (see below). But Greek history is not haunted by destruction of whole archives. The first deliberate burning of an archive I have found is in 115 BC,[10] and much of Roman history – as well as discussion of its evidence – revolves around the destruction of its records. This can hardly have been mere carelessness, but I would suspect must partly reflect a Roman reverence for written record, and in particular, its ancient traditions as embodied in the records. For example Suetonius lamented in moving terms the destruction of at least 3,000 bronze tablets on the Capitoline Hill, burned in the fire at the end of Nero's reign. As he expressed it, 'This was the most beautiful and most ancient record of empire (*instrumentum imperii*), comprising senatorial decrees, decisions made by the Roman people . . . dating back almost to the foundation of Rome' (*Vesp.* 8.5).

Rome's history is also peppered with book-burning, from the destruction of the Sibylline Books to the deliberate censorship of the Principate. The only indication of book-burning in classical Greek history is the supposed burning of Protagoras' works in the second half of the fifth century, but the

---

[7] Lambinudakis and Wörrle (1983).
[9] Linders (1975: 43 and refs. there).
[8] See Thomas (1992: 133–4, 140–1).
[10] *Syll.* (3) 684; Harris (1989: 128).

sources for that are comparatively late (from the third century BC) and unreliable, and, most significantly, largely of the Roman period.[11] One can only imagine that books as such were not seen as a threat by the Greeks, partly because they were only one way amongst many of circulating ideas compared with the more book-dominated Hellenistic and Roman cultures; and that written documents in archives were either totally extraneous to the main functioning of the city-state or, again, that their authority was simply not conceived as fundamental.

Indeed the element of control often associated with modern documentation was not necessarily connected with writing at all in the Greek world. Sparta, widely admired for the rigid domination she exerted over (and by) her citizens, achieved this almost entirely without writing. She had laws or *nomoi*, but they were unwritten: her legendary lawgiver Lycurgus was said to have disdained written law, trusting rather in education (Plut. *Lyc.* 13.1–3), and the comparative paucity of documents – even inscriptions – in Sparta is notorious.[12] Similarly, Plato's authoritarian scheme in the *Laws*, intended to control every aspect of citizens' lives, does not, so far as I can see, think entirely in terms of written laws (see especially *Laws* 822d ff., and cf. 788b, 793a–d). The very term *nomos* extended, of course, in meaning from custom to oral, customary law, and written law. Greek writers are often proud of the *polis* being governed by law (e.g. Phocylides fr. 4; Hdt. on Spartans, 7.104; Eur. *Medea* 537), but it is by no means certain that this always denoted law in written form. Writing, then, is not necessarily part of the identity or ideal of the Greek *polis* and one can excuse Greek political thinkers for not associating the cohesive power of the *polis* with writing when there lay before them the example of Sparta – according to popular rumour, Spartans were illiterate. Those who were interested in total control looked elsewhere for the mechanisms than the written word.

Publicity and inscriptions: memorials and laws

There is plenty of evidence, however, that Greek *poleis* were alert to certain possibilities of asserting authority that writing offered, whether one looks at the relations between citizens of the same state or between different city-states. *Polis* authority could be emphasised through display of its decisions or laws in monumental stone form – this is what the fifth-century stone law-code of Gortyn in Crete does by its repeated demands for obedience to what is written – or through attempts to limit memorials, in which the written word is only part of the whole memorial, effectively a sub-species of memorial.

[11] Dover (1975: 34–5); cf. Cramer (1945) for book-burning in Rome.
[12] See Cartledge (1978), Boring (1979).

It is the memorial which is the main realm in which the Greek city tried to limit and control writing. Thus Sparta forbade named tombstones except for those who had died in war or childbirth.[13] But this is not merely an example of peculiarly Spartan paranoia about writing. In an obscure and undatable law, Athens seems to have forbidden funerary monuments from perhaps *c*. 500 or 480 to *c*. 430 (these dates reflect the archaeological record).[14] This sumptuary legislation is usually attributed to Cleisthenes and is reflected in the total absence of private funerary monuments and tombstones down to about 430. The prime focus of attack here was probably memorials of any kind, but it would affect the use of writing. What is particularly striking is that Athens here seems to be moving along similar lines to Sparta. It is conspicuous that this is precisely the period when the public funeral ceremony and funeral speeches of the war dead began in the Kerameikos (perhaps from a little before the Persian Wars), and the huge stone lists of the dead are set up in the Kerameikos at least from the 460s if not earlier. In other words the only Athenians granted memorials at their death between the 480s and *c*. 430 were those who had died for Athens. This exception seems also to allow memorials for foreigners who had died for Athens: a list of Argives was erected (ML 35) and a memorial for a Megarian named Pythion (ML 51).

Here, then, is the *polis* attempting to extend its control over memorials and memory, and indirectly, therefore, over the written word. In the case of Athens this conforms with Athenian official ideals, and I wonder if it is attempting to associate the inscription entirely with the public activities of the *polis*.

Several cities were most concerned to protect the stones on which their decisions or laws were written. In a treaty between Elis and Heraia, inscribed at Olympia *c*. 500, a sacred fine is threatened 'for anyone who injures this writing' (ML 17). There are heavy penalties in a fifth-century Argive inscription for traitors and anyone who makes the letters on the stele illegible.[15] The Tean curses issue the direst threats against anyone who breaks the stelai, cuts out the letters or makes them invisible (ML 30). Another set of legal pronouncements from Teos (*c*. 480–50 BC), characteristically also in curse form, adds more: imprecations are directed against certain officials 'who do not read out (*analegein*) the writing on the stele to the best of their memory or power'. It probably continues with curses against anyone who does not write the words up or who spoils the stone.[16] Protection of writing (along with many other things) by means of curses continues into the Hellenistic period.

[13] Plut. *Lyc*. 27.3; Cartledge (1978: n. 71).
[14] Cic. *De Legibus* 1.26.64, with Stupperich (1977: 71–86).
[15] Mitsos (1983), ed. pr. (= *SEG* 33.275).   [16] See Herrmann (1981) for ed. pr.

This implies, of course, that the stone inscription authorises or embodies the law and that the inscription is meant to give permanence to the enactment – one important potential of writing. But so many early laws employ curses or oaths to make the law more effective, or are actually dedications to the gods – who are often enlisted as guarantors – that more seems to be at stake. If we can assume that most laws probably remained unwritten (i.e. customary laws),[17] it seems that these cities were attempting to use the monumental form of writing to impress and display their authority, to reinforce the curses or oaths. These would be more impressive if visible, and especially if they were read out repeatedly, like the Tean curses (cf. also a Delian inscription which writes out a curse twice[18]). They also intended to dedicate the inscription to the gods and therefore presumably still further sanctify it. This may be what is meant by a fourth-century inscription (Tod II 142) which says that it is to be inscribed 'in order that the oaths be valid (*kyria*)'.

Alongside this are attempts to ensure that secretaries did not abuse their (presumably superior) knowledge of writing. We have encountered the Tean curses against anyone who 'does not read out the writing on the stele'. Erythrae tried, probably in the fifth century, to prevent secretaries from serving the same magistrate twice and to curb their power in various ways.[19] On the other hand, Spensithios the remembrancer and scribe, *mnemon* and *poinikastas*, from an unknown city in Crete, *c.* 500 BC, was an exceedingly powerful man. He was able to participate in sacred and secular affairs in all cases wherever the highest official or *kosmos* might be involved, he was granted extensive honours and tax-immunity, and his privileges as well as his office were hereditary. The community of Spensithios seems to be heading in the opposite direction. But the point I would like to make is that even from our rather slight evidence for archaic and early classical secretaries, they seem to be regarded as highly responsible – if not as powerful as Spensithios: they are officials, not merely scribes, and there are hints that some cities were alert to their power and tried to regulate it.[20] There was little point in recording the law in writing if the secretary would not read it out accurately, or could not otherwise be scrutinised by the *polis*. I am not sure whether they are being regulated primarily because they are officials, or because they are in charge of written records, but the effect probably amounts to the same – and at least underlines the fact, often ignored, that the efficacy of written records was linked closely to the

---

[17] This is discussed at more length in a forthcoming article; cf. Ostwald (1973).
[18] Vallois (1914: 250–2).
[19] Erythrae: *Die Inschriften von Erythrai und Klazomenai* I (Bonn, 1972), ed. H. Engelmann and R. Merkelbach, no. 2 and 17; cf. protection of the *grapheus* at Elis, *c.* 475–450: Hainsworth (ed.), *Tituli ad dialectos Graecas illustrandas selecti* II (1972), no. 19 (= *SEG* 29.402). See generally, Ruzé (1988).   [20] Cf. Ruzé (1988).

character of the officials administering them. Written law would not promote fairness (if that were its aim) if officials were not themselves checked.[21]

What is at stake here, however, is writing in its publicly visible form. The Greek city harnessed the written word to impress its authority and record its laws, and they were probably the most important form of public writing in most cities. But this was done almost exclusively through the public inscription (or else wooden boards, which I return to below), rather than hidden documents. This is the characteristically Greek way of using writing in the service of the *polis*, and I would suggest that, in effect, the *polis* was here extending the role of the memorial to its own enactments. That is, the *polis* inscriptions borrowed and extended the habit of using writing for memorials for private individuals to its own decisions. Public inscriptions might, for instance, confer honour, and, by their very existence, public inscriptions on stone seem to have an authority beyond their literal content. Some of the earliest inscriptions are very like marker stones, tall and thin, and tapering at the top, which reminds one that inscriptions probably began as marker stones. So while these documents would also function to preserve or convey information, their public and visible nature is enlisted in a sense quite close to that of the memorial. This is exactly what one would expect in a society where so much emphasis is laid on outward and public reputation. As one honorific inscription from Erythrae in the 330s puts it, two stelai are to go up 'so that all may know that the People knows how to return appropriate thanks for the benefits conferred on it'.[22] In more precise examples (below) we can see how the public written word is used to confirm, publicise and protect the values of the community (above I was mainly concerned with the limitation of writing and memorials). The role of the private stone memorial was in some sense replicated by the city-states when they began to set up written versions of their own enactments.

Athens: public inscriptions and lists in the democracy

When we turn to the richer evidence from classical Athens, Athenian proxeny and honorary decrees show exactly this importance of the inscription as a public memorial of honour. In some of the most utterly formulaic of Athenian inscriptions, the focus of their formulae is precisely on the erection of the stone itself. Often very little is mentioned in the decree

[21] Cf. chapter 7, below.
[22] *Die Inschriften von Erythrai und Klazomenai* I, no. 21.

except for the erection of the stone, and the phraseology signifies that the honour consists precisely in being put up on a stele. For instance *IG* I³ 91 (*c.* 416/15): after the name in large letters and the prescript, it is proposed 'since Proxenides is a benefactor . . ., to praise him and inscribe him as *proxenos* and *euergetes* on a stele on the Acropolis'.²³ The phrases about erecting stelai familiar from the longer decrees tend to swell in these cases to fill the whole inscription. It was important to get the name right. An individual from Skiathos is honoured in 408/7 (I³ 110), but was sensitive about his origins, and a proposal is added to the stone to alter his origin from 'Skiathos' to 'Palaioskiathos' (or Old Skiathos). An inscription praising Polyklytos and others (I³ 106) adds, 'Those things written about Timanthos on the Acropolis are to be chiselled out by the Treasurers of the god from the stele' (lines 21ff.). But at least they do not record what is being chiselled out. Another does. A decree concerning Neapolis in northern Greece (*IG* I³ 101, 410/9 BC) adds a proposal that the decree inscribed above should be corrected by the secretary to the *boule*, so that it should not say (as it was going to) that the Neapolitans were colonists of Thasos. It is to be stressed that they carried on the war together with the Athenians. It is the publicly visible inscriptions which are conveying the honour and which must be correct. But the despised phrase '*apoikia* of the Thasians' is preserved for ever in stone in the latter proposal!²⁴ The Athenian assembly had the last laugh.

Compare the use of lists. Public disgrace as well as honour revolves around open and public documents, particularly lists, which are surprisingly frequent in Athens. So far I have been concerned simply to stress how it was the public inscriptions, rather than archival copies, that were considered powerful. But the public nature of these lists can also be used by the *polis* most effectively to shame its malefactors and ill-wishers. These lists, in stone or wood, were carefully scrutinised, perhaps some of the few inscriptions that were.²⁵

One of the most famous in Athens was the public list of traitors. Thrasyboulos, for instance, accused Leodamas of being on it in the early fourth century, of 'being inscribed on the stele' (ὅτι ἦν στηλήτης).²⁶ Its counterpart is the stele of benefactors which Demosthenes granted an important exemplary role (Dem. 20.64). The list of public debtors on the Acropolis, probably a wooden tablet, was where you would go to seek information to blacken your opponent: as does, for example, the speaker of

---

²³ Cf. *IG* I³ 24 on engraving (but beginning is missing), or *IG* I³ 123.
²⁴ Cf, also *IG* I³ 118 (= ML 87), list of hostages and sureties to be erased from where they are inscribed, in a decree about the Selymbrians, 408 BC.
²⁵ See Thomas (1989: 64–7).   ²⁶ Lyc. *Leocr*. 1.117–19; Arist. *Rhet*. 2 1400a32–6.

[Dem.] 58.14–16. Names would be erased as debtors paid up, so that the process of checking could hardly be easier.[27]

Once we start looking more carefully, other lists come to light. The Amnesty Decree of Patrokleides, passed in 405 and used (or misused) by Andocides for his own case (*De Myst.*), prescribed a wholesale obliteration of names on various lists (it is unclear if they are all lists, and Andocides (§76) seems to take it that decrees were also obliterated). The language is compressed and obscure but it implies that there were names on stelai of those in exile for murder, those guilty of attempted massacre or tyranny, and of members of the recent oligarchy of the 400 who did not remain in Athens. It also, incidentally, mentions lists of various kinds of debtors kept by the appropriate officials, tablets (as Boegehold shows) recording charges connected with *euthynai*, lists of *graphai* and a few other types of records.[28] All are to be destroyed in order to reunite the city. I find it astonishing that it also ends by threatening dire penalties for anyone who secretly (*idia*) keeps a copy of the records that are to be cancelled or who speaks maliciously (*mnesikakesai*) – presumably about the past.

For what it is worth, Isocrates, rather later, indicates – in typically opaque language – a range of other publicly visible lists (*Antid.* 15.237): not all sophists are intriguers and sycophants; *these* you will find on the wooden boards (*sanides*) set out by various officials – public offenders and sycophants (set out by archons and thesmothetai), malefactors and their instigators (kept by the Eleven), private offenders, initiators of unjust complaints (kept by the Forty). By his use of ἐκτίθημι (ἐκτιθεμέναις) he implies they were set up outside, probably outside the various courts.

In addition there were yet other lists: lists of metics, deme members (a focus of much manipulation), perhaps those who could attend the assembly.[29] The point is that there is evidence of a surprising number of lists set out by various officials or by the assembly. Most of these seem to gain their force from being publicly visible and therefore capable of being checked. And, while officials keep most of them separately, the *polis* (or assembly) assumes complete power over their content. The mass amnesty offered by the decree of Patrokleides involves the power to destroy the records and prevent anyone keeping copies of them, the obliteration of the criminal records of individuals, the opposite, as it were, of the *damnatio memoriae*. As with the practice of *damnatio*, not only does it show an attitude to written records rather alien to the modern mind (for the

---

[27] There was also a list of Plateians granted Athenian citizenship in the Peloponnesian War, inscribed on a stele on the Acropolis 'so that each should be able to prove his relationship', [Dem.] 59.105.   [28] Andoc. 1.76, 77–9, with Boegehold (1990).

[29] For the *lexiarchikon grammateion* (and elusive *pinax ekklesiastikos*), see *IG* I³ 138.6, and Whitehead (1986: esp. 103–6); for metic lists, Whitehead (1977: 83); for cavalry lists, Thomas (1989: 82–3) and Kroll (1977); Boegehold (1990) discusses all the lists mentioned by the decree of Patrokleides; Thomas (1989: 64–6) for publicly inscribed lists.

records *are* the offence), but it underlines the state's attempt to control the past.

Public inscriptions and the Athenian empire

Let us turn to the assembly decrees of the fifth-century democracy. It has often been noted that Athenian inscriptions increase greatly in number with the radical democracy founded in the 460s: the democratic ideals perhaps demanded greater publicity for the assembly's enactments. Inscriptions recording assembly decrees are repetitiously concerned with stipulating that they be erected on stone on the acropolis, and there is a standard clause for this. It is unclear how many decrees were inscribed. Obviously the ones we have preserved are precisely those deemed appropriate for stone – and the fact that they seem to record the whole of a decree, regardless of its immediate or eternal usefulness (e.g. clauses about dining in the Prytaneion 'tomorrow'), suggests that they were also regarded as embodiments or memorials of assembly business. It is impossible to make much of these erection clauses by themselves. But closer scrutiny reveals some important distinctions and suggests further reasons for this increase in documentation.

Many concern allies of the Athenian empire (478–404 BC), decreed for a specific allied city after a revolt, or for general application over the whole empire. The mechanisms and development of the empire have been much studied, but surprisingly little attention has gone to the specific contribution of written records to imperial control.

For instance, it is interesting to see how the erection clauses are adapted for those decrees which were imposing a settlement on a recalcitrant ally. For one thing, the allies usually have to pay for the stele. Thus the first statement after the prescript in the Phaselis decree declares that it should be engraved on the Acropolis for the Phaselites (*IG* I³ 10, ML 31; *c.* 469–450 BC). At the end of the decree, the Phaselites are to pay. By contrast, the inscription of the treaty with Egesta about the same time (pre-450) is paid for by the Athenians (*IG* I³ 11). The Erythrae decree after Erythrae's (probable) revolt (*c.* 450 BC) says that 'these things and the oath of loyalty are to go on a stone stele on the Acropolis, along with the oath of the *boule*', and as for Erythrae, the phrourarch, an Athenian official, is to engrave them on the Acropolis at Erythrae (*IG* I³ 15, lines 42ff.). Colophon pays for the Athenian inscription (*IG* I³ 38, l. 38–40), and the oikists in Colophon are to inscribe the decree and the oath in Colophon 'where it is the custom' (*IG* I³ 38, lines 38–40; 447/6 BC). After the Euboean revolt, the Chalcidians pay for the Athenian inscription we have as *IG* I³ 40, and the Chalcidian *boule* is to set it up in Chalcis in the temple of Zeus.[30]

[30] Cf. also Neapolis, *IG* I³ 101: stele to go up in the temple of the Virgin Goddess and they to pay for the stele in Athens.

These inscriptions spread over the empire would surely have been impressive, and D. M. Lewis has suggested that the very stoichedon style itself, characteristic of fifth-century Athenian inscriptions, would have been associated in the Greek world with democracy.[31] But they were obviously not merely associated with democracy, nor erected merely for information. The Coinage Decree in which Athens tried to impose Athenian coins, weights and measures on the allies, was communicated through heralds, and they are specified elaborately in the decree. But the decree also declares that 'the *archontes* in the cities are to inscribe it on a stone stele in the agora of each *polis* and the *epistatai* in front of the mint. The Athenians are to do it if they will not' (ML 45 § 10). Later, there is more, heavily restored, about putting up a stele in front of the mint, probably to record the deposits of foreign currency made by individuals (§ 14). Whatever the content of this further written record, it is erected 'so that anyone who wants may see' (the phrase σκοπεῖν τῶι βου[λομένωι... can be made out). This latter phrase is easily, and very often, taken as a declaration of democratic openness and accountability when it occurs on Athenian decrees erected in Athens. The circumstances here, however, give it quite different connotations: the decree was to be visible to impress on the allies the weight of Athens' authority, like a settlement after a revolt, to intimidate as well as to communicate, to impress as well as to record on stone.

What deserves more emphasis here, is that the Athenian democratic organs are effectively causing their decrees to be set up in stone in allied territory, making the allies pay for the privilege and even, on occasion, telling the subject state where to place them. They are presumably meant as permanent stone reminders of the crushing of the revolt and the oath the allies had to take. Indeed it was surely particularly important that the oath of obedience was written up publicly. (Lists, incidentally, are made on these occasions of those who swear the oath, but not on stone: this is specified for Eretria in 446/5 (*IG* I³ 39) and Chalcis (*IG* I³ 40, lines 18–20), just as lists of swearers were usually added up on the stone inscription in the case of treaties.[32])

That at least one Athenian thought that these inscriptions were to intimidate rather than simply to convey information, is suggested by the wonderful parody of the Coinage Decree in Aristophanes' *Birds* (lines 1020ff.; performed in 414). 'Nephelokokkugia' has barely been founded when the *episkopos* and decree-seller arrive (1021ff.). One of the new laws the decree-seller has states that this new city 'shall use [what are clearly Athenian] measures, weights and decrees' (1040). More parodies follow of

---

[31] Lewis (1984).
[32] Cf. also the list of oath-swearers in treaty with Samos, *IG* I³ 48 (439/8); alliance with Perdiccas has a list, *IG* I³ 89; *IG* I³ 11 (Egesta).

the official language of Athenian decrees and one decree begins, until the reader is interrupted, 'And if anyone expels the *archontes* and fails to admit them according to the stele...'[33] (ἐὰν δέ τις ἐξελαύνη τοὺς ἄρχοντας καὶ μὴ δέχηται κατὰ τὴν στήλην ...). Finally, in almost exact confirmation that cities were right to try and protect their inscriptions in whatever way they could, the decree-seller accuses the founder, Peisetairos, of relieving himself against the stele one evening (1054).[34]

Given the close identity in Greek eyes between the decision, law or treaty, that has been made, and the inscription that records it, these Athenian inscriptions could only be a potent symbol of Athenian power and a physical reminder of her interference in their affairs, even their civic space. The most impressive inscriptions in the allied cities may well have been Athenian decrees.

Non-epigraphic documents and accountability in fifth-century Athens

So far we have been dealing almost entirely with documents on stone, and a state use of writing which seems closely bound to that of the memorial. But was there not an explosion in the number of other types of documentation in the fifth century as a response to the growing complexity of democracy and empire? Evidence is rather slight and our main evidence is in any case inscriptional, but we do happen to hear about some non-epigraphic records: at various points, the inscribed decrees evince concern to create more documentation. Why?

First, some more of the background. I have argued elsewhere[35] that from the end of the fifth and early fourth century, there was an important development in the use of documentation, a new acceptance of writing as proof in the lawcourts, and during the fourth century a new awareness of the value of past written documents and archives. But that mainly concerns the fourth century, for which we also have richer evidence. What of the fifth? From the 460s with the establishment of the radical democracy, there was an explosion of decrees erected on stone. It is often commented that this profusion is expressive of a democratic concern with accountability and openness, and it is, for instance, in the latter half of the fifth century that massive yearly inscriptions are put up recording (in excessive detail) the votive offerings in the temples, the accounts of the *poletai*, or the accounts of the temple treasuries.

---

[33] Cf. clause in Brea inscription, *IG* I³ 46 lines 21ff.: if anyone votes against the stele, their property shall be confiscated.

[34] Meiggs (1972), 587 suggests the same risk is recognised in the regulations for Miletus, *IG* I³ 21, lines 47–9.   [35] Thomas (1989: ch. 1).

But such 'accountability' often had a religious dimension: often what goes up on stone is meant for the gods, like the great stone tribute lists which recorded the sixtieth dedicated to the goddess Athena. Also important, the increasingly frequent inscription of decrees in this period does not in a sense, really represent a new kind of document, or even a new use of written record. Rather, it could be seen merely as an extension of the idea that laws and treaties should be inscribed, with which we are familiar from the archaic period, another manifestation then of the characteristic Greek version of the 'epigraphic habit'. Thus the inscribed decrees may not be administrative documents so much as laws and memorials (of assembly business which everyone knew anyway). Or, as we have seen, memorials of the conferment of honour.

However, there is also some evidence for an extension of record-keeping in this period, for a clear concern with certain sorts of records on *pinakia* or wooden tablets. The evidence lies in the stone-inscribed decrees of the fifth century recorded in *IG* I³, for certain decrees contain elaborate instructions about making written records on *pinakia*. I must stress that these are instructions which we simply happen to have precisely because they were written up on stone, but that these epigraphic decrees do contain indications of anxiety about records which would *not* be kept on stone, which deserve more attention.[36] What emerges is a concern in the period of the Athenian empire for closer control of financial affairs via written records.

So the Cleinias decree of 448/7 (*IG* I³ 34) arranges for a system of collecting the tribute which is proof against corruption. *Symbola* or identification seals are to be agreed with each city so that the carriers cannot defraud Athens. The amount each *polis* pays is written down on a *grammateion* (tablet) in that city itself and sealed; the document is then read out in the Athenian *boule* when the money is delivered, a simple system. The Hellenotamiai are to read to the Assembly who paid the full tribute; receipts go to the cities (ἀντιγραφσομένος). Someone – probably one of the Hellenotamiai – records the tribute on a whitened board (*pinakion*) city by city; there are lists on the *pinakion* in the *boule* of those who owe money, and the *boule* is to publish these (ἐπιδεῖχσαι, line 60) to the people, listing city by city. Thus the stone tribute lists recorded the sixtieth which went to Athena, but here it is decreed that there should be other written records kept (for the first time?) which are concerned with ensuring financial probity and efficient, full collection of the tribute.

The written record of the debts (of tribute) is mentioned in the Methone decree (*IG* I³ 61),[37] and in the Neapolis decree (*IG* I³ 101) some money is

---

[36] I omit unintelligible fragments, of which a considerable number seem to make some mention of writing or documentation.

[37] Lines 9, 14–15; the mention of *sanides* is restored.

owed by the Neapolitans: the generals in Thasos are told to record the money as it is received (lines 25–30). The Neapolitans have given money willingly to the Hellenotamiai and the envoys are to have (records) kept and handed over to the *boule* (lines 39–40). In the Kleonymos decree of 426/5 (*IG* I³ 68), it is decreed that the Hellenotamiai should make lists on a *sanis* of those in default of tribute and those who bring it ... to be put up on each occasion in front of some building, perhaps a temple. Heralds are to go out to the cities and arrange (?) for the election of those to collect the tribute, 'and they shall be written in the *bouleuterion*' (52ff., lines 56–7 restored: κ[αὶ ἀναγραφōσι ἐν] [τō]ι βολευτερί[ο]ι).

Two other decrees are also concerned with the recording of debts, though this time not of tribute. The Kallias decree of 434/3 BC, concerning loans to the state from the treasures of the gods arranges for the *logistai* to calculate 'what is owed to the gods precisely' (*IG* I³ 52). Repayment of the money shall be made by the Prytaneis together with the *boule*, and they shall cancel records of debts as they pay them back, 'after seeking both the *pinakia* and *grammateia* and wherever else claims are written down'. The priests, *hieropoioi* and anyone else who knows are to produce the written records (τὰ γεγραμμένα, lines 12–13). Elaborate arrangements follow for counting out the money before the *boule* (on the Acropolis); then the Treasurers take them over and are to record on a single stele everything according to the individual gods, how much belongs to them, and the entire sum with silver and gold separately. 'In future, the Treasurers are to record on a stele' and give accounts, of the money that is there and that going to the gods (i.e. revenue), and whatever is spent during the year (lines 24–7). The stelai go onto the Acropolis.[38]

In a similar vein, perhaps, a decree about the first-fruits offerings to Eleusis declares that heralds are to go to the cities, and a *pinakion* is to be made to record the offerings from the *demos* and the cities – to be listed individually and displayed in Eleusis (the Eleusinion) and in the *bouleuterion* (*IG* I³ 78). There is to be an inscription of the votive offerings dedicated out of the first-fruits with the names of every Greek who made the offering (line 43); and there are to be two stelai recording the decree, one for Eleusis, one for the Acropolis.[39]

These pronouncements are disparate, slight and each preserved because they were part of a decision deemed worthy of stone. But they do at least

---

[38] Cf. the Reassessment Decree (*IG* I³ 71, ML 69, 425/4), mostly on assessors and suits relating to the tribute, which is important enough to go up on two stelai, one on the Acropolis as usual, but also one in the *bouleuterion*.

[39] NB also *IG* I³ 64 about Athena Nike; *IG* I³ 76, treaty with Bottiaeans; *IG* I³ 84, shrine of Neleus – inscribing on a wall what is owed, and the clause 'so anyone who wants can see'; *IG* I³ 138, contributions to Apollo, from each sector of the city, with records, according to those listed on the *lexiarchikon grammateion*.

provide some background to the increasing profusion of inscriptions, and particularly the new fifth-century habit of inscribing temple accounts and inventories. It is hardly surprising that accounts were being kept of state and temple finances; after all we have some of the results in the elaborate inventories and accounts which were inscribed. What is striking is the extent to which accountability and recording of contributions are exercising the assembly at this period, and that the state is turning to written records to attempt to control the activities of officials, to ensure that they are not embezzling – and also to create more lists: lists of debtors, lists of payers, lists of votive offerings, and so on. As usual the final decrees are to be inscribed, but that is no surprise,[40] nor is the rule that the temple inventories and accounts should go up on stone, for they were of concern to the gods. (It has been pointed out that many Greek inventories are so inexact and inconsecutive that they were unusable as inventories or 'records' and were primarily meant as a symbolic record of the official and honest handing over of the temple treasures from one treasurer to another,[41] but some account should be taken of the fact that it is easier to make lists than to make usable, functional records.)

What I think is more surprising is that in these decrees, so anxious about making further written (non-epigraphic) records, it is *financial* accountability and honesty that is at stake. More extensive recording is being enforced not simply for all official activity but in the two areas of tribute collection and the property of the gods. This may be going too far on the basis of such slight material, but these are the main intelligible and non-fragmentary pieces of evidence for the *boule* and the assembly in the fifth century turning their attention to the tightening up of administration through the written word. The written decrees which proliferate in the fifth century are essentially a similar kind of written record to what was produced before – written, monumental laws. But publishing accounts and inventories on stone is a radically new activity and must be the epigraphic expression of this preoccupation with financial tightening up and probity that we see in these regulations about written record on *wooden* boards. The inscriptions of accounts or of the sixtieth of the tribute to Athena were public, monumental signs that the finances of the gods were being looked after – and debts on stone, as with many public inscriptions, tended to concern the gods.[42] But there is a more practical side, and in that, accountability and honesty were being ensured through more humble documents. Nor do

---

[40] It is also notable that the elaborate arrangements for keeping records of the transactions involve their production before the boule and assembly, *and* public posting for all to see.

[41] Linders (1975) and Burford (1971).

[42] Then only later, as David Lewis has pointed out to me, for secular buildings like the Piraeus walls of the 390s.

these deal with purely divine matters: it is the tribute, not merely the sixtieth for Athena, which is being tightened up by more careful record-keeping.

I would suggest, then, that the other main area in which Athens is prompted to extend the use of writing in the fifth century to ensure its control is the sphere of taxation and revenue. Thus it was not so much the more complex administration of the empire in general that generated the extension of written records, but an obsession with accountability that was especially severe in the realm of public finance; the need to ensure that the allies were paying the tribute they were supposed to (with humiliation for the defaulters), and that the collectors were not embezzling it. This suggests that the need to collect taxes might very often be the catalyst to more extensive production of written documents and that this was one important area where Athens (at least) used the written word to enhance its control.[43]

Conclusions

The Greek city-state lacked any elaborate bureaucratic apparatus – even Athens' attempts to tighten up tribute collection used extremely simple forms of record-keeping and many such records were destroyed as soon as the debt was paid. But the city-state did exploit a certain potential of writing: in so far as it did try to enforce or extend its power through the written word, it did this almost overwhelmingly by means of the public, visible and usually inscribed record, rather than hidden archival documents. In most cases we have very little idea of what a state used writing for exactly, and what we tend to see is what emerges on stone. Cities which have left little written record may often have used more perishable bronze (e.g. Argos).[44] But the wording in inscribed laws, archaic and classical, implies that those establishing the law were concerned to impress on the citizenry the importance of the stone version – very seldom is there any mention of other kinds of written documents (hence the interest of the Athenian imperial inscriptions which are enforcing more 'paper-work'). Inscriptions are referred to as if they are memorials or even embodiments of the decision they record. The continuing existence of the stone meant the validity of that decision. Their value lies partly in being public and hard to destroy, but the Greek cities also exploit their monumental value, and even confer divine protection on them by dedicating them to a god or placing them in temples. Both Sparta and Athens tried to limit the use of

---

[43] Cf. the increasing use of documentation for financial transactions among individuals. Similarly, there is evidence from rather early on for written accounts in the demes: see now, the example from Rhamnous: ΕΡΓΟΝ 1985 (1984) p. 55 and plate 78; ΠΡΑΚΤΙΚΑ 1988 (1984), pp. 192–5 with illustrations at p. 188 and pl. 121; SEG 38.13.

[44] See Thomas (1992), 82–4.

inscriptions as memorials to private individuals; Athens' public inscriptions and benefactors could also do the same. The state used the written word for power almost entirely in its public, and usually monumental, guise.

There are tenuous signs, however, that one impetus to extend the non-epigraphic documentation kept by the state was to ensure accountability and probity in the realm of public finances: the ideal of accountability in the Athenian democracy and the urge to collect as much tribute as possible generated deliberate attention to the keeping of more records (which we only just happen to hear about). These then generated more documents, more lists (though rudimentary), and official records are being initiated on wooden boards. In the Persian empire, the development of elaborate bureaucracy is generated by the taxation and distribution system. In other words, it seems likely that it is not so much the existence of writing which often generated the increase of records, but the exigencies of state taxation which might itself encourage a greater exploitation of writing. At the risk of setting out an extreme position, I would suggest, then, that Athens' democracy followed and enhanced, in its use of writing, the fairly simple Greek idea that *polis* laws should be written; that its moves to more elaborate state record-keeping were prompted by financial anxiety; but that elaborate records of the citizen body itself were not made necessary – as they often have been in other states – by a taxation system. The ingenuities of financial record-keeping were directed towards those who did most to finance the city-state, that is, the gods, and non-citizens, metics and the allies of the Athenian empire. The lack of any bureaucracy may be connected as much to the privileged position of the citizen in the *polis* as to the general Greek approach to state records and the epigraphic habit.

But we should be wary of overemphasising the sophistication of these 'hidden' records. The assembly still comes back to the final proof of accountability, the erection of the final accounts for the god on stone. These accounts may seem utterly impractical as accounts (or inventories) but yet they served the same symbolic, public and monumental function as the other decrees of fifth-century Athens.

4 Literacy and language in Egypt in the Late and Persian Periods

John Ray

Egypt in the Late Period was not the power it had been in the days of its imperial splendour, but it was still one of the most important countries in the Mediterranean. Once Psammetichus I, the founder of the Twenty-sixth Dynasty, had succeeded in the work of reunifying the country (a task which was complete by about 640 BC) the natural economic strength of Egypt was able to assert itself. At most periods of Egyptian history Pharaoh must have been one of the richest men in the world, if not the wealthiest, with the strength to command loyalty and to buy the technology needed to uphold his supremacy. The agricultural potential of the country, and its considerable natural resources, made it an envied place to live, and immigrants in tens of thousands were attracted to the land of the Nile. It is in fact one of the paradoxes of Egyptian archaeology that more is known about some of the foreign peoples who settled in the country from the records they have left in Egypt than from what remains in their own homelands. A list of the foreign languages and scripts found in Egypt from the period of the New Kingdom down to the Arab conquest would total well over forty, and this includes the longest texts known in some languages – for example, Aramaic and Etruscan – and some of the earliest attested in others, such as Carian, Greek and possibly Dravidian. Late-Period Egypt was a cosmopolitan place, and questions of its language and its literacy must be seen in this light.

The principal language of the country was of course Egyptian, in spite of the increasing numbers of foreign settlers. Egyptian has the longest recorded history of any of the earth's languages: by the beginning of our period it had already been spoken for at least three millennia, and it was still to be in use in Coptic Egypt fifteen hundred years later. The Egyptians were keenly aware of the antiquity of their civilisation, and the ruling religious and political élite made considerable use of this. The medium for official pronouncements, and for important public inscriptions, remained the hieroglyphic script, with its ability to impress, attract and mystify at the same time. A fine example of the use of hieroglyphs is the stele set up by Pharaoh Apries in the temple at Memphis, recording donations of land to the cult of the god of the city, Ptaḥ. The following king, the usurper Amasis, used a similar stele to record the events of his predecessor's demise, an attempted Babylonian invasion, and the unrest which followed. The Persian conquest in 525 BC, and the official promotion of Aramaic that went with it, made little difference to this tradition in practice, and Darius I lined the banks of his canal linking the Nile to the Red Sea with a row of stelai recording the opening of this great waterway in hieroglyphs as well as in cuneiform. Even such an important innovation needed to be commemorated in this most traditional of forms. A comparatively humdrum event, such as the making over of customs dues from the Greek emporium at Naukratis to the cult of the goddess Neith, could be turned by Nectanebo I in the first year of his reign (379/8 BC) into one of the finest creations of the Egyptian artist.[1] Here elegance in design was used to enhance public impression, in a way that was thoroughly traditional.

However, there was more to hieroglyphic than mere impressiveness. The connotations of the script were religious in the extreme; it was known to Late-Period Egyptians as 'the writing of the speech of the gods' (*sh̲ mdw-n̲tr*). The religious and ceremonial weighting applied to hieroglyphs is unparalleled in other societies, except possibly by the Chinese script. Since hieroglyphs were the prerogative of the gods, invented at the beginning of time by Thoth himself, the language which they recorded was also deemed to be important; it could not be contaminated with the mundane. Late-Period inscriptions are written in Middle Egyptian, a canonical form of the language which was already fifteen hundred years old, and which may have been spoken in a pure form even in its earliest days. All the same, it was thought necessary at least to approximate to this stage of the language. This use of archaic language and idiom had important consequences for Egyptian culture, as will be seen later in this chapter.

Hieroglyphs were a beautiful but clumsy medium, and most of the daily business of Egypt was conducted in hieratic. This is simply a stylised cursive script, formed by writing hieroglyphs quickly with pen and ink on papyrus. The Egyptians did not formally differentiate the two scripts, although hieratic had long lost much of its pictorial character, but in practice the distinction is a useful one, and may have been felt by the Egyptians themselves. Hieratic was not merely the medium for everyday transactions; it had long since also become the way of recording literary and intellectual works. An interesting example from our period is *Papyrus Vandier*, a literary tale involving a magician, a debauched Pharaoh, the magician's wife, and a descent into the Underworld.[2] From the point of view of this chapter the most important aspect of this text, which may date from the end

---

[1] A convenient photograph of this stele, now in the Cairo Museum, can be found in Brunner (1965: pls. 23–4). A translation is contained in Lichtheim (1980: 86–9).
[2] Posener (1985).

of the sixth or the first half of the fifth century, is linguistic. A. Shisha-Halévy has argued that the language of this narrative is close to early demotic – in other words to the spoken language of its day; nevertheless, it shares several features with the elevated idiom derived from earlier literary tales.[3] Such a text was presumably the usual medium for 'polite' literature during most of our period: language which was recognisably vernacular, but restrained by notions of literary decorum. Here there is clearly some form of censorship at work, though it may well be an unconscious one. Unformulated assumptions are sometimes the strongest, at least in matters of literary taste.

Hieratic, however, was in the course of being replaced. At the beginning of the Twenty-sixth Dynasty (664–525 BC) a new script appears, known as demotic. F. Ll. Griffith[4] was the first to suggest that this new script arose in the Delta, and slowly spread into the south of the country, and recent discoveries of hieratic inscriptions at the Serapeum of Memphis seem to bear out this interpretation. Over the previous centuries, hieratic had divided into two mutually unintelligible systems, used separately in the Delta and in Upper Egypt. While the country was politically divided this state of affairs was tolerable, but with the reunification of the land a central administration was essential. This entailed a common script, and demotic, which is a deliberately stylised version of lower Egyptian hieratic, bears some indication of being deliberately created to supply this need. If this interpretation is correct, demotic would be an early example of a script introduced by a regime in order to propagate its own interests and values, in which case Psammetichus I can be seen as something of an Egyptian Atatürk.

There is an interesting corollary to this. The later form of the Egyptian language, Coptic, preserves a series of dialects which differ especially in the vowels they adopt. Most of these dialects can be assigned with some accuracy to the various areas of Egypt, but the one which is hardest to locate is the 'official' one, known as Sa'idic. Sa'idic has some affinities with the dialects of northern Middle Egypt, but it seems to have been deliberately standardised at some point. Recently, H. Satzinger has made the interesting suggestion that Sa'idic is in fact the received pronunciation of earlier Egyptian, preserved phonetically in the Coptic script.[5] The most likely candidate for the ancestor of such a dialect would be the idiom of the Late-Period royal court, either at the original capital, Sais, or more likely at the seat of government in Memphis. If this is true, it is quite possible that this received pronunciation spread with the assertion of Saite control over Egypt, and therefore with the spread of the demotic script. This idea is still

[3] Shisha-Halévy (1989). Useful additional points are contained in Vernus (1990).
[4] Griffith (1909: 1–35).   [5] Satzinger (1985: 307–12).

sub judice, but it explains several features of Coptic linguistics, and it deserves serious consideration. It certainly brings us face to face with the control of language and idiom which is characteristic of ancient Egypt at most periods, and it also reminds us of the centripetal tendency of Egyptian government.

There is another aspect of this control which is worth investigating. Ancient Egypt shared a tendency, common in the eastern Mediterranean, to preserve or create elevated forms of language which were thought suitable for formal use; the everyday language is rarely permitted in such contexts. Modern Standard Arabic is a good example of this, and in modern Greece the debate between supporters of *dhemotikē* and those who favour the artificial *katharevousa* still leaves its traces. The 'Middle Egyptian' in use in the Late Period is one such *katharevousa*, and a certain element of linguistic snobbery can be detected throughout Egyptian history.[6] On the other hand, a text such as *Papyrus Vandier* can be described as vernacular coloured by the existence of a *katharevousa*; the essential innovation which allowed such a text to arise is presumably the invention of the demotic script, and the acceptance of vernacular language in legal and administrative contexts which this implied. If Satzinger's theory about the origin of Sa'idic is correct, the existence of a courtly or received pronunciation for the vernacular would have helped in this acceptance; a rough parallel would be with the so-called 'radio Arabic' commonly used in the Middle East for popular, but semi-official discourse, although it might be better to compare the language of *Papyrus Vandier* with that of the literary folktale tradition which flourished in mediaeval Cairo. This at least gives an idea of the complexities which can form in a tradition such as ancient Egyptian.

Within the Pharaonic state there flourished many immigrant communities, with the same combinations of assimilation and separateness, not to mention feelings of exclusiveness towards other immigrants, which are found in any cosmopolitan society. The best-known of these must be the Ionian community, the first of which arrived as mercenaries during the reign of Psammetichus I. Merchants and other traders soon joined them, and before long the regime found it necessary to regulate their activities.[7] An inscription from Priene, recently published, sheds new light on the

---

[6] Cf. the Middle Kingdom official who recorded in his autobiography that he 'never said *pa 's*', by which he meant the vulgar definite article which was beginning to appear in the vernacular; Parkinson (1991: 19). The degree to which avoidance of the vernacular can go used to be seen on buses in Athens, which until recently bore notices forbidding passengers to spit, in language which would have been understood by Plato. Strangely, these notices were not in *dhemotikē*.

[7] A good treatment can be found in the monograph of Austin (1970); also Lloyd (1975: 1–60) and Lloyd (1988: 116ff.).

growth of the Ionian presence in Egypt. This describes how one Pedôn son of Amphinnes was rewarded by King Psammetichus with a golden bracelet and the command of a city, presumably in Egypt.[8] Such awards were standard Pharaonic practice. If the king mentioned is Psammetichus I, the inscription is the earliest historical one known in Greek, antedating the celebrated Abu Simbel text, but it is worth asking the question whether the king referred to in the Priene inscription is not Psammetichus II, who employed Ionians in considerable numbers on his great Nubian campaign. In this case, the text would date from nearer 593 BC. The subsequent history of the Ionian community is one of considerable assimilation into the Pharaonic state. A group who settled in Memphis were known to later ages as *Hellenomemphitai*,[9] and one of the earliest Greek papyri, the Curse of Artemisia dated to 311 BC, is an appeal by the daughter of one of these Ionomemphites against the father of her child.[10] Although written in good Greek, it can be turned almost word for word into Egyptian demotic; indeed, the Curse of Artemisia can almost be said to be an ancient Egyptian text written in Greek. Surely this is assimilation to a remarkable degree.

The Carian community in Egypt has a similar history to that of the better known Ionians.[11] The limited texts at our disposal show the Carians as mercenaries, leaving their names in stone quarries or along desert *wadis* in the service of their royal masters. A remarkable series of stelai from a necropolis at Saqqâra shows the adaptability of the Carians to Egyptian religion and artistic motifs; these stelai date to the years immediately following the Persian conquest in 525 BC.[12] The Carians continued to serve the new overlords of Egypt, although about this time they abandoned the name Pesmašek (their form of the name Psammetichus). This was either because of political expediency – the name was a reminder of the previous dynasty, and was in fact assumed by several pretenders to the throne – or more simply because of a change in fashion. The city of Memphis became a home for a large part of the Carian community, and it is no surprise to find a colony of *Caromemphitai* mentioned in later texts alongside their Greek counterparts.

An interesting figure in this context is the lady Takheta, whose name means 'she of the Hittites'. This woman married Pharaoh Amasis, and became the mother of Psammetichus III, the last Pharaoh before the Persian conquest. Takheta appears to be the daughter of a wealthy family of immigrants, either from Syria or Anatolia, who were able to make use of

---

[8] Masson and Yoyotte (1988). The inscription, on an Egyptian block statute, surfaced in the antiquities market; it is to be hoped that the text is genuine. The editors date it to the reign of Psammetichus I, c. 635 BC.   [9] Thompson (1988: 82–6, 95–7).

[10] Wilcken (1927: text 1, pp. 97–104).

[11] Cf. most recently Ray in Sasson (forthcoming) and literature cited.

[12] R. V. Nicholls in Masson (1978: 57–87).

her to forge links with the royal house.[13] It follows that Psammetichus III was partly foreign; whether he was the first Pharaoh to have been so can be doubted, but it is equally clear that he felt no need to disguise his mother's name. Whatever her exact origin, the fact that there were foreign elements within the country who were thought fit to enter royalty deserves to be stressed. This raises a question of more than genealogical interest. Immigrants came into Egypt for a better life. What happened when they became rich? Cultural assimilation, as we have seen, was a powerful force, but on its own it was probably insufficient to prevent wealthy and influential foreign communities from being a threat to Egypt's stability. Marriage into ruling circles would have been useful here, since the regime would find it easier in this way to draw on the community's loyalty; on occasions the power of such communities may have been such that it might even have been necessary.

This may as well bring us to the story of Joseph. The best treatment of this novella, embedded in the Book of Genesis, is still that by D. B. Redford.[14] The hero of this story is an immigrant who succeeds in beating the Egyptians at their own game – interpreting dreams and running the country – while remaining true at heart to the values of his own community: a role-model for the aspiring foreigner in Egypt. Joseph even succeeds in receiving an official Egyptian name in an audience with a grateful Pharaoh; this is the equivalent of naturalisation and a knighthood.[15] Here too we are brought face to face with the process of immigrants being absorbed into Egyptian society, even at the highest levels. The narrative is presumably fiction, but even fiction needs to make a bargain with reality. There may well have been junior Josephs in Late-Period society.

Another important group in Late-Period Egypt were the Phoenicians.[16] The role of this group was essentially mercantile, and traces of their activity are probably best sought in the archaeological record: amphorae and other Near Eastern storage jars are frequent at several Late-Period sites. From the point of view of assimilation to Egyptian values, there are important Phoenician graffiti in the temple of Osiris at Abydos, a testimony to their devotion to the god. This may be surface conformity (impiety would be bad for business), but it could well be a sign of deeper involvement in things Egyptian. An indication that this is so can be gained from the considerable material surviving from fifth- and fourth-century Egypt which is written in Aramaic. There are numerous short inscriptions from the town of Syene

---

[13] Ray (1990).

[14] Redford (1970) is surely right in seeing this composition, in the form in which we have it, as a creation of the Late Period, although the essence of the story may be older.

[15] On the Egyptian name of Joseph see Schulman (1975).

[16] This topic is dealt with most recently by Leclant (1991).

(Aswan), but for our purpose probably the most informative text is the one known as the Carpentras stele.[17] This reads as follows:

Blessed be Tabâ daughter of Taḥapi, devotee of the god Osiris. Nothing evil did she do, nor utter calumny here on earth against any man. From before Osiris be thou blest, from before Osiris receive water. Serve the lord of double truth (*nm'ty*) and live among his favoured ones (*ḥsy'*).

Here we have good Egyptian names, a dedication to Osiris, invoked under an epithet – lord of double truth – which is purely Egyptian, and a form of the negative confession which is familiar from the Book of the Dead. The words in italics are good Egyptian as well. It is difficult to avoid the conclusion that the Carpentras stele is an ancient Egyptian text which happens to be written in Aramaic. As with the Curse of Artemisia, which is also a text which concerns an immigrant woman, we can see that adaption to Egyptian culture could go to remarkable lengths.

Much has been written about the main source of Aramaic documents from Egypt, the archives of the Jewish colony on the island of Elephantine, and this is not the place to enlarge upon it. A notable feature of these archives is the use of Aramaic, rather than Hebrew; this can be seen as a form of incomplete assimilation to Near Eastern culture rather than to Egyptian. The survival of family documents from this community is not surprising; these argue for a level of literacy on a par with, or perhaps better than, that of the Egyptians among whom the Jewish settlers found themselves. This, however, may be the result of the accident of discovery, and not much can be made of this point in isolation. More significant for us is the existence of what might be termed 'intellectual documents' among the Elephantine archives. These include the biography in Aramaic of the Persian king Darius, which suggests, if not loyalty to the Achaemenids, at least a certain curiosity about them; the wisdom-text known as the Story of Ahiqar, which is known to have influenced later Egyptian literature, and the tale of a magician, Ḥor son of Pawoneš, which is clearly an Egyptian romance translated into Aramaic.[18] In combination, this is remarkable evidence for cross-cultural interest and alertness, in a small community which was not one of the wealthiest in Egypt.

In short, the evidence from the various foreign communities in Late-Period Egypt shows a consistent pattern of adaption to, and adoption of, Egyptian culture and ways of thought. The Jews of Elephantine seem to be something of an exception; Zeus and Ba'al, for example, could readily be referred to by the name of the Egyptian god Amun, but the Jewish deity

[17] Grelot (1972: text 86).
[18] This Aramaic document from Elephantine is being prepared for publication by B. Porten and K.-Th. Zauzich.

appears to hold aloof from such syncretism. The limited material from fourth-century Edfu suggests that the Jewish community in that city was harder to distinguish from the rest of the native population, but this is an impression rather than a clear picture.[19] However, the same fourth century is the likely date of the most remarkable Aramaic text found in Egypt, the now notorious *Papyrus Amherst*.[20] This is the longest extra-Biblical text in this language, extending over twenty-two lengthy columns of writing. The script in which this narrative is written is Egyptian demotic, with phonetic groups used according to Egyptian principles (e.g. the group *rn* which means 'name' in Egyptian, used, purely in accordance with its sound, for the Aramaic syllable *rin*). It is worth speculating on the reasons for this. The writing-system could have been designed for an Egyptian who knew no Aramaic, but it is difficult to see why such a person would want to read, and presumably recite, a lengthy text which meant nothing to him. A more likely customer is a Near-Easterner, probably born in Egypt, who lived in a community already on the way to being Egyptianised. The use of demotic to write a foreign language is most easily explained if the potential reader, or readers, felt at home in this script. Such a community might still have had need for its own Aramaic rites, and the text (or at least the published parts of it) does bear a certain resemblance to the miscellanies of myth, ritual and incantation which characterise the later Graeco-Roman magical papyri. Cross-writing is in fact well attested in the Near East: Copts in modern Egypt use their ancient language in prayer-books in Arabic transcription, the Arabic script was used in renaissance Spain to assist in the conversion of Muslims, and the mediaeval and early modern texts from the Cairo Genizah show an almost bewildering variety of scripts and language, some in extremely unusual combinations. The common factor appears to be partial loss of an earlier language or tradition, and adaptation to a surrounding language and culture.

Any community which welcomes foreign settlement is faced with problems of administration. How, for example, did the late Egyptian legal system work? Egyptians were clearly bounded by their own laws, but the archives of Elephantine suggest that the Jews kept their own family traditions. This was no doubt convenient, but what happened when such traditions conflicted with Egyptian laws, as for example in a mixed marriage? And what about criminal law, which one would imagine to have been the same for everyone, regardless of origin? Was criminal law differently applied when one of the parties was Egyptian from the situation

---

[19] The standard introduction to this subject is still Kornfeld (1973).

[20] The literature is considerable, though at present devoted more to scholarly disagreements than to publishing the text. See for example Vleeming and Wesselius (1985), especially the treatment of script and language on pp. 13–27.

applying when no Egyptians were involved? Finally, what about cases involving members of different foreign communities within the country? A comparison with Ptolemaic Egypt, where these problems recurred in an acute form, suggests one solution: to treat cases by the language in which the various documents were written. This is a simple criterion which cannot be evaded, but it was reached in Hellenistic Egypt only after the better part of two centuries. Can we be sure that the same applied to the earlier Pharaonic state?

With these questions we can leave the immigrants to their own problems; the bulk of the population of Late-Period Egypt was, after all, Egyptian. Increasingly the majority of our records are in demotic, in the north and in Middle Egypt by the middle of the Twenty-sixth Dynasty, and in the south after the accession of Amasis in 570 BC. The masterpiece of early demotic, and one of the most informative texts to have come from any period of ancient Egypt, is *Papyrus Rylands IX*, which dates to the ninth year of Darius the Great.[21] The language of this text – a rambling and slightly self-righteous appeal by an elderly priest named Petiēsi – is generally taken to be close to the spoken language, with characteristic repetitions and strained syntax. Yet it is also formalised, reflecting the fact that the writer (or dictator) was a provincial priest. In addition, there are extracts from oracles given by the local god, and these are clearly couched in an archaic idiom which is not that of daily speech. In general, one has the impression that the language of *Rylands IX* is not far removed from that of *Papyrus Vandier*, once allowance is made for the very different subject-matter of the two texts. This may be seen as the normal written language of the educated; the whiff of formality which runs through this idiom is characteristic of a society which produces *katharevousas*, and the latter occur only when there is a literary tradition to revere.

The history of Egyptian demotic is an interesting one, on which much remains to be said. It is normally taken for granted that the language which is written in the demotic script is that of the ordinary Egyptian going about his (or occasionally her) ordinary business, and that it changes and develops accordingly. This is what the name 'demotic', and its older variant 'enchorial', implies. However, we have already seen the tendency of Egyptian to produce levels of language which are extremely formal and resistant to change, and it is worth asking whether demotic is really an exception. Much of the surviving corpus of demotic consists of legal documents, which are by their nature conservative and formulaic; in a sense, it would be surprising if such texts did reflect the spoken language. More disturbing is the evidence of demotic letters. Here too we find

---

[21] Text published in Griffith (1909: 218–53). See also Sauneron (1967: 17–21), and more recently Ray (1988) and literature cited.

considerable use of stock formulae and received phrases, and it is likely that in Egyptian society, where most people were presumably illiterate, there was general recourse to the public letter-writer (*epistolographos*; the Egyptian equivalent, *sh n hyr*, literally means 'scribe of the street'). It is interesting to note that Greek letters from Egypt tend to contain more gossipy details than Egyptian ones; the reason for this may well be that in an Egyptian village a letter, once it reached its goal, would have been read out by a scribe to the recipient, within the hearing of several prying neighbours and numerous children. On the other hand, a Greek letter may have had more chance of being read in private by the person for whom it was intended.

Legal texts are conservative for reasons of their own, and private letters may be subject to the limitations of a scribal class and a low level of literacy; it is therefore likely that these are special cases. However, suspicions about demotic deepen when we look at the evidence from Roman Egypt, and especially from Coptic. By the time that Coptic texts appear with any frequency, Egypt had been part of the Greek-speaking world for more than seven centuries. Throughout this period, Greek was the language of government, and much of intellectual life. The normal effect of such a state of affairs is that the language of the peasantry is seen as socially inferior, and becomes permeated with vocabulary and phrases from the dominant language. Modern Persian is full of Arabic words and Japanese shows the impact of Chinese; modern English is similarly imbued with French and Latin. The same is largely true of Coptic. The prominence of Greek words in Coptic is sometimes explained by the influence of theology, and the adoption of Christian religion. However, the influence of Greek goes noticeably beyond this, extending even to the replacement of everyday words and the adoption of sentence-particles such as δέ, ἀλλά or γάρ. It is difficult to resist the feeling that this infiltration was not introduced suddenly by some Hellenophile priest, but is the result of a long process over the preceding seven centuries. Nor is it simply a matter of vocabulary. Coptic knows constructions, methods of word-formation, even the occasional tense, which must have developed organically over a long period of time within the Egyptian language. Nevertheless, when we return to pagan texts, we find hardly any of this. Demotic, throughout the period of Greek and Roman rule, behaves as if Greek does not exist. There is the occasional loan-word, as Clarysse has shown,[22] but the total effect is almost insignificant. In addition, the linguistic changes which have clearly arisen within Egyptian, and appear firmly rooted in all dialects of Coptic, are almost unknown to earlier demotic. What is the reason for this?

[22] Clarysse (1987). Other information can be found in Johnson (1975) and Johnson (1977).

Part of the answer seems to lie in a curious exception: a series of ostraka from the Italian excavations at Medinet Madi in the Fayum.[23] These ostraka, which seem to have been written in the first half of the second century AD (one text is dated to the ninth year of Antoninus), are extremely difficult to decipher; however, it seems clear from the preliminary publication that some at least of these texts are the products of an elementary stage in a priestly school. It is the very ineptness of the hands which is interesting: several mistakes occur which can only be the product of dictation, where one word is written for another because it sounds identical. The impression that in the Medinet Madi ostraka we are hearing the sound of spoken Egyptian is strengthened by the frequent appearance of Greek words, embedded within the language in the way that we later find in Coptic. Greek infinitives, for example, are combined with Egyptian auxiliary verbs in a series of periphrastic tenses, in a way that would be unthinkable in a standard demotic text. In addition, there are details of the spelling in some of these ostraka which correspond closely with the later Fayumic dialect of Coptic. In short, it looks as if the Medinet Madi texts have broken loose from the constraints of normal demotic writing, and in so doing have revealed the true state of the spoken language underneath.

Another feature of Coptic which is worth mentioning is the existence of a considerable body of words of Aramaic origin. Egyptian has some Semitic loan-words which entered the language during the New Kingdom or even earlier, but the Aramaic representation in Coptic is strong, and seems to be *sui generis*. In addition to this, there are several words which are clearly of Persian origin.[24] These words seem to have been in the language for some time, and this rules out the possibility that they were borrowed during the Sasanian conquest (AD 616/17 – 627). Not only is this too recent, but it is far too short a period for our purpose. The majority of these Persian words must have entered that language at the time of the Achaemenid domination of the country, and in general they refer to a limited range of exotic items such as hares or a particular word for glass. Some of these appear in early demotic, as does a series of words which refer to details of the Achaemenid government: most of these, understandably, disappear from the language in the fourth century BC. The larger range of Aramaic words can broadly be described as mercantile, and a fair proportion of these appear in earlier demotic; because they were commercial and carried no political messages, they were able to secure a permanent place in the language. It therefore appears that spoken Egyptian, in its pre-Hellenistic stages, was not averse

[23] Bresciani et al. (1983), and subsequent volumes in the series *Quaderni di Medinet Madi*. For an introduction see Donadoni (1955).

[24] The Persian words in Coptic, as well as the Aramaic ones, can be obtained from Černý (1976); note especially the indexes on pp. 372–84.

to incorporating foreign words, or at least some categories of them. The later intolerance of Greek is all the more marked, and may well have a political motive (refusal to recognise the dominant alien). The reluctance to record changes within the Egyptian language itself, on the other hand, can hardly have been political; the reason for this is far more likely to be the linguistic conservatism which characterises Egyptian writing at most periods of its history. The fact that demotic was also bracing itself against the wholesale influence of Greek idiom may have strengthened this conservatism, in a general hardening of the linguistic arteries, but it was not the principal cause of it. This clearly lies elsewhere.

Another feature of demotic texts is the wide diversity of hands which they display. This is true even before the late Ptolemaic period, when the script moved upwards into the sphere of literary compositions, a place previously occupied by hieratic. With very few exceptions (some of which are ephemeral jottings such as tax receipts), demotic texts are well written. It is difficult to convict a demotic text of bad spelling, even if one were to be attracted by such an arrogant course. This is one of the many exceptional features of the Medinet Madi texts; they are demotic in the making, so to speak, and therefore not subject to many of the forces which shape a finished text. This suggests that the majority of our texts are the product of a competent 'élite': public scribes, temple personnel, and representatives of the propertied classes.[25] In addition to this social conformity, regional and local variants are also difficult to detect. This may improve as knowledge increases, but in general one is impressed by the synchronic, as opposed to the diachronic, uniformity which appears in demotic texts.

Most demotic is of course the work of anonymous professionals. However, it is possible to distinguish some individual 'authors'. Petiēsi of El-Ḥibeh in Middle Egypt wrote, or at least dictated, the *Papyrus Rylands IX* which was discussed above (see p. 59). This text is dated to 513 BC, although it also refers to events which took place long previously. The personal and idiosyncratic style of the narrative suggests that the writer had considerable control over its contents; it may even be a free composition. Another creator of demotic texts is Ḥor of Sebennytos in the central Delta, who flourished in the first half of the second century BC.[26] This man's handwriting – as opposed to his spelling – is atrocious, but he is literate in a wide variety of texts, ranging from litanies to gods and accounts of dreams to minutes of committee meetings. He even kept written job-references from the early part of his career. As befits a priest, he can compose magical incantations in Middle-Egyptian *katharevousa*. He is clearly aware of his bad hand, and dictates whole memoranda to a secretary, whose elegant

[25] A preliminary attempt to estimate the wealth of one section of this class (the priesthood) can be found in Johnson (1986).   [26] Ray (1976).

writing looks almost like the product of machine technology. These two hands can be found on the same ostraka, which is fortunate, since it is far from certain that we would be able to date these hands to the same time and place if we were confronted by them separately. So much for our knowledge of palaeography.

While bad demotic is extremely rare, there are several examples of limited literacy to consider. There are dockets of various kinds, acknowledgements on tax receipts, names of witnesses accompanying legal contracts, and possibly some mummy-labels, where the impression is hard to resist that the writer is competent in this sort of text, but little else. Since this state of semi-literacy was sufficient for the everyday needs of the writer, it may not have been felt as a deficiency. To see it as such would be to import a twentieth-century preference into an ancient society.

In view of all this, can we identify what causes the conformity of a script such as demotic? One clear factor is teaching method. We can see this at work in the ostraka from Medinet Madi, and in a more professional and schematic form in the large number of scholar's exercises which survive from other sites.[27] Education seems to have been largely a temple preserve, and this might tempt us to think that demotic was in some way centrally controlled. This, however, is unlikely to be true in anything but the vaguest sense. The government of ancient Egypt did not have the technology to exercise surveillance over every village along the Nile. We do hear of officers such as 'inspectors of scribes' (_shd shw_), but it is doubtful whether their functions were solely, or even slightly, concerned with correcting spelling. A stronger form of control is probably an unconscious one: convergence upon the notion of an ideal script, whether real or imaginary. This is the counterpart in the realm of calligraphy to the existence of a _katharevousa_ – a purified, canonical idiom – in the world of language. Calligraphy, or the notion of how the written word should appear, is characteristic of Egyptian writing at all periods, and its application to demotic, a potentially hideous script, is one of the Egyptians' more considerable achievements. Hand in hand with this would go a notion of what sorts of text were suitable to be written, although new discoveries of Egyptian literature regularly remind us that our concept of what was canonical is often too limited.[28] In both these fields, control is more likely to have been produced by voluntary pressure, exerted upwards by a scribal profession, rather than by government commands directed downwards. In

---

[27] See for example Kaplony-Heckel (1974), and the lists published in Helck et al. (1982: 750–898). There are also useful observations in Devauchelle (1984: 47–59).

[28] The subject-matter of the late hieratic snake-bite papyrus published in Sauneron (1989) may have been predictable; on the other hand, its range, and the thoroughness of its classification, come as a surprise.

this context it is worth recalling the possibility, described earlier, that the use of demotic carried with it a received pronunciation, and perhaps a preferred idiom. This too would have increased the spread of standardisation.

So far we have been discussing literacy in Late-Period Egypt, but it remains to decide how widespread this literacy was. It is worth recalling the truism that ability to read and ability to write are not the same; certainly they do not correspond exactly in any society. This is even more likely to apply when dealing with a complex writing-system such as demotic. The number who could read demotic, at least for simple economic purposes, is likely to have been considerable, although still far below that which is supposed to apply in the modern West. On the other hand, the number of demotic writers was doubtless far more restricted; this can be deduced, among other reasons, from the competence of the surviving texts. Below, or rather around, this 'professional' group, there must have been a penumbra of functional but limited writers, such as the docket-scribes who were mentioned previously. The essential difference between these two groups is that the first could create original demotic texts according to demand, whereas the second could do so only within the narrow limits of their functions. In practice, there is certain to have been an overlap between these categories, but the distinction, like most social judgements, may serve as long as it is not laboured. Demotic, like other scripts, was employed in a wide variety of situations, and the need for literacy, as well as the uses to which it was put, would have varied correspondingly widely. It is a difficult business to put numbers to these social categories. The best treatment of the population of Late-Period Egypt is by Lloyd.[29] Lloyd's estimate of approximately 3 million for Saite Egypt is likely to be conservative, and it probably needs to be raised to allow for the foreign communities we have been discussing. A figure of 3.5 or 4 million may be preferable. Recent discussions on the rate of literacy in Egypt have produced a working figure of 1 or 2 per cent.[30] In a population of 4 million, these figures would produce a total of 40,000–80,000. If we apply this figure to the wider category of demotic users (the 'penumbra'), it is likely to leave us with rather grim statistics; on the other hand, it is probably generous as a measure of the fully literate demotic class. It may well be that we should double the overall figure for the rate of literacy in limited situations, but reduce it when discussing the narrower category of fully competent professionals. More detailed estimates are so subjective that they are best buried away in a footnote.[31]

[29] Lloyd (1988: 189–90), and Lloyd in Trigger et al. (1983: 299–300).

[30] Baines (1983); Baines and Eyre (1983); Eyre and Baines in Schousboe and Larsen (1989: 91–120).

[31] Numbers are extremely difficult to provide for any period of Egyptian history, but the Late

The small proportion who were fully literate in demotic can be termed an élite, if it is necessary to use this word. However, it is important not to equate this proportion automatically with the ruling classes. Kings and similar figures can always dictate their correspondence to secretaries and listen to their favourite readers. It is probably better to think of the literate élite and the governmental élite overlapping, although one has the impression from literary references that Egyptian rulers traditionally prided themselves on at least some knowledge of reading and writing. The overlap between rulers and literate classes may therefore have been greater in ancient, and possibly Hellenistic, Egypt than it was in early mediaeval Europe. All the same, it was possible for a ruler in ancient Egypt to clash disastrously with the literate classes, as is shown by the conflict between Pharaoh Teôs (361/0 BC) and the priesthood of the temples which he chose to plunder in order to finance his Phoenician campaign.[32] Here Pharaoh was the loser, and the behaviour of the subsequent ruler, Nectanebo II, shows that the lesson was taken to heart.

In conclusion, although Late-Period Egypt contained, and generally welcomed, large communities of immigrants, it is worth remembering that the demotic script largely excludes the foreign. Literary hieratic, as far as we can judge, does this even more thoroughly. There is an analogy here. The country's foreign elements grew wealthy, and were even able to form small states within the state; but they did so on Pharaoh's terms. Even Joseph, clever though he was, had to put up with an unpronounceable Egyptian name. Egyptian culture was so distinctive, all-pervading and visually appealing that pressure to assimilate to it was overwhelming. Pharaoh could not marry every daughter of a successful immigrant, even if he had a mind to; and in practice he did not need to do so. Pharaonic culture did the job for him. Pharaonic culture similarly worked its influence on

---

Period is the best documented, and the following may be taken as tentative upper estimates for the middle of the fourth century BC:

population	4 million
Egyptian population	3.5 million
readers of demotic, passive or otherwise	1/4 million (?)
(*including* limited use of demotic	100,000
fully literate in demotic	10,000 or less)

This gives us some 250,000, or 7.14 per cent of the Egyptian population (6.25 per cent of the whole, including non-Egyptians), who can be described as having something to do with the process of writing; the remaining 93 per cent would be illiterate in the full sense. Of the proportion which were involved with demotic writing, some 10,000 could be described as fully conversant with the script and the writing of literature. The last figure represents some 0.29 per cent of the Egyptian population, or one in 350. This corresponds to 0.25 per cent of the total population, or one in 400. The literacy figures for the various foreign communities are even more difficult to estimate.

[32] Kienitz (1953: 95–8); Ray in Sancisi-Weerdenburg (1987: 83 ff.).

demotic. What began as a language of the people, or at least the people who administered the people, rapidly became an ideal idiom, a sort of Platonic form of Egyptian. Demotic is what the Egyptians would like to have spoken in a perfect, Greekless, world.

5   Literacy and power in Ptolemaic Egypt

Dorothy J. Thompson

It is hard to imagine a more striking symbol of Ptolemaic power and of the dominance of Greek culture than the new Library of Alexandria. Here, and in the closely related Museum, Greek literature was to be collected and selected, the Old Masters were to be stored, studied and sanctified, existing knowledge was codified and new knowledge encouraged. In the new Greek capital city of Alexandria, among the scribblers and scrolls, translations were made, literature was dissected and explained and new writers received support and speedy success. As the archaic Greek tyrants before them, so the early Ptolemies put their resources into books and literate culture with an energy and drive which was fortunately matched by their passion for the accumulation of wealth and its display. In the competitive world of Hellenistic kings, libraries became symbols of status and objects of prestige and pride to their founders. And in this world Alexandria was now the arbiter of taste and the leader of literate fashion.[1]

Alexandria, however, was the centre – not physically so since the new Greek capital, founded by Alexander in 332 BC on the Mediterranean coast, was far to the north of the kingdom it ruled, but none the less the centre of administration and rule for Egypt as a whole. For once Ptolemy I left Memphis and moved to the 'city by the sea',[2] then Alexandria became the centre of government, a focus for the new administration but also accessible to other Hellenistic kingdoms. In such a city, facing both up-river to Egypt and out to the Aegean, Greek culture could flourish and develop. But what of the rest of Egypt, the *chora* up-country from Alexandria?

This is the focus of the present investigation – the Egyptian base to the

---

[1] See Fraser (1972; 305–35); Canfora (1989), a somewhat speculative reconstruction; el-Abbadi (1990); Most (1990), on canonisation; Athenaeus, *Deipn.* 5 196–203e, for wealth; Strabo 13.1.54 (C609), on Hellenistic royal libraries. For abbreviations of editions of papyri see the works cited in chapter 8, n. 1, and note, in addition: *P. Lille dém.* III = *Papyrus démotiques de Lille III*, ed. Fr. de Cenival (Mémoires Publiés par les Membres de l'Institut Français d'Archéologie Orientale du Caire 110), Cairo 1984; *P. Lond. dem.* IV = *Catalogue of Demotic Papyri in the British Museum*, IV. *Ptolemaic Legal Texts from the Theban Area*, ed. C. A. R. Andrews, London 1990.
[2] *P. Oxy.* XXII 2332.59 (third century AD), in the Potter's Oracle.

new-found wealth and power of the Ptolemies. Through looking at the role of writing, and particularly of writing in the Ptolemaic administration outside the capital, I shall investigate the nature of Ptolemaic rule in Egypt. Through consideration of what was written, by whom, in what context and what language, as these changed over time, I hope to illuminate and to help evaluate the changing relations between conqueror and conquered, between Greek and Egyptian, between ruler and ruled. It is the changes as seen through writing, in the multifarious and multifaceted character of Ptolemaic rule of Hellenistic Egypt, which are my concern, and the complex relationship between language, literacy and culture in this, the best-documented of the Hellenistic kingdoms.

We may start on the eve of conquest in the last third of the fourth century BC. It was the antiquity and wisdom of Egypt which had always fascinated the Greeks, and part of that antiquity had been the invention of writing.[3] The ready availability too of the papyrus plant and its use as a writing material had been an early and important development. The different scripts of Egypt, the sacred script or hieroglyphs, the hieratic and the demotic scripts had different but complementary functions: writing was a skill limited to a very few, to some princes, to priests and, above all, to scribes.[4] How important a role was really played by writing within this society is hard to judge since it is the scribes' view that survives; and scribes were insistent in writing up their profession.[5]

The uses of writing were many and varied. Besides its use for sacred records and for literary purposes, writing was employed for more straightforward documentation, for the listing of objects and events, and, within the centralised administration, for communication and rule. The more cursive hieratic script, used at first for religious and literary texts, was later put to more mundane purposes. Finally, in the Late Period, the standardised demotic form took over as the standard script for regular writing of Egyptian, when hieroglyphs were not required.[6]

The use of writing for literature and memorials had developed over almost three thousand years and the role of writing for legal purposes, to register ownership and to define the role of personal property, of the individual and of the family within the state, was well established by the time of Alexander's conquest. Written contracts, witnessed by copy and by signature, were standard among the élite members of society, the priestly families, the necropolis workers and others with temple connections:

---

[3] Herodotus 2.177.2; Plato, *Phaedrus* 275c–d, located in the Greek city of Naukratis.
[4] On writing in pre-Ptolemaic Egypt, see Baines (1983, 1988); Baines and Eyre (1983); Ray (1986); Silverman (1990).   [5] Lichtheim (1973: 184–92); (1976: 113–14, 167–78).
[6] See Ray in ch. 4 above.

To you belong their documents, their titles in any place in which they are: every document which has been drawn up regarding them and every document which has been drawn up for me regarding them and every document by virtue of which I am entitled in respect of them, they belong to you and the rights conferred by them ...

runs an Egyptian demotic document from 198 BC in which a Theban priest renounces claim to profitable funerary services connected with certain (named) tombs in the region.[7] That this particular example is actually post-conquest in date is irrelevant. The wording is standard Egyptian and the message is clear. Documents were prized and treasured; they changed ownership with property and served in legal contexts. Whether or not their owners could read them was, I suspect, secondary to the importance with which they were endowed as written records. In a society of literate experts it was their simple existence that mattered. Whilst for their owners they may have served primarily as symbols of ownership, what is important is that they were symbols in *written* form.

An analysis of surviving demotic documents from the period before Alexander's conquest shows writing used for a range of personal activities including letters, lists, memoranda and the record of information; to record a wide variety of legal dealings, from marriage, divorce, sales, gifts, property divisions and other contracts to loans, witness lists, self-sale documents and slave transactions; and even for some religious uses such as temple records, oracles and petitions to the gods.[8] The range of recorded uses of writing is wide but, as always in the ancient world, it is equally important to remember that what survives, on papyrus and broken pot, is only a chance sample of what once was there. Conclusions based on this surviving sample are always liable to correction. The combination however of a ready supply of writing material and a range of Egyptian scripts, reflected in the range of experts who practised them, resulted in a society in which writing was well embedded.[9] And, although its practice might be limited, with literate skills confined to a small royal and priestly élite with a sub-élite of scribes, the number of those who recognised its importance and who took part, even at one remove, in a culture of which it formed part will have been much greater than the narrow band of scribes who practised literate skills.

Then came the Greek conquest, the capture of Egypt in 332 BC by Alexander of Macedon who, in his pursuit of the Persian enemy, took this Persian satrapy as a prelude to taking their king. Three hundred years later, when Kleopatra's kingdom fell in turn to Rome, Egypt had become a Mediterranean power – a country ruled by Macedonian kings and

[7] Andrews (1990: no. 3.9 (11 December 198 BC)); cf. Pestman (1983: 293–4).
[8] Listed by Thissen (1980).
[9] On the different literate traditions of Egypt and Greece see Thompson (forthcoming).

governed by an administration which functioned in Greek. So standard now was Greek as the language of the administration that the Roman take-over made no difference to the written language of Egyptian government. For in 332 BC what was new with the Greek conquest was not the domination of the country by a foreign power – that had happened before and the Greeks after all were replacing the Persians – but rather the impact of the new power. Once Ptolemy son of Lagos replaced Kleomenes as satrap and, some time later, was finally recognised as king of Egypt, Egypt was again ruled by a pharaoh resident in the country. This pharaoh however spoke Greek, and Greek was in time to become the new language of the administration, at least in written form.

The change from demotic to Greek was no overnight change. The continued use of the written script of the language of the existing personnel should cause no surprise, especially given the small numbers of immigrants compared with native Egyptians.[10] Similarly, some thousand years later on the Arab conquest of Egypt, Greek in turn remained in partial use for a century before finally being supplanted by Arabic.[11] What I shall focus on here is the apparent change in the nature of government which accompanied the new Macedonian regime. By far the most striking feature of this change is the change in the extent of documentation, or rather of the documentation that survives. From the third century BC onwards papyrus records in an ever-increasing quantity, the majority of them in Greek, form testimony to a bureaucratic administration involved in an ever-increasing number of aspects of the life both of the individual and of the community. And now, for the first time under the Ptolemies, are found recorded new operations of government and new controls, elaborate census listings, surveys, crop orders and many new central directives and taxes. Possible explanations and implications of these changes must also be considered.

First, however, we must face the problem of the documentary evidence for these changes. How far may this picture of bureaucratic change reflect a change not in documentation but in the pattern of survival of papyri from this period? May the changes be apparent rather than real, chimeric not substantial? These are complex questions, yet in answering them we may be in a better position to evaluate the extent of administrative and bureaucratic innovation that followed the Greek conquest. We may also be able to make more sense of the areas where, through looking at what is written and the language in which it is written, we find real changes in relations between the different groups within the population of Ptolemaic Egypt.

The first problem therefore to be considered is the fundamental question of whether there really was an increase in writing within the Ptolemaic and

[10] Bagnall (1984: 16–20); cf. Clarysse (1987), on the paucity of Greek loan-words in demotic.
[11] El-Abbadi (1990: 179–80).

later the Roman administration. Is the apparent upward curve of written material produced within the Greek administration anything more than the simple result of changes in practice, from the use of wooden tablets to papyrus perhaps, or of a change in funerary practice which resulted in the survival of that papyrus? For the reuse of waste papyrus to form mummy casing or cartonnage is a new feature of the Ptolemaic period. Most of the early Ptolemaic papyri come from cartonnage from cemeteries, particularly in the newly-developed Fayum, from Ghoran in the south-west and Gurob to the east, while the Tebtunis papyri are from that village's crocodile cemetery in the south. The Zenon papyri from the mid-third century BC and the Memphite Serapeum papyri from the second are unusual as representing caches of documents discovered together in their original form.

So, how far is it simply the survival of cartonnage which provides the picture of an increase in the volume of writing? Having raised the problem, I wish to discount it. The further increase in written material from the Roman period, when recycled papyrus was no longer used for cartonnage, suggests that the trend is real. On the more general question of the typicality of what has survived, there exists of course a whole range of reasons for the discovery of papyri, preserved through the dry desert conditions of Egypt – the fellahin searching for *sebakh* (fertiliser), the excavation of town sites or cemeteries, the borrowing and digging in search of food of the desert foxes, legal and illegal antiquities dealing, the construction of modern buildings or clearing for development purposes – and it is always possible to discount as atypical what has survived. To do so, however, is in my view perverse when dealing with such quantities. It is certainly the case that the spread of surviving Ptolemaic papyri is uneven, with very few from Upper Egypt, some from the Nile valley in Middle Egypt and none from the Delta; like the mummy cartonnage, most do indeed come from the Fayum, from the villages and village cemeteries that surround the cultivation in an area developed under the Ptolemies. In the Roman period a disproportionate number come from the excavations of Oxyrhynchus. To what extent this unevenness of survival reflects actual usage cannot of course be checked but, although our knowledge may be limited by locality, as more material is either found or published a coherent picture does take form. Whereas the Fayum probably was exceptional in the extent of Greek innovation and penetration found in that area, nevertheless a gradual extension of Greek writing and Greek ways may be documented, throughout the country, from the Ptolemaic to the Roman periods.

Aware then of possible slants to the survival of the written material and therefore to the hazards of interpretation – the comparative scarcity of documents from the reign of Ptolemy I may, in part, derive from the fact that recycled papyrus was not yet used for cartonnage – I would still wish to argue for a real increase in what was written down on papyrus following the introduction of Greek as the language of administration. It is the implications of this change which must be considered further.

Many questions may be asked. The most obvious area to start is with the relationship between the increase in surviving papyri and the change in ruling power. In simple terms, how far, as has been argued for the Normans in Britain after 1066,[12] did immigrant Greeks increase use of the written form in an attempt to establish a rule which owed its only legitimacy to the fact of conquest? Does an increase in writing reflect any increase in power? Closely related are questions of language and script, of different traditions of literacy within the two societies, Egyptian and Greek. How far is the apparent increase in bureaucratic records connected to the gradual change in the language of administration from Egyptian to Greek? And, if such a connection is postulated, we may further ask how far this was a directed change, the result of central government policy, or how far a spontaneous one. Was it simply the consequence of the employment of Greek officials? Did it reflect the different traditions of the new rulers? Or does it represent a Darwinian triumph of the simpler alphabetic script?

Some preliminary observations are needed to summarise what I have argued in greater detail elsewhere.[13] First, the question of language. Under Ptolemy I Soter very little survives that is written in Greek; official documents are in Egyptian – on papyrus demotic and generally hieroglyphs on stone. Even if pronounced in Greek, surviving royal decrees from these early years were displayed in Egyptian, in traditional hieroglyphic script.[14] That the earliest royal decrees from Ptolemaic Egypt treat relations with the temples is not surprising. Even under foreign rule temples remained key institutions in Egypt. The need of any Egyptian ruler to recognise his position of responsibility for the divine order of which he formed part was essential to his acceptance both by the people of Egypt and by the priestly élite. Furthermore it was from this priestly milieu that the early Ptolemaic administrators were to come, scribes trained in the temple schools[15] and literate in demotic, who in time would learn Greek in order to function in the bureaucracy of the new administration.

An exception in these early years to the normal use of Egyptian for official writing is Peukestas' warning posted up in Greek at Saqqara and addressed to his soldiers, the troops of Alexander, to keep well clear of a

[12] Clanchy (1979: 18, 74).   [13] Thompson (1992a).
[14] Sethe (1904: II 11–22, no. 9) (310 BC), the Satrap Stele translated in Bevan (1927: 28–32); Freud Museum Catalogue no. 14 (301 BC). The Rosetta Stone, Sethe (1904: II 166–98, no. 36) (196 BC), is the best-known example from later in the period.
[15] Williams (1972); Kaplony-Heckel (1974); Bresciani (1984); Devauchelle (1984).

priestly dwelling. From the first generation of post-conquest Egypt, the order shows how early the invaders were made aware of the importance of temples in Egypt. Memphite priests scored an early success in influencing the new power to their own advantage.[16] At the same time these instructions from Saqqara, written in a firm clear hand and fixed up with two nails, provide an interesting comment on literacy levels within the Macedonian army. In this case the instructions were directed at the Greek-speaking force of occupation, but within the new regime of the Ptolemies the posting of written orders – 'keep-off' orders – became adopted as a standard form of protection for Egyptians too.[17]

Within one hundred and fifty years of the conquest surviving papyri suggest that Greek had become the main language of administration, at least at its upper levels. With the capital firmly fixed in Alexandria, a centralised bureaucracy had come to function in the language of the conquerors. For administrative purposes instructions now emanated from the capital and were publicised in Greek and, at least at the level of the nome (one of the thirty administrative districts into which Egypt was divided), records were kept in this language; from the villages written reports in Greek were returned by officials. At the same time surviving ostraka show the continued, but by no means exclusive, use of demotic for tax receipts in the towns and villages of Egypt – an indication of the spoken language of the majority of the population, including local officials. Bilingual receipts are also found both on papyrus and ostraka but to argue from these to the literate competence of the taxpayer would be unwise.[18] For the illiterate, receipts bearing the scripts of both languages may well have been preferred. Over time however Greek became the favoured language for administrative documents, and surviving records suggest a significant increase in what was now being written down. Both aspects should be considered further – first, the adoption of Greek for official purposes and, secondly, the development of new bureaucratic institutions which functioned in writing.

The spread of the use of Greek for official purposes may be viewed in several ways. On the colonial model it may be seen as the imposition by a ruling power of its own language and system of writing. Alternatively, from the Egyptian side, the adoption of Greek by Egyptian priests and scribes, to be found both in temple environs and scribal offices, may be interpreted as evidence for flexibility and adaptation on the part of existing élites which

---

[16] Turner (1974); Thompson (1988: 106–54).

[17] E.g. *UPZ* I 108.14–18, 25–30 (99 BC), protection for Petesis, undertaker-in-chief for the Apis and Mnevis bulls, to be posted in both Greek and Egyptian scripts.

[18] E.g. *BGU* VI 1319–35 (third century BC), bilingual salt-tax receipts from Elephantine. Hanson (1991: 192) draws attention to the clarity of the names written on such ostraka; these alone might be read by the taxpayer.

enabled them to continue to hold prestigious (and lucrative) office within the new system. Finally, the growing use of Greek as the language for bureaucratic communication may be viewed as an autonomous development, an almost inevitable result, in a society where literacy was highly valued, of the introduction of a simpler alphabetic script.

Greek imposition, Egyptian collaboration and alphabetic superiority have, all of them, drawbacks as sufficient explanation, and as always the process of change is likely to have been a complex one, with different factors affecting different groups within the society as a whole. A reluctance at the top for learning Egyptian – note the much-quoted report that Kleopatra VII was the first in three hundred years of the Ptolemaic dynasty to learn the language of the country[19] – combined with the presence of Greek communities in Egypt, already established before the Macedonian conquest, to promote Greek as the administrative language. Just as the Persians earlier had used Aramaic, so the Greeks – or, rather, the Macedonians and Greeks – were to govern in Greek, and the earlier Ionian settlements in the eastern Delta and at Naukratis and, since the sixth century, at Memphis, produced a ready supply of information and administrators. Kleomenes from Naukratis, left in post by Alexander with overall financial responsibility for the country, would on this hypothesis be representative of the home talent available to Alexander and to the Ptolemies who followed.

Against such an interpretation with its emphasis on the role of Greeks is the fact that the early administration seems on the whole to have been carried out in demotic. The first surviving mention, for instance, of the Ptolemaic institution of the land survey is an ostrakon from Karnak in Upper Egypt carrying a *demotic* copy of an order of Ptolemy II Philadelphos for a general survey of the country completed for the first month of Year 28, October–November 258 BC.[20] It was not only the land but also the population that was subjected to a thorough census, and third-century BC census documents, the basis for individual taxation, were produced in both demotic and Greek within the same office. Some, if not most, of the scribes employed in the local offices where these lists were prepared were, on the evidence of the documents which survive, originally trained in demotic. When writing Greek some would use a rush, Egyptian-style, instead of a reed, the normal pen for Greek,[21] and the Greek they wrote, with practised hand but shaky spelling abounding in errors of syntax, suggests a second language. Whilst at a high level priests such as Manetho might be instructing the rulers in the traditional ways of

[19] Plutarch, *Antony* 27.3–4.
[20] Bresciani (1978) and (1983), translated in Burstein (1985: 122–3, no. 97).
[21] Tait (1988).

Egypt in Greek, other Egyptians made a career at court or in the army; and in the countryside existing scribal offices serviced the early activities of the new administration, often in demotic.[22] Like many of the tax and census lists, guarantees underwriting the village brewers for the payment of their taxes were still under Ptolemy III recorded in demotic, even when the parties concerned bore names that were Greek.[23] The use of the existing scribal class seems clear. What is less clear is where the balance lay. Was it a case primarily of collaboration, with the initiative from opportunistic Egyptian priests and scribes, or the result rather of interference from the immigrant power? Probably both were involved.

Given the numerical inferiority of the Greeks, reliance on the existing structures of government was probably unavoidable. Yet at the same time there exists striking evidence for a positive assertion of Greek language and identity within their new country. At least from the reign of Ptolemy II the existing scribal class started to learn to function in Greek. By a combination of tax-concessions and a widespread programme of education the new Greek rulers attempted to establish a new administrative class of 'Hellenes'. The exemption from the salt-tax of school teachers (*grammatadidaskaloi*) together with teachers of physical education (*paidotribai*) and victors in Alexandrian games has long been known.[24] What has recently become clear, as the result of the publication of third-century BC census lists drawn up in both Greek and demotic, is the privileged position of both 'Persai' and 'Hellenes', who were not required to pay the obol-tax, to which all other male adults (with the exception of those exempted from the salt-tax) were liable.[25] The exact identity of these two groups is still in question but, on the basis of details within the lists themselves, I have suggested elsewhere that Hellenes were defined in terms not of origin but rather of either their education or a post in the administration.[26] These were the men required to run the complex written administration in process of development. As members of the gymnasium, these new Hellenes would play an important role in the Ptolemaic administration.

The training of these new scribes seems in practice to have been a fairly thorough Greek education. Census lists again are important in showing the distribution of Greek teachers in the countryside. Since however totals given under a particular professional heading in these lists include all adult members of a family where the family head belongs to that profession, such totals may serve only as an indication of levels in an area; but in Egypt

[22] Thompson (1992c: 44–5), for Egyptians in the early Ptolemaic administration.
[23] De Cenival (1973) nos. 34–96, often with Greek abstracts, see Clarysse (1978).
[24] *P. Hal.* 1.260–5.
[25] *CPR* XIII; *P. Lille dém.* III. Further texts will be published in a corpus under the joint editorship of W. Clarysse and myself.   [26] Thompson (1992b: 326).

occupations did tend to run in the family. In the village of Trikomia for instance in one particular year in the mid-third century BC there were 3 adults listed under the heading of teachers in an adult population of 331 (i.e. 0.9 per cent of the adult population), in neighbouring Lagis within the Themistos division of the Arsinoite nome 3 under this heading in a total adult population of 323, and 24 out of 10,876 (0.2 per cent) within a complete toparchy or tax area.[27] That the existing evidence is primarily from the new settlements of the Fayum basin is, as already noted, a feature of the pattern of survival of Ptolemaic papyri. When more of the demotic material from the Nile valley is published this picture of an emphasis given to education may well be extended.[28] The situation in the Delta is unknown and Upper Egypt remains a mystery.

What was taught in school in this period may be seen from a Ptolemaic Greek school book. Published as *Un livre d'écolier*, this third-century BC papyrus roll contains rather a teacher's manual which may have served for several years.[29] Reading was taught on the a–b–c system; arithmetic and dating systems formed part of the curriculum as did lists of rivers and the Greek gods. The most notable feature of the manual is the Greek literature to which schoolchildren were introduced – Homer of course, the tragedians and New Comedy, together with more contemporary poetry from Alexandria; no prose writing is found in this manual. The pattern of literary papyri found in Egypt and contexts from which they come[30] suggests that the concept of a national curriculum may be as relevant to Ptolemaic Egypt as to post-Napoleonic France and her empire overseas. Whether the origins of this system of education were Macedonian[31] or more generally Greek, the inclusion of Alexandrian literature – and especially that which commemorated Ptolemaic buildings: temples, for instance, the Pharos, a fountain – gave a particularly contemporary emphasis to the new programme of schooling. The elements of reading, writing and arithemetic were, in this educational system, joined by instruction in Greek poetry. Literacy in Ptolemaic Egypt involved a knowledge also of literature.[32] We should ask what effect this may have had on the nature of that administration.

Although scribes and others working within the royal administration may have acquired a knowledge of Poseidippus and Callimachus,[33] it was of little practical application. Indeed, the language of surviving Ptolemaic documents, of decrees and depositions, of applications and appeals, lends

---

[27] Thompson (1992b: 325).
[28] For census material from Lycopolis (to be included in the corpus) see Sir Herbert Thompson in Petrie (1907: 31–9).   [29] Guéraud and Jouguet (1938).
[30] Clarysse (1983); Thompson (1987).   [31] As argued by Hammond (1990).
[32] Compare Heather (below ch. 12), on the role of literary texts in late Roman education.
[33] Thompson (1988: 260–1); Youtie (1970).

support to the argument of Wilcken for further technical training for would-be scribes and bureaucrats.[34] This is a subject on which there is more work to be done, but the complex vocabulary and syntax of both official communications and legal writings suggest the development of both a legal and a bureaucratic jargon. Existing Greek vocabulary was extended in meaning (*skepe* for example coming to mean not 'cover' but 'patronage' or 'protection'), and the use of unusual vocabulary, of abstract nouns for instance (*sykophantia*, 'sycophancy', *philautia*, 'selfishness', or *antilepsis*, 'defence' or 'succour') or colourful and unusual verbs (*skullesthai, diaseiein* or *perispan* are all terms used for 'to harm'), in legal and in bureaucratic writing suggests a professional system in which training and practice served to complicate and even to mystify.[35] If some of the bureaucratic words and phrases are found also in contemporary literary usage, in the Septuagint or in Polybius, suggesting their adoption into the language of the time, the *koine* of the Hellenistic world, the same fortunately cannot be said of the complicated sentence structure which combines with linguistic usage to typify the documents of the Ptolemaic administration. To take just one of many possible examples, *UPZ* 110 recording instructions of the *dioiketes* Herodes from 164 BC, at a time of dynastic struggle and trouble in the countryside, reads as a masterpiece of bureaucratese. Those who dealt in these writings learnt the jargon with the job and made it difficult for any outsider to gain access to the system and the information they controlled. And alongside the development of a Greek bureaucratic language came greater precision, at least in the recording of time. Dates, for instance, in demotic contracts recorded the season (three seasons with four months each) and the year; in Greek, all months were separately named, the day of the month was also added and, for some time at least, attempts were made to co-ordinate the different calendars in use – the Macedonian and the two Egyptian calendars, with reckoning by either the financial or the regnal year.

Through education therefore and tax-breaks, the new Greek rulers encouraged the adoption of their language within the administration of Egypt. At the same time Egyptian priests and scribes had everything to gain by collaboration and adaptation. For rather than standing apart, these two elements in the picture – Greek imposition and Egyptian collaboration – can be seen to reinforce each other. That mutual interest is essential to success in the extension of literacy and literate practices has been discovered the hard way in more recent literacy programmes.[36] Within the Ptolemaic bureaucracy the speedy spread of Greek and apparent multiplication of records made on papyrus will have served a purpose for those involved, both for the ruling

[34] Wilcken (1927: 474–5).
[35] Crawford (Thompson) (1974: 169), on *skepe*; *UPZ* I indices. On a similar development under the Roman empire see Kelly pp. 174–5 below. [36] Street (1984: 183–212).

power and for those who were its instruments. Mutual interest is an important feature of the development and the increase in what was now written down reinforced the interdependence of ruler and ruled.

But what of the third explanation for the extension of writing and the adoption of Greek: the role of the alphabet? It was, it has been argued, the greater simplicity of Greek which facilitated a further growth in bureaucratic practices in a country where recording had been well established already for almost three thousand years. Greek was an easier language to learn than was Egyptian, the alphabetic script simpler to write than demotic. Such a claim seems attractive to those whose prime familiarity is with an alphabetic script, but I should like to question its validity, both as a more general assumption and in this particular case. First, demotic script may be hard, but a complicated script is not in itself a bar to literacy. Japan is one of the countries today with the highest literacy rate – 99 per cent compared with 96 per cent in the USA[37] – yet in order to read the newspapers a knowledge of 8,800 characters is required. Graduated learning is simply built in to the system of education (with 500 characters to be learnt by the age of 12 and 2,800 by age 15). The Chinese script suits the language well and an alphabetic form has not been adopted. Secondly, the argument that Greek triumphed because of the greater simplicity of its alphabet implies that those who learnt it were not literate in Egyptian. But, as we have already seen, the rush, the Egyptian writing instrument, used instead of the reed for writing Greek in bilingual offices suggests rather the employment of scribes literate in both languages. In the Ptolemaic case, it may be that the somewhat formal nature of the demotic language had something to do with its ultimate demise, but I suspect that the Egyptian scribes who wrote in Greek did so primarily because this was the conquerors' language. As we have already seen, their spelling and syntax often suggest that Egyptian remained their first spoken language. Yet many must have been bilingual and literate in both Greek and Egyptian. In many countries of the world throughout history interpreters, officials, scribes, tradesmen and many others have, without difficulty, functioned in more than one language and script. Contemporary Egypt, Russia or Greece would all provide examples. But the answer to the question of why, over time, Egyptian was abandoned in favour of Greek within the administration is likely to have less to do with whether or not a script was easier or more difficult than with other factors concerning the nature of the ruling power and the structure of Ptolemaic society.[38] It is however not just the adoption of Greek, both spoken and

---

[37] As reported in *The Economist* 26 May (1990) 11.

[38] See Clanchy (1979: 165), on the need for a powerful authority behind a standard literary language to maintain it in use; cf. Ray, pp. 53, 58–66 above, on demotic as a standardised language.

written, but also the spread in bureaucratic activity which comes into question here. Even if a close link between the nature of the script, here an alphabetic script, and its adoption for written records is not accepted, we may still ask what lay behind the extension of bureaucratic records identified in this period.

Egypt, with its priestly/scribal élite, had always been a country in which the numbering and notation of many aspects of life had played a familiar role in the daily life of its inhabitants. What perhaps was new with the Ptolemies was not just their language but also their literate tradition and programme of education which led, I suggest, to a new generation of bureaucrats. And hand in hand with a growth in literacy there came perhaps, as in Norman Britain, a growth in documentation.[39] The new administrators of Ptolemaic Egypt – many of them Egyptians – trained now in the language of the occupying power, itself in the process of transformation into an integrated dynasty, needed new ways in which to express the skills that they learnt. And if an increase in written records was a function which might define the new administrators, so too it might serve to legitimate and enhance the image of the new rulers of Egypt.

And so, if this interpretation is correct, the first century of Ptolemaic rule saw an increase not only in writing but, through this, also in the extent of royal concern with many aspects of life of the country's population – census lists for all adults, a complete land survey of the country, the seed order and the crop survey. A centralised system was being developed based on a variety of territorial units – meris, toparchy, nome – which seem to have changed over time. The system bore all the characteristics of a bureaucracy, with its concern for detail whatever its use. So in 258 BC in the Karnak demotic ostrakon already mentioned (n. 20), recording the royal order for a comprehensive land survey, many different features are listed. The survey is to cover irrigation works, the distribution and cultivation of all land, field by field with measurements given, defined both by administrative category and nature of produce; vineyards, orchards and individual fruit trees, footpaths and water channels, are all to be listed, together with details of rents and revenues and of their destination. Two consequences of such a system of recording may be identified. First, for those working in such a system local knowledge was no longer a prerequisite; the compilation of such detailed records might allow, over time, the development of a new administrative class. Secondly, working in such a system, a new class of scribes and bureaucrats could identify with the new system of rule. And the records that they wrote may be seen to play a part in endorsing the new ruling power.

Alongside the administration, developments in the legal systems of

---

[39] Clanchy (1979: 14).

Egypt are equally relevant. The Ptolemies did not abolish the Egyptian legal system; they simply added their own Greek system of law. And the roles of these two systems changed over time. In an attempt to illustrate the complex process of change which slowly took place, and which affected language, form and procedure of legal transactions, we may look in some detail at one particular form of Egyptian contract, that which involves 'witness-copies'. These are demotic contracts in which, in addition to the standard 16 witnesses listed on the verso, the contract itself is copied out four (or more) times by different witness-copyists.[40] So, for instance, late in 265 BC in the Egyptian town of Thebes the funerary worker Neskhonsu, daughter of Teos, disposed of her property and assets. In return for regular subsistence, a clothes allowance and promise of proper burial on her death, her son Panas was to receive one and a half houses in Thebes, half of a house in Djeme, half of the revenues from his mother's funerary duties in nearby Hermonthis and all of the revenues from duties at certain specified tombs in the Theban necropolis. One of the documents recording this agreement is now preserved in the British Museum.[41] Written in demotic, the contract was once made up of 20 sheets of papyrus pasted together in a larger sheet approximately 40 cm high and three metres in width. On the back of this text are listed the standard sixteen witnesses to the deed, but the main body of the document contains the more remarkable feature: witnessing not just by name but by copying. Alongside the original text four of the sixteen witnesses have, in their own hands, each copied out for themselves, with only minor variants, the complete text of the contract, ending with the words: 'X has written this' The whole contract with its four finely-written witness-copies adds up to an impressive document, and on the verso the names of the full sixteen witnesses serve to endorse the spoken word to which they stand witness here. The document is thus doubly validated – both in writing and through the actual presence of the witnesses.[42]

Today value is often in inverse proportion to the elaborate layout of a certificate or label – wine labels, for instance, or degree certificates – but when most cannot read the layout and appearance of the writing is crucial. Large-scale documents covered in writing with witnesses named and acting also as copyists make an impressive record for their owners who, according to the wisdom they were taught, for generations kept safe their titles and legal deeds. And each time the contract was copied out, the start was marked by the ideogram for the year. Written in an enlarged form,

---

[40] Besides the examples in Andrews (1990), see Smith (1958: 87) (one example with 6 copies besides the original); cf. Baines and Eyre (1983: 74–7).

[41] *P. Lond. dem.* IV 1 (265 BC).

[42] Compare McKitterick (1989: 73–5), on the symbolic role of written legal transactions; (1989: 92), on witnesses essential for validity.

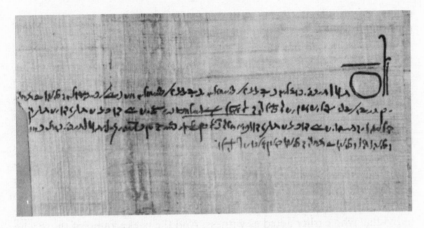

Fig. 2. A demotic papyrus showing an initial year sign. (British Museum papyrus 10464 (210 BC) = Andrews (1990) no. 26. Reproduced by Courtesy of the Trustees of the British Museum.)

comparable perhaps to an illuminated initial letter, the year-sign ⌐ (see fig. 2) presents a strong visual impact. Even those illiterate in demotic could, through recognition of this sign, easily make out the start of each copy; the fourfold reiteration of the contract itself might add validity and force. Whilst the practice of multiple versions, the witness-copies of contracts, may therefore be seen also to have served a practical end – as writing practice for junior scribes – its effect on the final appearance of the contract was of equal importance. Since often the contract's owner would not be able to read, the formal aspect of that contract was crucial. The symbolic force of such records should not be underestimated.

Contracts with witness-copies date from shortly before Alexander's conquest until the late third century BC. This form was later replaced by demotic property contracts of the simpler sixteen-witness form. The presence and listing of witnesses remained important, and on the verso the list of sixteen names was carefully placed in such a way that the start of the list comes just where on the front is written the verb _ḏd_, 'to speak'.[43] So, in the field of private legal contracts, traditional forms continued in use, and amongst the Egyptian population of Egypt the traditional scribe still had a role to play. By leaving intact a traditional legal system which functioned in Egyptian, the Ptolemies avoided too speedy a change and possible conflict. Substantial Egyptians, the priests and embalmers throughout the Nile

[43] Pestman (1978: 203).

valley, continued in these centuries to manage their legal affairs in traditional ways.

Yet, as in the administration so in the law, the Greek-language way began to impose itself. Just two examples may serve to illustrate this trend. The first is the office of *agoronomos*, an innovation known from the third century BC but whose regular function, in Greek, is known only from the second. *Agoranomoi* were state officials who acted as legal notaries rather than simple scribes. Greek documents drawn up in their bureaux were more than simple records; they had some legal standing. Increasingly, contracts drawn up in this office replaced the older forms – the Egyptian sixteen-witness contract and the standard six-witness Greek contracts, the *hexamarturoi sungraphai*. Once the *agoranomos* was involved there was no further need of witnesses. A state official had replaced the private individual who earlier acted as witness. And the background of those who held this post was often Egyptian. In an interesting discussion of the role of *agoranomos* Pestman portrayed this development as the take-over by Egyptians of a Greek office which had perhaps been set up to counterbalance the strength of the traditional Egyptian scribes.[44] I prefer to understand this development as one of Hellenising Egyptians being appointed to the office of *agoranomos* as the successful result of the Ptolemaic programme of training and education, specifically instituted with a view to the needs of the administration and the law. The new administration was increasing its control over the earlier system.

A second development, which in the legal sphere encouraged the move to the Greek way of things, was the requirement instituted late in 146 BC that all Egyptian contracts drawn up in demotic should now be registered in Greek in an official registry-office or *grapheion*.[45] Once a contract had been registered in this way, it was easier then to cite it in a Greek-language legal case before the *chrematistai*.[46] Like the existence of state *agoranomoi*, the registration of contracts in Greek may be viewed as an enabling factor in the move towards Greek ways. Once the Greek language and written legal forms were those of the ruling power, surviving papyri document a one-way move. Slowly the old skills of the Egyptian scribe came to be less in demand, while the scribes themselves had all to gain by retooling themselves in Greek. By the time the Romans came, the final take-over of Greek legal forms would seem to have been a straightforward move.

What I have tried to show in this chapter is that the Ptolemies used education combined with tax incentives to encourage Hellenisation among the majority population of Egypt. Greek became adopted in an intensified

[44] Pestman (1978) and (1989: 148–52).
[45] Wilcken (1927: 596–603). Hopkins (1991: 153) draws attention to this requirement as encouraging literacy.   [46] See Thompson (1988) 189, on *UPZ* I 118 (83 BC).

bureaucratic form of government in which written records played an important part in the control of the ruling power. From the Egyptian side there were positive reasons for co-operation, but the continuation of Egyptian legal forms was important for Egyptian identity and for the survival of demotic. In a non-violent and progressive development over three hundred years, the gradual move from Egyptian to Greek was but one aspect of a complex scene in which education, literacy and literate personnel were affected and changed by the Macedonian conquest and the establishment of a new dynasty in Egypt.

6   Power and the spread of writing in the West[1]

Greg Woolf

Romans believed that barbarians spoke strangely but were not illiterates. Just as classical education culminated in the study of speech not of texts, so barbarians were imagined, not as unlettered savages, but as imperfect speakers. Europeans since the seventeenth century have presumed connections between writing and civilisation that contrast strangely with the central place occupied by orality in ancient culture.[2] The idea that literacy implies higher levels of modernity and rationality remains deeply ingrained in our consciousness, popular as well as academic,[3] but for the Greeks writing was invented and imported by barbarians, and most Roman accounts followed in that tradition. Even if *litterae* were thought in some contexts to be connected with civilised knowledge,[4] barbarians were distinguished from civilised men by language, along with appearance and temperament, and their innate irrationality was not attributed to a lack of letters.[5] Roman views reflected their experience. Few of the groups eventually incorporated within the empire were ignorant of writing prior to conquest, and many had developed scripts and literacies centuries beforehand. Nevertheless, virtually all the scripts used in the West were descendants of the same Phoenician alphabets, and the spread of writing in the West might seem to be reasonably treated, as it usually is, as just one aspect of the expansion of the classical world.[6]

But on closer examination, the history of non-classical writing is more

---

[1] This paper has been much improved by the comments of Cyprian Broodbank, Rosalind Thomas and the participants at the Oxford seminar. The following abbreviations should be noted: *DAF = Documents d'archéologie française*; *ILN = Inscriptions latines de Narbonnaise*; *ILTG = Inscriptions latines des Trois Gaules*; *RAN = Revue archéologique de Narbonnaise*.

[2] Harbsmeier (1989) on illiteracy and savages in European ethnography, contrasted with classical stereotypes by Hartog (1988: 287–9). The primacy of orality in classical culture is a theme of Thomas (1992).

[3] Lévi-Strauss (1958: 347–60), Goody (1977, 1986), Ong (1982) argue varieties of this view. For critical overviews locating these ideas in Eurocentric views of literacy Graff (1979), Street (1984) and Bloch (1989).

[4] Desbordes (1990: 135–46) on Roman views of the origins of writing and their relation to Greek tradition. For the connection between *humanitas* and *litterae* cf. e.g. Pliny, *Epistles* 8.24.2. Hartog's (1988: 277–9) argument that barbarians used writing in strange ways is a little forced.   [5] Dauge (1981) and Wiedemann (1986).   [6] Lejeune (1983).

complex. If classical literacies were imitated by some groups, they were rejected by others, and where they were adopted they were adapted as well. The idea of a classical civilisation invented by Greeks and propagated by Romans, is in any case a myth, one that has effaced the contributions of groups like the Phoenicians and the Etruscans, and disguised cultural discontinuities that accompanied shifting configurations of power. My aim in this chapter is to illustrate this interplay between power and the spread of writing in Gaul by focussing on a series of these discontinuities, sharp differences in the use (or non-use) of writing between societies adjacent in space or in time.

The myth of classical civilisation, as an entity with a history of its own, is still influential today. The conventional history of writing in Gaul is a case in point. The first texts, inscriptions written in a Celtic language using Greek script, are termed Gallo-Greek and are held to be replaced first by Gallo-Latin (Celtic texts written in Roman script), and finally by true Latin ones. The process is envisaged as a slow progression, beginning in the fourth century BC, with a time-lag of a century or so between Mediterranean and non-Mediterranean France, so that Narbonensis was completely Latinised by the time of Caesar and the rest of Gaul by the reign of Claudius. The schema is the conventional one of Gaul civilised first by the Greeks of Marseilles, and then by the Romans, culminating in the happy fusion of Gallo-Roman civilisation. Gallo-Greek has even been described as 'l'écriture nationale des Gaulois', and as in the study of other aspects of the archaeology of the period, there is a tendency to overstress the contributions of France's approved ancestors, Celts, Greeks and Romans, and to suggest the phenomenon was nationally circumscribed.[7] The operation of national power on cultural history since the nineteenth century has drawn on the Roman idea that *humanitas*, civilisation, invented in Greece, was propagated and protected by Roman rule. One obvious discontinuity in this cultural genealogy of European civilisation is the shift in the moral valency of writing. Because writing did not signify civilisation to the Romans, they felt no need to conceal the existence of non-classical scripts, although their interest in it, as in most things barbarian, was minimal. As a result, a few materials survive on the basis of which it is possible to sketch the outlines of a history of non-classical writing in Gaul before, during and after the Roman conquest.

---

[7] Lejeune (1983: 744). cf. the *Recueil des Inscriptions Gauloises* (*RIG*), currently in production, which defines its subject as all Celtic texts from within the borders of modern France, together with some from northern Italy, thus excluding non-Celtic texts from France, such as the Iberian texts listed by Untermann (1980), and also Celtic and possibly Celtic texts from Spain (Lejeune 1973), Britain (Tomlin 1987) and Germany (Krämer 1982).

The earliest writing in Mediterranean France

The last few decades of archaeological research in southern France have made clear what should perhaps have been expected, that the foundation of Marseilles, traditionally dated to 600 BC, was only one episode in a long series of contacts between the communities of southern France and the wider Mediterranean world. Etruscan amphorae of the seventh and sixth centuries BC have been found on more than 90 sites between the Hérault and the Rhône while Greek amphorae from the eastern Mediterranean appeared in the sixth century and were not completely replaced by Massiliot wares until the mid-fifth century. Throughout this period Punic amphorae were also reaching southern French sites.[8] These distributions cannot be easily co-ordinated with historical events such as the battle of Alalia, as the excavation of several shipwrecks of the period has revealed cargoes of mixed Greek and Etruscan wares. Behind histories largely written in terms of ethnic conflicts, we must envisage complex patterns of exchange and colonisation in which Carthaginians and Etruscans may have played greater roles than those allowed them by Greek and Roman writers. Certainly the earliest history of writing in the region suggests the interplay of a variety of cultural traditions.

The earliest known scripts invented in the western Mediterranean were developed by Iberian speakers from Punic models in Mediterranean Spain.[9] An eastern Iberic script developed, probably towards the end of the fifth century, and is known from a series of hillforts in Catalonia and the Languedoc in the fourth century. By the end of the third century, variants of the script had been adopted inland, in Celtiberian Spain and at Vieille-Toulouse on the Gallic Isthmus. Celtic-speaking groups in northern Italy adapted a north Etruscan alphabet in the fourth century BC, creating a script that was used on some coins by the Cavares of the lower Rhône valley.[10] The adoption of a Greek script in the vicinity of Marseilles, creating the first Gallo-Greek inscriptions, was in fact relatively late, probably in the late third or early second century BC. Even so there remained anepigraphic zones, for example the area inhabited by Ligurians or Celto-Ligurians east of the Rhône and north of Massiliotis.[11] Much remains unclear or at least provisional in this account. New finds may well transform our understanding both of the relative chronology of these scripts, and of the uses to which they were put. But the overall picture that emerges is probably correct. Over the last five centuries BC, various

---

[8] For what follows Laubenheimer (1990: 12–20).
[9] Tovar (1961), Maluquer de Motes (1968).
[10] *RIG* II 1 on the Gallo-Etruscan texts with Bats (1988: 130–1).
[11] Bats (1988) is fundamental, cf. also Untermann (1969) and Goudineau (1989).

western Mediterranean communities, in contact with Greeks, Etruscans, Carthaginians and of course each other, adapted existing scripts to produce texts written in their own languages.

There was nothing inevitable or automatic about these developments. If Punic contacts with Spain were followed fairly rapidly by the creation of indigenous Spanish scripts, the reverse seems to be true for the groups in closest contact with Marseilles, some of whom did not adopt the Greek alphabet for more than three centuries after the arrival of the colonists, while others never developed writing. The time-lags in the picture are, as has been pointed out, the key to understanding the process of change.[12] The presence of visitors from literate cultures was a necessary precondition for the adoption of writing, but it was not a sufficient one. Punic, Etruscan and various Greek traders and settlers provided models that might be imitated, but some groups seem deliberately to have rejected those models.

What was writing used for by those who adopted it? The answer seems to be different for Iberian Catalonia and Languedoc, on the one hand, and for the Gallo-Greek zone east of the Rhône, on the other. Our inability to read Iberian poses a number of problems, as does the tendency of the literature to treat French sites and finds separately from Spanish ones. But a fairly wide range of uses seems likely. A little lapidary epigraphy is known and graffiti on potsherds are ubiquitous. Very large numbers of texts have been recovered from some sites, including 372 texts from Ensérune, an extensively excavated but still quite small hillfort.[13] Iberian coin legends are also known, both from coins produced in Spain and from the *monnaies à la croix* which circulated widely between the Garonne and the Pyrenees.[14] Most examples of Iberian writing are short texts, probably mostly names, but a series of long Iberian texts on lead sheets have been recently found, probably all produced in the third century BC. Six derive from Pech-Maho at Sigean near the present-day border between France and Spain. Another example has been found on Ensérune, one from a wreck at Gruissan and one from the Greek colony of Emporion, present-day Ampurias.[15] Although the texts are undecipherable they appear similar to two fifth-century Greek commercial documents also on lead, one from Emporion, and the other found at the Iberian hillfort of Pech-Maho on a reused Etruscan text.[16] Etruscan graffiti have also been claimed for the

---

[12] Bats (1988: 142–4).
[13] Untermann (1980) gives the following totals, which must certainly now be incomplete: Ensérune 372, Pech-Maho 33, Ruscino 20, Elne 17, Montlaurès 9, Lattes 3, Mailhac 3, Gruissan 1, La Lagaste 1, Aubagnan 1.   [14] Untermann (1975), Allen (1980: 109–13).
[15] *RAN* 12 (1979) 55–123, *RAN* 21 (1988) 61–94, 95–113.
[16] On the Emporion letter cf. *RAN* 21 (1988) 3–17 with a series of articles *ZPE* 68 (1987) 119–20, *ZPE* 77 (1988) 100–2, *ZPE* 82 (1990) 176. On the two texts from Pech-Maho: *RAN* 21 (1988) 19–59.

Iberian site of Lattes.[17] Only the Greek texts are legible, but suggest a picture of commercial ties uniting Greeks and Iberians and stretching from sites like Pech-Maho to Ampurias and perhaps Saguntum beyond. The period covered by all these graffiti is a long one, but the suggestion that Iberian usage derives in part from that of Emporitan Greeks seems plausible.[18] Further commercial uses are attested inland at Vieille-Toulouse, where 30 early second-century BC Italian wine amphorae bear Iberian *tituli picti*, names and numbers painted on the amphorae in red, along with some Latin labels. The precise significance is unclear but some system of allocation for delivery after unloading is possible, whether indicating the use of Iberian at Narbo or some other port or at the point of consumption.[19]

Less can be said about the Gallo-Greek inscriptions from east of the Rhône. The record is again dominated by a few sites, St Rémy, St Blaise and Cavaillon accounting for two-thirds of the graffiti on ceramic between them. Again, most texts are probably names. Of the 224 known examples, some 139 are graffiti on sherds of imported Campanian ware, and only thirteen are recorded from other forms of pottery.[20] Campanian ware was probably a luxury tableware in this society, judging by its rarity, possibly associated with the importation of Italian wine and new élite social rituals. Marking these vessels with names may have been a means of associating the owner or user with these rituals or with the prestige of possessing imports, although equally it may have been a means of appropriating alien artefacts and investing them with local meanings. Other uses of the script include lapidary inscriptions, some on stelai but others carved into rock-faces. It is unclear how far these are intended to echo Greek practices.

The contrasts between the Iberian epigraphy and that of the Gallo-Greek zone may be interpreted in a number of ways.[21] Writing may have been one means of signalling ethnic differences between the competing Iberian and Celtic populations who divided the band of hill settlements that dominated the coastal plains from the Alps to the Pyrenees and beyond. Conceivably the late appearance of Gallo-Greek may reflect a deliberate rejection of the culture of both Iberians and Massiliot Greeks. It is certainly interesting that Greek scripts were adopted not in the period of Massiliot imperialism but after the political decline of the city, raising questions about Massilia's civilising role in the region as portrayed by classical sources.[22] Possibly groups west of the Rhône were more ready to adopt

---

[17] *Lattara* 1 (1988) 147–60.   [18] Bats (1988).   [19] *RAN* 16 (1983) 1–28.
[20] *RIG* I for Gallo-Greek texts from France supplemented by *Etudes Celtiques* 25 (1988) 79–106.
[21] Bats (1988) for various suggestions.
[22] Strabo 4.1.5 on Gauls learning to write contracts in Greek under Massiliot tuition.

writing because their contacts with Greeks were more commercial than military. Ultimately, such interpretations can only be plausible hypotheses, at least in the present state of the evidence.

But one important point does emerge very clearly from this material. Writing was adopted in different periods by different groups who used it for different ends, while other groups rejected it altogether. That pattern of cultural change reflects the highly fragmented and local nature of social power in the region in late prehistory. Contacts with outsiders were optional and were not backed up by military or economic power, as is graphically illustrated by the text of the Greek letter from Emporion, which complains of business agreements reneged on. Neither Massiliot imperialism nor the long-distance trading systems, that clearly did exist, generated systems of power that could determine how writing was used and what meanings were assigned to it. Within and between the Iberian- and Celtic-speaking communities that inhabited the southern French hillforts, competition for power and status may well have influenced the ways writing was used or the reasons why it was rejected. Distinctions between neighbouring zones may even reflect ethnic or political tensions. But in so far as writing spread in the West during this period it was a slow, discontinuous and imperfect process.

Writing in temperate Europe on the eve of Roman conquest

No trace of writing survives from temperate Europe until the late La Tène period of the European iron age, roughly equivalent to the last century before Caesar's invasion of Gaul. Non-Mediterranean France was not isolated, but the scale of contacts with literate societies was of a different order from that experienced by the communities of southern France and eastern Spain. Texts and writing equipment have now been found in contexts securely dated to the pre-conquest period, and classical authors occasionally mention non-classical writing. Literate barbarians seemed unremarkable to Greek and Roman writers, but iron-age literacy has assumed a new importance for those who see late prehistoric Europe as a periphery of Mediterranean civilisation, where towns, states and market exchange appeared on the eve of the Roman conquest.[23] The relationships proposed between literacy and power are twofold. First the appearance of literacy, along with state-formation, urbanisation and increased trade with the south, is seen as a product of Europe's subordination to an expanding Mediterranean economy. Second, the development of literacy is seen as a

[23] The classic statement of this view of late iron-age society is Nash (1978a) and (1978b) reproduced most recently by Cunliffe (1988: 92–105). For doubts Bintliff (1984), Haselgrove (1988), Ralston (1988) and Woolf (1993, forthcoming a, b,).

sign of socio-political development, particularly by those who see literacy and the state as inseparable.[24]

Evidence of writing in iron-age Europe is poorer both in quantity and quality than in the south, and its chronology is much less certain. Three passages in classical writers mention Gallic literacy. Diodorus, in the context of a discussion of the Gauls' belief in the immortality of the soul, writes that 'for this reason, it is said, some of them throw letters written to their deceased relatives onto the pyre, so that the departed might read them'.[25] His account almost certainly derives from Poseidonius and so probably refers to southern France in the early first century BC. The other two passages are both Caesarian. In his ethnographic excursus, Caesar describes how the Druids:

> do not think that it is right to entrust their lore to writing, although they make use of Greek letters for their records (*rationes*) in almost all other matters, both public and private. It seems to me that they have this rule for two reasons, firstly because they do not want their doctrine to become common knowledge and secondly so that those who learn it should not become reliant on writing and neglect the faculty of memory. This does in fact happen to many people, that once they have writing to help them, they do not labour so hard to learn things and allow their memory to decay.[26]

Earlier in his narrative, Caesar relates how *tabulae* were found in the camp of the defeated Helvetii, which 'written in Greek letters, name by name, recorded how many fighting men had left their homeland, and listed separately, how many children, women and old men there had been'.[27]

It is striking how little importance is accorded to the fact of writing in these passages. Diodorus' interest is in the psychology of the Druids and Caesar deploys the topos of writing erasing memory, but the ability of the Gauls to write letters or *rationes* is viewed as unremarkable. The precision of the Helvetian census tablets arouses some suspicion, as does the circumstance that the total of fighting men is exactly one-quarter of the total and that Caesar cites the tablets primarily to calculate that he had killed 258,000 of the enemy. As he was attempting at the time to justify his actions in terms of the scale of the threat to the Republican province, so representing himself as a new Marius, it is tempting to dismiss the *tabulae* as an invention contributing to the general political ends of his *Commentaries*. On the other hand, whether true or false, the claim was certainly intended to be plausible, indicating again what little surprise the idea of literate barbarians occasioned Greeks and Romans.

---

[24] Emphases vary: Jacobi (1974), Krämer (1982) set iron-age literacy in the context of increased economic links with the south, Champion (1985: 10) makes connections with the appearance of archaic states as does, more tentatively, Goudineau (1989: 238).
[25] Diodorus 5.28.6.   [26] Caesar, *De Bello Gallico* 6.14.   [27] Caesar, *De Bello Gallico* 1.29.

Archaeological evidence of writing comprises finds of writing equipment, and Gallo-Greek texts similar to those found in the south. Bone styluses have been found in modern excavations at Manching in Bavaria, at the Bern-Engehalbinsel and (possibly) at Basel.[28] Fragments of two writing-tablets and a number of styluses are also among the published material from Stradonice in Bohemia.[29] On the whole, the amount of equipment is surprisingly small, considering the large number of sites that have been excavated from the period, and, even allowing for those like Mont Beuvray where soil conditions do not favour the preservation of bone, it is peculiar that extensive excavations, like those at Manching, have produced so little if this sort of equipment was in wide use. The similarity of the styluses and tablets to those found on Roman sites suggests the possibility that this material actually reflects the use of writing by Roman merchants operating in iron-age settlements.[30] Certainly neither the Gallo-Greek graffiti on potsherds nor the rare lapidary inscriptions could have been produced with equipment of this sort.[31]

Gallo-Greek texts are rarer in temperate Europe than in the south and appear much later.[32] Some fifty-odd examples are known, almost all of them short graffiti on potsherds and most of them from just a few sites in Burgundy: twenty-one were found on Mont Beuvray and fifteen from Alesia, both being sites extensively excavated in the nineteenth century. The remaining finds are from the same area of France. There are a few inscriptions on portable objects, including a sword labelled KORISIOS and a torque with the tribal name of the Nitiobroges. The few lapidary inscriptions also come from central and eastern France. Overall the French distribution suggests an extension of southern writing practices up the

[28] Jacobi (1974).

[29] Píč (1906) publishing material bought on the local antiquaries market, much of it modern forgery, but presumably based on categories of artefact actually found. Píč comments pp. 87–8, on the rarity of writing equipment among the finds.

[30] Jacobi (1974: 174) notes that he identified the styluses on the basis of their similarity to the Numantia example. Wells (1972: 40) cites the example from Bern as evidence for a Roman occupation of the hillfort. One possible context for their use would be a colony of merchants like the Julio-Claudian entrepôt on the Magdalensberg in Noricum (Egger 1961, Obermayer 1971) which has produced a large number of commercial graffiti. One final piece of writing equipment from an iron-age site in north-west Europe is an iron stylus among the material from Traprain Law (Burley 1955–6) but as with all the finds from this site, both the chronology and the precise provenance are very uncertain.

[31] Mooseleitner and Zellner (1982), in a preliminary report of excavations of a mid-La Tène site below the Dürrnberg bei Hallein near Salzburg, publish a sketch of what they describe as a clay writing-tablet, originally covered in a wax slip, but itself incised in a cursive script apparently bracketed by two crosses. Both the use and the proposed date of this artefact seem implausible as described, cf. Megaw (1985: 185), and it seems safest to reserve judgement pending final publication.

[32] The texts are collected in *RIG* I with the exception of the two examples from Manching published by Krämer (1982).

Rhône valley. Two graffiti have been recently found in the large-scale excavations at Manching in Bavaria, one bearing the ethnonym BOIOS and the other a fragment of an *abecedarium*, consisting of the Greek letters zeta, eta and theta in alphabetical order. The rarity and restricted distribution of the material can be compared to the record of the (later) pre-conquest graffiti from southern Britain, this time in Gallo-Latin. Although a number of tally marks and possible letters have been found, only 12 graffiti certainly come from pre-conquest levels, all from the site of Sheepen near Colchester.[33]

The chronology of Gallo-Greek epigraphy is difficult as few sherds have been recovered from stratigraphic excavations, and the possibility cannot be excluded that texts continued to be produced long after the Roman conquest. But some at least of the graffiti from Roanne come from a context that probably dates to the middle of the last century BC. That same context also marks the first appearance on the site of coins bearing Gallo-Greek legends. Indigenous legends, as opposed to the copying of legends from the classical originals on which the earliest Celtic coins were modelled,[34] appeared late in Gaul, associated with the settlement shift from open villages to hillforts that takes place in much of France probably in the second quarter of the last century BC.[35]

Coin legends make up the bulk of the surviving Gallo-Greek texts from temperate Europe, but consist only of the names of individuals. Some names are recognisable as those of chiefs mentioned in Caesar's *Commentaries* but most are unknown and conventionally, if speculatively, identified as moneyers or magistrates after the model of Roman coinage. Coin legends

---

[33] Hawkes and Hall (1947: 284–6) note that all the graffiti were on fragments of imported Arretine ware which 'suggests that the need for owners' marks was only felt in connection with this choice foreign fabric, and probably that the necessary literacy only existed within its circulation range, namely, no doubt, the wealthier classes and the trading community, whether native or foreign. The graffiti cannot indeed be proved to be the work of natives.' No other British graffiti are certainly pre-conquest, although scratchmarks are known from pottery from Bagendon (Clifford 1961: 249) and Skeleton Green (Partridge 1982: 104), similar to scratches on vessels from central Europe (Krämer 1982).

[34] Nash (1978a: 33, 38, 76) on these pseudo-epigraphic issues on which legends were eventually stylised and became part of the design.

[35] The absolute chronology of the late iron age is currently fiercely debated, cf. Duval et al. (1990). In the meantime, relative chronology using the small number of stratigraphically excavated sites is the safest strategy. Epigraphic coins do not appear in the levels known as Roanne 1, Aulnat, Basel Gasfabrik, Basel Munsterhügel 1 and 2, Feurs and Levroux les Arènes but do appear in Roanne 2 and 3, Villeneuve Ste Germain, Basel Munsterhügel 3 and Levroux Colline de Tours (data from Furger-Gunti 1979, Nash and Collis 1983, Gruel and Brunaux 1987, Vaginay and Guichard 1988). Epigraphic coins also appear unstratified on a number of sites including Mont Beuvray, Manching and Stradonice. Pending the publication of *RIG* IV which will be devoted to monetary epigraphy, the best guides are the series of papers by Colbert de Beaulieu in *Etudes Celtiques* 8 (1958) 141–53; 9 (1960) 106–38; 9 (1961) 478–500; 11 (1964/5) 46–69; and 11 (1966/7) 319–43.

do have the advantage, however, that they enable a much wider survey to be made of the scripts used by different groups in Europe. Mapping the location of the groups using particular scripts on coins assigned to them suggests that Gaul included anepigraphic areas, areas which used Iberian or north Italian scripts, areas that produced coins with Latin legends, and others that used Greek script, while some coinages appear in Greek and Latin variants or even use both scripts on the same issues, sometimes mixing scripts in the same words.[36] This pattern is a microcosm of the variations within temperate Europe as a whole. A number of areas continued to produce coins without legends, long after they were familiar with epigraphic coins produced elsewhere, like the coinage labelled KALATEDOU in either Greek or Latin script, which circulated throughout Europe.[37] Up to a point, it seems that numismatic epigraphy provides some sort of guide for the uses of writing in society as a whole. The correlation of coin scripts with those attested on graffiti in the same areas and at the same periods seems quite good. Gallo-Latin coin legends appear in pre-conquest Britain at much the same period as the Sheepen graffiti.[38] But on the basis of the evidence so far available it would be rash to assume a perfect fit between coins and other kinds of writing.

At least a generation before Caesar's invasion of Gaul, then, some groups were using scripts adapted from those used in Mediterranean France, by then a Roman province. The presence of Roman-style writing equipment suggests that even if these groups were not using writing tablets and styluses, they were probably familiar with their use by merchants of Mediterranean origin visiting or possibly even resident in a few of the larger settlements. Arguments *e silentio* have been shown to be risky on many occasions in the study of ancient writing, but it is striking that graffiti on sherds and coin legends both appear in the same restricted geographical and chronological bracket. It is possible that wooden tablets or other perishable materials were used earlier and elsewhere in late prehistoric Europe, but as yet there is no evidence beyond the Caesarian texts,[39] while the paucity of the texts and writing equipment recovered from huge excavations like Manching and Mont Beuvray suggests that the evidence may simply not be there to be found.

Of course, this minimal quantitative assessment need not imply that writing was of little significance in these societies. It has even been suggested that the very rarity of texts, combined with Caesar's comments

[36] Allen (1980: 108) but note Moberg's (1987) point that Allen's map, being based on areas of coin production rather than actual distributions, is potentially vulnerable to any misattributions of unprovenanced coins.   [37] Moberg (1987).

[38] Haselgrove (1987: 201–2).

[39] Wild's (1966) suggestion that impressions on some coins indicate the existence of papyrus in pre-conquest Britain is now challenged by Van Arsdell (1986).

on the Druids, suggests restricted, palatial literacy used as a means of social control, while the appearance of lapidary epigraphy might reflect the replacement of this regime by political forms similar to those of archaic Greece or Rome.[40] The picture is more plausible than the notion of Celtic bureaucracy, based largely on the Helvetian tablets.[41] But these snippets of classical testimony are capable of multiple interpretations. More fundamentally, numerous studies have challenged the equation of either bureaucracy or writing with statehood: classical Greek states had no recognisable bureaucracy and the New World empires of Teotihuacan and the Inca were notoriously illiterate.[42] It is quite conceivable that late prehistoric states may have existed in Europe without using writing either as a means of organising resources or as technology of symbolic production. In fact, on quite different evidence, it is my impression that states did not exist in the region before the Roman conquest.[43]

If literacy and power are not connected in the development of writing to build and govern states in late prehistoric Gaul, what of the proposition that the spread of writing is a cultural consequence of the growth of the Mediterranean economy? The presence of Mediterranean merchants in these communities is well attested, as is the existence of exchange networks linking iron-age Europe with the Mediterranean,[44] but the same might be said for southern France three hundred years before. Arguably the picture suggested by the diversity of scripts used on late Celtic coinage, by the persistence of anepigraphic coinage in some regions and by the highly local distribution of Gallo-Greek epigraphy, is very similar to the picture built up of writing in southern France, and the relation between political power and writing seems no different in temperate Europe in the last century BC from what it had been earlier in the south. The increased scope of Mediterranean commerce had probably spread the knowledge of writing more widely, but as long as social power remained fragmented and locally based, the acquisition of writing remained just one option, one taken or rejected in accordance with essentially local needs and values.

Barbarian writing under Roman rule

The most dramatic discontinuity in the uses of writing in Gaul occurred after the Roman conquest, not before it. Roman rule replaced a mosaic of local societies and autonomous groups with a new configuration of power,

---

[40] Goudineau (1989).

[41] Champion (1985: 10), although it is true that lists are among the earliest uses of writing attested by Goody (1986).

[42] Thomas (this volume) on Greece. Larsen (1988) surveys the issue.

[43] Cf. n. 23 above.   [44] Fitzpatrick (1989), Woolf (forthcoming a).

within which cultural differences were not obliterated, but rather were co-ordinated into a new imperial geography of culture. Local writings became barbarian, as a new imperial set of values was asserted against which local choices and preferences might be definitively measured. Writing itself, according to this ideology, was neither civilised nor barbarian, but it did matter what language was used, whether in texts or in speeches.

The most striking feature of these changes is the sudden and complete disappearance of both the Iberian and the Gallo-Greek scripts throughout Gaul. The change is difficult to date precisely, but it is reasonably clear that from the middle of the first century AD the only non-classical texts produced in Gaul were Gallo-Latin texts that used Roman script to write a Celtic language or languages. None of these texts has been found in Mediterranean France and the total number known is tiny compared with that of Latin inscriptions in France. The extant Latin epigraphy of the Gallic provinces is meagre compared with that of Rome's Mediterranean or Danubian provinces;[45] yet, even so, surviving Latin inscriptions are numbered in tens of thousands rather than in hundreds. More than twenty Gallo-Roman sites have produced over 100 inscriptions, more than forty have produced 50 or more, and almost a hundred sites have produced 20 inscriptions or more.[46] Only sixty-eight Gallo-Greek lapidary inscriptions are known, of which all but three are from the south. Only fourteen Gallo-Latin lapidary texts are recorded, all from non-Mediterranean Gaul.[47] It is against this background of Latin epigraphy that the significance of Gallo-Latin texts must be assessed.

Gallo-Latin texts are very varied in nature and seem to have been produced over a very long period. The graffiti are said to be three to four times as numerous as those in Gallo-Greek in the Three Gauls, which would suggest a total of between 150 and 200 examples. Like both Gallo-Greek and Latin graffiti, most are simply names, but a small number of longer texts exist. A lead curse tablet from the late first century has been found at Larzac[48] and another lead tablet, probably including magic spells, was found in a watery deposit at Chamalières. That tablet included the names of several Claudii, suggesting a late first-century AD date.[49] Most famous are the bronze calendars from Anse and Coligny. The latter is now

---

[45] Harris (1989: 266–8) gives the following figures for inscriptions per 1,000 km²: Belgica and Germany 18.3, Aquitania 11.2, Lugdunensis 10.3 compared with Africa Proconsularis 127.3, and Campania 410.9. Only inland Spain, Britain, Raetia and Mauretania Tingitana (3.3) rank lower than the Gauls.

[46] Figures from *CIL* XII and XIII with supplements but without subsequent publications, whether in *AE* or in collections such as *ILTG* or *ILN*.

[47] *RIG* I for Gallo-Greek inscriptions, *RIG* II 1 for lapidary texts in Gallo-Latin. The Gallo-Latin calendars are published in *RIG* III, but for a full corpus of non-lapidary Gallo-Latin we await the publication of *RIG* II 2.

[48] Lejeune (1985).   [49] Lejeune and Marichal (1976–7).

dated to the early third century AD.[50] The lapidary inscriptions include grave stelai, and in one case, at Genouilly in the Berry, two Gallo-Latin stelai are associated with one Gallo-Greek one, just as Gallo-Latin and Gallo-Greek legends occasionally appear on the same coins.

Gallo-Latin texts exhibit a complex relationship with the Latin epigraphy of Gaul. The common use of Roman script suggests a familiarity with Latin texts, and the genres of texts are clearly related: graffiti, funeral stelai, religious calendars and curse tablets are all well known in Latin versions. While scratched owners' marks are also characteristic of pre-conquest texts, the more elaborate documents derive from deliberate imitation of Roman models. The calendars must have been produced by individuals who could not only read Latin, but were also familiar enough with Roman religious ideas about time to produce a non-Roman version of them.[51] The epigraphic medium is itself thoroughly Roman, and if we are to believe Caesar, the very idea of writing down religious lore is fundamentally un-Druidic. The appearance of the names of Roman citizens in the Chamalières tablet, at a time when there were few Roman citizens in Gaul, also suggests that these texts were produced by Gauls who knew Roman culture well. The chronology of the phenomenon is more puzzling: the earliest examples overlap with Gallo-Greek texts, but if the calendars are correctly dated, Gallo-Latin continued in use into the third century. Until the graffiti are better understood, it is impossible to be certain whether we are dealing with two distinct groups of texts of Gallo-Latin – a first-century AD group closely linked with Gallo-Greek and the appearance of lapidary Latin, followed by a second batch in the third century connected to new attitudes to Roman culture – or whether writing in Celtic followed the familiar rhythm of the epigraphic habit.[52] Equally, the publication of the graffiti may indicate whether or not it is significant that the few surviving examples of Gallo-Latin lapidary epigraphy are from areas where Latin epigraphy is scarce: the Massif Central, the Berry and western France. Gallo-Latin graffiti are certainly present at Alesia in Burgundy, so further work may strengthen the impression of a close relationship between Gallo-Latin and Latin writing in Gaul.

Despite these uncertainties it is possible to reject some current interpretations of Gallo-Latin epigraphy. Gallo-Latin was not a transitional

---

[50] *RIG* III (dated on epigraphic grounds).

[51] For more recent examples of new writing systems being created by appropriation and adaptation of a script used by invaders, Harbsmeier (1988).

[52] At least some of the texts are late enough to be considered in relation to MacMullen's (1965) ideas of a 'Celtic Renaissance', or to the alleged revival of local cultures and languages more generally in the later empire, cf. MacMullen (1966), Millar (1968). Alternatively, artefacts like the Coligny calendar may reflect the continued extension of Roman culture in the third and fourth centuries. The issue requires a proper study.

stage between Gallo-Greek and Latin writing, but appeared about the same time as Latin epigraphy and flourished in parallel to it. Nor was Gallo-Latin a popular pidgeon, a mixture of Latin and Gallic, used by the semi-Romanised commons.[53] Some such texts may exist. The corpus of firing records and tally marks from the pottery production site at La Graufesenque consists largely of Latin notes, recording the contents of firing-batches in large kilns, but Celtic words sometimes slipped in and a few texts seem more Celtic than Latin.[54] But most Gallo-Latin texts imply a much closer familiarity with Roman writing and are more likely to have been produced by or for Gallic élites, like the Claudii of Chamalières, than by the culturally disenfranchised. The safest course might be to regard Celtic written in Latin script as a mixed bag, including poor imitations and deliberate substitutions. What Gallo-Latin was definitely not, was the written language of groups socially, culturally or politically half way between Gauls and Romans.[55] Rather these texts were produced by those who were in some senses both Roman and Gallic.

Gallo-Latin texts cannot be understood without reference to Latin epigraphy. That fact distinguishes this barbarian writing from all earlier non-classical literacies in Gaul. Gallo-Latin writing was non-classical and barbarian in a new sense because it was produced in relationship to classical writing, whether in imitation, in rejection, or both. What altered was the context within which decisions and choices about writing were made, and in particular the way in which power shifted in Gaul following its incorporation into the Roman empire. The mosaic of local literacies was replaced by an imperially constituted system of differences within which cultural choices were still possible, but were made in the knowledge that they would be assessed in relation to an externally imposed regime of values.

Power and the spread of writing

The spread of writing in the West has a complex history. Two quite different processes contributed. The first comprised a piecemeal series of adoptions, adaptions and rejections at a local scale in the context of a world where social, political and economic power was very fragmented. The second process was a consequence of rapid imperial expansion accompanied by widespread cultural change which destroyed writing practices and changed their meaning as well as spreading new ones. The spread of writing

---

[53] Meid (1983).   [54] Marichal (1988).
[55] The relationship between epigraphy and spoken language, like that between epigraphy and literacy levels, is clearly a complex one and it may well be impossible to infer anything certain about the spread of spoken Latin in Gaul or the survival of spoken Celtic from these inscriptions. On those issues cf. the papers collected in Neumann and Untermann (1980) and in *ANRW* II 29.2 (1983).

cannot be seen as one component of the spread of classical civilisation. Ancients would not have been surprised, as they did not see literacy, civilisation, political maturity and progress as connected in the same way that Europeans tend to see them.

Power and literacy are connected, in this instance, less by the instrumental advantages of the technology for early commerce, states and empires than by the importance of power relations as a context shaping the way that writing was adopted, adapted, used and rejected. The punctuation of the history of the spread of writing resulted from shifts in power, while the spread of writing does not seem to have greatly affected Roman expansion or the resistance to it. In this respect, then, writing seems no different from other aspects of culture, for example the potter's wheel, viticulture or stone architecture. If writing was more important as a symbolic medium than as a bureaucratic technology, perhaps this is unsurprising. But our ignorance of all but the general lines of the uses and meaning of barbarian writing makes argument along those lines difficult.

Nevertheless, writing did (and has) spread in a manner that seems cumulatively irreversible. However slowly and discontinuously, writing was being adopted by more and more groups across Europe when the process was interrupted and diverted by Roman conquest, and the collapse of the empire did not result in permanent setbacks. Similar sequences elsewhere in the world confirm the suspicion that the cultural relativism, that has now widely replaced earlier over-generalisations about the implications of literacy, leaves some important questions unanswered, questions arguably more the responsibility of historians than of anthropologists. Not the irradiation of barbarian Europe by classical civilisation, not Roman imperialism, then, but not a random and unpatterned series of cultural choices either. Writing retains at least the power to puzzle.

7 Texts, scribes and power in Roman Judaea

M. D. Goodman

No ancient society was more blatantly dominated by a written text than that of Jews in the Roman period. The most influential text was of course the Hebrew bible, of which many thousands of copies must have existed by the first century AD, scattered throughout the Jewish world. Since such great authority was attributed by Jews to the bible, it is a reasonable hypothesis that the ability to read, write and interpret biblical texts will have brought prestige to those who possessed it within Jewish society.

The survival from antiquity of much evidence about Jews in this period through the continuous Jewish and Christian religious traditions down to modern times, and the discovery of archaeological finds in the Judaean Desert over the last half century, make it possible to test this hypothesis. My suggestion at the end of this essay will be that among Jews reading did not in itself bring power, but that writing – or at least writing of a particular kind – probably did.

The date of the canonisation of the Hebrew bible and its Greek translation, the Septuagint, is much debated, but disagreement revolves primarily around the questions of what books were contained within the canon at which period and what precisely a canon of the bible should be understood to be.[1] No one doubts that, by late Hellenistic times in Judaea, a select core of texts, more or less corresponding to those eventually enshrined within the bible, was recognised by all Jews as the main foundation of their theology and the source of authority for almost all their civil, criminal and religious laws and customs.

These texts were taken so seriously by Jews that everything written in them was assumed to be valid and important in contemporary life. Apparent discrepancies within the texts were regularly explained away by ingenious interpretation. New laws and customs were either generated or justified by subtle exegesis of biblical passages.[2] According to the rabbis, an ability to read scripture was thus a prime aim of education (cf. *Mishnah*

[1] Contrast Beckwith (1985) to Barr (1983) and Barton (1986).
[2] Vermes (1970, 1973).

Abot 5.21). But writing was less common,[3] not because it was thought unimportant but, on the contrary, because the production of religious texts was a specialised task.

When Josephus claimed in the first century AD (*C. Ap*. 1.37–41) that Jews venerated their religious texts with a zeal which far surpassed the nonchalant attitude to their own traditions of other peoples in the ancient world, he may have had partly in mind the serious attention paid by Jews to the contents of these texts: regular reading by Jews of the laws ensured, so he claimed, both accuracy and unanimity in their interpretation (*C. Ap*. 2.175–81). But Josephus' boast at *C. Ap*. 1. 37–41 may also have reflected a different and even more striking peculiarity of Jewish culture, a peculiarity about which he wrote in the immediately following passage in *Contra Apionem*. This was the belief that religious power was enshrined within the physical object on which the divine teachings were inscribed.

Josephus wrote that Jews were prepared to risk their lives to preserve the scrolls of the Law (*C. Ap*. 1.42–4). When a Roman soldier destroyed a text, the result was a riot (*B.J*. 2.229–31; *A.J*. 20.115). Josephus claimed with pride that he had used his privileged position to rescue books from destruction in Jerusalem in AD 70 (*Vita* 418). A scroll of the Law could be a rallying sign for the seditious (*Vita* 134) or, in the eyes of the victorious Romans, a symbol of the defeated nation, paraded at the culmination of the triumphal procession of Titus and Vespasian in Rome (*B.J*. 7.150).

The sacred text *par excellence* was the Pentateuch, properly inscribed in the stipulated Hebrew lettering in ink on parchment, but other books from what was later described as the canon of scripture could, if correctly written, also share in the numinous quality obscurely defined by the rabbis as the ability to 'defile the hands'.[4] The religious power of such written objects may have been only loosely connected to the meaning of the words they contained, since few of the works now included within the corpus of the prophets and (in particular) the writings were ever subjected in antiquity to the intense study and interpretation accorded to the Pentateuch. The symbolic significance of the texts used as *tefillin* (phylacteries) was particularly blatant, since they were encased in leather in such a way that they usually could not be read at all.[5]

The origins of this reverence for physical texts can perhaps be traced back to biblical times. The two tablets of stone brought down from Mt Sinai by Moses had enshrined a powerful religious charge; carried in the specially devised ark (Exodus 25.10–22), they had formed the focus of Jewish veneration, and those who lacked sufficient respect for them were liable to divine punishment, like Uzzah who unwisely touched the ark in its

[3] Schürer (1973–87: II 420).   [4] Goodman (1990).
[5] See Benoit, Milik and De Vaux (1960–1: 80–5).

journey from Gibeah to Jerusalem (II Samuel 6.7). In one symbolic passage in the book of Ezekiel (3.1–3), prophetic utterance was said to have been achieved by swallowing a written text on parchment (cf. also Jeremiah 15.16).[6]

According to the later rabbinic view of such attitudes, one of the reasons was simple. At least by the fifth century AD, if not earlier, the Hebrew alphabet was reckoned by Jews to be sacred in itself: the tabernacle had been created out of the letters (*Babylonian Talmud Berachot* 55a), each letter had a symbolic meaning (*Babylonian Talmud Shabbat* 104a), every stroke made by a scribe in the creation of a text had its significance (*Pirkei de R. Eliezer* 21). Such numinous qualities seem to have adhered only to sacred texts in Hebrew. Despite the widely attested belief that the Septuagint translation of the bible into Greek had been divinely inspired (cf. Philo, *Vit. Mos.* 2.41–2), there is no evidence that Greek biblical scrolls were ever afforded the same reverence.

However, in the early Roman period it is wrong to suppose that Hebrew functioned *only* as a sacred language. On the contrary, texts found in the Judaean Desert reveal Hebrew in secular use, at least among *some* Jews, well into the second century AD.[7] The sound of spoken Hebrew became in itself sacred, and therefore worrying (and indeed dangerous), only when the Divine Name was pronounced. The author of *Targum Jonathan* to Deuteronomy 32.3 neatly linked the taboo against uttering the Name to that encapsulated in the notion of sacred texts, by asserting that Moses, who did utter the Holy Name, only dared to do so after he had dedicated his mouth with eighty-five letters (which was the minimum quota of letters from a sacred text which had to be inscribed for the parchment on which it was written to defile the hands, cf. *Mishnah Yadaim* 3.5). It is possible that this reverence for the Name was also sometimes one of the causes of Jews' respect for their written texts, since, as the documents preserved in the Cairo Genizah in the early Middle Ages amply illustrate, any writing which contained the name of God was treated as too precious for deliberate destruction when no longer needed.[8] But the inclusion of the Divine Name cannot have been the only reason for treating some texts as holy, for the texts which defiled the hands could acquire this power by containing any eighty-six consecutive letters from the appropriate book. In the case of the book of Esther, notoriously, the Divine Name did not occur at all.

It is worth asking whether this high valuation ascribed to religious texts as objects had any effect on Jews' use of secular written documents, but the

[6] Davis (1989).

[7] On languages used in Roman Palestine, see, e.g., Schürer (1973–87: II 20–8).

[8] On the Cairo Genizah in general, see Reif (1988). On the writing of the Divine Name in Hebrew manuscripts, see Sanders (1965: 7); on the Name in Greek manuscripts, see *P. Oxy.* 3522; Tov (1990: 12).

answer is mostly negative.[9] The private documents, recording loans, marriage contracts and so on, which have been found in the Judaean Desert, seem to have served the same function as documents in contemporary Greek and Roman society – essentially, to act as a record of agreements between individuals.[10] This was, for instance, the purpose of the *ketubah* (meaning, literally, 'written object'), which recorded the stipulation made by a husband to his wife as to the recompense she could expect upon divorce or widowhood; the use of writing to confirm that stipulation seems to have been a practice borrowed by the Jews from Greek customs.[11] The archive of the unfortunate and litigious woman Babatha, who left her private documents wrapped up in a sack in a Judaean Desert cave in the last days of the Bar Kokhba war,[12] reveals even a remarkable lack of concern about the language to be used in such documents. She preserved legal agreements in Greek and Aramaic as well as in Nabataean. The language used may have depended sometimes on the preferences of the parties involved, but it may also simply have reflected the expertise of the scribe.

The exceptions which prove the rule are the secular documents to which power was accorded when this notion was inherited from biblical law, as in the use of a *get* (divorce document) to effect a valid break between a married couple (cf. Deuteronomy 24.1–4), or the document dissolved in water and given to a *sotah* (suspected adulteress) to drink (cf. Numbers 5.11–31). In both these latter cases, precise formulation and production of the documents was reckoned crucial to their validity.[13]

The need for precision would seem necessarily to give a role to experts, as in any legal system, but in the second half of this paper, I shall argue specifically that the special Jewish attitude towards religious texts may have given peculiar prominence and power to the scribes who produced them.

Even the secondary role of scribes in recording oral transactions could of course be highly important in societies which attributed strong evidential value to written documents, as was evidently the case among Jews in the Roman period. Babatha presumably believed that her scrolls of papyrus and skin could ensure her status and her property rights. It was assumed in rabbinic texts that scribes (*soferim*) could be found in village markets with blank forms to record loans and sales.[14] Such services could be essential for normal life: a vow taken not to benefit in any way by a named individual

[9] Schams (1992).
[10] Documents in Benoit, Milik and De Vaux (1960–1); Yadin (1989).
[11] Archer (1990) 171–3.
[12] Yadin (1971). For the Greek documents, see Yadin (1989). The semitic documents are so far unpublished.   [13] See discussions in the *Mishnah*, tractates *Gittin* and *Sotah*.
[14] Cf. Goodman (1983: 57–9).

could, according to one rabbinic opinion, be cancelled if he turned out to be a scribe (*Mishnah Nedarim* 9.2). But, important though this function was, there is no evidence that it was more vital in Jewish society than in other contemporary societies. It is thus plausible to seek a religious explanation of some kind for the common modern assumption that scribes had a central role in Jewish life in first-century Judaea.

This view that the authority of scribes was paramount in almost all areas of Jewish behaviour[15] derives primarily from the New Testament. In the gospels, the term *grammateis* ('scribes') was used frequently in references to the opponents of Jesus. In twenty-two places, Jews depicted as acting as the authorities were described as 'high priests and scribes'. Eighteen times they were named as 'scribes and Pharisees'. The authors of the synoptic gospels seem clearly to have thought of scribes as a separate class within the Judaean religious establishment.

But when attention is turned to the precise religious role of Jewish scribes as pictured in the New Testament, oddities emerge. Most strikingly, scribes are never depicted as writing anything. In so far as they are said to undertake any specific religious activity, it is teaching (Mark 1.22; Matthew 7.29, 17.10). Thus the standard histories of Judaean society before the destruction of the Temple in AD 70 explain the prominence of scribes by equating them with Pharisees.[16] As the argument was formulated by Jeremias, scribes won influence as expert interpreters of the Mosaic Law, which they exegeted in the light of Pharisaic traditions which were specifically preserved in oral form.[17]

This standard view is odd in a number of different ways. First, the correct Greek for an interpreter of texts, rather than a writer of them, should have been *grammatikos*, not *grammateus*. Secondly, the notion that scribes had authority specifically because of what neither they nor anyone else wrote down seems rather bizarre.[18] It is true that some later rabbinic texts (e.g. *Babylonian Talmud Temurah* 14b) emphasised the importance of preserving traditions by word of mouth, master to pupil, rather than in written form.[19] But in practice, and regardless of later rabbinic beliefs about the oral publication and transmission of their most influential document, the Mishnah,[20] at least some of the smaller, less popular rabbinic compositions must have been written down, as were those writings of the sectarians at Qumran which have been discovered in the Dead Sea caves.

Thirdly, it is by no means clear that scribes should be equated with

[15] See, for example, Saldarini (1989: 241–76).
[16] See, for example, Jeremias (1969: 243–5, 379–80).   [17] Jeremias (1964).
[18] See Bickerman (1988: 161–76, esp. 163).   [19] Strack and Stemberger (1991: 35–49).
[20] For arguments in favour of accepting such beliefs, see Lieberman (1962: 83–99), but the issue is still debated.

Pharisees, not least because that would render otiose the collocation 'scribes and Pharisees' found in the gospels.[21] Fourthly, it is uncertain that Pharisees in the first century subscribed to a concept of an oral Torah alongside the written Torah. Explicit formulation of this notion is found only in rabbinic texts of the third century AD.[22] Fifthly, neither Josephus nor Philo suggests that a class of scribes had religious authority in Judaean society. According to Josephus, there was no need for lay scribes as legal experts because the main teachers and interpreters of scripture were priests (cf. *C. Ap.* 2.165, 184–7; *Vita* 196–8; *B.J.* 3.252). As E. P. Sanders has trenchantly remarked, most of the persons described as 'scribes' in modern scholarly works were not so designated in any ancient text.[23]

The standard view of the role of scribes in first-century Judaea is thus rather dubious. But the prominence of scribes can hardly be dismissed altogether. The New Testament picture of Jewish scribes must have come from observation of some facet of Jewish life. It can hardly have been an anachronism under the influence of the organisation of Christian communities, for within those communities scribes are not attested as a defined group. Nor can it have derived from the pagan Greek environment within which much of the New Testament was composed: in civic Greek society, a *grammateus* could be an important administrator, like the town clerk in Ephesus described in Acts of the Apostles 19.35, but no class of scribes (in the plural) existed. What in the Jewish background could have come through to the early Church to encourage them to depict Jewish scribes as they did?

References to scribes in surviving Jewish texts from antiquity are rather sparse, in marked contrast to their ubiquity in the synoptic gospels. In few cases is an interpretation of their role as that of a legal expert totally precluded, but in most cases it is by no means obvious. Thus some scribes (*soferim*) in the Hebrew bible could be government officials rather than legal experts (e.g. II Kings 22.3–13). Ezra may have won his reputation for deep understanding of the law not by virtue of his role as scribe but because he was a priest (Nehemiah 12.12–13); in any case his designation as scribe may have been an official Persian title as well as a description of his role within Jewish society.[24] In the royal charter for Jerusalem issued by the Seleucids at the beginning of the second century BC, the 'scribes of the sanctuary' were, according to Josephus (*A.J.* 12.142), granted privileges as officials of the Temple, but, like the scribes described in II Chronicles 34.13 as a class of Levite, these individuals seem to have been on a fairly low

---

[21] This is not to say that scribes could not be confused with Pharisees in different versions of the same story in different gospels. Cf. Cook (1978: 88–95).
[22] Sanders (1990: 97–130).   [23] Sanders (1992: 174–81).   [24] Cf. Schraeder (1930).

social level and in my view are more likely to have been bureaucrats than religious leaders or *iuris periti*.[25]

It seems hard to imagine that the polemic in the New Testament can have been aimed simply at such people. Thus nothing much is gained by asserting that the scribes of the gospels and the Acts of the Apostles should be identified as Levites.[26] Even if the suggestion is correct, it leaves open the question why the particular functions of these Levites laid them open to such antagonism. Only occasionally does the role of scribes as interpreters rather than simply writers of religious texts emerge as clearly from Jewish texts as from the Christian gospels. The rabbis, in texts compiled in the late second century AD and later, ascribed some specific religious teachings to the *soferim* of a distant, but evidently post-biblical, past (e.g. *Mishnah Tohorot* 4.7; *Abot* 6.9), even though in the same texts the term *sofer*, when it was applied to their own day, was reserved for descriptions of technicians or schoolteachers.

But the best example of a scribe's profession being described as that of a religious teacher may be found in the extended praise of the scribe's life to be found in the treatise of Ben Sira (38.24–39.11), composed in the early second century BC. The passage is worth quoting at length (Anchor Bible translation):

> The scribe's profession increases wisdom;
>   whoever is free from toil can become wise.
> How can one become wise who guides the plough,
>   who thrills in wielding the goad like a lance...?
> So with every engraver and designer
>   who, labouring night and day,
> Fashions carved seals...
> So with the smith sitting by the anvil,
>   intent on the iron he forges...
> So with the potter sitting at his work...
> All these are skilled with their hands,
>   each one an expert in his own work;
> Without them no city could be lived in,
>   and wherever they stay, they do not hunger.
> But they are not sought out for the council of the people,
>   nor are they prominent in the assembly.
> They do not sit on the judge's bench,
>   nor can they understand law and justice.
> They cannot expound the instruction of wisdom,
>   nor are they found among the rulers.
> Yet they are expert in the works of this world,
>   and their concern is for the exercise of their skill.
> How different the person who devotes himself to the fear of God

[25] *Contra* Bickerman (1988: 162–3).   [26] Schwartz (1985).

and to the study of the Law of the Most High!
He studies the wisdom of all the ancients
　　and occupies himself with the prophecies;
He treasures the discourses of the famous,
　　and goes to the heart of involved sayings;
He studies the hidden meaning of proverbs,
　　and is busied with the enigmas found in parables.
He is in attendance on the great,
　　and has entrance to the ruler.
He travels among the peoples of foreign lands
　　to test what is good and evil among people.
His care is to rise early
　　to seek the Lord, his Maker,
　　to petition the Most High,
To open his lips in prayer,
　　to ask pardon for his sins.
Then, if it pleases the Lord Almighty,
　　he will be filled with the spirit of understanding;
He will pour forth his words of wisdom
　　and in prayer give praise to the Lord.
He will direct his counsel and knowledge aright,
　　as he meditates upon God's mysteries.
He will show the wisdom of what he has learned
　　and glory in the Law of the Lord's covenant.
Many will praise his understanding;
　　his fame can never be effaced;
Unfading will be his memory,
　　through all generations his name will live.
The congregation will speak of his wisdom,
　　and the assembly will declare his praises.
While he lives he is one out of a thousand,
　　and when he dies he leaves a good name.

The term used for 'scribe' at the beginning of this panegyric (38.24) is, in the Greek, *grammateus*. Such a man, according to Ben Sira, is devoted to study and wisdom (38.34–39.3).

It is true that much of Ben Sira's treatise was compiled from highly traditional clichés culled from the wisdom literature of the Near East, and it is quite possible, as E. P. Sanders has recently stressed,[27] that Ben Sira's own authority derived in part from the fact (if it was a fact) that he was a priest. It is worth noting that the praises accorded by Ben Sira to the life of the scribe are closely paralleled in other wisdom texts, most strikingly in an Egyptian text, *The Instruction of Khety, Son of Duauf*.[28] But it seems inescapable that Ben Sira meant his praises to apply at least in part to his own society. If so he must have thought that the role of scribes was (or

[27] Sanders (1992: 181).　　[28] Skehan and Di Lella (1987: 449–50).

should be?) to dispense wisdom at leisure, not just to be engaged in the copying of sacred texts.

It is likely enough, then, that some individuals in Jewish society called scribes had prestige in that society because of their legal expertise. But in the rest of this paper I shall explore the possibility that they may also have gained prestige by virtue of the main function suggested by their name, that is, writing.

I discussed in the first part of this paper the numinous qualities attributed by all Jews to the parchments on which biblical and some other texts were inscribed. Large numbers of such texts must have been produced, since all sources agree that all, or at any rate all adult male, Jews had regular access to at least a Pentateuch scroll, since they could expect to hear it read aloud in synagogues at least once a week, on the Sabbath.[29] The onus of producing a valid text, and therefore a sacred object, presumably lay entirely with the scribes.

There is no evidence that any system existed for checking texts once complete. In any case this would be an exceptionally laborious task for texts as long as the Pentateuch. It is quite possible that archetypes of some (all?) biblical books were kept in the Temple (cf. *Mishnah Kelim* 15.6).[30] But there is no reason to suppose that all copies in use were made by consultation with these archetypes: the gospel references to scribes presuppose their wide dispersion around the country. In practice, numerous variants in biblical texts were preserved at Qumran, probably by a single group of Jews, if the Dead Sea sectarians were responsible at least for the preservation, if not necessarily the production, of all the scrolls found in the nearby caves.[31] So far as is known, no-one fixed any seal on finished texts to certify their accuracy. This is not because all copies were *assumed* accurate, for the rabbis had traditions about the activity of *soferim* (scribes) in correcting texts into which errors had crept, in a fashion similar to Hellenistic scholarship on the text of Homer.[32] It is worth remarking that such scribal activity seems to have been accepted by the rabbis without complaint. What made a parchment scroll holy was therefore presumably the authority of the scribe who *said* that he had copied a sacred text correctly onto it.

It requires little imagination to suggest the prestige which might accrue to a scribe who can produce a holy object, for which Jews might be prepared to die, simply on his own authority by the marks made on

---

[29] Schürer (1973–87: II 447–54).   [30] See Leiman (1976).
[31] On biblical texts from Qumran, see Vermes (1977: 198–225); for current uncertainty about the origins of the scrolls, see (most radically) Golb (1989).
[32] Lieberman (1962: 20–37).

parchment. For 'people of a book', the writer's function was bound to seem admirable. On over twenty of the inscriptions set up by Jews in the city of Rome, the title (or description?) *grammateus* was displayed.[33] When the *targumim* referred to Moses as the scribe (*safra*) *par excellence*,[34] they thought of him perhaps not only as interpreter of the Divine Law but, more prosaically, as the man who wrote down the words of God (Exodus 34.27).

Perhaps the two roles of scribes, as writers and interpreters, were mutually reinforcing. An expert *sofer* who was trusted to produce valid manuscripts for worship might well also be a learned exegete of the biblical texts he assiduously copied. Such learning must have been presupposed by the author of the post-talmudic tractate *Soferim*, whose detailed regulations for the production of texts belong in their present form to the early mediaeval period, if he really expected the rules which he laid down to be scrupulously followed.[35]

It might be precisely for such learning that a scribe was trusted as a scribe. In that case, perhaps there never existed a *class* of scribes whose main function was to teach the Law, as the scholarly consensus has it. Hence the silence of Philo and Josephus about such a class. But those pious scholars whose expertise in producing holy copies of the sacred texts was renowned may also by definition have been treated as authorities in other aspects of religious life. Hence, when scribes laid down their teachings, their words had power.

[33] Leon (1960: 183–6, 265–331).   [34] Vermes (1973: 52).   [35] Higger (1937).

8 The Roman imperial army: letters and literacy on the northern frontier

Alan K. Bowman

The context

The wooden writing-tablets with ink texts which were discovered at Vindolanda, a fort near Hadrian's Wall, in the excavations of the 1970s and 1980s constitute a unique body of documentation, quite obviously so for the north-western Roman empire for we have had no collection of Latin cursive texts remotely comparable in quantity from this area and this period. It is thus by far the most important and coherent body of material for the study of literacy in the western part of the early Roman empire.[1] It must be emphasised that these tablets can be dated archaeologically to a relatively coherent period (*c.* AD 90–120) during which the character of the northern frontier zone in Britain was being forged, just before the building of Hadrian's Wall.[2] What we have is a succession of deposits of discarded letters and documents in an area which was occupied, during the first two periods of occupation (*c.* AD 92–102/3), by the residence (*praetorium*) of the commanding officer of the unit or one of the units stationed at Vindolanda. There are groups of letters associated with particular

---

[1] For some preliminary remarks on the value of these texts for the study of literacy see Bowman (1991). I am grateful to Dr J. D. Thomas for his comments on a draft of this chapter. The ink texts are published in Bowman and Thomas (1983) and (1994), where bibliographical references to preliminary publications and discussions may be found. Hereafter the texts are referred to by their publication numbers in Bowman and Thomas (1994). Comparable material is cited by Bischoff (1990: 13–15) and Cugusi (1983: 271–84), cf. Cugusi (1992). Abbreviations for editions of papyri may be found in J. F. Oates, R. S. Bagnall, W. H. Willis and K. A. Worp, *Checklist of Editions of Greek Papyri and Ostraka* (4th edn, Atlanta, 1992) and E. G. Turner, *Greek Papyri: An Introduction* (2nd edn, Oxford, 1980). Note also: *O. Claud.* = J. Bingen et al., *Mons Claudianus, ostraka graeca et latina* I (IFAO, Documents de fouilles XXIX, Cairo, 1992); *BASP* = *Bulletin of the American Society of Papyrologists*; *ChLA* = *Chartae Latinae Antiquiores* (eds. A. Bruckner, R. Marichal, Olten–Lausanne, 1954–); *O. Bu Njem* = R. Marichal, *Les Ostraca de Bu Njem* (Tripoli, 1992); *P. Qasr Ibrîm* = M. E. Weinstein, E. G. Turner, 'Greek and Latin papyri from Qasr Ibrîm', *JEA* 62 (1976) 115–30; *Tab. Vindol.* I = A. K. Bowman and J. D. Thomas, *Vindolanda. The Latin Writing-tablets* (Britannia Monograph 4, 1983); *Tab. Vindol.* II = A. K. Bowman and J. D. Thomas, *The Vindolanda Writing-tablets (Tabulae Vindolandenses II)* (London, 1994); *VRR* I = *Vindolanda, Research Reports, New Series*, vol. I: *Introduction and Analysis of the Structures*, by R. E. Birley et al. (Hexham, 1994).

[2] *VRR* I, Jones (1990).

individuals as well as groups of texts connected by type or subject-matter, offering an album of snapshots over two decades or more which reveal Vindolanda and its occupants mainly through the documents and letters generated or retained in the commander's house, a very different matter from the official archives of the military unit. In the subsequent periods the area seems to have been occupied by a barrack-block and a workshop and the tablets associated with these structures must, at least in part, reflect a different section of the community at Vindolanda.[3]

The range and diversity of the subject-matter of the texts is very important. There are military documents and reports, accounts of cash and commodities relating both to the military unit and to the domestic organisation in the *praetorium*, large numbers of personal letters, the occasional literary text and the earliest known examples of Latin shorthand. Diversity of provenance is also relevant, although in most cases we cannot be very specific. The documents, reports and accounts we may take to have originated at Vindolanda or possibly in outposts in its penumbra. As regards the correspondence, the situation is more complicated. Clearly we have some drafts or file copies of letters written by people resident in the *praetorium*. We also have, naturally, a large number of letters sent to people at Vindolanda by correspondents living elsewhere: that might presumably be anywhere within the occupied area of Britain – Corbridge (Coria), Carlisle (Luguvalium), Ribchester (Bremetennacum), Catterick (Cataractonium), Binchester (Vinovia), Aldborough (Isurium) and London (Londinium) are all mentioned in the tablets. The range of communication surely also embraces north-western Gaul at least and probably extends to Rome itself. There is at least one letter which was probably sent by someone at Vindolanda to a recipient in London who then brought it back to Vindolanda where it was eventually discarded.[4] Finally, the palaeographical range is of the utmost importance. There are several hundred individual cursive hands, not to mention different types of writing (capital, cursive and shorthand) – a phenomenon quite unparalleled in our Latin evidence, especially at this early period.

The value of this material may be further emphasised by two other

---

[3] For the dating of the periods of occupation and the identity of the buildings see *VRR* I. There are small groups of letters associated with Julius Verecundus and Priscinus, prefects of cohorts, another with Cassius Saecularis, whose position is unknown. By far the largest group is that associated with Flavius Cerialis, prefect of the Ninth Cohort of Batavians. It contains 66 texts but it is probable that many more texts from Period 3 belong to it. Note also the small dossier of correspondence of his wife, Sulpicia Lepidina (291–4).

[4] Drafts and file copies: 225–41. Corbridge, 154, 175; Carlisle, 211, 250; Ribchester, 295; Catterick, 185, 343; Binchester, Aldborough, 185; London, 154, 310; Gaul, 255; Rome, 283. Unknown place-names include *Cordonovi* (or *-vae*, or *-via*) (299), Briga (190, 292) and *Ulucium* (?) (174). Letter brought back from London, 310 (*Londini* on the back must be regarded as part of the address, see *Tab. Vindol.* II, note *ad loc.* and pp. 57–61).

features. First, all of this written material was generated or circulated in the northern frontier zone within a very short time of its first occupation by the Romans and it was a region which, as far as writing was concerned, was to all intents and purposes practically a *tabula rasa*.[5] Second, we are surely not dealing, for the most part, with Romans, Italians, or even long-acculturated Gauls. A good deal of the central core of the material is connected with an officer called Flavius Cerialis, prefect of the Ninth Cohort of Batavians. His name and the known practice of putting Batavian units under the command of their own élites indicates that he is a native Batavian and that he or his father was the first in his family to gain Roman citizenship, surely as a reward for loyalty to Rome and the Roman general Petillius Cerialis during the Batavian revolt of AD 69/70.[6] Thus, in northern Britain, the army of occupation included units from the areas of the empire most recently absorbed, northern France, Germany, the Netherlands; at Vindolanda there were sections of at least two Batavian cohorts, the Third and Ninth, and one Tungrian cohort, the First, during the period which produced the tablets.[7]

The light which the Vindolanda texts throw on the relationship between literacy and power can be illustrated by four themes which recur in the following sections: (1) the power of Latin literacy as an instrument of acculturation; (2) the use of literacy by the imperial power as a tool of institutional control through the army; (3) the power of the army and its penumbra to generate written material which promotes the cohesiveness of the institution; (4) the power of individuals to generate and control texts beyond the restrictive bounds of a 'chancery' or record-office. The value and significance of the tablets is increased by the fact that they illuminate a stratum of society below the social and literary élite, operating in an area very far from the centre of the empire or the already literate Greek east.

Technology and education

Even if the high Roman imperial era is taken to be the period at which literacy achieved its zenith in the ancient world, the ability to read and write will still have been confined to a relatively small percentage of the population. The size of the literate group itself may be less important than

---

[5] On Celtic literacy in general see Woolf (ch. 6 in this volume), Tomlin (1988: no. 14), Evans (1990: 158–9). On the creation of Roman schools in Britain see Tacitus, *Agr.* 21.1–2 (cf. *Ann.* 3.43 for Autun under Tiberius).

[6] Batavian revolt, Tacitus, *Hist.* 4.12–37, 54–79, 5.14–26. Nobles commanding units, Tacitus, *Hist.* 4.12. Loyalty to Rome, cf. Claudius Labeo, Tacitus, *Hist.* 4.18. For possible evidence of Batavian culture or habits at Vindolanda see 208.

[7] There is some evidence for Celtic and Germanic names (e.g. 184, 310, 350). The explicit evidence for the origin of an individual, Sabinus, from Trier (182.i.4), is unique.

the fact that a very much larger proportion of the population lived according to rules and conventions established on the presumption that written communication was a normal and widespread form of regulating and ordering (in the broadest possible sense) its life. In the army, we might see a microcosm, where élite literacy in the officer class regulated the lives of the rest. In fact, there is strong evidence for literacy among centurions, decurions and *principales* and some evidence for its presence at lower levels, but it is certainly impossible to claim *mass* literacy in the army (which must, in any case, be envisaged as a more literate world than the civilian).[8] There are other ways of approaching the issues.

In this world, the technology of manufacture was not a restricting factor as might once have been thought, as it presumably was not in Egypt where papyrus was cheap and plentiful. Instead of the relatively expensive, manufactured and imported stylus-tablets, these thin leaves of wood must have been simple to cut from remnants of local timber (alder, birch and oak have been identified). The surface is reasonably smooth and can be rubbed, the ink appears to be a standard carbon-based mix. Writing was thus not restricted to those who could afford expensive materials. On the other hand, these are not simply casual offcuts and scraps; they are frequently made with tie-holes and V-shaped (or occasionally semi-circular) notches in the edges, probably for holding a binding cord, and were pierced and cut before the leaf was used, as is shown by the frequency with which writers avoid such holes. Clearly, then, we have a simple manufacturing technology combined with physical features which are disciplined and function-specific; this enables and encourages people to produce documents and letters outside the context of an official record-office. Despite the paucity of archaeological data from other sites, the use of this type of wooden-leaf tablet cannot have been peculiar to Vindolanda – the mass of correspondence, of broadly similar format, which originated elsewhere guarantees that and examples have turned up at other sites.[9]

The geographical spread of evidence in an area which has hitherto produced nothing comparable emphasises the fact that habits of use and methods of writing do not develop randomly but within the framework of conventions and expectations, to which a distinguished palaeographer has aptly applied the phrase 'the grammar of legibility'.[10] The tablets from Vindolanda illustrate both discipline and diversity in this area and warn against defining rigid categories and classifications.

[8] See Gilliam (1986: 379–85), Breeze (1974), Bowman (1991), and below pp. 119–22. The presence of a blank notice-board *tabula ansata*, probably from the Flavian period, in a workshop at Carlisle is suggestive, see Caruana (1987).   [9] Tomlin (1986, 1992).
[10] Parkes (1991: 2), cf. Bischoff (1990: 20–37). For Greek papyri see Turner (1987: 1–23).

The documents and accounts from Vindolanda do not exhibit the same degree of formality as texts such as the third-century papyri from Dura-Europus on the Euphrates which belong to the official records of the Twentieth Cohort of Palmyrene archers. The strength report of the First Cohort of Tungrians from Vindolanda is written across the grain and parallel to the short edge on a huge diptych. A memorandum describing the fighting characteristics of the native *Brittunculi* also runs across the grain. Some other, shorter reports are written along the grain. Many of the accounts are written in the same format as the strength report, with narrow columns; one is put together in a concertina arrangement which remains unique. We have, however, several accounts written across the grain including one in a two-column format like a letter (see below) and one in a unique three-column format.[11] The latter certainly relates to the soldiers listed by their centuries, but several of the smaller accounts might well concern the domestic organisation of the *praetorium*. In sum, there seems to have been a broad commonality of convention which was not unduly restrictive, but no standard format to which the writers of these reports and accounts were confined.

From the point of view of format the letters are perhaps more interesting. In the commonest arrangement (fig. 3a) the leaf is used with the broad dimension running horizontally and the text is written in two columns along the grain from left to right, the first often broader than the second and extending beyond the centre of the leaf. It is to be noted that the heading is usually written on the first two lines and that the first line of the message is more often than not indented, with an enlarged initial letter. The leaf is scored vertically down the centre and folded and the address is then written on the back of the right-hand half, the name (and normally the rank) of the addressee in large, spindly letters (which is technically better *not* regarded as a capital script), and below that the name of the sender of the letter, with *a* or *ab* in normal cursive, but almost always sloping upwards from left to right.[12] The two-column format, with the left broader than the right, and the address convention on the back can be paralleled in Greek papyri but it is worth noting that the double-column layout is comparatively very rare; it may be commoner in Latin papyrus letters but so few examples survive (and those biased towards the military context)

---

[11] Dura-Europus, Welles, Fink and Gilliam (1959). Strength report, 154. Memorandum, 164. Reports, 156–8. *Renuntium*, 127–53. Concertina format, 190, cf. Bowman (1975); 180/344 may be a triptych, folded in the same way, but not made up of several leaves tied together. Two-column account, 182. Three-column account, 184. Note that Bischoff (1990: 27) thinks that the use of columns in the codex was a legacy of the papyrus age.

[12] The question of layout is considered by Bischoff (1990: 27–30) but only with reference to books. The literary evidence is cited by Cugusi (1983: 30).

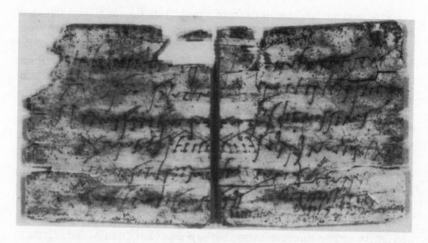

Fig. 3a. A letter from Niger and Brocchus to Flavius Cerialis: *Tab. Vindol.* II 248 (see n. 1). Scale 1:1. (Photo: E. Hitchcock, University College London.)

that it is impossible to be sure.[13] This arrangement is, however, not universal and the variations are interesting. A letter may be written on two or three leaves, folded together. The first part of a letter from Claudia Severa is written in one column across the whole leaf, the remainder in two columns, and the closing greeting is actually on the back. Octavius writes to Candidus on two leaves, two columns on each leaf, but the sequence runs from right to left, which must be explained by the supposition that Octavius was a left-hander. Some writers conclude their text by writing at a right angle between the columns or occasionally in the left margin, others continue on the back of the leaf. A draft of a petition or letter is written on the back of an account and probably occupies more than one leaf. An address is once written on the back of the left-hand half of the leaf.[14]

As far as the layout and appearance of the text are concerned, the matter of columns has already been dealt with. In by far the majority of cases the first line of the text contains the name of the author and the addressee, sometimes with *suo*; the second line *salutem* or *suo salutem* at the far right. There are, again, a few exceptions. In one case the address on the back is written not in the usual elongated letters but in ordinary cursive.[15]

---

[13] Columns, *P. Oxy.* 18.2192, *P. Wisc.* 2.84. Addresses, Welles, Fink and Gilliam (1959: pl. XXXIII). Latin letters, *ChLA* VI 300, X 452, 457, XI 487.

[14] Severa, 292; Octavius, 343; right angle, 302, 311, 316; backs, 305, 307, 340; petition on the back of an account, 344; address on back of left-hand side, 319.

[15] Exceptions, 212, 214, 275, 311. Address in ordinary cursive, 352.

Fig. 3b. A cash account from Vindolanda: *Tab. Vindol.* II 181 (see n. 1). Scale 1.2:1. (Photo: Alison Rutherford, Audio Visual Centre, University of Newcastle upon Tyne, reproduced by permission of the Vindolanda Trust.)

Although there is a good deal of ancient evidence for the principles and practice of epistolography, there is, as far as I know, no ancient text which describes the characteristics of the layout of a letter. An important development may have been initiated by Julius Caesar, who sent letters to the senate *quas primum videtur ad paginas et formam memorialis libelli convertisse, cum antea consules et duces non nisi transversa charta scriptas mitterent* ('which he seems to have been the first to change to the form of a paginated notebook, whereas previously consuls and generals had only sent despatches written with the roll rotated through 90 degrees'). The relationship between these features of layout in our Vindolanda letters and the layout of a 'literary' letter is of major interest but must be left open.[16]

Equally interesting are the practices of abbreviation and punctuation,

[16] For epistolography see Cugusi (1983: 43–145). Caesar, Suetonius, *Iul.* 56.6, cf. Turner (1978: 32).

notably the use of apices to mark vowels and interpunct between words. *n* with a superscript bar for *noster* is common, as are standard abbreviations for *numerus* and *modius, pondo, praefectus, cohors, collega* and so on. The only reasonably clear instance of abbreviation of a *gentilicium* occurs in a woman's name. The common *cos* for *consulibus* occurs once. The apex was normally used as a marker for long vowels and it is therefore remarkable that its use in Vindolanda texts extends to short vowels and, even more unusually, apparently as a sort of full stop. The employment of interpunct seems to fit the evidence from the other end of the empire – it is frequent in a few texts and occasional in a few more, which seems to confirm the belief that its use was in decline at this time. In one interesting example the second hand which wrote the closing greeting imitated the first writer's regular use of interpunct.[17]

What can this tell us about the diversity of writing practices and the diffusion of literate skills? The Roman army is a limited context, though broader than might at first appear, since our documentation certainly represents not merely officers and soldiers but also wives, slaves and possibly even some civilians; it is very difficult to perceive any reflection of the local British context except in the third person.[18] Our evidence suggests that technology is less of a limiting factor than we might have thought. On the other hand, the diffusion of literate skills seems to take place within a framework of broadly standard conventions, some of which can be detected at the other end of the empire. It looks as if the recipient of a letter or the user of an account would in general terms know what to expect to see, but this does not mean that there is no room for individuality and manipulation of the medium, that is power over the production of the text. The standardisation of particular forms emerges from a literate milieu which is characterised by a breadth of practice but it may still be one in which the *sort* of thing which people read and write is constrained. The degree of inventiveness implied by the concertina-form account tells us something about the use of notebooks (*pugillaria*) which may be relevant to the context in which the development of the codex took place. Octavius' letter and many other examples have to be set against the implications of rigidity and restrictiveness implied by the idea of an institutionalised 'chancery' or *officium* of clerks. Finally, and of the utmost significance, these texts are the productions not of the world of Cicero or Pliny but of the vitally important sub-élite literate inhabitants of the empire.[19]

---

[17] *noster*, 248.ii.10, 260.7. *numerus*, 207, 309. *modius*, 186, 190, 192. *pondo*, 192.4, 186.10. *praefectus, cohors, collega*, 260 back. *gentilicium*, 291.i.1. *cos*, 186.14. Apex, 248, 265, 291, cf. Wingo (1972: 95–6), Kramer (1991), *Tab. Vindol.* II, pp. 57–61. Interpunct, 297, 345, cf. *Tab. Vindol.* I, p. 69, II, pp. 56–7.

[18] The petition on the back of an account (344) may well be from a civilian, but not a Briton. Third-person reference to *Brittunculi*, 164.

[19] Concertina, Bowman (1975), cf. Tjäder (1986). Octavius, 343. Sub-élite, Hopkins (1991).

Writing techniques

The enabling factor which underlies and promotes these phenomena is the ability to write and to communicate over a broad range, temporally, spatially and psychologically. Whatever percentage of this population was literate, it is crucial to ask what they learned and how, an area in which we particularly need to bear in mind the assumed Batavian and Tungrian context of at least a proportion of our material. Palaeographical matters are very important here but can be presented summarily and without too much technical detail.[20] We perhaps have direct references in the texts to writing-tablets and to books (*libros*). Be that as it may, someone in the *praetorium* wrote a line of Virgil's *Aeneid* in rustic capitals mixed with more cursive forms. If this was one of the children of Cerialis and Lepidina, he or she will be a second- or third-generation 'Roman', but it might be Cerialis himself and, indeed, it is far from certain that this was simply a writing-exercise. Another fragment may contain the beginning of a poem of Catullus and repetition of the word more strongly suggests a writing-exercise.[21] The use of capital script in literary texts is expected, but less attention has been paid to a phenomenon which strikes us very forcibly at Vindolanda: the mixture of capital and cursive script in documents. Furthermore, there are some cursive hands which are 'almost literary' and one thoroughly cursive but strikingly calligraphic text is a routine military report.[22] It is precisely in this welter of evidence provided by several hundred different individual hands that we must examine the relationship between the so-called Old Roman Cursive and New Roman Cursive scripts. We can observe features which should make us more reluctant to identify fundamentally different types of writing – or at least to see elements of relationship between what have been thought to be fundamentally different types of writing. And, finally, perhaps one more unique category of evidence. A handful of tablets appear to contain the earliest known examples of Latin shorthand writing, perhaps the form known as Tironian notes. Some have thought it likely that this will have originated in the military bureaucracy. This certainly suggests the use of stenography or dictation and the latter is strikingly illustrated in a letter in which the scribe has corrected an obviously phonetic error, from '*et hiem*' to '*etiam*'.[23]

The totality of evidence suggests a context in which the idea of a literacy

---

[20] See *Tab. Vindol.* I, pp. 51–71, II, pp. 47–61.
[21] Writing-tablets, 217. Books, 333; Virgil, 118. Quintia in 119, the name at the beginning of Catullus 86.
[22] Consular date, 186. Account with some capital script, 206. Almost literary hand, 120. Calligraphic report, 152; 147, another text of this type, has letter-forms which are very close to capitals.
[23] Shorthand, 122–6, cf. Ganz (1990: ch. 1), Teitler (1985). Dictation error, 234.

taught exclusively through formal schooling does not necessarily apply; the extended *familia* of the officer may be complementary to, and as important as, the *tabularium*. This has an important bearing on the whole question of the development of Latin writing and the ways in which literacy spread. The analysis of letter-forms and the relationship between capital and cursive scripts is of particular importance, especially for the disappearance of Old Roman Cursive (in which the Vindolanda texts are written) and its replacement by New Roman Cursive in the late third century. The change has been related to the difference between official cursive (which we might expect to find in documents) and 'private script' (written by the educated classes); the private script was joined by a more elementary self-taught 'popular script' based on simple capital forms, and the coalescence of the two produced New Roman Cursive.[24]

In the Old Roman Cursive of the Vindolanda texts several forms of individual letters were in use at one and the same time, and there is some evidence of importance for the development of New Roman Cursive. Most striking is the first appearance, in a capital text, of a form of *e* which so far has appeared only in incised texts (stylus tablets or graffiti).[25] In general, the mixture of forms which others have tended to classify more exclusively as private, popular or official, even in one and the same text, suggests that the distinctions are less clear-cut than some think.[26] This is natural in a context in which many private letters were probably being written or copied by people accustomed to writing official documents and in which many 'private' writers may have learned to write from those people or at least have been in close contact with them. There is another general consideration which points in the same direction, and which highlights the relationship, or at least the contact, between capital and cursive hands. Normally these are studied in different kinds of texts, literary and documentary respectively. Scholars have occasionally commented that the development of capital hands might be illuminated by consideration of the headings in military texts, principally pay records. Vindolanda provides examples of the use of capital script in non-literary texts and of writers switching from capital to cursive in the body of one text.[27] This is not unique to Vindolanda and it is a point of absolutely crucial importance, for it suggests the intermix of what are thought to be parallel developments in a milieu which was primarily military but included literate women, slaves and probably also traders and

---

[24] For a summary see *Tab. Vindol.* I, pp. 55–9, II, pp. 47–8.

[25] *Tab. Vindol.* I, pp. 69–70, Bowman and Thomas (1987: 132); there is a second example in a military duty roster on an ostrakon from Mons Claudianus in Egypt (I am grateful to Hélène Cuvigny for this information).

[26] The evidence of the Bath curse-tablets also suggests that the distinction was not always clear-cut, see Tomlin (1988: 225).

[27] 162, 163, 186, 206. Cf. e.g. *P. Qasr Ibrîm* 38, *O. Wâdi Fawâkhir* 6–7.

artisans. It also has extremely important implications for the possible developmental connections between literary texts, documents and letters which have too often been considered in isolation from each other.

This may help us to illuminate the relationship between the different kinds of writing in the process of learning to become literate. All seem to have been commonly in use in the army, which was certainly one milieu in which provincials could acquire literacy in Latin, along with the *familia* and the schools like those established in Gaul and Britain.[28] The progression will run from the record of the military essentials to an aspiration to 'polite letters' and the transcription of literary texts.

Organisation and power

The development of literacy, bureaucracy and documentation reinforces the autonomy of the institution in which it exists. The Roman army was notorious for its tendency to record its operations and administration in a mass of paperwork.[29] The content of the official record-office at Vindolanda would, if we had it, give us a detailed picture of the work of the military clerks. What we do have – written material dumped in the area of the *praetorium*, and later a barracks and a workshop – may be even more useful. Control of a unit's operations, knowledge of its strength at particular times or regular intervals, disposition of the personnel and the duties which they were performing is to be expected. All units must have recorded these details and, given the clear evidence for a high degree of fragmentation, flexibility and movement of units and parts of units, it seems obvious that such records were an essential means of keeping track of what was going on. Even more, this degree of precise and detailed communication goes a long way to explain how the Roman military presence exerted such effective control over such large areas with so few troops – and perhaps made them seem more numerous to the natives than they actually were. The connections between literacy and numeracy in this particular context are crucial and it is important not to assume that the former implies the latter.[30]

On the other hand, it is not simply a matter of a standard range of documents prepared by military clerks in a prescribed form – we should again set the restrictive tendency of the institution as a whole against the degree of flexibility and inventiveness which can be employed within it.

[28] Above, n. 5. The remark of Hopkins (1991: 138 n. 11) that the variety of handwriting in *P. Hamb.* 39 shows that soldiers learned to write prior to joining the army depends on the idea that the army teaching would create uniformity. The evidence from Vindolanda suggests the opposite (cf. pp. 121–2 below).   [29] Goody (1986: 90), Vegetius 2.19.

[30] Control of space: cf. Nicolet (1988: ch. 6) and note the early evidence for a census in the frontier region (304).

Military strength reports from different places, though broadly comparable in type and purpose, do not perhaps allow as clear and precise a typology as has sometimes been thought. Some of our brief duty reports from Vindolanda compare closely with texts on ostraka from Bu-Njem in Africa. The strength report of the First Cohort of Tungrians is what one would expect but is difficult to classify precisely.[31]

There are two new and interesting groups of short texts relating to the military organisation. First, short reports with the *renuntium*-heading, of which there are 27 examples with a more or less identical text which can be reconstructed in the form: *X K(alendas) Iulias, renuntium cohortis viiii Batavorum, omnes ad loca q(ui) videbunt et impedimenta (? praesentia), Candidus et Vitalis optiones renuntiaverunt* (or *renuntiauerunt optiones et curatores, detulit Iustinus optio (centuriae) Crescentis*). These must be routine reports on the state of the unit or perhaps of small groups outposted to nearby fortlets. The date and heading ('Report of the Ninth Cohort of Batavians) and the closure ('Candidus and Vitalis the *optiones* made the report') are straightforward enough. What is particularly interesting is the standard use of the word *renuntium* which has not occurred elsewhere, the repeated and idiosyncratic formula with the abbreviated *q(ui)* followed by *videbunt* in the sense 'see to', suggesting the meaning 'all are at their posts and they will also see to the baggage (?which is present)'. Above all, we should note the fact that they are not mass-produced chits but are all written by different hands, presumably those of the reporting *optiones* themselves. It would be interesting to know to what extent this could be ascribed to local initiative devising its own methods of control. Be that as it may, it is worth emphasising that such documentation fits into the picture of a frontier as a communication system, rather than a barrier – a zone of intensive troop mobility and information exchange which simply could not function without written documentation.[32]

Second, there are a dozen examples of letters requesting leave of absence (*commeatus*). These are again formulaic and seem to begin with the name and rank of the applicant, followed by *rogo domine Cerialis me dignum habeas cui des commeatum* ('I ask, my lord Cerialis, that you consider me worthy to be granted leave'), sometimes further qualified by the place at which the leave is to be taken. Again, these are not simply chits filled in but

---

[31] *O. Bu Njem* 1–62. Bowman and Thomas (1991: 63–6).

[32] 127–53, cf. Bowman and Thomas (1987: 132–5, 1991: 65). These may be compared with the practice described for the army of the Republic by Polybius 6.34.7–36.9. Almost all these texts are assigned to the Period 3 occupation when the Ninth Cohort of Batavians was at Vindolanda. Frontier zone, cf. Isaac (1992: 102–3).

letters written in different hands (several of them quite good) and at least some coming, we may assume, from lower ranks.[33]

Neither of these groups of documents proves mass literacy in the army (that is not my point) but they offer texts which are more than bare signatures in individual hands and indicate a literate milieu which does not simply operate with forms and formulae which could not be understood by those whose lives were regulated by them.[34] This may perhaps be taken as an indication of a tendency on the part of the institution to open up channels of communication and methods of organisation rather than to restrict, in a sense to create and encourage communal use of texts.

The accounts are no less interesting in this context. Some of these clearly relate to the fort as a whole or to the needs of the soldiers at Vindolanda, at amenities in its vicinity or in contact with more distant places including Catterick (Cataractonium), Aldborough (Isurium) and Binchester (Vinovia). It is interesting and significant that documentation clearly includes communication with the presumption of financial credit through the military network. How far this may have involved civilians is difficult to tell, but the draft petition which is written on the back of an account of wheat states that the writer was from abroad (*homo tra(n)smarinus*) and strongly implies that he was a civilian, probably a trader, who had been maltreated by the military.[35]

Several of the accounts are likely to relate to the domestic administration of the *praetorium* rather than the central administration of the unit. This does not mean that they are non-military, for the *praetorium* is of course an integral part of the fort and the military establishment. But it does have a broader significance, if only because the *praetorium* was occupied by the family of the unit commander, supported by slaves who may also have played a role in the broader context of the fort.

The detailed accounting of the organisation of foodstuffs in the *praetorium* through the domestic slaves will cause no surprise.[36] Equally interesting is a group of fragmentary texts apparently containing inventories of clothing and household equipment, mainly culinary.[37] The nature and quantities of items recorded assure us that these must relate to a small establishment within the unit and to the relatively luxurious lifestyle of the officer class. The clothing lists, in particular, reflect concerns found in other accounts and in letters recording or requesting the despatch of such

---

[33] 166–77. Contrast *O. Claud.* 48–82, and for an example of a pre-written chit with the name filled in see Bagnall (1976: no. 1).

[34] Signatures, Hopkins (1991: 138).

[35] Fort revenues at Vindolanda, 178; unit accounts, 184; local supplies, 182. Catterick, Aldborough and Binchester, 185. Credit, 343.ii.21–3. Draft petition, 344.

[36] 190 and perhaps 302.   [37] 194–7.

items.[38] One would expect the clothing to be strictly personal, but the household lists might be inventories of equipment belonging to the residence.

The first temptation would be to argue that this gives us an excellent example of the way in which military record-keeping practices spread into the private or semi-private sphere and became central to the organisation and control of the establishment. This, then, would have implications for assumptions about the spread of such practices beyond the walls of the fort and into the civilian population. But can we be sure that the influence is entirely one-way? Might not the Roman tradition of domestic organisation through literate slaves have influenced the operations of the military bureaucracy?

It is perhaps easier to be certain that the correspondence provides us with evidence of an increasing breadth of literacy emanating from the military. Even if we observe a distinction between 'official' and 'private' correspondence, which is not always easy to do, the character of the correspondence as a whole is mixed. The letters of September and Karus to the prefect Cerialis, for instance, might be described as official business, the letters of Claudia Severa to Lepidina and of Chrauttius to Veldeius are clearly social and private, the letter of Octavius to Candidus concerns matters of business and trade.[39] As in many other aspects of the activities of the army and its personnel, it is very difficult to draw a precise line of demarcation between military and non-military. It is, indeed, precisely this feature which lies at the very centre of the way in which the Vindolanda texts help us to understand the relationship between literacy and power in the institutional context of the Roman army. It is absolutely crucial to this approach to see the significance of the fact that we have in the same context some material which reflects the self-contained organisation and institutional autonomy and some which clearly goes beyond that. In both cases, however, the access is strictly controlled, if only in the banal sense that letters have to be delivered via the institutional communication network.

The power of communication

It is hardly original to claim that the embedding of literacy in the institutional organisation of the Roman army rendered it a more effective presence in an otherwise largely illiterate area. This institutional literacy enabled a broader spread and gave to the lives of individuals a social, economic and psychological coherence within the framework of Latin culture. This is an important clue to the reasons for the rapidity and success

---

[38] 192, 207, 255, 346.

[39] For classification of letters see Cugusi (1983: ch. 4). September to Cerialis, 252, Karus to Cerialis, 250. Severa to Lepidina, 291–2. Chrauttius to Veldeius, 310. Octavius to Candidus, 343.

with which the army achieved the acculturation of peripheral communities and used them in turn as instruments of furthering those processes. It must again be emphasised that we are here not dealing with the context of the already literate Greek East.

The way in which individuals use their literacy to manipulate institutional power is well brought out in the letter of recommendation from Karus to Cerialis, in the letter of Niger and Brocchus, and in the draft letter in which Cerialis attempts to secure access to the patronage of the provincial governor. The literate foundation of social and economic coherence is illustrated in the correspondence of Severa and Lepidina and in Octavius' business letter.[40] A more subtle and interesting aspect of the correspondence is the evidence it gives us for the psychological and cognitive factors involved in letter-writing in a world in which letters are a form of gift-exchange and dialogue, infrequently going beyond the polite cliché or the request for some particular service.[41] These features are very much in evidence at Vindolanda, but some evidence of individuality can be detected by examining the facility with which our letter writers manipulate the medium of expression through the written language.

Occasionally personal feelings are shown, by addressing someone as *homo inpientissime* ('most neglectful man'), beginning a letter with the unceremonious and acerbic *opto tibi male eveniat* ('I hope that it will turn out badly for you') or the excusatory *nihil malo animo feci* ('I have done nothing with malicious intent'). These can be contrasted with the examples of more elegant and formal Latin and the more matter-of-fact forms of expression which occur when writers deal with business matters in rather neutral language. From the psychological point of view the element of dialogue or supposition of verbal contact is significant, but for Claudia Severa, the wife of a prefect, there are perhaps some things which cannot be put in a letter and must be discussed in person. Nevertheless complaints about a correspondent not having written frequently enough imply quite a high level of expectation and probably implicate a fairly broad range of people (not just the equestrian officer class) in the literacy-using network.[42]

The opening and closing formulae of the letters offer interesting evidence for individuality and variation of expression, which is absent from literary epistles of the early empire but compares well with Latin letters on papyrus.

[40] Karus, 250. Niger and Brocchus, 248. Cerialis' draft, 225. Severa and Lepidina, 291–2. Octavius, 343.

[41] Gift-exchange and dialogue, Demetrius, *On Style* 223–4. Note the immediacy conveyed by the instruction *illum a me salutabis verbis meis* (310 cf. 353). Subject-matter, Demetrius, *On Style* 231–2; in general, Parsons (1980).

[42] 311. 321, 297. Elegant Latin, 225. Business language, 343. Personal contact, 292. Complaints, 310, 311.

The austerity of *Claudius Karus Ceriali suo salutem* ('Claudius Karus to his Cerialis, greetings') is amplified in examples such as *Chrauttius Veldeio suo fratri et antiquo contubernali plurimam salutem* ('Chrauttius to Veldeius his brother and old messmate, very many greetings') and *Vittius Adiutor aquilifer leg(ionis) ii Aug(ustae) Cassio Saeculari fraterclo suo plurimam [salutem]* ('Vittius Adiutor eagle-bearer of the Second Augustan legion to Cassius Saecularis, his little brother, very many greetings'). The closing greetings are often variations on a standard theme, in its simplest form *vale, frater* ('farewell, brother). But note *opto sis felicissimus quod es dignissimus* ('I pray that you enjoy the best of fortune because you are most worthy'), *opto felicissimus vivas* ('I pray you live in the best of fortune'), *bene valeas frater domine opto* ('I pray that you are in good health, my lord and brother'). Most striking of all is the elaborate and elegant expression of Claudia Severa to Lepidina: *sperabo te soror. vale soror anima mea ita valeam karissima et have* ('I shall expect you, sister. Farewell, sister, my dearest soul, as I hope to prosper, and hail'), showing the unusual use of *spero*, the somewhat convoluted *ita valeam* which may be taken with *karissima* or with *ita* looking back to *vale*, and the very rare *have* added at the end. Compare Severa again ending another letter with a verbose and enthusiastic greeting, addressing Lepidina as *anima mea desideratissima* ('my most longed-for soul').[43]

The closures are almost always written in a hand different from that which wrote the main part of the letter and must be that of the author, as opposed to the scribe. They can thus be taken, like a signature, as a clear expression of individuality. The letter of Claudia Severa is written in a very refined cursive, her own closure in a hesitant, ugly and unpractised hand but very elegant Latin. Other closures, however, and some of them very cursive, should not be taken to indicate a lower level of expertise or literacy. Those texts which are the work of only one hand might of course be taken as entirely 'scribal', indicating an illiterate author. But in this context, it seems much more likely that the letters of Octavius to Candidus (perhaps both centurions or *optiones*) and Chrauttius to Veldeius the governor's groom, where the closures are in the same hand as the rest, were actually written by Octavius and Chrauttius; the same is surely true of the letter written by Severus, a slave, to another slave belonging to the officer Genialis.[44] The correspondence of Cerialis includes sixty-six texts of which seventeen are drafts or file copies of his own letters. Of the latter, eight are written in a hand which is probably Cerialis' own; the rest by probably five

[43] Opening formulae, 251, 310, 214. Closures, 301, 364, 346, 258. Severa, 291–2. Cf. *P. Mich.* 8.467–72. In general, Lanham (1975).

[44] 343, 310, 301. For examples from Egypt see *P. Oxy.* 1.32, P. J. Sijpesteijn, *Talanta* 5 (1973) nos. 13–14, cf. Gilliam (1986: 379–85).

different hands of which one provides clear evidence of dictation. Aelius Brocchus and his wife Severa could both write but used at least two different scribes. It is absolutely crucial to avoid inferring either that an individual could not write from the fact that he or she did not write on one or more occasions or that bad handwriting is a sign of 'illiteracy'.[45] The interpretation of these features, as of the more formulaic texts, is indeed crucial for assessing the power of literacy and observing its centrality at the geographical periphery of the empire. It embraces not merely equestrian officers (including native Batavians) but centurions, decurions, *optiones*, slaves, wives, and perhaps traders, and probably also draws in friends in other postings and families in the homeland.[46] Given the variety, the range, the individuality of the texts and their writers in this corpus of material it perhaps does not really make all that much difference if we do not always know precisely who performed the act of writing; it is enough that several hundred individuals could do it within a framework of convention and expectation which would have rendered their texts easily comprehensible at the other end of the Roman empire.

[45] Correspondence of Cerialis, 225–90. Cerialis' hand, 225–32. The presence of so many drafts at Vindolanda makes one wonder how many texts conventionally described as 'writing-exercises' (e.g. *ChLA* XI 493) are in fact simply drafts. Dictation, 234. Brocchus and Severa, 244–7, 248, 291–2. Bad handwriting, cf. R. Thomas (1991).

[46] The Vindolanda material does not enable us to test the remark of Richmond (1953: 206–8) that the evidence of a writing-tablet from London shows members of Celtic society conducting their business in Latin in the Flavian period.

9   Literacy and power in early Christianity

Robin Lane Fox

I

Like the Jews in their synagogues, early Christians gave a distinctive twist to the place of literacy in ancient societies: they met to read, hear and discuss their holy texts, the 'word of God'. Among pagans, textual communities were very rare and marginal to the main patterns of worship. Written records did indeed feature in the practice and organisation of pagan cults: pagans might list their priests or prophets, inscribe rules of practice, preserve oracles or hymns or even use a written text as a means of divining the gods' will.[1] The practical and symbolic importance of such records was sometimes great, but their role is quite different from the role of 'sacred literacy' in Christian and Jewish communities.[2] The most frequent use of a text in pagan worship was as a guide to practice, much as we use a cookery book or a gardening dictionary;[3] such were the texts of the most bookish manipulators of the gods, the sorcerers and masters of spells. Only among a few optional minorities were texts regarded as sources of divine wisdom: the supposed words of Orpheus had divine authority for some people, while the few devotees of Egyptian Hermes read their god's words in texts.[4] Among the wide range of pagan mystery cults, too, there were some in which texts were specially important.[5] Those in honour of Dionysus are the best attested: when Ptolemy IV wished to regulate private celebrations of Dionysiac mysteries in the Egyptian *chora* (*c.* 200 BC), he ordered that celebrants must register and hand over the 'sacred writing' (*hieros logos*), sealed with their individual names.[6] This 'sacred writing' would presumably be more than a guide to practice: it would probably contain prayers and songs of praise, to be read, perhaps, in the context of an initiation. The famous wall-paintings in the Villa of the Mysteries at Pompeii may show us just such a text at a later date: a

[1] Beard (1991).
[2] Nock (1972: 344–5); Fontaine and Pietri (1985), and Mondésert (1984) are the most helpful recent survey-volumes of the Christian evidence.   [3] Liepoldt and Morenz (1953).
[4] West (1983: 25–7); Fowden (1986).   [5] Burkert (1987: 70–1).
[6] Hunt and Edgar (1934: 1 no. 208).

scroll is being read by a young boy in what is probably an initiatory rite.[7]

The differing role of texts shows up in a differing pattern of persecution. In the fourth and fifth centuries, when Christians attacked pagans, they attacked their shrines and holy places: the exceptions were sorcerers, who were best attacked, as always, by seizing and burning their books. When pagans attacked Christians in the last 'Great' persecution, they did try to go for their books:[8] they attempted to confiscate Christians' scriptures and burn them.[9] The task was not easy because Christians had produced so many different books and might hand over something considered 'heretical' instead. There was plenty to offer up. Besides the books of the New Testament, almost every Christian minority, heresy and independent teacher had written texts of their own. The very existence of widely accepted sacred texts impelled them to do so. As a textual community Christians could be heretical or radical in their reinterpretations, as no pagan priest ever was.[10]

None the less, sacred scriptures did not constitute Christianity, and even if pagans had seized all the copies, the religion would not have died. A brief history of Christians' sacred texts may help us to see why.[11] At first, antiquity's two religious 'textual communities' shared the same texts, a range of older Jewish writings which were the inheritance of Jesus as of any fellow-Jew. This sharing quickly provoked disputes: in Acts, we read of Paul's great marathons with these set-texts, held for three consecutive Sabbaths in Thessalonica (17.2) or 'from morning till evening' in Rome (28.23) in which he tried to connect Christianity to bits of older sacred text which had never predicted it. Nothing similar ever did happen, or could have happened, in pagan cults.

As for the emergence of the Christians' own holy texts, Jesus himself is nowhere recorded as authorising, or encouraging, the writing of a memoir, or Gospel, about himself. Instead, among early Christians, his sayings were transmitted orally, and oral tradition continued to carry special authority well into the second century. From the 60s, perhaps even earlier, Christians did none the less begin to write texts, or Gospels, about their founder, but these Gospels, too, were valued as sources of Jesus' sayings, perhaps more so than as biographies or narratives of his mission. Various Gospels soon circulated, but by the third quarter of the second century the four which we now recognise were widely, though not universally, regarded as special. As texts took over and the length of the oral tradition grew, respect for orally transmitted sayings diminished. Meanwhile, disputes with Jews had made Christians aware that some of the older Jewish texts were thought by their

[7] Herbig (1958: pl. 19).   [8] Speyer (1970: 123–52).
[9] *Acta Purg. Felicis*, ed. C. Ziwsa (CSEL XXVI, Optatus, Vienna, 1893) 198–9 for clear evidence.
[10] Barr (1966).   [11] Lane Fox (1991: 120–54).

opponents to be less authoritative than others. Here, too, an inner core of texts began to be marked out during the second century. From these two streams of development a narrower range of scriptures emerged in the Churches, still fuzzy at the edges but with the main core which characterises Christian Bibles to this day.

Whether or not Christianity could have survived and cohered without this 'sacred literacy', it could not have cohered even as far as it did without its distinctive history of power. Unlike Judaism, the other great textual community, Christianity quickly developed a widespread structure of authority. By *c.* 100, some (not all) of the Churches had developed the office of bishop, to be held by incumbents for life: Jewish synagogues had no such lifelong 'commanding officer'.[12] This combination of sacred text and an increasingly standardised pattern of authority make the early Church a unique subject for studies of literacy and power.

For religious historians, these two key words are a large pair which leave great freedom to the imagination: I will explore them by exploiting it. First, I will consider literacy as an enhancement of power: power, here, is the power which was acknowledged to belong to special Christians, through merit, position or both. Then, I will reverse the relationship and look at the power of literacy as evinced in the mentality of early Christians. This theme is almost unlimited, but it brings us near to questions which are otherwise poorly documented in the ancient world. Many Christians came from a social class and a sex (female) where literacy would be least widespread, yet as Christians they had sacred texts of the utmost authority and value which were important to their own identity. These texts were not restricted to officers or bureaucrats: anyone could own and read one, just as anyone, even an Ethiopian eunuch in Acts 8.27, could have owned and read a Jewish text in the period when Christianity began. The relationship of orality and literacy takes on new contours if it is seen in the context of conversion to a new sacred literacy in a new textual community.

Connections between literacy and power surface in almost any Christian text, but modern scholarship has tended to treat them piecemeal. There have been fine studies of the use of scriptural quotations by individual writers. There has also been vigorous discussion of the extent of private reading of the scriptures (most notably by A. Harnack),[13] of Christian sources as evidence for the degree of literacy in ancient society and of Christianity's role, or lack of it, in spreading literacy through an otherwise 'illiterate' audience (most recently by W. V. Harris).[14] I will presuppose these strands of scholarship, adding only a few pertinent comments to the latter two. Here, one of my main points is that reading and writing are

---

[12] Lane Fox (1986: 495–517).   [13] Harnack (1912).
[14] Harris (1989); Wipszycka (1984: 279–96).

separate skills and that in antiquity, too, the inability to write does not entail the inability to read. Literacy is certainly a matter of degree, as so many of its studies have argued, but it is also a term with two distinct constituents, as historians of early modern Europe have been quicker to recognise than historians of antiquity.[15]

In Christian company, literacy also has a double reference. Like many other groups in this book, whether Hellenistic Greeks in Egypt or late Roman bureaucrats, Christians made use of the convenience of literacy as a means of exerting power or maintaining solidarity. I wish to emphasise how widely and skilfully Christians exploited literacy as a convenience, but I should stress that these uses were common to secular groups too and only by historical accident did it have to be literacy which they exploited. If there had been some other medium of communication, by broadcasting perhaps, it could have served many of these purposes instead.

Sacred literacy is another matter: like Jews, Christians had texts which were believed to give the word of God, and these texts were not replaceable by some other medium. The belief cannot remove the fact that, by origin, the Jews' sacred texts were all the work of human authors. However, as written texts they had long outgrown their origins. By the Christian era, Jews had long been regarding the words of their scriptures as words of God, even when we know their authors by name (like Nehemiah) or infer them by conjecture (like D or P). In the Gospels, Jesus is shown doing likewise (at Matthew 19.5, he quotes the author of Genesis as if God, not the author, is speaking). Christians rapidly extended this same divine coating to their own 'apostolic' authors, even though these authors were much less remote in time and occasionally, like Paul, had marked a distinction between their own words and those of God or their Lord Jesus. This divine whitewash made Jewish and Christian texts unlike any other epistles or narratives in antiquity.

I will touch on both types of literacy, the convenient and the sacred, and on both of their constituents, reading and writing: my first part says more about writing, my second about reading. As for power, there were Christians who exercised earthly power over fellow-Christians, in much the same sense as a governor, tax-collector or military superior from Ptolemaic Egypt to Vindolanda. However, there was also power from God. Sometimes, this power enhanced one man's power over other men (and women): the classic instance is the power of kings to which Christians added ideas new to pagans, the ideas of anointment, election and power from God, ideas which were only to be found in such a clear form in the texts of their sacred literacy. There was also the prospect of power before

[15] Many of the studies reprinted by Graff (1981) emphasise this fact.

God, won by special merit on earth. This power enabled its earners to bless or curse, forgive sins, see into hearts, heal sicknesses, pray effectively and, after death, to intercede with God in heaven. Most often, this power was earned by merit, although Christian orders of merit set a very high value on non-acts like suffering or fasting or abstaining from sex. Meritorious Christians also enjoyed prestige, like meritorious scholars, athletes or soldiers in the secular world. I will end by referring to prestigious Christians, but here, too, there was a divine dimension. Christian prestige was earned before God, not merely before men and women, and as God's favour was so potent, it is always important to consider (as it is not for an athlete or a scholar) whether power and prestige were kept separate among the particular Christians in question.

II

Among Christians before Constantine, power was the attribute of three particular groups: it was achieved by visionaries; it was ascribed to martyrs and confessors; it was vested above all in bishops. Literacy assisted the exercise of power by all three, but we should also note some significant absentees, especially in the light of Goodman's chapter (ch. 7). Among Christians, there is no evidence of any respect or undue prominence for scribes. Like their Jewish contemporaries, Christians did show reverence and a certain scruple when writing out holy names in a text: not just the name of God, but of Christ and Jesus too. The evidence lies in the earliest surviving Christian papyri, whose writers followed a regular pattern of shortened 'sacred names': they have been fully studied and their historical significance has been emphasised most recently by C. H. Roberts.[16] Like Jews, Christians also showed scruples when disposing of texts which contained such sacred names: they left them in jars, the regular 'morgue', as Roberts has well called it,[17] for texts with holy words in them.

Among the Jews, the high status of scribes is implied only in the Christian Gospels, and Goodman suggests that it may rest essentially on the scribes' role as writers of holy texts with holy names in them. This view needs a slight adjustment for the Christian side of the matter. The practice of Christian copyists shows that for them, too, texts of scripture had holy words in them, yet the copyists of these texts never attained any undue status in the Christian communities.[18] Part of the explanation must be the early importance of oral tradition, so forcefully attested by Papias (*c.* 125);[19] perhaps there had also been more to a Jewish scribe than copying,

---

[16] Roberts (1979: 26–48).   [17] Roberts (1979: 6–8); Robinson (1988: 21).
[18] Roberts (1963: 11–14) suggests only the greater readiness of scribes to name themselves in Christian texts from the third century.   [19] Euseb. *H.E.* 3.39.15.

and that extra aspect (answering points of casuistry which arose from the Torah?) was less relevant among early Christians. For them no Torah was so authoritative both for conduct and the sense of national identity. To judge from the very small sample of early Christian papyri, Christians' holy texts rank not as fine scrolls or works of calligraphy but as humdrum books, copied in everyday hands. I conclude, then, that scribes did not command partieular respect among Christians because, at first, the oral prevailed over the Christian written; texts were not sumptuous nor supreme symbols of Christian identity, let alone a source of pollution for hands which touched them; if Jewish scribes did indeed do more than merely copy, Christian scribes did not.

Like the early Christians, therefore, I will leave scribes on one side and instead, explore the relation of literacy to the power of visionaries, martyrs and bishops respectively.

According to Revelation chapter 10, John, 'in the spirit on the Lord's day', saw an angel in heaven holding a little scroll, apparently opisthographic (written on front and back):

The angel saith unto me, Take it and eat it up; and it shall make thy stomach bitter, but in thy mouth it shall be as sweet as honey ... And I took the little book out of the angel's hand and ate it up ... and it was in my mouth as sweet as honey ... And they said to me, Thou must prophesy ...

Nowadays, prominent authorities try to deconstruct texts: in the earliest Churches, they seemed to consume them. Dreams of book-eating were not peculiar to Jews and Christians. A generation later (c. 130), the pagan Artemidorus noted them in his great collection of past and present dream-types: 'to dream of eating a book is good for people in education, sophists and all who make a living from lecturing on books...' (2.45). Perhaps we should try it more often.

Behind John's vision, however, lay a different model, the words of Hebrew prophets, especially Ezekiel's vision in chapters 2 and 3 (although his textual roll had a sweeter taste).[20] The logic, here, is obvious. The prophet who 'swallowed' a heavenly scroll spoke with impersonal, digested authority: much that he wrote was not his own personal opinion, but the very words of God or his angels. However, he could not rely on contemporaries to leave the words of his vision exactly as he reported or regurgitated them: in his final sentences, John pronounces an awful curse on anyone who 'adds or takes away' from the text of his book.[21] The claim to have digested sacred literacy adds authority to a vision; writing then allows it to circulate in space and endure in time, but in Christian company it does not fix it: it gives others a chance of rewriting it. Those who know the

[20] Davis (1989: 58–64).   [21] Van Unnik (1949: 1–36).

early Christians' talents for constructive forgery will agree that John's concerns were not misplaced. Yet his curse, too, gained power from literacy. If he had merely uttered it over the finished text, it would have dwindled with the words and their audience. By being written, not spoken, it endured, like the curses inscribed on pagan, Jewish and Christian tombstones.[22]

Within twenty or thirty years, Christians could read another such visionary report from heaven, the work of Hermas, the richest of our early sources for literacy and visionary power.[23] In his first vision (Hermas, *Vis.* 1.2), Hermas writes how he had seen an aged lady, sitting with a book which she was reading with an awesome expression, while telling him to pay attention. On his way to Cumae, he sees her again: she tells him to take the little book and copy it, which he does, 'letter by letter' because he could not 'distinguish the syllables' (2.1), and then the original is snatched away. Fifteen days later, after fasting, the text's meaning is revealed, including a rude rebuke for a backsliding Christian, Maximus, and a quotation from the book, now lost to us, of Eldad and Modat (2.3).

After more visions, the sub-plot of literacy and power develops. The elderly woman, the Church in disguise, is pleased that Hermas has not yet publicised the text to the 'elders': she wishes to add to it, whereupon Hermas must write out two little books, one for Clement and the 'cities outside' which are his concern, the other for Grapte and the 'widows and orphans'. As for Hermas' own, he is to read it to the elders who are heads of the Church (2.4.2.3).

When the old lady gives way to a visiting Angel of Repentance, Hermas' visionary literacy is still kept exercised. This Angel reveals the Commandments and Parables which fill the rest of our text, but we only have them (Hermas implies) because the Angel told him to write them down 'so that you may have them to hand and keep them' (5.5).

Here, too, we find the interplay of sacred literacy and convenient literacy, combined in the imagery of a vision. On the highest authority, Hermas can assure us that his text is not his own invention and that his motives are not questionable. He has copied down the text of the Church herself and the very words of an angel: he has copied and circulated them, not out of pique or ambition but because the Church herself has told him to do so. Sacred literacy lent impersonal power to Hermas' text, while earthly literacy allowed it to circulate impeccably.[24] As a text, not a mental video, it could reach widows, orphans and 'churches outside', but as good Mother Church had dictated, the text was coming round to them only on the highest authority. The success of Hermas' heavenly dictation is shown in the high

[22] Feissel (1984: 228–9).   [23] Brox (1991) for commentary on each passage.
[24] Compare Luttikhuizen (1985) on the book of the vision of Elxai, apparently written in 116.

respect and breadth of circulation accorded to it by later centuries. In view of it, might not a Christian go one step further and artfully exert power by distributing anonymous letters as if they were letters directly from heaven? In the early Church, it is surprising that we have no evidence of this further step. We have it, however, rather later, in early mediaeval Saxony, where anonymous heavenly mail warned contemporaries about such grave concerns as Sunday observance and excessive feasting.[25]

In their texts of their mental videos, both John and Hermas refer to another heavenly book, although neither of them was able to transcribe it. Dictated texts from angels circulate with evident power, but there is also power in the idea of a text which angels are keeping but do not reveal for publication. Both of these early visionaries mention the 'book of life' (Hermas, *Vis.* 1.3; John, Rev. 20.12); good Christians are listed in it, whereas sins, even sinful thoughts, may be written down in heaven for the opposite reason (Hermas, *Vis.* 1.2.1). The idea of these 'secret files' in heaven goes back to Jewish visionary texts, to Enoch and Daniel 7.10. Its cautionary power is obvious; around 200, Tertullian could tell Christians in Carthage (*De Spectac.* 27) that they should not attend pagan games because, among other ghastly reasons, the angels will notice members of the crowd and write down their names, *singulos denotantes* ('noting them down one by one').

Recording angels were a constant, literate police force, active above early Christian saints and sinners. According to Paul, a 'written bond' had been cancelled for Christians by Christ's death (Coloss. 2.13–15); many of the Greek Fathers were so sure of these records in heaven that they understood this written bond as the angels' ledger of our sins.[26] Bede, *Eccles. Hist.* 5.13 has a vivid story of the imagery of the two heavenly books, good and bad, being balanced against each other by angels during a Christian's dying hours. Before a New Testament existed, Christians were already a 'people of the Book' in this neglected sense: the book of their Recording Angel.

As for martyrs, they too saw visions and some of them recorded them in personal diaries which underlie one or two of our written accounts of their suffering.[27] Literacy, here, enhanced their prestige, just as the circulation of early accounts of their deaths extended their fame and encouraged their honouring on 'saints' days' in the calendar. In the newly published *Passion of Athenogenes* (he was martyred in Cappadocia in the Great Persecution) Christians are told to have the martyrdom read in their homes so as to earn intercession by the saint himself.[28] None the less, prestige might not be immediate: nearly a century after Polycarp's death, his follower Pionius

[25] *Epist. Liciniani, PL* 72.699 Leclercq (1899).   [26] Koep (1952: 55–7).
[27] Lane Fox (1986: 439–40, 469–72).
[28] *Passio Athenogenis* (ed. P. Maraval, 1990) 78, with pl. 21.

tells us how he found the text of his martyrdom neglected and in need of recopying.[29] But literacy eventually worked, and Polycarp became a widely remembered saint.

In the making of a historical martyr, literacy had little place or power before 250. Until then, letters from the Emperors limited persecution by forbidding anonymous letters of accusation: prosecutors of a Christian had to appear and state their case, not write it. From 250 onwards, Imperial literacy initiated persecution: uniquely, a Reader and a cleric in Athenogenes' church are said to have provoked attention by their own literacy, using it to write a hostile pamphlet and send it boldly to their governor.[30] For all other would-be martyrs, meanwhile, the one convenient power of literacy lay in its use for notes of intercession and forgiveness.[31] These notes remitted fellow-Christians' sins and, like written visions or curses, they could endure and circulate, alternative visas to the judgements of bishops and clergy.

In the ideals of a martyr, however, sacred literacy did have important power. Determined martyrs read their sacred texts and found support for their own ambitions or predicaments. Some of them found role models, as did the authors of their martyrdoms: they gave power to stories of execution by turning them into something higher with the help of scripture.[32] If there had been no Gospels and no framework of Jewish texts, it seems unlikely that the execution of a Christian could have had such overtones of power won by triumph over Satan, intimacy with the Holy Spirit and intercession before the heavenly throne.

As for bishops, neither visionaries and their books in heaven nor martyrs and their notes of forgiveness made the task of ruling a Christian flock any easier. Yet for them too, literacy became a powerful ally. The everyday convenience of literacy allowed them to involve the 'Church universal' in the affairs of their own diocese and indeed, to maintain and exploit the power of the idea of One Church. It allowed them to maintain contact with a diocese's individual communities, which were otherwise scattered, like the domestic centres of 'new Christianity' in modern China or parts of South America. Before the 250s, Christians met in scattered little house-churches, not in central purpose-built cathedrals. Literacy also allowed bishops to outmanoeuvre opponents, display a solid front of opinion, abjure or curse mistaken Christians or 'sign up' lists of names for creeds and disciplinary rulings, texts which allowed yet more power to be mobilised. As for sacred literacy, it allowed bishops to cite impersonal sources for their own authority: like visionaries, bishops profited from texts in which God's word, not their own, was made public. Like martyrs, they

---

[29] *Mart. Polycarpi* 22.5 (ed. Musurillo, 1972).
[30] *Passio Athenogenis* (ed. P. Maraval, 1990) 50–2.   [31] Lane Fox (1986: 448).
[32] Saxer (1986); Deleani (1985: 315–39); Dolbeau (1983: 65–82); Siniscalco (1975: 595–614).

also gained new ideas of their power from their community's sacred texts. There was one major difference. Unlike martyrs, bishops had nowhere been mentioned or foreseen by the texts which they cited.

By the mid-third century, these connections of literacy and power are all beautifully visible in our evidence. We catch echoes of them from Dionysius, bishop of Alexandria: we find him circulating approved views and advice, through the institution of the Easter encyclical letter; we find him mobilising and circulating the views of a bishops' synod; during the great controversy over whether or not heretical Christians needed to be rebaptised, we can deduce the existence of at least seven letters, in the space of not more than four years, sent to bishops and clergy in Rome.[33] Two are said to have been 'lengthy' and a third was a 'protracted demonstration' on the matter at issue. Nearer home, the existence of a book on the nature of the millennium provoked Dionysius into a polemical dispute and refutation lasting three full days.[34] Cameron's chapter below (ch. 13) emphasises the importance of polemic, dispute and the circulation of approved views and testimonies in the Greek Christian world of the seventh and eighth centuries. These features may be prominent in that period but we should not see them as new to it: they are prominent in our evidence for the 250s and, in practice, go back to the Apostolic Age.

In the third century, probably in Syria, Christians still reckoned with the possibility that a bishop might be illiterate:[35] little bishoprics were multiplying in the provinces of north Africa and who knows what lowly level of culture some of their holders had attained? In a great city, however, there would usually be no question: bishops were literate and articulate, as we can see from the richest of all our sources, the letters preserved in Cyprian's correspondence, radiating in and out of Carthage in the 240s and 250s. Here, G. W. Clarke's admirable edition helps historians to see literacy and power at work in a major bishop's life.[36]

Like emperors or army-commanders, Cyprian used the convenience of literacy to enhance his power. His circumstances made it unusually welcome. During persecution, he withdrew into hiding and yet needed to maintain and exercise power in his Church while absent: letters allowed him to maintain authority. As the very process of his election showed, a bishop was both a local and a universal figure: here, literacy helped to maintain his links to the wider Christian network. By the 250s, it was the 'ancient custom' for other bishops to write 'letters of communion' to a new incumbent, on news of his valid appointment (Cyprian, *Epist.* 45). If an incumbent later fell into local suspicion or faction, these outside letters of welcome could be useful allies. Allies were particularly necessary because

---

[33] Feltoe (1904: 40–59).   [34] Euseb. *H.E.* 7.24.6.
[35] *Didascalia* (ed. R. H. Connolly) p. 30.   [36] Clarke (1984–7).

Christians' unique combination of cult, doctrine and clerical authority led them into feverish struggles for recognition by fellow-Christians against heretics, schismatics and outright 'usurpers'. The fever of these struggles naturally enlisted literacy to a degree unparalleled in any other ancient cult.

Here, Cyprian's evidence is marvellously illuminating: as Clarke aptly remarks, 'what we have almost entirely from Cyprian and mostly from his correspondents are not private messages but public letters, written and designed from the start to be encyclical in the full sense, to be circulated and to be copied freely'.[37] A good sample would be Epistles 45, 49, 55, 59 and 67. To uphold his own position, we find Cyprian sending an entire dossier of 13 of his previous letters across 'for information' to the Church in Rome (Epistle 20). From Carthage, he writes to Spain, Gaul, Rome and Cappadocia. Against the schismatic Novatian, he sends to Rome a list of all 'politically correct' bishops and their sees and the minuted opinions of 46 elders, who are all named and listed. The 'circulatory habit' was not peculiar to Cyprian or Carthage: Eusebius, *H.E.* 6.43.27 reveals Cornelius sending a similar dossier of approved names and views at this time from Antioch to Rome. Cyprian's Epistle 55 tells us how Epistle 30 (by Novatian) has been 'circulated throughout the entire world and reached every Church and all the Brethren'. Like scholars' offprints, selected letters kept authors' views known outside their local patch. During the flurry of petitions and rescripts which is amply documented in Fergus Millar's *Emperor in the Roman World*, a parallel flurry of much longer texts – epistles, martyr-stories, 'protracted demonstrations' and so forth – was circulating round the Mediterranean between Christians. The roots, as so often, lie right back in the New Testament: Paul, Coloss. 4.16, already requests a mutual exchange of epistles and their reading out before another Church. Among the Jews, we know of texts circulated in the context of festivals, to encourage them in the recipients' communities (2 Macc. 1.9, Greek Esther 11.1). What we do not have is more significant: we know of no contemporary analogies in the synagogues to the Christians' flurry of epistles.

In the year 256, our evidence shows Cyprian in one of his most active flurries. In that one year, the crisis over rebaptising heretics led to the summoning of three councils of bishops, culminating at Carthage on 1 September. It caused Cyprian to write and circulate tirelessly, as our Letters 69 to 75 still reveal so vividly. Copies of old letters accompanied each new one. Letter 70, from thirty-two bishops, accompanied Letters 71, 72, 73; Cyprian sent Letters 71 and 72 with Letter 73 to the bishop of Rome in 256 and then read out 72 (probably) and 73 (certainly) to bishops at the September meeting. Letter 75 is a translation into (markedly Cyprianic)

[37] Clarke (1984–7: I 8).

Latin of a helpful letter in Greek from Firmilian in Cappadocia: again, the point of translating it was to allow it to be circulated from Cyprian's seat.

Literacy, here, was being used for 'the organization of opinion', in Sir Ronald Syme's fine phrase for the era of Augustus. In Epistle 74, Cyprian circulates a text from another Christian, but only after annotating it with his own comments. At the September Council, the power of all this literacy then becomes evident: Cyprian reads out his major texts on the issue all over again; during the year support for him has crept up: at the Council, it reaches the total of 86 bishops, the minutes of whose opinions are all recorded and, naturally, circulated widely in Cyprian's cause.[38] This use of a Council and its itemised minutes leads on to the pressures exerted through literacy at major Christian Councils from Nicaea onwards.[39] Frequently, they are held (like Nicaea) under the forceful eye of the Emperor or his senior officials. The parading of signatures leads to the pressure to sign an agreed statement or to 'sign away', or abjure, a heresy. Literacy here sets the seal on coercion: we still have the great formulae of abjuration which Manichaeans were obliged to recite and then sign personally.[40]

Where there is such power in literary circulation and in signatures, there is ample scope for abuse of both. Cyprian found his authority dogged by fellow-Christians' forgeries: in Epistle 9, he is even reduced to appealing to the test of handwriting, to establish authenticity. While opponents tried to destabilise him by putting their words under his name, Cyprian had to use his own trusted 'postmen', like one of John le Carré's secret agents: he specially trusted Niceforus the acolyte, among others. One of the Readers, *lectores*, in his Church at Carthage was in charge of the distribution and publicising of Cyprian's authentic letters: visitors could thus be acquainted with Cyprian's views even when Cyprian himself was absent, avoiding arrest.[41]

These problems are as old as Christianity itself. Forgery would not have surprised the author of Revelation, nor would the art of suppression have surprised the author of the Third Johannine Epistle. There (3 John 9–10) we learn that Diotrephes, probably the head of a local church, had forcibly 'shut out' a letter from the Johannine circle and prevented it from being read out in Church: perhaps it is one of the very letters which our Churches now read from their Bible. In Epistle 43, we find Cyprian up to the same arts. The bishop decides what shall circulate and be heard in his Church: from this power it is an easy step to the rulings by bishops at the Church Council of Elvira, dated (I have suggested elsewhere) to the years soon after Constantine's conversion.[42] At Elvira, not only are bishops agreed to be

[38] Von Soden (1909: 247–307) gives the best text, as Marin (1989: 331–3) rightly emphasises.
[39] Williams (1987: 67–81, for a sample).
[40] Lieu (1983: 152–218, esp. gen. introd. at 152–5).
[41] Cyprian, *Epist.* 29; 49.3 with Clarke (1984–7: II 107).

able to check Christian visitors' written 'credentials' and to veto letters which may be brought from outsiders, as if from martyr-confessors: they are also to bear down heavily on letters for women. Women are not to write letters in their name or to receive 'friendly' ones, except jointly with their husbands. Here, bishops' power is even turned on the literate culture of the billet-doux.

These particular powers concern literacy as a means of circulation: if there had been a swifter means of circulation, some of them would have depended on that 'medium' instead. In Christian circles, however, literacy also drew on the power of an irreplaceable text: the scriptures, in which, it was accepted, God spoke to men. Quotations, therefore, from scriptures could both support and encourage a bishop's claims to rule, a power which is seen most clearly and deeply in Cyprian's writings. Frequently, Cyprian adduces texts about priests from the Old Testament to support the power of the bishop; the classic case is his Letter 3 to the elderly Rogatianus, who was under attack, not least for his advanced age. Cyprian adduces a cluster of texts about the High Priesthood among the Jews and a particular favourite, Deuteronomy 17, on the penalty to be paid for opposing a priest's authority. As S. L. Greenslade established, and M. F. Wiles has endorsed, these texts from the Old Testament are not simply the back-up for a position which Cyprian wished to argue anyway,[43] as such texts so often are in Paul's Epistles. They emerge as the origin of Cyprian's idea of the bishop's role in the first place. And yet, no text in Hebrew Scripture, nor even in the New Testament, had addressed the role of the single bishop as leader of the Church: Cyprian's views on a bishop's power are false at their very foundation.

Scriptural texts could also support a bishop's specific rulings as well as his general position. J. Gaudemet has recently surveyed explicit citations of scripture in the surviving acts of Church councils, from *c.* 300 to *c.* 600.[44] We might expect texts to be explicit supports, or origins, for many of the rulings issued here. Gaudemet rightly emphasises the incompleteness of the surviving acts and minutes and their variation from place to place, but the picture is unexpected. In our surviving texts, scripture is rarely cited for conduct in acts of councils from the Greek East: Gaudemet lists only six non-doctrinal citations in councils before 600. In north Africa and Gaul the figures are slightly higher. In general, scriptural texts are cited on points of doctrine, but rarely on points of conduct. Of course the scriptures influenced the minds, correspondence and positions of many of the

---

[42] *Canons of Elvira* 25, 58, 81 in Hefele (1907: I 221–64) with Lane Fox (1986: 664–5); note also Canon 52, against people who put 'libelli famosi' in churches.
[43] Greenslade (1943: 171–6); Wiles (1963: 146–7); in general Fahey (1971).
[44] Gaudemet (1985: 289–307, esp. 293–4 on the Greek East).

participants, but this influence happens not to be strong in our written records. Where it is strong, Gaudemet points to the role and presence of particular individuals at the Council.

In the third century, our slight evidence is more explicit. Elsewhere, I have remarked on the prominent role of scripture in the disciplinary rulings of Gregory, bishop of Pontus in the 250s.[45] In a fine study, M. Marin has recently examined the acts of Cyprian's Council of Carthage in September, 256.[46] The question of the baptism of heretics was doctrinal and we find quite a copious quotation of scripture by bishops whose views are minuted. Marin emphasises how many of their chosen texts are texts exploited by Cyprian in the controversy. He suggests that Cyprian's Biblical views are seen here at work, not that Cyprian is echoing an existing consensus in north Africa: the suggestion suits Gaudemet's point about the importance of individuals at later Councils. Bishop Cyprian, it seems, drew on sacred literacy to build up a consensus which could then be paraded against opponents.

There was a further advantage. In the Bible, God spoke to Christian readers: as Cyprian reminded Donatus, 'in prayer you speak to God; God speaks with you when you read the scriptures'.[47] Citation of Biblical texts took the personal edge from a bishop's rulings: Augustine is explicit, here. 'If threats are made, let them be made from the Scriptures, threatening future retribution, that it should not be ourselves who are feared in our personal power, but God in our words.'[48] We are back with the advantage of impersonality which a sacred text also gave to Christian visionaries. Bishops did not eat it, but they certainly quarried it for effective weapons.

III

Most Christians were not bishops or visionaries and went to considerable pains to avoid being martyrs: were there connections between literacy and power for them too? Here, the most significant connections are those between power and 'sacred literacy', not the literacy of everyday convenience. In their textual community, Christians had texts of God's word, and nothing except expense and bother prevented them from owning or studying copies for themselves. If we accept the ingenious reckoning of T. C. Skeat, a standard papyrus-roll of twenty sheets would cost about $1\frac{1}{2}$ drachmas in the second century: 'it follows that books in the ancient world were not very expensive, at least for the sort of people likely to need them'.[49]

For a start, many people believed that there was an inherent power in

---

[45] Lane Fox (1986: 539–43).   [46] Marin (1989: 329–59).
[47] Cyprian, *Ad Donatum* 15.1.   [48] Augustine, *Epist.* 22.5.
[49] Skeat (1982: 172); I quote Skeat again, in Lewis (1989: 41).

holy words. Not every Christian would have seen them in the same light, but many did believe that words from scripture, written or recited, had power against demons or in rites of exorcism.[50] Among theologians, Origen remarks (*Homilies* 20.1, on Joshua) that 'just as pagans have incantations with a healing or effective power, so much the more, when we recite scripture, even if we do not understand it, the angels will be present for us, *velut carmine quodam invitati*'. Others did not even believe that the words had to be recited: we happen to know from John Chrysostom that women and children in Antioch in the later fourth century might wear a small codex of a Gospel round their necks for its protective powers.[51] The most powerful piece of Christian literacy, in this sense, was the (fake) letter to King Abgar of Edessa, written as if from Jesus himself.[52] In the late fourth century, its text acquired a further sentence: 'Your city shall be blessed and no enemy shall ever be master of it.' By the late fifth century, it had been inscribed on Edessa's wall, like a security alarm. It circulated to other cities, Ephesus, Philippi and so forth, but like other security alarms it failed to work: Edessa fell several times to invaders, lastly to the Arabs in 638.

Those who wore a tiny codex must have believed that it had holy power, but it does not seem that this belief was universal. John Chrysostom did also know of Christians who thought that they must wash after handling a text of scripture or abstain from sex before touching God's word: he regards them as wrongly influenced by Jews or as a misinformed minority.[53] Earlier in the fourth century, much fuss was made in north Africa against those who 'handed over' scriptures to the authorities during persecution: it was not, however, that the physical objects themselves were holy, in the rabbinic sense that they polluted the hands which touched them, but rather that the contents were God's words and the handing-over was a symbolic betrayal. The key point here is that although texts were surrendered in the Greek East too, the issue of 'handing over' was never even raised there as an act of sacrilege.[54]

Among potential converts, holy texts did have power too but not quite the power of a holy charm or object. None of the earliest surviving Christian texts on papyrus is a fine book or work of art.[55] The scrolls of scripture in a synagogue must have seemed much more impressive; indeed, R. L. Wilken has suggested that their special aura may have been one reason why Christians in Antioch continued to be drawn to attend Jewish worship on a sabbath.[56] Hard evidence for the appeal of a fine book can be found not in Antioch but rather earlier when followers of Mani began to

[50] Thraede (1969: 65–105, esp. 65 on the use of the Creed and the 'Rule of Faith' in exorcism).
[51] Joh. Chrys. *Hom.* 72.703B.   [52] Segal (1970: 73–5).   [53] Wilken (1983: 73–83).
[54] De Sainte Croix (1954: 84).   [55] Roberts (1979: 14–25).
[56] Wilken (1983: 80–3).

preach his new Gospel of Light in the eastern Roman provinces from the 250s onwards.[57] Professional scribes and portrait painters accompanied Mani's missionaries in order to illustrate their texts. The writing was on parchment; the bindings were very fine and the pictures derived from Mani's own 'Picture Book'. These fine folios were intended to be impressive to hearers and non-readers and we can catch a hint of their impact in comments by Augustine, a former convert to their new Gospel. During the third century, Christian teachers had no such folio art-books, although Origen is implied by Eusebius to have worried about some of his own texts' appearance.[58] A rich patron gave him trained calligraphers and shorthand secretaries to work on the texts of his scriptural commentaries. Books on God's book it seems, should be good-looking books, for His sake, probably, rather than for the sake of winning readers. The gender of Origen's copyists is worth noting: the shorthand secretaries were male, but the calligraphers were young ladies, 'the earliest known instance of woman's invasion of the book trade, and it must be regretfully recorded that it set a precedent hardly taken up again before the nineteenth century'.[59]

Like Protestants' texts in Europe just after the Reformation,[60] Mani's books existed to be seen, not merely to be read: among the Christians, was their sacred literacy more often read or heard? One power of scripture might be that it made more people learn to read in order to know God's word. Christianity has certainly had this role in areas of its long history, especially in Sweden during the seventeenth and eighteenth centuries: in 1707, Defoe describes the consequences in Scotland. 'For a whole church full of people, not one shall be seen without a Bible ... if you shut your eyes when the minister names any text of Scripture you shall hear a little rustling noise over the whole place...'[61] His eye-witness impression has been upheld by social historians, not least by using the testimony of Scottish Christians interrogated for religious deviance in the early 1740s: personal statements of the 'Cambuslang revivalists' about Christianity's role in teaching them to read are direct and unsophisticated.[62] 'By reading much and oft in it when I hear passages of it cited as I am hearing sermons I can now turn to them. And O how wonderful is the change now with me.'

Among the early Christians, the 'little rustling noise' of books, at least, has been championed by C. H. Roberts and T. C. Skeat as a significant Christian innovation.[63] In their view, Christians actually pioneered and influenced the spread of a change in book production, from cumbersome

[57] Lieu (1985: 139–40); Augustine, *Contra Faust.* 13.6.   [58] Euseb. *H.E.* 6.23.2.
[59] Roberts (1963: 15–16).
[60] Parker (1992: 64, with the Catholic Counter-Reformation's retort, 74).
[61] Smout (1982: 123).
[62] Smout (1982: 114–27): I quote the unique testimony, cited on his p. 126.
[63] Roberts and Skeat (1983).

scrolls to convenient codices (or books), but this theory can no longer be taken on trust: much depends on the open question of the dating of the earliest surviving Christian codices, recently cast into doubt again.[64] Christians perhaps joined a fashion which was already spreading among pagans and applied it to their scriptures (most probably for ease of reference to particular passages): the evidence is still almost wholly from Egypt and here, too, we must be wary of generalising it.[65]

None the less, the codex was indeed adopted and as anyone could own a text of scripture, the rustle of pages could, in theory, have become widespread. According to Harnack, the Church became 'the elementary schoolmistress of the Greeks and Romans',[66] but W. V. Harris has rightly attacked the extreme interpretation that Christianity 'promoted literacy' widely.[67] There was no early Christian 'Church Law,' like the law which linked Christian membership and reading ability in Sweden in 1686.[68] To Harris's discussion, we might add a little evidence for Christians starting up 'primary schools', but it is either late (Symeon the Mountaineer, in John of Ephesus' *Lives*, c. 550) or legendary (a *Life of Lucian of Antioch*, purporting to refer to c. 310).[69] Harnack's remark, however, can be taken in a weaker sense: sacred literacy was not altogether powerless over ordinary Christians' abilities.

Most of the evidence for keen Christian teachers or readers belongs in settings where literacy would be a social accomplishment anyway. However, we should allow for the special impetus which 'sacred literacy' gave such people. Harnack's fine collection of the evidence can be plundered for examples. Eusebius honours Pamphilus, the scholar and eventual martyr, whom he describes as copying and distributing texts of the scriptures to interested parties: according to Jerome, he gave out 'many codices' not only to men but to women too 'whom he had seen to be dedicated to reading' (women suspiciously after Jerome's heart, however).[70] The reading of scripture in the family is a practice with a long history of exhortation in our texts, going right back to Clement's *Paedagogus* (c. 200).[71] Mothers and fathers could plainly be important, as they must have been for literate Jewish children: in 2 Tim. 3.15 Timothy is said to have had knowledge of the scriptures since childhood and if this is true, he presumably owed it to his mother, a Jewish woman (Acts 16.1); according to Eusebius, Origen's father made him learn daily 'saying lessons' from the

---

[64] Van Haelst (1989: 13–35); MacCormick (1989: 150–8).
[65] Den Boeft and Bremmer (1991: 116–17) emphasise *Acts of the Scillitan Martyrs* 12, where the 'capsa' in this north African court-room ought to mean a circular holder, for rolls, therefore, not codices.   [66] Harnack (1912: 85).   [67] Harris (1989: 285–322).
[68] Johansson (1981: 165).
[69] Lane Fox (1986: 288–9, with refs.); Eyice and Noret (1973: 373–4).
[70] Jerome, *Adv. Rufin.* 1.9.   [71] Harnack (1912: 56–63, 122–34).

scriptures.[72] Domestic relations were not always so harmonious. The most thought-provoking examples are the girls from Thessalonica whose martyrdom occurred in the 'Great Persecution'. They had their own cache of Christian texts and confessed to be afraid when reading and studying scriptures at night 'because of their parents'. One of the girls, Irene, had Christian 'parchments, books, tablets, codices and pages' although she denied that they were her own.[73] Their origin was never revealed but she did acknowledge them after being caught 'in possession' by the authorities.

The girl martyrs of Thessalonica would presumably have been basically literate by upbringing, but Christianity turned them into habitual readers: without its sacred literacy, these girls would not otherwise have been reading after 'lights out' at home. This power would be even more effective outside the Greek cultural areas in which the Christians' sacred texts arose. The main point of a translation is to reach people who cannot otherwise join in: the very style of 'Christian Latin' has been interpreted as a simpler literate language in which people who were not habitually literate would have found it easier to participate.[74] In Egypt, the passage of Christian texts and teaching into Coptic dealt the final death-blow to the older Egyptian scripts. 'The simpler Coptic writing and its adoption consigned the whole world of pagan Egyptian literature, lore and records to oblivion. Christian Egypt shut the door upon the past and threw away the key which was not to be recovered till the nineteenth century.'[75] In Syriac, Christianity did not create a literature from nothing, but it did vastly increase what was available, not least by its own translations of scripture, commentaries and so forth. From the fourth century onwards, the Christians' sacred literacy can sometimes be seen inventing a written language and a script for the first time, among Ethiopians or Slavs or Goths.[76] In the mid-fourth century the Goths were given the first ever book to be written in Gothic: it was the work of the heroic Ulfilas, their Christian evangelist, and some of its later textual development can be followed in papyrus-fragments and that great survivor among early scripture-books, the purple Codex which is now in Uppsala.[77]

The survival of several papyri of the Gothic Bible might suggest that individual Goths came to acquire and study their own copies, but here we need to be cautious. Ulfila's initiative must have been heard much more widely than it was ever read in private: our texts may all have been copies for reading in Church. Even in user-friendly Christian Latin, the importance of listening greatly outweighed reading. During the Great Persecution, the authorities were told to hunt out texts of Christian scriptures and at Cirta in

[72] Euseb. *H.E.* 6.2.8.
[73] *The Martyrdom of Agapê, Irenê and Chionê*, in H. Musurillo, *Acts of the Christian Martyrs* (Oxford, 1972) 5.1.   [74] Brown (1968: 90).   [75] Barns (1978: 20).
[76] Metzger (1977: 215–23, 375, 394–404).   [77] Friedrichsen (1926, 1939, 1961).

north Africa we have marvellous evidence of the results.[78] Thirty-seven different codices are shown to have been 'brought out' by various Christians and handed over for destruction, but in each case, the Christian is a *lector*, or Reader, in the Church's hierarchy. Then, too, Readers were special people, but remarkably, among Christians, Readers might be little boys. As E. Peterson showed, their attested ages in epitaphs include examples from 5 to 18: in the early Church, the holy innocence which Christians nowadays ascribe to choirboys rested on boys who were reading God's word aloud to their audience.[79] In Cyprian's Letters, there are hints that Readers were also involved in teaching candidates for baptism: one reason would be that some of the candidates did not read for themselves, another that they lacked the necessary texts (the large size of lettering in some of our Christian codices has been explained as a device to help Readers).[80] However, there is no need to assume that Readers could always write: indeed, there is plain evidence, and a mass of comparative case-studies, to imply that they might not. Much has been made recently of Ammonius, the Church Reader in Egypt, known in a papyrus of the year 304, who could not even write his own name.[81] In Cyprian's Letter 38, we find another illiterate being promoted up to the rank of Reader. Recent scholars have tried to explain these sources by ingenious further conjectures, but the obvious answer is right: readers, even the chosen Readers in a Church, could not necessarily write, as writing was a separate skill. Where we have large samples of evidence, in eighteenth-century Sweden for instance, this fact is taken for granted: the records of the Cambuslang Christians, interrogated in Scotland in the 1740s, led T. C. Smout to the conclusion that 'reading and writing are no more closely or necessarily associated than horses and carriages or lovers and marriages'.[82] It was no different in the early Church.

In Jesus' Judaea, people honoured scribes; in the early Churches they had a special rank for Readers. What we have, then, is a cult with texts of the highest authority, the 'word of God', none the less fitting into the abiding pattern of all culture in antiquity: much more was heard and circulated orally than was ever read in private by individuals. This conclusion need not imply a very limited awareness of the contents of scripture among individual Christians. Individual texts and competent readers may have been scarce, but a single book can always be shared more

---

[78] *Gesta apud Zenophilum*, ed. C. Ziwsa (CSEL XXVI, Optatus, Vienna, 1893) 187–8: there, Readers also practise secular trades, naturally enough.
[79] Peterson (1934: 437–42); Paoli-Lafaye (1986: 59–74, esp. 63–4 on the verb 'resonare' and musical metaphors applied to Readers); at ibid. 67–70, she notes that a Reader should not remarry a second time.   [80] Turner (1977: 84–5).
[81] Most recently, Wipszycka (1983: 117) and Clarke (1984: 103), on *P. Oxy.* 33.2673; earlier, Roberts (1979: 65). All are misled.   [82] Smout (1982: 121).

widely, like a weekly magazine, and one reader can suffice for a much larger audience. In another 'textual community', the Cathars in the village of Montaillou, we have detailed evidence of the travels of books and complex information by word of mouth round the village: Le Roy Ladurie, however, reckons that only 4 people were literate in a community of 250.[83] In the mid-third century, we might think of Nepos' book on the millennium in this light: it circulated among the villages of the Arsinoite nome in Egypt and caused such misplaced interest that bishop Dionysius had to go and harangue its audience for three whole days to win them back to sound opinion.[84] Yet very few people will have read it.

In the absence of personal reading, we must allow for the power of sacred literacy on Christians' other senses. They may not have read and rustled the pages of codices in Church, but they certainly sang with gusto. In this light van der Meer's fine presentation of Augustine's audience in Hippo becomes intelligible.[85] Their participation was every bit as noisy as a jury's in classical Athens: they acclaimed, applauded and interrupted their preacher and beat their breasts in a great rumble of fists at the mention of deadly sins like adultery. However, they also applauded, or even capped, concealed quotations from a Psalm in a sermon: in Oea, they shouted out 'Wrong!' when the New Jerome Bible made Jonah sleep under ivy, not a gourd (they knew the gourd, surely, from seeing it so often in early Christian art, rather than from minute study of the Biblical book).[86] In Hippo, there may have been no singing in Church before the 390s, and even after its introduction people sang refrains to solo psalm-singers or followed antiphonally-led chanting.[87] None the less, it was surely this singing which formed the audience's ear for scriptural allusions. Sung words stuck, as Arius and Augustine knew, authors of doctrinal songs for popular usage, like their heirs in Protestant Europe, apostles of the Reformation. So did symbols and stories which were seen, like Jonah's traditional gourd. Unlike pagan worshippers (except Mithraists), by the fourth century Christians were sitting in Churches decorated with symbolic or narrative scenes from Scripture. Like some of the scriptural scenes in synagogues' mosaics or on the walls of Dura-Europus, important Christian figures were captioned in user-friendly lettering:[88] theologically positive poems were sometimes added by gifted bishops.[89] The relative claims of text and image were to become one of the liveliest topics in later Christian theology,[90] but already

---

[83] Le Roy Ladurie (1982: 358 n.2 and on 352), 'Précieux ils sont, ces livres, car presque personne n'y touche.'   [84] Euseb. *H.E.* 7.24.6.   [85] Van der Meer (1961: 339–42).
[86] Augustine, *Epist.* 71.3, 75.6.
[87] Van der Meer (1961: 325–37, with 326 nn. 37–8).
[88] Pietri (1985: 194–8); Monfrin (1985: 233–9).
[89] Prudentius, *Dittochaei* 1–49; Paulinus of Nola, *Epist.* 32, for examples.
[90] McKitterick (1990b: 297–318) and others in McKitterick (1990a).

in the earlier congregations, simply-captioned images helped to fix scenes from a story in a seated audience's mind.

The Christians' sacred literacy was supremely authoritative and seriously powerful in setting Christians' ideals of conduct; however, much more was known through listening, singing, and looking than through personal textual study: sacred texts encouraged some readers to read rather more, but they did not make ordinary Christians into readers in the first place. If early Christian texts had had no more power than this summary suggests, Christianity would bear out the truth that a new force for literacy has to fit into the 'cultural ancestry' of its recipients. But the picture is not quite so simple.

If the general practice of Christians stood in an inverse relation to the exhortations written on it, scriptural study must have ranked almost as low in daily life as sexual fidelity. The Church order, wrongly ascribed to Hippolytus and datable c. 200, already urges Christians to study scripture daily.[91] Thereafter the barrage of encouragement continues, urging scripture on married couples and families, before and after meals, before the servants and at bedtime. However, in life's hierarchy scripture often seemed awfully dull: the 'taedium verbi divini' was a complaint acknowledged by Origen;[92] women might prefer to read light literature in Church; 'Which of you ever takes up a Christian book at home?' protested John Chrysostom to his hearers. 'You have dice in most homes, but not books.[93] Harnack judged that exhortations to read the Bible in the family are even rarer in texts from the Latin West.[94] Certainly, our best later evidence bears him out: in the early sixth century, Caesarius, bishop of Arles from 503 to 543, was a tireless circulator of sermons and texts, excelling even Cyprian and leaving a lasting mark on the complex manuscript tradition of his own writings. However, he knows he is fighting an uphill battle: he has to exhort his Christians firmly to read the Scriptures aloud to servants and families because otherwise they will have no idea of the divine word.[95] No doubt they resisted: when Caesarius began to preach in Church after the lessons from Scripture had been read, we find him locking the door to stop his audience from leaving early.[96]

Where the majority backslide, there is scope for what I have elsewhere described as Christian 'over-achievement'. Literacy joins virginity, martyrdom and poverty on that new and important scale, the double standard between good and less-than-ordinary practice. 'I am a man of business', John

[91] Hippolytus, *Trad.* 36.1 (ed. G. Dix and H. Chadwick 1968); also 35.2.
[92] Harnack (1912: 69 n. 2) lists several such passages.
[93] Joh. Chrys., *Hom. in Johann.* 32.   [94] Harnack (1912: 94).
[95] Morin (1939–40: 481–6); note esp. Caesarius, *Sermo* 2.6 (esp. 6.3), 7 (esp. 7.4), 8 (esp. 8.2) and 73.1–2.   [96] *Vita Caesarii* (ed. G. Morin 1942) 27.

Chrysostom imagines a protestor telling him; 'it is not my trade to read the Bible ... that is the business of people who have renounced the world and devoted themselves to a lonely life on mountain tops.' Demands to read more met a brisk answer: 'We are not monks.'[97]

It was, above all, among those who withdrew to be perfect that literacy gained a new power. The most explicit early text is the Rule for the monastic communities of Pachomius' followers: the Rule is perhaps not Pachomius' own formulation but it is true to his heirs' aspirations.[98] When a candidate for a monastery has heard and agreed to the Rule

they shall give him twenty Psalms or two of the Apostles' epistles or some other part of Scripture. And if he is illiterate he shall go at the first, third and sixth hours to someone who can teach and has been appointed for him. He shall stand before him and learn very studiously and with all gratitude. The fundamentals of a syllable, the verbs and nouns shall be written for him and even if he does not want to, he shall be compelled to read. (Rule 139)

There shall be nobody whatever in the monastery who does not learn to read and does not memorise something of the Scriptures, at least the Gospels and Psalter. (Rule 140)

As a result, we find that parts of Scripture are known (in Greek) as the 'off-by-hearts';[99] the borrowing and return of the community's texts is regulated in accompanying 'Library Rules'; hours of the day are set aside for textual recitation and that act of monastic 'meditatio' whose scope has been well emphasised in studies by H. Bacht.[100] As he points out, the rule of Horsiesios, one of Pachomius' successors, is a living witness to this meditative routine. Apart from its stress on reading and pondering scripture, its own language is shot through with scriptural allusions, absorbed by its author.

Monastic meditation, memorising and copying spread from the early Pachomian foundations through the rules of other communities;[101] communities of women followed the same path. 'Pale, hollow-eyed and thin-faced,' Evagrius urges in his important *Sentences To a Virgin*, 'virgins must rise at dawn and read the scriptures.'[102] The growth of monasteries is not just a chapter in the changing history of Body and Society: it picks up yet another thread first exemplified by Origen and his ideals.[103] Thanks to Christian perfectionism, the map became dotted with something quite new:

[97] Harnack (1912: 118, for sources).
[98] *Pachomian Koinonia* (transl. A. Veilleux, 1981) II 166.
[99] Veilleux (1968: 309–12).
[100] Bacht (1972: 244–64); *Pachomian Koinonia* (transl. A. Veilleux, 1981) II 202.
[101] De Vogüé (1977: VII 334–59).
[102] Evagrius, *Sent. ad Virginem* 4, with Elm (1991: 97–120).
[103] Vessey (1988), with further material for the Latin West; Koenen (1974: 347 on monks as copyists).

arsenals of sexually frustrated readers, stretching from Egypt to the coasts of Scotland.

In their daily company the written word had its widest and deepest power. W. V. Harris has recently doubted the 'stupendous feats of memory about which Christian authors had fantasies';[104] he is too sceptical. Already in Rome, Novatian (*c.* 250) had attacked those Christians who could not recall Scripture but who had memorised the form and breeding of every racehorse in the games.[105] In an oral culture, such feats are not rare, and Christian perfectionists soon applied them to learning the word of God. Harris doubts the story of Blind John from Egypt who memorised and recited whole books of scripture, according to Eusebius, *Martyrs of Palestine* 13.6–8, but the key point is that Eusebius himself had seen him, in amazement; he is speaking from his own experience, having watched while the blind man recited in a Church before an audience of sharp-eyed Christians. It even seems that perfectionists set new standards for the clergy: in a Coptic papyrus, of the early fifth century, we find the bishop in Oxyrhynchus defining that a Deacon must learn to recite one Gospel, 25 Psalms and 2 Epistles while an Elder should also manage the books of Deuteronomy, Proverbs and Isaiah.[106] Literacy, here, connects with spiritual power, but again, the connection depends on the Christian belief that in their text, they listen to the word of God. Here, too, the emphasis is on memory and recitation, oral arts although a text lies behind them.

Among ordinary Christians, I have emphasised the power of their sacred texts against demons and invaders; their symbolic power for converts and lay members; their power in oral and visual culture more often than in individual, close reading. Their most conspicuous power, however, was among Christians who were not content to be ordinary. Those who memorised, read and meditated did not therefore wield power over fellow-Christians: their literacy connected with prestige, not power, with spiritual merit which was won (they believed) before God. By meditating on scripture, they drew nearer to His presence and His will. It took the distinctive institution of the monastic community to ensure that this spiritual prestige did not burst out into individual power and become disruptive.

---

[104] Harris (1989: 301).

[105] Novat. *De Spectaculis* 5.3–4.

[106] Rossi (1887: 87–8), cited by Wipszycka (1984: 291 n. 23), with her important pages 291–4 on monastic literacy in the seventh and eighth centuries; Merkelbach (1980: 291–4) notes 17 'analphabetisch' monastic leaders at the Council of Constantinople in 536, but does not consider that they may have been readers, though not writers.

10   Greek and Syriac in Late Antique Syria

S. P. Brock

Language and geography

In the Eastern Roman Empire the language of political power was predominantly Greek, although Latin long retained a presence in the army and in the law.[1] In Ptolemaic Egypt Greek had encountered a language of former political power, which nevertheless retained great cultural prestige; how Egyptian Demotic fared in this encounter has been discussed by Ray and Thompson in earlier chapters (chs. 4 and 5). What happened when Greek met with another language, Aramaic, that had once served alien masters – the Achaemenids – as the language of power in the Near East? The case of Aramaic happens to be more complicated, thanks to the variety of different written dialects in use in different areas and in different times; accordingly, for practical reasons, discussion will be confined to the interaction of Greek with the Edessene dialect of Aramaic, known today as Syriac, which in the second and third centuries AD became the literary language of Aramaic-speaking Christians both inside and outside the Roman Empire.

Although Aramaic had been eclipsed during the Hellenistic period, the century or so either side of the turn of the Christian era witnessed the emergence, around the arc of the Fertile Crescent, of a number of written local Aramaic dialects, Nabataean, Palmyrene, Syriac and Hatran, each possessing its own distinctive script. These written dialects, known almost exclusively (except in the case of Syriac) from inscriptions, witness to the fact that Aramaic continued to be spoken very widely outside the Hellenised towns; generally described as ἡ Σύρων φωνή, 'the language of the Syrians', it was employed, we are told by Theodoret,[2] by the Osrhoenoi, Syroi, Euphratesioi, Palestinoi and Phoinikes, though, he adds, there was considerable difference in dialect. The question of who spoke or wrote which language, Greek or Aramaic, and where, is a complex one, and the

---

[1] An illuminating discussion of the gradual displacement of Latin by Greek as the language of the state is given by Dagron (1969). It is significant that almost all Latin words taken over into Syriac come by way of Greek.   [2] Theodoret, *Questiones in Librum Judicum* 19.

evidence is scattered and often elusive. Though our primary concern here is with written Aramaic in the Edessene (Syriac) dialect, it will be necessary first to look at the more general situation as regards spoken Aramaic.

A number of references in John Chrysostom's writings[3] indicate that the demarcation between spoken Greek and spoken Aramaic is essentially provided by the distinction between *polis* and *chora*.[4] Even in the *polis*, however, Aramaic was clearly the normal language of the lower classes.[5] It is in fact likely that large numbers of people, especially in the towns, will have been bilingual, with in most cases Aramaic as the mother tongue; no more tangible witness to this situation can be found than the inscriptions of Palmyra, where many – including the Tariff of AD 137 – are bilingual. For the fourth century, Theodoret offers a number of incidental sidelights on the question in his *Historia Philothea*. Thus the hermit Macedonius, who came from outside Antioch, spoke only Aramaic, and so needed an interpreter in order to intercede with the *strategoi* on behalf of the people after the episode of the statues.[6] Abraham of Cyrrhus, who was even summoned for an audience by the emperor, and who ended up as bishop of Harran, likewise knew no Greek.[7] On the other hand, another hermit, Aphraates, 'knew a few phrases in Greek', and preached in Antioch in a 'semi-barbarous Greek'.[8] Even those who had enjoyed a Greek education and become skilled rhetors, such as the preacher Severian of Gabala, might sometimes betray their mother tongue by their strong Aramaic accent.[9]

Severian will have belonged to the richer Aramaic-speaking families who could afford to give their children a Greek rhetorical education, a *sine qua non* for anyone who aspired to any kind of preferment in government service.[10] It is important to realise that not everyone had aspirations in this way, and the fifth-century Syriac poet known as Isaac of Antioch recounts for his audience the miseries endured by the sons of ambitious parents of this sort: 'The children of the female slaves have a more enjoyable time in the house of their masters, acting as though they were the heirs: their master has gone off on his wandering travels in search of education – and he has a hard time of it!', while his mother is left 'as though she had become

[3] *Patrologia Graeca* 49, col. 188: the country people who come into Antioch for festivals 'have a different language from us, but share the same faith'; compare also *Patrologia Graeca* 50, col. 646. In general, see Bardy (1968: 18–31), Bowersock (1990: 29–40) and Poggi (1990).
[4] For a discussion of the general background, see Kennedy and Liebeschuetz (1988).
[5] Libanius, *Oratio* 42.31 (tinkers).   [6] Theodoret, *Historia Religiosa* 13.7.
[7] Theodoret, *Historia Religiosa* 17.9. Later it was rare for a bishop not to speak Greek; thus, at the Council of Chalcedon Uranius bishop of Himeria needed (or maybe, preferred) to speak through an interpreter (a priest from Edessa): *Acta Conciliorum Oecumenicorum* II 1, pp. 98–9.   [8] Theodoret, *Historia Religiosa* 8.2.
[9] Socrates, *Historia Ecclesiastica* 6.1.   [10] See Heather, chapter 12, below.

barren'.[11] It is this pull between the attractions of the language of political power, on the one hand, and the language of cultural prestige (in our case, Syriac), on the other, that will chiefly occupy us below, but before turning to the question of which literary language people chose to use, the evidence of the use of Greek and Syriac in documents and inscriptions requires brief consideration.

Particularly interesting witness to literacy in the two languages in Osrhoene is provided by a group of documents for the most part dating from the 240s. In the case of *Dura Parchment* 28, written in Edessa on 9 May 243, we have a Deed of sale, by Aurelia Mat-Tar'ata, of a slave girl. The document is written by a professional scribe in Syriac, with the husband adding in his own hand a declaration 'that I have written on behalf of Aurelia Mat-Tar'ata, my wife, because she is illiterate'. The witnesses all sign in Syriac – with two exceptions, both officials of the Colonia, Aurelius Mannos ὁ ἐπὶ τοῦ ἱεροῦ καὶ τοῦ πολιτικοῦ and Abgar the *strategos* (their status is significantly also given in Syriac).[12]

The cache of two Syriac parchments and 17 Greek parchments and papyri, known as *P. Mesopotamia*, linked with a place called Beth Phouria in Osrhoene, is especially intriguing. Among the Greek documents[13] it is not surprising that the five petitions addressed to Roman functionaries should be in Greek, and there is no doubt that these were written by professional scribes; in two cases the petitioner, Abdisauta, a *bouleutes* of Neapolis, has provided a subscription in Syriac. What is unexpected is the presence of two private letters[14] and ten private documents (e.g. buying and selling of slaves) in Greek; in the case of the latter, several have Syriac subscriptions, and for two documents the five witnesses all sign in Syriac. One wonders what circumstances led to *P. Mesopotamia* 6–7, the sale by a woman[15] of a slave girl dated 6 November 249, being written in Greek in Marcoupolis (otherwise unknown), whereas *P. Dura* 28, written in Edessa, capital of Osrhoene, six years earlier, is in Syriac: maybe the reason lies in the fact that Marcoupolis (known in the Syriac documents as 'New Town') was a recent foundation connected with the suppression of Edessa's native dynasty and its transformation into a colonia. Syriac, however, is also evidenced in Marcoupolis / New Town by the presence of two parchment documents in that language, a transfer of debt dated 28 December 240, and

---

[11] *Carmen* 31, ed. G. Bickell in *S. Isaaci Antiocheni Doctoris Syrorum Opera Omnia* (Giessen, 1873–7) II 106.   [12] Photographs in Bellinger and Welles (1935).

[13] See Feissel and Gascou (1989).

[14] Like the petitions, these are on papyrus; it would seem that papyrus in Osrhoene is a writing material introduced by the Roman administration, whereas the local practice was to write on skin.

[15] Her brother subscribes in Syriac on her behalf, since she is illiterate.

a lease of land dated 1 September 242;[16] both documents are written by a professional scribe who also gives his name, perhaps an indication that Syriac scribes enjoyed a higher status than their Greek counterparts.

The new evidence provided by *P. Mesopotamia* indicates that the linguistic situation was more complicated than the picture suggested by the incidence of inscriptions in Greek and in Syriac: here the Euphrates serves as an effective dividing line,[17] and Greek inscriptions east of the river, in Osrhoene, are rare (and what does exist normally reflects the Roman administration in some way), while Syriac ones west of it are non-existent until the very end of the fourth century, when there is a bilingual from the Jebel Barisha:[18] all the early Syriac inscriptions come from east of the Euphrates, though the earliest one, dated AD 6, happens to be from Birecik, on the river. It is only in the sixth century that Syriac starts to appear much more frequently to the west of the Euphrates (mostly confined to northern Syria).

The absence of early Syriac inscriptions from the area west of the Euphrates happens to fit in well with the early history of Syriac literature, for it is only in the first half of the fifth century that Syriac authors living to the west of the river emerge.[19]

Greek and Syriac: the literary level

References to 'barbaric Syriac' in Greek writers should not mislead one into thinking that literature in Syriac was undeveloped or uncouth. On the contrary, it was a literary language which could boast writers of wide fame, men like Bardaisan (died 222) and the poet Ephrem (died 373). Nor was the movement of translation in a single direction, from Greek into Syriac; especially in the fourth and fifth centuries, it seems, a number of works by Syriac authors were translated into Greek,[20] and we learn from a fragment by Theodore of Mopsuestia that Flavian bishop of Antioch and Diodore bishop of Tarsus had Syriac antiphonal liturgical poetry translated into Greek.[21] Indeed, so great was the prestige of Syriac poetry in the fifth century that this posed a source of embarrassment for Greek cultural chauvinism, which could not bear to see literary excellence issuing from

---

[16] See Teixidor (1990) and Brock (1991).

[17] Further south, however, Palmyrene flourishes this side of the river (but disappears shortly after 272). For Aramaic in the Hauran, see Contini (1987).

[18] Babisqa, *Inscriptions grecques et latines de la Syrie* II 555.

[19] Notably Balai, associated with Chalcis/Qenneshrin, and John the Solitary, associated with Apamea; on the latter, see below. On the pre-Constantinian period, see especially Millar (1971: 2–5) and (1987: 159–62).

[20] Notably the *Liber Legum Regionum*, from the school of Bardaisan, various works by Ephrem, and several hagiographical texts (for which see Peeters (1950)).

[21] Theodore of Mopsuestia *apud* Niketas Akominatos, *Patrologia Graeca* 139, col. 1390C.

barbary: the neat way round this problem was to claim that Syriac verse form was actually derived from Greek![22]

What is important to realise in this connection is that we are dealing with two literary cultures, each with its own prestige, and that Syriac literary culture had behind it its own educational system, of which the best-known witness is provided by the 'Persian School' at Edessa,[23] which in due course, after its suppression by Zeno in 489, transmitted a synthesis of Syriac and Greek theological tradition to Nisibis, across the border in the Sasanian Empire, and thus to the Church of the East in general. Nor was Syriac solely a language of Christianity, for there once existed Manichaean and pagan literature written in it, but of this only diminutive relics survive. Greek, then, although it was undoubtedly the language of power in the eastern provinces of the Roman Empire, was by no means the sole language of prestige, and it is this sense of prestige that had been acquired by Syriac, *qua* literary language, by the late fourth century that needs to be remembered when we consider the question of which language authors from bilingual areas choose to adopt for their writing.

It was undoubtedly the case that large numbers of people in Syria in Late Antiquity were bilingual in Greek and Aramaic;[24] what is more difficult to establish is whether some of the more educated among these could also be described as bi-cultural, that is to say, people who felt at home in both Greek and Syriac literary cultures. The evidence is tantalisingly elusive, and for the most part has to be extracted from those who also wrote, and so it is to these that we now turn.

At the outset we can separate out two basic categories, those whose mother tongue is Greek, and those whose mother tongue is some form of Aramaic. In the former case, whether or not some knowledge of Aramaic is present, Greek will be the language of writing as a matter of course. Typical of such authors will be John Chrysostom, whose father was a *stratelates*, and who learnt his rhetoric from Libanius and philosophy from Andragathius;[25] in his case, it seems likely that he knew little or no Aramaic. Much more interesting is the second category, those whose mother tongue was some dialect of Aramaic, and it is likely that this will have been much the larger category, and the majority of such people will have had at least some knowledge of Greek, while some will have come

[22] Sozomen, *Historia Ecclesiastica* 3.16, on which see Brock (1985).
[23] Vööbus (1965) may overestimate the role played by philosophy and medicine in the curriculum in the fifth century.
[24] Thus Schmitt (1980: 201) describes the situation as one of 'Diglossie'.
[25] Sozomen, *Historia Ecclesiastica* 8.2; for his father: Palladius, *Dialogue* 5. Note that the *strategoi* who spoke with hermit Macedonius needed an interpreter, Theodoret, *Historia Religiosa* 13.7.

from strongly Hellenised families. Here it will be helpful to consider briefly a few case histories, differentiating between four different sub-categories: (1) those who write in Greek; (2) those who write in both Greek and Syriac; (3) those who write in Syriac but who are also clearly well-read in Greek; (4) those who write in Syriac but who read little or no Greek.

(1) Well-off families who had ambitions for their sons' careers would need to ensure that they received a good education in the language of power for this was the *sine qua non* of preferment. Thus Theodore bishop of Mopsuestia, who was born of a wealthy family in Antioch *c*. AD 350, ἀνὴρ καὶ τῶν ἱερῶν βίβλων καὶ τῆς ἄλλης παιδείας ῥητόρων τε καὶ φιλοσόφων ἱκανὸς ἐπιστήμων 'was a man well conversant both with the holy scriptures and with rhetorical and philosophical culture';[26] Theodore, of course, chose an ecclesiastical, rather than a secular, career, and the same was the case with Theodoret, likewise born in Antioch (AD 393) of rich parents. As a result of their Greek education both men wrote exclusively in Greek, though it is likely that Theodoret normally spoke Syriac,[27] and both men made use of their knowledge of Syriac here and there in their biblical commentaries. Men of this sort by no means came only from Antioch: among Christian writers a notable example is the fourth-century writer Eusebius of Emesa (who in fact came from Edessa), who likewise displays knowledge of the Syriac Bible in his writings; and, among pagans, Porphyry (Malkos) from Tyre, and Iamblichus from Chalcis. A particularly intriguing case is that of the poet, Romanus, from Emesa, perhaps of Jewish origin; here is a man who perfected (but hardly originated) a new Greek verse form (the *kontakion*) that was in part inspired by Syriac models, and who introduced themes and motifs drawn from both Greek and Syriac homiletic tradition.[28]

It was presumably from among people of this category, almost all of whom could to some extent, at least, be called bi-cultural as well as bilingual, that translators from Syriac into Greek came.

(2) Although it is likely that quite a number of readers and writers will have been bi-cultural, only isolated instances can be found of people who actually wrote in both languages. Tatian, described with tantalising vagueness as Ἀσσύριος, 'an Assyrian/Syrian', may be the first Christian writer to have written in both Greek and Syriac; his *Oratio ad Graecos*, in Greek, is a fiery attack on (pagan) Greek culture by one who had obviously received a reasonable education in it, but reacted against it on his

---

[26] Sozomen, *Historia Ecclesiastica* 8.2.

[27] That he normally spoke Syriac is suggested by *Historia Religiosa* 21.15, where he tells of 'a demon' speaking to him in that language, urging him not to persecute the Marcionites.

[28] See further Brock (1989). For the interesting contrast between Emesa and Edessa see Van Rompay (1990).

conversion to Christianity. His other work, the *Diatessaron* or harmony of the four Gospels, is unfortunately lost in its original form, and it remains disputed whether he wrote it in Greek (where it has left hardly a trace) or in Syriac[29] (in which it is known to have circulated widely until its suppression by Theodoret). A much clearer instance is provided by Rabbula (died 435). Born of rich parents and belonging to one of the leading families in Chalcis/Qenneshrin, he was given a good Greek education and would no doubt have enjoyed a distinguished secular career had he not converted to Christianity, ending up as bishop (or to his enemies, 'tyrant') of Edessa. As shepherd of a Christian community Rabbula wrote in both languages (though nothing happens to survive in original Greek), and also translated from Greek into Syriac.[30] When he preached in Constantinople (in Greek, of course) he apologises, with rhetorical modesty, for being 'a country bumpkin, living among country bumpkins, where we mostly speak in Syriac'.[31]

(3) It will at once be obvious that it was Christianity which lent to Syriac the requisite prestige to enable it to compete with Greek as a literary language; although this competition was thus confined to the sphere of religious literature, within that sphere we encounter quite a number of cases where men who have a good Greek education nevertheless choose to write in Syriac, rather than in Greek.

Perhaps the most surprising case is the earliest in time, that of Bardaisan 'the Aramaean philosopher' (154–222), friend of Julius Africanus and courtier of king Abgar VIII of Edessa. Clearly very well informed on contemporary philosophical trends in the Greek-speaking world,[32] he wrote only in Syriac, using both prose and poetry. Sadly, apart from brief quotations, none of his writings survive, but it seems likely that his choice of Syriac was largely guided by the Christian content of his teaching (even though later generations came to consider this teaching unduly pagan). The same motivation probably underlies the choice of Syriac for the *Book of the Laws of the Countries*, by one of his disciples; here the cultural mix is even more intriguing, since the opening is modelled on the Socratic dialogue. The work, under the title *Dialogue on Fate*, was soon made available in a Greek translation, of which Eusebius made use.

The same use of dialogue form is also a feature of several writings by the Syriac monastic writer John the Solitary, or John of Apamea, who was connected with Theodoret's monastery at Nikertai and belongs to the early

---

[29] For Syriac as the original language, see the case made by Petersen (1986).

[30] According to his life (ed. Overbeck, p. 200), he wrote 46 Letters in Greek; his Rules, on the other hand, are in Syriac. Cyril's 'On Orthodox Faith', addressed to Theodosius II, was translated into Syriac by him.

[31] Only the Syriac translation of this sermon survives (ed. Overbeck, p. 241).

[32] See Drijvers (1970).

fifth century.[33] Nothing is known of his background or the circumstances of his life, but to judge by his frequent use of medical imagery and a quotation from Hippocrates' *Aphorisms*, it is possible that he had had a medical training.

Thanks to a Life by his disciple Elias,[34] we are much better informed about another, later, Syriac writer with a good Greek education, John of Tella, who belongs to the first half of the sixth century. Born of well-to-do parents at Kallinikos, his father died when he was a child; his mother and grandparents nevertheless saw to it that he received a good education 'in the wisdom of the Greeks', and at the age of 20 he is put into service in the *praetorium* of the *dux* in Kallinikos. To improve his education his mother also provided him with a *paidagogos*, but her plans to marry him off are foiled by his encountering a local ascetic, under whose influence he adopted a new life-style in an upper room at home, living off dry bread. His *paidagogos* obligingly consumed the meals sent up by his mother, reassuring her, when she asked why her son looked so pale, that it was because he was burning the midnight oil studying – not in fact the pagan Greek writers[35] as his mother was led fondly to suppose, but the Psalms which he was learning – in Syriac. Before long he exchanged home for a full monastic life, and ended up as bishop of Tella and one of the chief figures of the anti-Chalcedonian party; what writings he has left are entirely in Syriac.

Unlike John, who evidently never put his Greek education to specific use, another scion of Kallinikos and a contemporary by the name of Paul did so, serving as a translator into Syriac of many of Severus of Antioch's theological works. Although nothing is known of Paul's background, it is likely that he, along with the many other translators from Greek into Syriac, will have belonged to this third category, comprising Aramaic speakers with a Greek education. This certainly applies to the most famous of these translators, Sergius of Resh'aina (died 536), whose work covered both medicine (notably Galen) and philosophy (Aristotle), as well as theology;[36] Sergius was also a creative writer in his own right, providing introductory material to assist readers of his translations.

(4) For men in all three previous categories, Greek would have been a serious option as the vehicle for their writing; that they chose to write in Syriac serves as a clear indication that, for them at least, Syriac as a written language enjoyed a prestige that could rival that of Greek, the language of

---

[33] French translation of a group of three dialogues by Lavenant (1984), whose introduction also deals briefly with the difficult problem of his identity.

[34] Ed. with Latin translation by Brooks, *Corpus Scriptorum Christianorum Orientalium* 7–8 (1907); the episodes cited are to be found on pp. 27–30 of the acompanying Latin translation.

[35] Literally 'those outside', reflecting Greek usage οἱ ἔξω.

[36] Hugonnard Roche (1989). Sergius' translation of the Pseudo-Dionysian Corpus constitutes one of the earliest witnesses to that famous work.

political power. For our final category, to which belong a number of famous Syriac authors writing in Syria in the fourth to seventh centuries, this would definitely not have been the case. Three famous names can serve as illustrations. Ephrem, who died in Edessa in 373, in fact came there from Nisibis, where he lived most of his life, until it was ceded to the Persians in 363; although a building inscription, dated 359, on the baptistry at Nisibis where he will häve served as deacon was written in Greek, it would seem that the Christian community in that border town was predominantly Syriac-speaking, and the extent of Ephrem's own knowledge of Greek is uncertain:[37] in any case it will not have been sufficient for him ever to have considered writing in that language. The same applies to the voluminous Syriac author Philoxenus, bishop of Mabbug/Hierapolis (died 523), who certainly had a moderate knowledge of Greek, but lacked any kind of Greek education;[38] he had in fact been born outside the Roman Empire, but had come to Edessa to study at the famous 'Persian School', where he was one of its alumni who rebelled against its christological stance. Philoxenus' exact contemporary and fellow student at the Persian School, the poet Jacob bishop of Serugh (died 521), was born in Kurtam, a village on the Euphrates, and represents someone who lived all his life without being outwardly affected by the Greek cultural world: for him the Syriac cultural heritage was entirely self-sufficient (though his education at the Persian School had brought him into contact with a number of Greek Christian writers in Syriac translation).

It is no doubt significant that Jacob was a product of the *chora*, rather than of a *polis*: for such people, in particular, the Greek cultural world, despite the superficial presence of its outward trappings in day-to-day provincial life, remained an essentially alien entity. This should not, however, lead us to suppose that there was also an underlying sense of antagonism, or that behind the emergence of the non-Chalcedonian Churches as independent bodies lay latent 'nationalist' aspirations.[39] Here it is essential to remember that some of the main anti-Chalcedonian writers, such as Severus of Antioch, had written in Greek (though their works usually survive only in Syriac translation), and that it was only with the Arab invasions that these Churches became identified with particular 'national' languages. Indeed, even after the advent of Arab rule, there were also sizeable Syriac-speaking communities in Syria which adhered to the

[37] Evidence for Ephrem's knowledge of Greek comes largely from his *Prose Refutations*, though the Hymns contain a few indirect references.

[38] Although he was probably not capable of doing it himself, Philoxenus commissioned a number of revised translations from Greek, including the New Testament (the so-called 'Philoxenian', known only from his quotations of it and from its revised form in the 'Harklean', made just over a century later).

[39] This view was satisfactorily refuted by Jones (1959): see also Dagron (1969: 53).

Chalcedonian faith of the Byzantine Church. While it would definitely be wrong to read the situation, say, of modern French-speaking Canada, back into any time in Late Antiquity, when 'nationalism' was not a functioning concept, there is one modern analogy which could prove more helpful, that of Lebanon under and immediately after the Mandate. There too we have two cultural languages, French and Arabic, flourishing side by side, with extensive bilingualism, but only the former is the language of power. Investigation into the choice of language made by different Lebanese writers during that period would be likely to throw up the same sort of spectrum that we have encountered in the case of Aramaic-speakers in Late Antique Syria.

Greek and Syriac in the liturgy

Everything that we have seen points to the fact that it was Christianity which provided Syriac with the necessary prestige to enable it to compete as a literary language (in specific spheres) with the language of contemporary political power. Since the Church's main public message is expressed through the liturgy, the choice of language used there is obviously of considerable relevance to our topic. Though the details are unclear, Syriac must have already served as a liturgical language in the time of Bardaisan, since he composed hymns in that language. At this early period liturgical prayer will have been largely extempore (though based on a fixed framework), and the choice of language will have been dictated by local circumstances; in large cities like Antioch, where Greek was extensively used, it may well have been that there was also instantaneous translation of parts of the services into the local Aramaic dialect, as happened in Jerusalem in the time of Egeria's visit.[40] In Edessa of the 370s, on the other hand, Ephrem's liturgical poetry makes it clear that Syriac was the language of the liturgy, and indeed it is likely that the oldest of all extant anaphoras, that attributed to Addai and Mari, has its roots in Edessa.[41]

In mixed linguistic contexts problems could arise, as happened with a monastic foundation at Zeugma on the Euphrates: the community had been founded as a Greek-speaking one by a certain Publius (significantly of curial origin), but its way of life soon attracted Syriac-speakers as well; to accommodate these Publius built a separate dwelling for them, but they all worshipped together twice a day in a single church where services took place using both languages.[42]

[40] Egeria, *Itinerarium* 47.   [41] See Macomber (1973).
[42] From some three centuries later we hear of a more embittered case, reminiscent of some Belgian monasteries in recent years, where conflict arose between Syriac- and Persian-speaking monks in Fars: in that case the founder, John of Dailam, had to build two separate

Such use of two (or even three)[43] different languages side by side in the liturgy seems to have been not uncommon and is reflected in a number of the earliest surviving liturgical manuscripts from the region (dating from the early Arab period) where both Greek and Syriac feature, though the Greek is written in Syriac characters,[44] indicating that by this time it was the subordinate language, soon to be displaced altogether by Syriac (and then in turn, in Melkite communities, by Arabic in the course of the Middle Ages).

Finally, it is worth recalling that the Sasanian policy of mass deportations, in which many people from Syria, including Greek- as well as Aramaic-speakers, were caught up especially in the 260s, resulted in the presence of isolated pockets of Greek-speakers in the Sasanian Empire who sometimes retained their language for many generations: in the early fifth century the descendants of one such deported community in Fars still employed Greek in the liturgy and maintained a separate Greek-speaking hierarchy.[45]

Conclusion

The central place justly enough given to Greek and Latin in traditional Western education, combined with the fact that Syriac was effectively cut off in the seventh century from the Greek-speaking world by the Arab invasions, happen to make it difficult for the modern student of Late Antiquity to appreciate fully the role played in some of the eastern provinces by this literary language which, by the time of the Byzantine army's defeat at the battle of the river Yarmuk, had already travelled in the service of Christian missionaries right across Asia as far as China. Within the Roman Empire Syriac, which had started out confined to Osrhoene, had spread west, across the Euphrates, as the literary language of Aramaic-speaking Christians by the early fifth century, and it is ironic (though not entirely surprising) that its use should have continued to increase in this area over the course of the next two centuries precisely at a time when Syriac literature was itself becoming more and more philhellenic,[46] adopting not only large numbers of new Greek loan-words, but also many features of Greek style. The prerequisite for this phenomenon was undoubtedly the presence of a local population, large numbers of whom were, to varying extents, bilingual. Amongst these people, it is essential to distinguish between those who could speak, and those who could read,

monasteries, one either side of a river ('Life of John of Dailam', *Parole de l'Orient* 10 (1981) 123–89). For multilingual communities see Hendriks (1958) and Dagron (1969: 50–2).
[43] Jerome tells how at Paula's funeral Greek, Syriac and Latin were all used (*Letter* 108.29).
[44] A notable example, with the Liturgy of St James, is published by Sauget (1985).
[45] *Chronicle of Seert* (ed. Scher, *Patrologia Orientalis* 4: 222).
[46] For this aspect see Brock (1982).

both languages, for the latter group (in whom this chapter has been primarily interested) will have been very much the smaller, and within this group the number of those who could effectively write in both Greek and Syriac was smaller still. What is, however, perhaps rather surprising is the finding that even among the reduced number of people capable of writing in either language (all of whom will have come from a particular social background), only isolated instances can be found of men who chose to write in both: Syria can provide no equivalent of the sixth-century Egyptian littérateur, Dioscorus of Aphrodito.

11   Later Roman bureaucracy: going through the files[1]

C. M. Kelly

I begin in the Hippodrome at Constantinople: not to exercise any passion for horse-racing; but to pursue an interest in archives and document storage. According to the partly autobiographical account of the sixth-century bureaucrat John Lydus, the judicial records of the Eastern Praetorian Prefecture (the largest and most important administrative department in the later Roman Empire) were in the charge of an official known as an *instrumentarius*.[2]

From time immemorial a place has been allocated to him in the Hippodrome below the imperial box and southwards right down to the so-called Sling; and every matter since the reign of the emperor Valens [in the late fourth century] which has been dealt with in the greatest courts of justice (as they once were) is preserved here and is readily available to those who inquire – as if it had been dealt with only yesterday.[3]

The Hippodrome formed the south-western boundary of the Great Palace

[1] For their help and advice, I would like to thank Keith Hopkins, Justin Goddard and those who participated in the seminar and colloquium at Oxford. I am particularly grateful to Peter Garnsey for his ever prompt and perceptive criticism. The opinions and the flaws (of course) remain my own.

The following should be noted:

> Ammianus Marcellinus, *Res Gestae*: Teubner edn, ed. W. Seyfarth, 1978.
> Anonymous, *De Rebus Bellicis*: A. Giardina, *Anonimo: Le cose della guerra*, Fondazione Lorenzo Valla, Milan, 1989.
> St Basil of Caesarea, *Epistulae*: M. F. Patrucco, *Basilio di Cesarea: Le lettere* I, Corona Patrum 11, Turin, 1983.
> John Lydus, *De Magistratibus*: A. C. Bandy, *Ioannes Lydus: On Powers or The Magistracies of the Roman State. Introduction, Critical Text, Translation, Commentary and Indices*, The American Philosophical Society, Philadelphia, 1983.
> Symmachus, *Relationes*: R. H. Barrow, *Prefect and Emperor: the Relationes of Symmachus A.D. 384*, Oxford, 1973.
> *Theodosian Code*: T. Mommsen and P. Krüger, *Theodosiani Libri XVI cum Constitutionibus Sirmondianis*, 2nd edn, Berlin, 1954.

For abbreviations of editions of Papyri see chapter 8, n. 1.

[2] Stein (1922: 36 n. 2).
[3] Joh. Lydus, *Mag.* 3.19 καὶ χῶρος μὲν αὐτῷ ἐν τῷ Ἱπποδρομίῳ ὑπὸ τῷ τῆς βασιλείας βήματι ἐπὶ τὸν νότον ἄχρι τῆς καλουμένης Σφενδόνος ἐξ ἀρχαίου παρακεχώρηται, πάντα δὲ τὰ ἀπὸ τῆς βασιλείας Οὐάλεντος ἐν τοῖς τότε μεγίστοις δικαστηρίοις πεπραγμένα αὐτόθι σῴζεται καὶ τοῖς ἐπιζητοῦσιν οὕτως ἐστὶν ἕτοιμα, ὡς εἰ χθὲς τυχὸν πεπραγμένα.

Fig. 4. Chamber in the Sphendone of the Hippodrome at Constantinople.
(From Casson et al. (1928) fig. 20.)

at Constantinople. The Sling (ἡ Σφενδονή) was the colloquial name for the
semi-circular end of the U-shaped course.[4] The imperial box, in all
probability, was somewhere just short of midway along the south-eastern
side of the Hippodrome, with easy and secure access to and from the palace
proper.[5] Following John Lydus' description, the Prefecture's archives
should have been stored beneath the tiered seating stretching from the
imperial box to the curved end of the race-track.[6] A British expedition in
1927 recorded in the substructure of the Hippodrome's south-eastern side
five roughly rectangular rooms (about 3.5 by 8 metres) opening out on a
corridor lit by large, arched windows (fig. 4).[7] Following modern estimates
for the overall dimensions of the Hippodrome,[8] there could have been

[4] Guilland (1969: 375–6); Janin (1950: 183); Mamboury and Wiegand (1934: Taf. CIII–V).
   For a general description of the Great Palace at Constantinople see Müller-Wiener (1977:
   229–37).
[5] Dagron (1974: 327–8); Guilland (1969: 463–70); Janin (1950: 182); Piganiol (1936: 385–7);
   Vogt (1935: 482–8).
[6] Caimi (1984: 25); Dagron (1974: 317). For a possible parallel in the siting of the secretarium
   circi in Rome, see Chastagnol (1960: 252–3).
[7] Casson et al. (1928: 17, figs. 20–2). The chambers are nos. i–v on Casson's plan. See too the
   earlier German survey of 1918 in Mamboury and Wiegand (1934: 42–3, esp. Abb. 15, Taf.
   CII, CVII); Mamboury (1936: 242–3); Müller-Wiener (1977: 67 Abb. 44).

space for about twenty-five to thirty such rooms between the imperial box and the Sling – an impressive amount of storage space, at an even temperature and well protected from fire.

In themselves, thirty near-rectangular rooms under a Hippodrome are not, of course, cause for much excitement. But their presence in the Great Palace at Constantinople should not be passed over too hurriedly. The bulk of the topographical information for the reconstruction of the palace buildings and their functions is based on a tenth-century compilation of court protocols, the so-called *Book of Ceremonies* of Constantine VII Porphyrogenitus.[9] Unsurprisingly, this was little concerned with administrative offices or archives. After all, monarchs (even now) rarely process past filing cabinets on their way to state occasions. The rooms under the Hippodrome are a useful corrective to a view of the palace as a predominantly ceremonial or ritual space. The presence of a substantial archive depository on the palace site itself serves as a reminder that ruling the later Roman Empire was as much about administration, record-keeping and paperwork as it was about glitter, splendour and wonder-working. Alongside all its religious and ideological symbolism, Constantine's 'New Rome' was also the Empire's administrative head office. The concentration in the Great Palace of an imperial secretariat and its related archive buildings reinforced in concrete form the importance of the compilation and circulation of written documents as a means of expressing and exercising power. Records, reports, receipts – their collection, storage and retrieval – were fundamental to the proper functioning of Roman imperial government.

The later Empire presents some splendid examples of administrative detail lovingly documented. From fourth-century Middle Egypt survive the working notebooks for a register of landowners. The register covered the agricultural land in the Hermopolite Nome held by residents of the West Citadel Quarter of the town of Hermopolis and of the nearby provincial capital of the Thebaid, Antinoopolis. Individuals, their public and private land holdings, and some conveyances as well, were all listed in a dossier which gives a wonderfully detailed picture of how the land was divided and who owned what.[10] A similarly detailed record of private affairs was created through the public registering of wills, gifts, emancipations, adoptions and guardianships.[11] By the sixth century, copies of these and other transactions (contracts of sale and guarantees) were deposited with

[8] Guilland (1970: 9).

[9] See, for example, the reconstruction of Ebersolt (1910: esp. 180–216).

[10] *P. Flor.* 1.71 and *P. Giss.* 1.117 – now re-edited as *P. Landlisten F* and *G* in Sijpesteijn and Worp (1978); see too Duncan-Jones (1981) and the excellent discussion in Bowman (1985).

[11] Steinwenter (1915: 58–62); Wenger (1953: 744–58).

the municipal authorities, incorporated in official registers, and stored in local archive buildings.[12]

That basic pattern was repeated throughout later Roman administration. A brief (and unavoidably selective) catalogue of these examples gives an impression of a government heavily dependent for its operation on written reports, records and instructions. From its higher levels survive the reports submitted to the emperor Valentinian by Quintus Aurelius Symmachus (Urban Prefect of Rome in 384/5); the *Verona List* and the *Notitia Dignitatum* (which list some of the Empire's senior military and civil officials and those under their control); and the reports and requests for information preserved in the laws collected in the *Theodosian Code*.[13] Written documents were not only descriptive: they could also put into operation complex sets of organisational arrangements. When the emperor Diocletian visited Egypt in 298, a series of requisition orders sent in advance ensured that the troops escorting him were provisioned through additional supplies of lentils, meat, chaff, bread, barley, wine and wheat.[14] A bakery, a smithy and an armoury were ordered to be made ready.[15] Nile boats and their crews were to be kept on continual stand-by for the imperial post.[16] John Lydus (remembering his time in the judicial branch of the Eastern Praetorian Prefecture in the early sixth century) gives some idea of the sheer amount of paper later Roman government must have consumed annually: 'In those days there were so many matters that (even summarised) they could hardly fit into ten volumes... The number of matters was so great that the entire year was not long enough to complete them all.'[17]

Taken together, all these forms, claims, reports, orders, proclamations, files and archives convey something of the extent to which central government in the Roman Empire was dependent on paperwork – both for its knowledge of events and as a means of influencing their course. In major administrative headquarters (such as the Great Palace at Constantinople) an image of empire was compiled, collated and controlled through the written word. A continual flow of documents provided important information about the concerns pressing on those in the Empire, about the actions of government officials and about the aims, intentions and instructions of emperors. The exchange of written documents was an essential process linking rulers and ruled. Information submitted as petitions, or as reports from imperial agents in the provinces, was summarised by technically trained administrators and shorthand writers. In response, replies, instructions

[12] Posner (1972: 217–21); Rees (1952: 93–4); Steinwenter (1915: 74–82); Wenger (1953: 752–5).
[13] A few examples: *C. Th.* 1.8.1 (of 415), 1.15.3 (of 357), 6.30.8 (of 385), 7.4.12 (of 364), 8.4.4 (of 349), 8.4.29 (of 428), 10.9.2 (of 395), 11.29.5 (of 374), 11.29.6 (of 416), 11.30.34 (of 364), 11.30.41 (of 383), 11.30.65 (of 419), 11.36.31 (of 392), 16.2.37 (of 404), 16.10.1 (of 320).
[14] *P. Panop. Beatty* 1 lines 276–331.   [15] Ibid. lines 213–16, 332–7, 342–6.
[16] Ibid. lines 252–5.   [17] Joh. Lydus, *Mag.* 3.13.

or general laws were drafted, approved, issued, publicly posted and copied down by local scribes. Indeed, it might be argued that given the limitations imposed by the population and area governed, by drawbacks in the means, speed and reliability of communications, and by a dependence on the most basic information storage and retrieval systems, later Roman bureaucracy was a surprisingly efficient and effective gatherer and conveyer of information and instruction.

But how should one assess this flurry of documents and paperwork – this *paperasserie* – or as A. H. M. Jones wittily called it (in, as far as I know, the only joke in the fifteen hundred pages of his *The Later Roman Empire*) this *papyrasserie*?[18] From one point of view, it might have seemed surprisingly ineffectual. In the 430s, the compilers of the *Theodosian Code* (which was supposed to gather together all the legal decisions issued by emperors since Constantine[19]) were able to extract only more recent material from the central imperial archives. There seems to have been no complete, centralised register of laws issued by the various palatine departments. Some material was culled from provincial records (those of the *vicarius* and proconsul of Africa seem to have been particularly well combed) and even from the personal collections of academic or practising lawyers.[20] Following such an operation, the *Code*'s commissioners (after nearly seven years' work[21]) might perhaps justifiably have seen the central imperial archives as 'disorganised and inadequate'.[22]

That divergence – as revealed in the compilation of the *Theodosian Code* – between the seeming reliance of later Roman government on the written word as an important instrument of government and its failure to institute (or effectively to enforce) any correspondingly sophisticated archival practices is important; but the point should not be pressed too far. It is only one view. After all, the ex-bureaucrat John Lydus claimed that the Eastern Praetorian Prefect's archive under the Hippodrome was a model of administrative efficiency:

every matter since the reign of the emperor Valens which has been dealt with in the greatest courts of justice (as they once were) is preserved here and is readily available to those who inquire – as if it had been dealt with only yesterday.[23]

If for some reason that were not possible, the Prefecture could then fall back on the summaries made of each case.

---

[18] Jones (1964: I 602).   [19] *C. Th.* 1.1.5 (of 429); see n. 49 below.
[20] On the sources of the *Theodosian Code*, Mommsen (1900: esp. 163–76) and Seeck (1919: 1–18 esp. 11–13) remain fundamental; for more recent discussions see Archi (1976: 21–2); Gaudemet (1957: 53–9); Honoré (1986: 158–9, 161–2); Jones (1964: I 473–6).
[21] Honoré (1986: 162 n. 4).   [22] Posner (1972: 222).   [23] Joh. Lydus, *Mag.* 3.19.

For the most learned of the Prefecture's staff summarised in Latin the decisions which had been made in such detail that if, by chance, the original record were destroyed, then from the paraphrase alone (even though it was only an outline) the record of the decision could be recovered. I myself recall this actually happening.[24]

John presented his readers with claims of an administratively perfect world. It could (of course) have been mere idle bureaucratic boasting, akin to the defensive claims made by those people who, standing in front of a desk piled perilously high with paper, assert that they can find anything they need – in only a few seconds. That is perhaps unfair to John; but his claim does point up the difficulties (given the divergent experiences of those involved) of determining the effectiveness or efficiency of later Roman documentary and archival practices.

How then should we understand the impressive quantity of paperwork which circulated between emperors, officials, their departments and those they governed? What happened to a document or report after it had performed its immediate purpose? Perhaps the imperial chancelleries of the later Roman Empire were indeed like some great nineteenth-century European government department. The British Colonial Office had a room devoted to each part of the globe, where reports, letters and communications with foreign potentates were all carefully registered, docketed, recorded and meticulously filed. Did the rooms under the Hippodrome in Constantinople look something like that? Or were they simply stuffed with heaps of documents? Did they look more Kafkaesque – a series of subterranean rooms staffed by incommunicative bureaucrats, half-strangled by their own red tape, surrounded by useless pieces of yellowing paper stacked in long-forgotten dusty piles?

For its whole length the room is divided into two by a high desk which stretches from wall to wall; one side is so narrow that two people can hardly get past each other... On the desk there are large books lying open, side by side and officials stand by it, most of them reading... Meanwhile a clerk searches through a great many files and documents (which he has under his desk) and there is a letter for you, but is not a letter which has just been written, rather – judging by the appearance of the envelope – it is a very old letter which has lain there a long time.[25]

Any thinking about the uses of writing, documentation or archives in the later Roman Empire must be connected to a wider consideration of the possibilities, limitations and restrictions surrounding the exercise of power through bureaucratic or administrative means. Clearly, the expansion and centralisation of bureaucracy in the later Empire allowed imperial government to exercise an unprecedented level of control over the human and economic resources of empire. Above all, the ability of central

---

[24] Ibid. 3.20.
[25] F. Kafka, *Das Schloss* (Kurt Wolff Verlag, Munich, 1926) at 341, 344.

government to extract and concentrate these resources was greatly strengthened. Later Roman government paid for a professional standing army larger than that under the Principate, funded a greatly increased bureaucracy, founded a second imperial capital, supported a new religion and heavily subsidised barbarian tribes on its frontiers. The achievement should not be underrated. Despite obvious shortcomings and inevitable haphazard inefficiencies, the creation of an extensive bureaucracy permitted the later Roman state to maintain a level of control over empire not reached again in Europe until the eighteenth-century absolutisms of France and Prussia.

For emperors, the expansion of bureaucracy in the later Empire was a two-edged sword. While undoubtedly it allowed a more penetrating and detailed control over empire, bureaucracy also posed a serious threat to imperial power. At its simplest, the problem was one of delegation and independence. The efficient functioning of any bureaucracy requires the delegation of power in order to allow officials to take decisions in their own right. But, from an imperial point of view, delegation was also a dangerous and uncomfortable necessity. Too much delegation might so far remove emperors from the actual exercise of power that they could become the prisoners of an administrative system which monopolised and controlled important policy-making information. It was Weber who wryly noted Bismarck's annoyance upon finding that the Prussian bureaucracy (which he had been instrumental in creating) carried on – seemingly undisturbed – without him:

Upon his resignation, he saw to his surprise that they continued to manage their offices unconcerned and unaffected, as if he had not been the master mind and creator of these creatures, but rather as if one person in the bureaucratic machine had been replaced by another.[26]

But emperors' conflict with bureaucracy cut much deeper than the need to reconcile the necessity of delegation with the retention of an effective level of imperial control. It was also a problem played out in the seemingly more mundane matters of administrative language, documentation and the written word. Any move towards the fixity, predictability or regularity necessary for the more effective operation of a fully rational bureaucracy threatened, in its turn, the free play of imperial power. Bureaucracy's marked preference for order directly challenged the whimsicality and unpredictability of action fundamental to the unfettered exercise of imperial power; it restricted emperors' ability to act independently and to break through – at any time or on any pretext – the restrictions imposed by convention or established procedure. Meticulously ordered archives were

[26] Weber (1985: 570–1).

the most dangerous documents of all. The precedents they contained enabled present action to be constrained by past practice. For emperors that was not always desirable. It is a mistake to assume that all governments wish always to maintain an accurate, correct and easily retrievable record of their actions. Predictability is only one way of organising rule.

Against the limitations imposed by the expansion of bureaucratic power in the later Empire emperors constantly strove to reinforce their own stake in the system. Their word was to have unquestioned priority over all other competing or conflicting alternatives (past or present). The superiority of imperial pronouncements was underscored by their self-proclaimed sanctity; sacred documents were issued from the Imperial Oracle.[27] St Basil (bishop of Caesarea) writing to a friend in the early 360s joked that he treated the latter's previous letter as an imperial missive: 'I paid it due reverence as if it were some official proclamation, and when I broke the seal, I stood in awe at the sight of it.'[28] Faced with a report from Symmachus which criticised the imperial selection of officials for the Urban Prefecture in Rome and recommended revised criteria for future appointments, the emperor Valentinian witheringly observed: 'For it amounts to sacrilege to question whether the person, whom the emperor has chosen, is worthy.'[29] In the light of such a reaction, it comes as no surprise that the anonymous author of a mid-fourth-century pamphlet – which offered advice on a wide range of civil, fiscal and military affairs – should have tentatively advanced his case, observing the perfection of the emperors and their government, while, at the same time, nervously suggesting improvements.[30]

Enforcing the imperial will was no easy matter. By insisting on the primacy of the imperial word, emperors emphasised their own position; but in so doing, they unavoidably reinforced the importance and potency of official documents as a means of control. They risked becoming prisoners of their own strategy. That uncomfortable paradox was a recurrent theme in considerations of emperors' power by that shrewdly perceptive fourth-century historian Ammianus Marcellinus.[31] In his history, imperial inaction, ignorance or incompetence were frequently portrayed as the result of faulty sources, misinformation or the lack of reports.[32] Even more

[27] Some examples: *C. Th.* 1.15.8 (of 378), 2.1.9 (of 397), 2.4.5 (of 389), 11.12.4 (of 407), 11.13.1 (of 383), 11.16.16 (of 385), 11.21.3 (of 424), 13.11.12 (of 409), 16.7.7.3 (of 426), 16.10.8 (of 382).

[28] Basil, *Ep.* 3.1 Εὐλαβήθην αὐτήν, ὡς τι δημόσιον προσαγγέλλουσαν, καί, παρ' ὃν ἐξέλυον καιρὸν τὸν κηρόν, ἐφοβούμην προσβλέπων...

[29] *C. Th.* 1.6.9 (of 385) sacrilegii enim instar est dubitare, an is dignus sit, quem elegerit imperator; Symm. *Rel.* 17 with Vera (1981: 131–3).

[30] Anon. *De Rebus Bell. pr.*15–17.

[31] In thinking about Ammianus' portrayal of imperial power, I have benefited particularly from the discussions in Tassi (1967) and Valensi (1957: esp. 91–7).

[32] For a comprehensive collection of examples, see Noethlichs (1981: 203–5).

telling were his stories of the forging or misuse of imperial documents. In 355, Silvanus, the infantry commander at Cologne, became the centre of a complex and intricate plot.[33] A minor court official (Dynamius) had some time previously requested from Silvanus letters of recommendation. Keeping them, he effaced the writing, leaving only Silvanus' signature. Above it, Dynamius then wrote a new text indicating that Silvanus was relying on officials in the imperial palace at Milan to support his revolt. This packet of letters was shown to the emperor Constantius who immediately ordered Silvanus' arrest and recall. Several further forgeries eventually led to the documents being more closely scrutinised:

on examining the writing more carefully (and discovering a sort of shadow of the previous markings) what had happened was understood: that the earlier text had been altered and – in accordance with the aim of this patched-together forgery – other material, quite different from that which Silvanus had dictated, had been added.[34]

Central to Ammianus' account of this revolt is the power of the written word. It was a packet of documents which put the emperor in a false position in the first place and forced him to make incorrect deductions and to act wrongly. Pointedly, it is only when the written document was effaced that these limitations were removed. Constantius could then exercise imperial power unfettered and go on successfully to efface a usurper. In contrast, Silvanus was committed to a series of fatal actions by writings which (paradoxically) he had never seen. Only death expunged his mistake.

Ammianus' account neatly captured something of the uncomfortable and ambiguous relationship between autocracy and bureaucracy. A written document – even when false – could dictate imperial action. Only the reduction of the written word to a shadow of itself allowed the full assertion of imperial power. That is (of course) only one side of a difficult equation. It takes us to extremes. It is nicely balanced by Ammianus' account of Constantius' involvement in the execution of his heir apparent Gallus Caesar. In this version, written documents are again pivotal. Gallus was persuaded to return from Antioch solely as a result of a stream of letters from the emperor which assured him (wrongly as it turned out) that he would come to no harm.[35] But how should one understand these documents? Was Constantius again misled as to Gallus' true intentions by false reports submitted by untrustworthy bureaucrats and, as a result, forced (ironically) into writing misleading letters? Or was Constantius playing his own game, using correct administrative methods and channels

[33] For the whole story see Amm. 15.5.
[34] Amm. 15.5.12 ... contemplans diligentius scripta apicumque pristinorum quasi quandam umbram repperiens animadvertit, ut factum est, priore textu interpolato longe alia, quam dictarat Silvanus, ex libidine consarcinatae falsitatis ascripta.
[35] Amm. 14.11.1, 9, 16.

to keep tabs on Gallus before taking advantage of bureaucratic procedures by knowingly writing misleading letters to persuade him to return? Ammianus keeps the options open.[36] The truth or falsity of the written word was blurred. In other versions, that confusion was taken even further. A letter ordering Gallus' reprieve, which Constantius dramatically sends at the last minute, arrives (unsurprisingly) too late.[37] Was this genuine remorse by a sadly duped emperor? Or was it the last hollow word by a shrewd ruler skilled in creating, manipulating and, above all, (re)writing the records of his own actions?

These are attractive irresolutions. They reflect something of the continual manœuvring necessary for the maintenance of imperial power: a manœuvring both against the dangers involved in the creation of a bureaucratic system of rule and against the limitations inherent in the use of the written word. Something of these shifting patterns of support and subversion was also preserved in the *Theodosian Code* promulgated in 438. The laws it contained captured – like snapshots in a photograph album – another view of that complex and kaleidoscopic process. On one view, the *Code* (with its cataloguing and categorisation of over 2,500 laws, in sixteen books, and nearly four hundred chapters[38]) is a model of encyclopaedic order and methodical arrangement. It represents a rational approach to government and to the problems of administrative delegation and imperial control.

For this reason, a cloud of volumes has been dispelled, a cloud on which the lives of many people – who explain nothing – have been frittered away.[39]

In commissioning the *Code*, the emperor Theodosius II granted power to the *diligentiores*[40] whom he had appointed to sort through previous imperial legislation:

to excise superfluous words, to add necessary ones, to alter ambiguities, to emend inconsistencies, so that by these methods each individual constitution may surely stand out clearly elucidated.[41]

On receipt of the *Code* in the Senate at Rome in 438, the senators

---

[36] Amm. 14.7.9, 11.1–4, 21–3.
[37] Philostorgius 4.1 (*Die Griechischen Christlichen Schriftsteller* 21, ed. J. Bidez, Leipzig, 1913 at 58); Zonaras, *Ann.* 13.9 (*Patrologia Graeca* 134 1133B–1136A).
[38] Honoré (1986: 133).
[39] Theod. II, *Nov.* 1.3 (of 438) Quamobrem detersa nube voluminum, in quibus multorum nihil explicantium aetates adtritae sunt...'   [40] *C. Th.* 1.1.5 (of 429).
[41] *C. Th.* 1.1.6.1 (of 435)... demendi supervacanea verba et adiciendi necessaria et demutandi ambigua et emendandi incongrua tribuimus potestatem, scilicet ut his modis unaquaeque inlustrata constitutio emineat. I follow Archi (1976: 32–7); Honoré (1986: 164–7); Turpin (1982: 24–8) in seeing the instructions of 429 (*C. Th.* 1.1.5) and 435 (*C. Th.* 1.1.6) as complementary. For a good discussion of the principles behind the codification see Volterra (1980: esp. 125ff., 1981: 88–98).

enthusiastically shouted (twenty-three times): 'You have removed the ambiguities of the imperial constitutions!'[42]

Support (rhetorical, vocal, self-proclaimed) was in its turn matched by subversion. Concessions to the rationalist virtues of order, clarity and 'methodical provision'[43] were continually undercut by overlapping, inconsistent or contradictory legislation and by the inclusion of imperial laws 'which in silence have become obsolete since they were only applicable to matters in their own time'.[44] In practice, as a collection of legal or administrative documents, the *Theodosian Code* has a surprisingly limited use. It is difficult (for example) to establish with any certainty the criteria upon which promotions or appointments were made, or to define precisely the competence of any particular administrative department or official.[45] Any comparison between the *Theodosian Code* and a modern set of administrative regulations starkly exposes the extent to which the *Code* avoided precise definition or 'the formalism and the rule-bound and cold objectivity'[46] traditionally associated with rationally organised officialdom.[47] At best, it was 'un mosaico di brani',[48] simply 'a collection of constitutions. It did not aim to settle legal controversies. It marked out no general principles. It organised no system.'[49]

Within – and against – this elusive legal framework, later Roman emperors continually emphasised the primacy of their position. To

---

[42] *C. Th. Gest. Sen.* 5 Constitutionum ambiguum removistis. Dictum XXIII.

[43] Weber (1985: 551).

[44] *C. Th.* 1.1.5 (of 429) ... quae mandata silentio in desuetudinem abierunt, pro sui tantum temporis negotiis valitura; see generally Gaudemet (1957: 52); Honoré (1986: 162–4). Given that there was 'no attempt to iron out inconsistencies' (at 162) and 'no neat division between obsolete and currently valid laws' (at 163), I am less convinced than Honoré (at 164) that the resulting contradictions could be resolved by the application of the rule in *C. Th.* 1.1.5 (of 429) that a later statute (if inconsistent) repeals an earlier. For further unresolved tension (again, despite seemingly clear-cut prescriptions) between general laws (*leges generales*) and personal rescripts (*leges personales*), and between laws promulgated in the eastern and western halves of the empire, see Archi (1976: 39–42, 96–107); Honoré (1986: 176–81); Turpin (1982: 44–57).

[45] For a good example of a range of potentially conflicting criteria for promotion see *CJ* 12.19.7 (of 444); for ambiguous and overlapping administrative competences see *C. Th.* 1.6.5 = *CJ* 1.28.1 (of 365) and *C. Th.* 1.6.7 = *CJ* 1.28.3 (of 376) which refuse to define clearly the responsibilities of the Urban Prefect of Rome and the *praefectus annonae* (Chastagnol 1960: 297–300).   [46] Weber (1985: 565).

[47] See (for example) the description of functions, the division of responsibilities and the regulation of officials as set out by a modern bureaucracy in the *Civil Service Year Book 1992* (HMSO Cabinet Office) ch. III; *Handbook for the New Civil Servant* (HMSO Civil Service Department, 1980) 7–12, 33–7; *The Cabinet Office Staff Handbook pt IV Discipline and General Information* (HMSO Cabinet Office, May 1987); and the series of guides (published by the Civil Service Commission) under the general title *The Work of Departments*.

[48] Volterra (1983: 195).

[49] Honoré (1986: 167); Turpin (1982: 34). It should also be noted that the *Theodosian Code* (as it stands) only represents the first stage of an announced process of codification. In the second stage, the *Code* and its predecessors the *Codex Gregorianus* (*c.* 292) and the *Codex*

preserve their own power of independent action, they undermined at random the dependability and certainty of their own legal system. Imperial power was not to be restricted by force of law. That tactic was most forcefully on display in the most subversive category of legislation in the *Code* – those directives which announced that a previous imperial grant was to be treated as invalid even in a case where:

a person claims that, as a result of our decision, he has obtained imperial letters of appointment and either the outer seal of the documents or the writing inside confirms his claim.[50]

For those attempting actually to use the *Theodosian Code* to define their exact legal position, there can have been nothing more unnerving than those laws. After all, if once seemingly valid rescripts could be invalidated as 'fraudulent' or 'surreptitiously obtained'[51] how could anyone confidently determine that any imperial ruling would continue to have legal effect? Imperial letters of appointment properly submitted, signed and sealed might be ruled untrustworthy, although in some cases (by confusing turns) they still might have force.

To the Urban Prefect of Rome: If any department, person, association or profession should have procured a grant of imperial favour or any imperial authorisation concerning an immunity which is incompatible with the scope of this legislation, it shall have no validity; but if it should be the case that such grants have been presented, and have also been accepted by the most esteemed [senatorial] order, they may again be reconsidered, whenever appropriate.[52]

But, in the end, who could tell? The very nature of the *Code* and its arrangement made any reading uncertain. Lawyerly attempts at systematic interpretation were strongly resisted. Some jurists were rejected out of

Hermogenianus (c. 295) were to be amalgamated and harmonised: *C. Th.* 1.1.5 with Archi (1976: 24–31); Honoré (1986: 164); Turpin (1982: 25–7, 33–4); Volterra (1983: 195–7). One wonders what such a Code might have looked like, or how far it might have met the recommendation of the anonymous writer of *De Rebus Bellicis* for a work which would elucidate 'the confused and contradictory rulings of the laws' – confusas legum contrariasque sententias (21.1)? For me, at any rate, it seems only appropriate that this second stage was 'never spelled out in detail' (Honoré 1986: 164) and remained unfulfilled (see n. 53 below).

50   *C. Th.* 6.22.1 (of 325/6) Si quis iudicio nostro se adeptum codicillos adstruxerit et idem vel superna codicillorum inpressio vel scriptura adstipuletur interior ... – contrast *C. Th.* 1.3.1 (of 383) where those claiming direct authority from the emperor are to be believed only to the extent that they can prove their claims by written documents. Noethlichs (1981: 50–5) lists over seventy examples from the *Theodosian Code* and *Novels* of the invalidation of previously valid imperial grants.

51   See (for example from *C. Th.* 1) 1.2.9 (of 385) elicitum damnabili subreptione; 1.9.2 = *CJ* 1.31.2 (of 386); 1.11.2 = *CJ* 11.74.1 (of 398).

52   *C. Th.* 6.2.26 (of 428) ita ut omne beneficium omnisque adnotatio specialis super immunitate contra huius sanctionis formam a quocumque officio persona schola vel professione elicita nullam habeat firmitatem, sed allegata quoque et ab amplissimo, si ita contigerit, suscepta ordine denuo, cum libuerit, retractetur; see too *C. Th.* 6.27.3.*pr.* (of 380), 8.4.20 (of 407).

hand: 'Desiring to eradicate the endless disputes of the academic lawyers, we order the destruction of the notes of both Ulpian and Paul upon Papinian.'[53] Others were only acceptable on the basis of a system which, if tried, would probably have produced more haphazard inconsistencies than rational elucidations or reliable precedents.

We confirm all the writings of Papinian, Paul, Gaius, Ulpian and Modestinus, so that the same authority shall attend Gaius as attends Paul, Ulpian and the rest... But when conflicting opinions are tendered, the greater number of authors shall prevail, or, if the numbers should be equal, the group in which Papinian (a man of outstanding ability) is prominent shall have precedence: as he defeats a single opponent, so he yields to two.[54]

Confusion and complexity empowered emperors. These were important tactics in promoting and preserving their stake in the system. Emperors were not to be hemmed in by the formulation of inviolable legal maxims or restricted by the strict application of academic rules of construction. In such a capricious and ever-changing world, only emperors themselves could grant a greater degree of assurance. Certainty depended on them alone – and even that remained unsure. Sometimes emperors might question the authenticity of even their own documents and the edicts upon which reliable delegated authority depended. Sometimes they openly admitted that their own rulings or actions might run contrary to a strict interpretation of the written text.[55] Symmachus as Urban Prefect of Rome – suspecting the presence of '*inique elicita rescripta*' – had little alternative but to refer the matter to the emperors themselves: 'It is open only to your Clemencies to cancel rescripts illicitly obtained.'[56]

[53] *C. Th.* 1.4.1 (of 321/4) Perpetuas prudentium contentiones eruere cupientes Ulpiani ac Pauli in Papinianum notas ... aboleri praecipimus. This insistence by emperors on controlling the meaning and interpretation of their own laws presumably could have conflicted sharply with the instructions for the (unfulfilled) second stage of the *Theodosian Code* whose compilers were empowered to harmonise existing legislation. This second project – at the very least – presented a much more difficult (and dangerous) negotiation with imperial power than the irresolutions which mark out the 'reconciliation' of this conflict in the completed *Code*.

[54] *C. Th.* 1.4.3 (of 426) Papiniani, Pauli, Gai, Ulpiani atque Modestini scripta universa firmamus ita, ut Gaium quae Paulum, Ulpianum et ceteros comitetur auctoritas ... Ubi autem diversae sententiae proferuntur, potior numerus vincat auctorum, vel, si numerus aequalis sit, eius partis praecedat auctoritas, in qua excellentis ingenii vir Papinianus emineat, qui ut singulos vincit, ita cedit duobus. Cf. *CJ* 1.17.1.6 (of 530); for scholarly attempts to minimise, rationalise or explain away the difficulties this law presents see Honoré (1986: 142–4) and Volterra (1983: esp. 197–208 with bibliography at 197–9 n. 18).

[55] *C. Th.* 6.27.3. *pr.; CJ* 3.1.8 (of 314), 6.61.5.1 (of 473); further examples in Gaudemet (1954: 195 n. 176). Compare too the expression of *indulgentia* as a reason for the issuing of a law or rescript (Gaudemet 1979: 250 n. 67, 257 n. 94, 258–76). Again, what guarantee was there that an emperor would be so indulgent on a second occasion?

[56] Symm. *Rel.* 44.1 ... vestrae tantum clementiae liberum est inique elicita rescripta rescindere; Gaudemet (1954: 183); Honoré (1986: 168–9 n. 47).

But emperors did not have it all their own way. Obscurity also advantaged bureaucrats; it too protected their position. Above all, it allowed them to monopolise the channels of communication between emperor and subject. For most ordinary people, the very complexity of the administrative system made it impenetrable.[57] Few could find their way through the fantastically convoluted, baroque turns of later Roman legal and administrative rhetoric – 'lo stile magniloquente e ampolloso'.[58] John Lydus prefaced his account of the sub-divisions of the Eastern Praetorian Prefecture by remarking:

In order that the details of this division may not escape even outsiders (τοὺς ἔξωθεν) – since the common people, being ignorant and confused about the terminology I mentioned above, daily make pointless inquiries – I shall set out in my account the reason for the division of the one *corps* into two.[59]

Generally, John had little sympathy for those who got administrative details wrong. He complained that some could not even master basic bureaucratic vocabulary. For him, the use of *adsecretis* for *a secretis* reflected 'the usage of the uneducated';[60] the use of *privatoriae* for *probatoriae* was the result of 'an illiterate guess'.[61] To be sure, these are the snide remarks of an insider. But under the carapace of an increasingly technical language, a highly formalistic way of writing inevitably gave more power to expert administrators. That perhaps helps to explain why many high-ranking officials in the later Empire were well known for their poetic or rhetorical ability.[62] In the strengthening of bureaucratic rule, the manipulation of language mattered.

Emperors (in their turn) resisted. John decried Justinian's ruling that Greek – rather than Latin – could be used in administrative documents. For him, one of the mysteries of administration was in danger of being laid bare. He threatened the fulfilment of an old prophecy which foretold that Fortune would forsake the Romans when they forgot the language of their homeland.[63] A century earlier, Valentinian III's response to such special pleading by bureaucrats had been more explicit. A lurid description of the operation of a tax collector alleged:

The first signs of his coming are that he brings forth and unrolls terrible regulations under various and innumerable headings: he presents a miasma of minute calculations, confused with inexplicable obscurity, which, amongst men unused to such deceit, has the effect that they understand even less.[64]

That clear-cut invective is of course misleading. Such imperial statements

[57] MacMullen (1962: 372–5).   [58] Volterra (1981: 91).   [59] Joh. Lydus, *Mag.* 3.9.
[60] Ibid. 3.20.   [61] Ibid. 3.2; and see too 1.23, 2.4, 2.6, 2.9, 2.13.
[62] Jones (1964: I 388).   [63] Joh. Lydus, *Mag.* 2.12 = 3.42.
[64] Val. III, *Nov.* 1.3.2 (of 450) Prima sunt venientis exordia, ut proferat et revolvat super diversis numerosisque titulis terribiles iussiones: praetendit minutarum subputationum caligines inexplicabili obscuritate confusas, quae inter homines versutiarum nescios hoc amplius agunt, quo minus intellegi possunt.

were partly circumvented, partly contradicted by emperors' own need for complexity and ambiguity as a means of protecting and maintaining their position. The development of an obscurantist bureaucratese should be seen less as a sign of some later Roman intellectual malaise, than as a deliberate and sophisticated means of attempting to accommodate an uncomfortable and potentially explosive relationship between autocracy and bureaucracy. These conflicts pressed against the limits of both emperors' and bureaucrats' power. Even those imperial edicts which inveighed against bureaucrats' convoluted and overblown rhetoric were themselves excellent examples of the art; they were also (of course) drafted by bureaucrats in the service of the emperor.

Some understanding of this kind of manœuvring (by all parties involved) seems to me to be central to any understanding of later Roman bureaucracy and the role played by written documents within that system. Much is epitomised in the *Theodosian Code*; what first appears as an ordered, docketed and precisely catalogued administrative world dissolves on further inspection into a Looking Glass world of uncertainty, conflict and terminological inexactitude. From that point of view, the alternative models for imagining the working of later Roman bureaucracy – as a well-ordered room in the British Colonial Office, or as a sinisterly chaotic office in Kafka's *The Castle* – were both misleading in their clarity. Both rightly emphasised the importance of administration, documentation and the written word; but neither fully comprehended the byzantine complexity of a pattern of power which (with its inevitable self-contradictions) both promoted centralised, bureaucratic government and also aimed to protect imperial power from the strictures imposed by the written word.

These conflicting claims of autocrat and bureaucrat are the key to any understanding of the nature of both imperial and bureaucratic power in the later Empire. Any move towards a more rational or more systematically delegated pattern of administrative control was cross-cut by emperors' competing needs to enforce their own authority and to resist the restrictions imposed by a precise legal terminology or a bureaucratic insistence on precedent. That clash between the self-proclaimed freedoms of imperial power and the restraints imposed by the necessity to support and promote a complex and sophisticated administration resulted in a continually shifting pattern of rule characterised by conflict, negotiation and ambiguity. The tensions (and the random shifts and slippages they involved) were the cost later Roman emperors paid for insisting on remaining autocrats, while seeking to rule an empire more closely through a more permanent and highly organised bureaucracy. Effective imperial power was only to be maintained by an unpredictable manœuvring between support for bureaucracy and its subversion. These tactics were both pressing and important. They made the drafting, authorisation and promulgation of written documents – and their subsequent storage, cataloguing and recall – more than a matter of mere administrative efficiency. For later Roman emperors the growth of bureaucracy paradoxically both strengthened and threatened their rule. Their problem (if nothing else) was clear: a smoothly functioning, autonomous administration – with rules established, fixed, signed and sealed in written documents available from the archives – left little room for the caprice of autocracy.

12 Literacy and power in the migration period

Peter Heather

εἶναι γάρ τι καὶ ἐν ἑκάστῳ βάρβαρον φῦλον, λίαν αὐθάδες καὶ δυσπειθές, τὸν θυμὸν λέγω καὶ τὰς ἀπλήστους ἐπιθυμίας, ἀντικαθήμενα γένη τῷ λογισμῷ, καθάπερ Ῥωμαίοις Σκύθαι καὶ Γερμανοί.

There is in each of us a barbarian tribe, extremely overbearing and intractable – I mean temper and those insatiable desires, which stand opposed to rationality as Scythians and Germans do to the Romans.[1]

Self-styled philosopher, orator, and political propagandist, Themistius pronounced this sentence before the emperor Valens and the assembled Senate of Constantinople in 370, commenting on a peace treaty Valens had made in 369 with some Goths (in Themistius' classicising Greek, Goths are usually 'Scythians'). It reflects a general contention underlying both Themistius' expressed thoughts, and those of many of his contemporaries, that the inhabitants of the Roman Empire (or rather its élite) were actually made more rational by the classical cultural tradition in which they were customarily educated. Its accumulated *exempla* of human virtue and vice would, if properly digested, enable an individual to control his emotions.[2] 'Barbarians' not fortunate enough to share this education, remained prey to their every passion, unable to steer a sensible and rational course.[3]

Apart from anticipating Goody and Watt on the consequences of literacy by the best part of 1,600 years,[4] Themistius' writings set the agenda

---

[1] Themistius, *Or.* 10, ed. Downey, p. 199 lines 14–18; English translation: Moncur in Heather and Matthews (1991: 38–9).

[2] Thus Themistius continues: 'it is virtue's task to render [the passions] submissive and amenable to the dictates of the intelligence'. Themistius' whole conception of philosophy is precisely the ability to pull out historical examples to illustrate the correctness or otherwise of any course of action.

[3] For Themistius, 'barbarians' are men, but lesser men: *Or.* 10, p. 212 lines 1 1ff. (cf. *Or.* 16, p. 299, lines 14–15). This greater rationality is a common conceit, underlying the characterisation of Scythians (again = Goths) by the historians Eunapius and Zosimus as dishonest and faithless – i.e. unable to steer a consistent course; cf. Gregory Nazianzus, *Ep.* 36 on Modares: a faithful Goth and the exception to the rule – and the conception of Libanius and Synesius of Cyrene that the Goths' natural state was slavery (*Or.* 19.16, 20.14; *De Regno* 21, ed. Terzaghi, pp. 49ff. respectively). On Graeco-Roman perceptions of their own cultural superiority, see Dauge (1981); Teillet (1984: pt 1).

for this chapter. For the migration period (set in motion by the arrival of nomadic Huns on the fringes of Europe in *c.* 370) brought together the two culturally disparate groups Themistius defined so clearly, if one-sidedly, and eventually led to the replacement of the Roman Empire in the West with a series of Germanic successor states. In what ways did literacy continue, fail, or come to empower states, groups, and individuals in the course of this sea-change in European history?

Literacy and power in the non-Roman world

There is some evidence for literacy in the non-Roman, especially the Germanic, world before *c.* 370. Runes had existed for centuries, and were clearly in use. To take the Goths as an example, runes have been found on pottery, on a spindle-whorl, on a spear-head, and on a famous gold torque from the Pietroasa treasure.[5] The extent and variety of their use, however, is difficult to estimate. Tacitus famously describes the use of runes, or something like them, in divination (*Germania* 10), and later commentators ascribed a magical significance to the individual marks.[6] Perhaps considered a particularly powerful means of communication with the superhuman world, their control may have empowered a priestly class. The possibility that runes were also used for more mundane communication should not be excluded *a priori*. They were sufficiently well known for Ulfila's Gothic alphabet to borrow some letters from the runic futhark,[7] and were originally devised for engraving on wood, a material very unlikely to survive. It can only be an argument from silence, but later examples show that runes could have been used for messages and records (see further below).[8]

The most striking advance in Germanic literacy, however, was the creation of literary Gothic in the circle of Ulfila in the mid-fourth century. An exciting philological enterprise, its effect on the relationship between literacy and power is hard to estimate. All surviving remains of Gothic are linked to Christianity: mostly fragmentary Biblical texts, but also some commentaries and other liturgical materials (Biblical Gothic was probably rather different from the everyday language since word-order, idiom, and syntax followed the patterns of Ulfila's Greek model).[9] Thus Gothic

---

[4] Cf. Goody and Watt (1963).
[5] For refs.: Heather and Matthews (1991: 94, 154).   [6] Page (1987: 14–22).
[7] Heather and Matthews (1991: 154): how many is complicated by the heavy dependence of runes upon Latin characters.
[8] Cf. Kelly (1990: 37–8) on runes in early Anglo-Saxon England, citing the 500 or so runic texts surviving from 14th-century Bergen.
[9] Friedrichsen (1926: esp. 15–34 and 169ff.) on the Gospel text; Friedrichsen (1939: esp. 40–61, 111–27, and 257ff.) on the Epistle texts. For an introduction: Heather and Matthews (1991: chs. 6–7).

literacy in this form was probably largely the preserve of, and may have again empowered, a priestly class. In the long run, the creation of a Gothic Christian community around the Gothic Biblical text was to have profound historical effects, but this was largely accidental. The Goths' political leadership finally accepted Christianity as they crossed the Danube in 376, and, not surprisingly, adopted it in the form advocated by Ulfila. Ulfila and his supporters held to a pre-Nicene definition of Christianity which was also consonant with the form of Christianity preferred by the then emperor, Valens.[10] After Valens' death, the Theodosian dynasty decisively shifted the balance back in favour of Nicaea, but the Goths held to the faith they had received. As a result, an alien community within the Empire found itself equipped with a deviant form of Christianity, which was widely received among other Germanic immigrants into the Empire, creating a divide which on occasion led to considerable troubles within different successor states.[11] In 376, however, the Goths were just trying to adopt the religion of the emperor Valens, not use a variant of literate Christianity to strengthen their sense of identity.

Neither runes nor the Gothic Bible provide insights profoundly helpful to this enquiry, and the clearest evidence for literacy in the non-Roman world before c. 370 is actually for a functional knowledge of Greek and Latin, enabling different individuals to make their way in the Roman world. No doubt the majority were of humble status, such as the guardsman who, in winter 377/8, returned home to spark off an invasion of Raetia, or the troops of the Rhine army who had been promised that they would not have to serve too far away from home.[12] Many of these may only have spoken Greek and Latin, of course, but, particularly from the time of Constantine onwards, a string of senior generals of non-Roman origin appear in our sources. Sometimes this can be misleading, in that a non-Roman name might hide the Roman pedigree of someone born and bred in the Empire, but the truly foreign origin of some is attested to, and it seems likely that they could deal with written as well as spoken Greek or Latin. In the early 380s, for instance, the newly arrived Gothic renegade turned imperial general Modares received two letters from Gregory Nazianzus and replied in between.[13]

Such linguistic facility might seem surprising, but, by the fourth century, the Roman Empire had impinged upon the Germanic world for at least 300 years, and contact in a whole range of fields – cultural, economic, military,

[10] Heather (1986); Heather and Matthews (1991: ch. 5).
[11] A good survey is Schaferdiek (1970); an English translation of one central text – Victor of Vita, *Historia Persecutionis Africanae Provinciae* – has just been published: Moorhead (1992).
[12] Ammianus 31.10.3; 20.4.4.
[13] Jones (1964: 98, 619–23) on generals particularly of German origin; Greg. Naz. *Ep.* 36–7.

and political – meant that this frontier (like so many others) was no impenetrable barrier. In the fourth century, one Gothic prince spent time as a hostage in Constantinople, and, even beyond the frontiers, Germanic rulers had to cope with imperial diplomatic correspondence. In one famous incident, letters from the Alamannic king Vadomarius to Constantius II were intercepted by the emperor Julian.[14] Another interesting case involves the Gotho=Roman peace treaty with which we began. In 365, the relevant Goths interfered in the civil war between Valens and Procopius, sending the latter military support. After his defeat and death, they excused themselves to Valens on the grounds that Procopius – a member of the Constantinian dynasty – had sent them letters reminding them that their current peace agreement had originally been made with his relative, Constantine I, and that they should therefore support him. This has sometimes been interpreted to mean that the Goths were very literal in their understanding of written documents.[15] But their support of Procopius belongs to a much broader context of unrest; in 362/3 the Goths had tried to get Julian to change the nature of their obligations, and, in 364 took advantage of the Romans' defeat in Persia to stir up trouble. The Goths were probably calculating, therefore, that support for a grateful usurper was more likely to give them what they wanted than head-on confrontation, and the pious reference to Constantine was no more than a specious excuse.[16]

The evidence is spectacularly sketchy, but there is enough here to show that literacy of a number of different kinds was at work beyond the frontier, and was being manipulated by different individuals and groups according to their best interests. To place this material in a more interesting context, it is perhaps worth referring briefly to a quite different range of evidence. Imperial propaganda of all eras presents a fairly constant image of the inferiority of 'barbarians'; a series of fundamental changes had transformed the Germanic world beyond all recognition, however, in the first three centuries AD.

Taking the political map, first of all, the multiplicity of small groups encountered in Tacitus' *Germania* had given way, at least in the vicinity of the frontier, to a few much larger groups: Saxons, Franks, and Alamanni on the Rhine, with Burgundians further to the east, matched in scale by Goths on the Danube.[17] Consonant changes had occurred in political structures. In place of temporary war leaders, ruling dynasties had begun to appear. Among the Goths, power passed between three generations of the

[14] The hostage (*Anon. Val.* 6.31), was perhaps the father of Athanaric: Wolfram (1988: 61–4); letters of Constantius II: Ammianus 21.3.4–5.
[15] Ammianus 27.5.1–2; cf. Wolfram (1988: 65–6).   [16] Heather (1991: 115–17).
[17] There were others, and some older groups retained their identity within the larger formations, but the *Germania* refers to well over fifty independent political groups. Some relevant reflections: Heather (1991: 86–7); James (1988: 34ff.).

same family before 370.[18] There is also much archaeological evidence for increased social stratification; rich burials became more common, and the diversity between richer and poorer burials more striking. Literary evidence similarly provides examples of specialised warrior groups which by the fourth century were quite substantial; at the battle of Strasbourg, the Alamannic leader Chnodomarius had a personal retinue of 200 men (Ammianus 16.-12.60). All of this was powered by an economic revolution. The extensive agriculture and dispersed settlement patterns typical of the early iron age were increasingly replaced by intensive, integrated pastoral/arable farming, which was carried out from large, long-lived villages. There is even evidence of craft specialisation, most strikingly in the production of glass, which began for the first time beyond the Roman frontier in the late third century.[19] This adds up to a complete shift in the internal power relations of Germanic groups, creating large chieftainships or proto-states which were powerful enough to issue challenges to and make demands of the Roman Empire.[20]

The point of this brief excursus is precisely that literacy played no obvious part in what was clearly the big story of the Germanic world in these years, where the creation and maintenance of power seems to have involved flexing everything other than literary muscles. There is, however, one important caveat. It is inconceivable that these proto-states were not running tribute systems of some kind. Regular subventions would have been required to maintain specialist warrior retinues, and there is some archaeological evidence for larger settlements with considerable storage facilities, perhaps illustrating the type of centre from which such systems were run.[21] Such systems would obviously have required checking and enforcement, so that it is conceivable that literacy and/or record-keeping had some importance (perhaps even providing a non-religious role for runes). This is frustratingly speculative, but given such obvious advances in sophistication, it would be unwise to insist too fiercely on the non-existence of records.

Literacy and power in the Roman world

Shifting our sights to the Roman world, literacy was, by contrast, closely related to the exercise of power on a whole range of levels.[22] Indeed, there is

[18] Wolfram (1988: 61–3).
[19] See e.g. Hedeager (1988); Bloemers (1989); Pearson (1989); Myhre (1978); Fulford (1985); cf. the general comments of the introduction to Gledhill et al. (1988).
[20] Cf. above p. 180 on the Goths; on the similar activities of the Alamanni: Heather (1991: 120).
[21] For refs. to such centres relevant to the Goths, Heather and Matthews (1991: 57).
[22] While I accept the general picture painted by Harris (1989), I do not find the final chapter on Late Antiquity, arguing that a general decline had set in by 350, or even 400, convincing. A good discussion is Vessey (1992: 149–52); cf. further below p. 194.

far too much relevant material to do it justice here, and all I will attempt to do is highlight a few areas of critical importance.

Most obviously, literacy was central to the power of the imperial state machine. As Wickham has rightly emphasised, a distinguishing feature of the late Roman state was its ability to raise large sums of money from a land tax, precisely targeted upon the largest sector of the economy. This revenue paid for a large professional army (estimates range between 300 and 600,000 men), and a vast range of other governmental activities.[23] Even if the full complexity of the original design of the Diocletianic system – involving allowances for different qualities and categories of land – was not maintained,[24] the system still generated enormous amounts of paperwork, controlling both income and expenditure. Tax records were also subject – as they had to be to remain serviceable – to a continuous process of emendation as land moved in and out of production and population changed.[25]

The Empire's legal structures were similarly dependent on literacy. Late Roman legal codifications – those of Gregorianus and Hermogenianus at the turn of the fourth century, followed by those of Theodosius II and Justianian in the fifth and sixth centuries – are the most dramatic demonstrations of legal literacy, but represent no more than the tip of the iceberg. They were only necessary because a steady flow of written imperial edicts continually updated a system which was based on written law, with documentary evidence as the foundation of proof. The state also took responsibility for regulating the whole legal profession, and placed itself at the heart of dispute settlement in the Roman world by making sure that cases were settled in accordance with its regulations, in courts that it sanctioned, in front of judges who were state servants.[26]

Links between literacy and power in a bureaucratic state require no further belabouring. What I would like to draw attention to, however, is a second, and quite different, level on which literacy and power operated together. By the fourth century, a very particular kind of literacy, the product of an equally particular type of education, provided social cement for the entire Empire.

The general features of this education require only brief comment. Its characteristic method – whether in Latin or Greek – was a painstakingly thorough grounding in a small canon of literary texts: Virgil, Cicero, Sallust and Terence in Latin-dominated parts of the Empire, the Greek

---

[23] Wickham (1984).   [24] Cf. Harris (1989: 290–1).
[25] Jones (1964: esp. 448–62, 586–96).
[26] Basic account Jones (1964: ch. 14), though inclined, in my opinion, to overstate the propensity for chaos.

equivalents being Homer (above all), Euripides, Menander and Demosthenes.[27] Between five and ten years were spent in grinding through every line of these texts under the demanding eye of the grammarian, this labour having two main purposes. Above all, the student learnt 'correct' language; phonology, morphology and the rules governing individual parts of speech were laboriously and no doubt repeatedly explained. Kaster's recent study has brought the late Roman Latin grammarian and his linguistic rules beautifully to life, showing how a once controversial figure had, by the fourth century, established himself as the unique arbiter of 'correct' language. The linguistic aim of such an education was that the student should have a complete mastery of 'correct' language and a ready facility to compose in it himself. Such was the attention to detail that students came away knowing large amounts of their texts by heart; one friend of Augustine's could recite all of Virgil and much of Cicero from memory. At the same time, the grammarian also used incidental references within the texts to transmit a broader cultural education, instructing his students in ethics and history as the texts dictated.[28]

Two particular aspects are worth singling out. The regime has been criticised for its narrowness, and accused of producing individuals who were unfit to govern.[29] Fostering practical governmental skills, however, was not the point. As Kaster has recently re-emphasised, such an education actually functioned as a caste marker. The grammarians' rules created and maintained a totally artificial language – not susceptible to normal linguistic transformations over time – by which the ruling élite of the Empire could recognise one another. Graffiti from Pompeii, for instance, suggest that the linguistic changes which created Old Romance were already under way in the first century AD, but, thanks to the grammarian, were resisted by the imperial élite, in formal contexts at least, for as long as the Empire survived (their eastern counterparts held Greek in a similar straitjacket).[30] The amount of schooling required to master this artificial language meant that only fairly well-off families could afford to educate in it one or more children. Thus, while acquisition of this education could potentially generate social mobility, in practice mobility was strictly limited. Augustine was the son of a town councillor from a small North African municipality, and this clearly placed him on the fringes of those able to afford a full education. At one point, he had to cool his heels at

[27] Marrou (1982: 161–4), changing composition of the Greek canon; (ibid.: 277–8), Latin authors.
[28] Marrou (1982: 164–75), Greek, (ibid.: 279–83), Latin; Kaster (1988: esp. chs. 1–2). See also Desbordes (1990: esp. chs. 2–4). Cf. Dionisotti (1982) for examples of school texts. Augustine's friend: *De Anim. et Eius Orig.* 4.7.9; cf. Brown (1967: 36).
[29] MacMullen (1962, 1976: 48ff.); cf. Kaster (1988: 12–13 with other refs.).
[30] Wright (1982: 30, 48 with refs.); see further below n. 74. On the creation of this language: Desbordes (1990: pt 2, esp. chs. 7–8, 10–13, 15, 18).

home for a year while his father got the money together for him to go to Carthage.[31] By the later fourth century, this was an education affordable – with few exceptions – only by the curial classes and above.[32]

It is also worth reflecting on the intellectual content of this education. In fact, there was very little. The grammarians stressed toil, and much time was spent in memorising rules, and learning by heart examples of their application. Much of this must have been very dull, and its is hardly surprising that the schoolmaster and the cane went hand in hand. Cleverer students – like Augustine – must have become bored and disruptive, the less able were hit until they managed to force the rules into their memories. Indeed, where an educational system functions as a class marker, then its contents may be arcane, but must not be too intellectually demanding. Elite parents will become restive if their children regularly fail to acquire the requisite educational distinctions; the mark of élite status must be something that even the slowest children of the upper class can grasp (if hit sufficiently hard over a long enough period). In such circumstances, it is the stupidest children of the upper class who will dictate educational standards.

Such observations aside, the central point is that, by the mid-fourth century, this kind of education had become the *sine qua non* for a rewarding career in the imperial bureaucracy, the upper reaches of which were expanding steadily. The language of this burgeoning bureaucracy, and therefore of government, was precisely the 'correct' language of the grammarians, and, at a rough calculation, something like 3,000 good jobs existed in each half of the Empire by *c.* 400 AD.[33] A very particular kind of literacy thus empowered individuals in crucially important ways. Not only was it in itself a mark of distinction, but, when used to win a bureaucratic job, also brought further rewards: consisting not just of a salary, but of a series of rights and privileges which the individual could use to reinforce his claim to élite status.[34]

Knowing Virgil off by heart is not an obvious qualification for tax-collecting, however, and the bureaucratic structure of the Empire displays other odd features. Substantial numbers of the best jobs, for instance, were *dignitates* held only for short periods. Over fifty proconsuls of Africa are known to have held office between 357 and 417, averaging

---

[31] Brown (1967: 38).

[32] Cf. Nellen (1981: ch. 3); considerably modifying such studies as Hopkins (1961, 1965). See also Kaster (1988: 23ff.). On mobility and the Constantinopolitan Senate, with some comment on literary culture, see Heather (forthcoming a).

[33] Heather (forthcoming a: fig. 1) – defining a good job as one which brought the holder senatorial or top equestrian status.

[34] See generally Jones (1964: esp. 396–401, 535–42, 601–6); Heather (forthcoming a). I believe that Jones overstresses the desire of landowners to escape local office; the right office provided opportunities to dominate local society.

little over a year each. Even a much more important job, such as the Praetorian Prefecture of the East, saw little greater continuity. Between 337 and 369, eleven men held office, averaging three years each, while between 414 and 455 the average tenure was considerably less, at about eighteen months.[35] Another odd feature is that, in addition to their normal complement of staff, the great central ministries had large waiting lists of supernumeraries, queuing for an ordinary place within the bureau. In 399 AD, there were 224 established *largitionales* in the East, for instance, but 610 supernumeraries.[36]

The central structures of the late Roman state cannot, therefore, be characterised as a straightforward, well structured bureaucracy, and, as A. H. M. Jones commented,[37] the total edifice cannot have been very efficient. Efficiency was probably not, however, its main point. The peculiarities of the system (short tenures and large waiting lists) all tended to maximise the number of people able to hold office or at least have some interest in the bureaucracy, in any given period. At the same time, the educational requirement meant that all these people (or the vast majority of them) necessarily came from the élite landowning classes of the Empire. I would argue, therefore, that the odd structure of the bureaucracy actually addressed the main internal political problem of the later Empire. By the fourth century, what had originally been a conquest state had long since evolved into a community of relatively equal communities. The slowness of communications also meant that much power had necessarily to be devolved from the centre. The main structural problem in such a context was how to achieve devolution without generating political fragmentation.[38]

A totally artificial, shared literary literacy gave a sense of identity to a landowning class widely dispersed between Hadrian's Wall and the Euphrates; it also incidentally provided them with an enemy to unite against, in the form of 'barbarians' considered the antithesis of their cultural tradition. At the same time, the fact that this shared artificial literacy was the key to rewarding careers, both gave mastery of it an extra functional point, and meant that the landed classes had every interest in involving themselves actively in the state. A shared literacy, the key to élite status and rewarding careers, was thus the cornerstone of the social fabric of the late Empire.

This structure was only in part created from the centre. In many cases, emperors were responding to mass demand when creating jobs, or allowing

[35] Jones (1964: 380–1).
[36] *C.Th.* 6.30.16; cf. Jones (1964: 584–5). Supernumeraries are also known in the *sacra scrinia* and the *agentes in rebus*, and similarly gathered around legal courts (ibid. 507–10).
[37] (1964: 383).
[38] The magnitude of the problem is underlined by, for instance, the inability of the Carolingians to hold together a substantially smaller area for more than two generations.

them to continue, but this very fact reflects a strong interest at the local level in involvement at the centre, which can only have added to the overall health of the imperial organism.[39] Some areas were seemingly under-represented. Few Romano-Britons, for instance, appear in fourth-century sources holding high office, and it may well be no accident, therefore, that Britain generated more political unrest in the fourth century than most other areas.[40] Nor, of course, were there enough jobs for everyone. There were, however, plenty per generation: quite enough to make most members of the élite think it likely that they *might* get one, and this would have been the crucial point. Overall, we can think of the late Roman landowning élite very much in terms of a textual community, as defined by Brian Stock.[41] Characterised by their possession of an intimate knowledge of the same small corpus of literature, these people had their lives fundamentally shaped by this knowledge.

There are obviously many other areas in which literacy impinged upon power. Other, less distinguished, teachers of language operated at lower levels, offering to a more modest clientele approximations of the grammarian's wares. A whole range of other literacies were the result, which trained individuals for technical scribal and notarial jobs, and were no doubt a path to reasonable prosperity for individuals, as well as reinforcing the literate infrastructure of the Empire.[42] It is high time, however, to look forward to the collision of the two quite separate cultures we have briefly surveyed.

States beyond the Roman frontier

In states which emerged outside the old Roman frontier in the course of the migration period, literacy seems to have played as marginal a role as it had done in the Germanic polities of the fourth century. Our best evidence comes from Attila's Hunnic Empire.

Here literacy continued to play an important part in diplomacy. Attila kept a Roman prisoner from Upper Moesia, one Rusticius, precisely for his skill in drafting letters in Greek and Latin (Priscus, ed. Blockley fr. 14). Otherwise, we know that Attila extracted Roman secretaries from Aetius (one of whom met a sticky end[43]), and there is some evidence of

---

[39] Heather (forthcoming a); cf. *C. Th.* 12.1 for laws attempting to keep town councillors out of central government jobs. These laws are well known, but usually given a thoroughly negative gloss as 'the flight of the curials': cf. (e.g.) Jones (1964: 737–63).

[40] Campbell et al. (1982: ch. 1).   [41] Stock (1983: esp. 90–2 and conclusion).

[42] On the lesser guardians, see Kaster (1988: 44ff.); cf. on shorthand specialists (*exceptores*), Teitler (1985: esp. chs. 2 and 7).

[43] Cf. *Prosopography of the Later Roman Empire* II 319, Constantius VI and VII (separate figures); Constantius VI was crucified.

list-keeping. When the embassy which included Priscus the historian arrived at Attila's court, its members were belaboured, amongst other things, with a list of refugees whose return Attila demanded. What evidence there is suggests that this list contained relatively few names of prominent individuals; two unfortunate renegade princes were returned with Priscus' embassy (and subsequently executed), and the specific discussions we know of all concerned small numbers.[44]

The question of scale has broader relevance, because the Hunnic Empire certainly operated tribute systems (Priscus, ed. Blockley fr. 49). An obvious question, therefore, is whether this involved bureaucratic control of however rudimentary a kind – the operation of lists[45] – or whether surpluses were collected on an *ad hoc* basis. At this point the question is unanswerable, and what indications we have raise as many questions as they answer. One of Bleda's wives, for instance, ruled a particular village, and several more were controlled by Berichus, 'one of the leading men of Scythia'[46]; how much organisation did this kind of allocation require? The Hunnic Empire – like other nomadic Empires[47] – was capable of exercising power on a considerable scale, but military hegemony was the basis of it, and there is no clear evidence of an important bureaucratic, hence literate, component. Similarly, the individual's road to high status was a martial one. The case in point, of course, is the former Roman merchant captured by the Huns, whom Priscus met in Attila's camp. By the time they met, the prisoner had won freedom, wife, and fortune through martial endeavour (Priscus, ed. Blockley fr. 11.2, pp. 266ff.). Links between literacy and power in such contexts were clearly not very direct.

Successor states

In the medium term

Within states which emerged inside the old Roman frontier, literacy remained much more closely associated with power, except in Anglo-Saxon England, where there is no evidence at all of continuity in Roman learning. Even in the west of the island, their Latinity suggests that both Patrick (*c.* AD 450) and Gildas (*c.* 550), despite all the disruption, received good-quality Roman educations, and, on the continent, the prestige value attached to 'Roman' learning everywhere remained strong. Merovingian

---

[44] Priscus ed. Blockley fr. 11.2, p. 246 (17 fugitives mentioned, in addition to those already handed over), p. 249 (5 of the 17 sent on the embassy), pp. 254–6 (the list).

[45] Cf. Goody (1977: 90ff.); Goody (1986: esp. 37–56) on the importance of lists.

[46] Priscus ed. Blockley fr. 11.2: Bleda's wife (pp. 260–2); fr. 14: Berichus (p. 292).

[47] Cf. *Miracula Sancti Demetrii* 284–5, ed. Lemerle 2.5, pp. 227–8 on the Avar reorganisation of Bulgarians and Roman prisoners into a new social group.

kings customarily learnt to read in the sixth century, and some verses of two 'barbarian' royal poets have survived: the Visigoth Sisebut and the Merovingian Chilperic, who also attempted alphabet reform, ordering four extra letters to be taught in schools.[48] Successor kings likewise patronised classical poetic grandiloquence. The *Latin Anthology* was put together in Vandal Africa, where Luxorius achieved considerable success, one Lampridius won favour with his verses at the court of Euric the Visigoth (where Sidonius Apollinaris also tried to use poetry to win relief from exile), and Venantius Fortunatus was welcomed in sixth-century Frankish Gaul.[49] In these and other ways, the self-proclaimed superiority of classical culture was accepted on its own terms: nowhere more so than in Ostrogothic Italy. Different letters of the *Variae* collection, for instance, have Theoderic supporting all its central pillars: the rule of law, literary education, and the claim that these maintained an order put in place for mankind by the Divinity. He even used this as an ideological stick with which to beat the rulers of other successor states, who were explicitly cast as inferior (morally as well as technologically) to the extent that their rule failed to maintain the Roman way.[50] Classical literary culture, then, was still highly admired, and still the vehicle for individual advancement. A civilian upper-class career structure even survived in certain areas. The *Variae* are full of references to civilian bureaucratic posts, and the *Breviary of Alaric* implies a similar continuity in southern Gaul and Spain.[51]

What one might term administrative literacy – the more obviously functional pursuits of the Roman bureaucracy – were also taken up in some of the successor states. The land tax was inherited directly by Franks, Visigoths, and Ostrogoths (though not, it seems, by Anglo-Saxon and British kings). Amongst other things, the land tax made successor kings much richer in relation to their own followers than ever before, and parvenu royal dynasties (Merovingians, Balthi, and Amals respectively) attempted to use this extra power to distance themselves from potential rivals. Theoderic used Italian tax revenues, for instance, to fund a hierarchy of posts for which Gothic nobles could compete. To this extent, Roman bureaucrats could be allies of kings against their original followings.[52]

[48] Britain: Lapidge and Dumville (1984). Gaul: Norberg (1954: 131ff.); Wood (1990: 67, 73). Spain: Fontaine (1980); Collins (1990: 115–16); cf. Riché (1976: 256ff.).

[49] Luxorius: Rosenblum (1961: 25ff.). Euric: Nixon (1992: 73–4 with refs.); cf. Sid. Ap. *Ep.* 8.9. Venantius: see now George (1992: passim).

[50] Heather (forthcoming b). See especially *Variae* 3.3 and 2.40 on Clovis, together with 1.46 on Gundobad, on the varying inferiorities of other kings. Usage in the *Variae* is totally consistent: the Goths are never 'barbarians', other peoples always are. The refs. in nn. 48–50 considerably modify the still essential account of Riché (1976: ch. 2, esp. 53–60).

[51] On the *Breviary*, there are useful comments on Jones (1964: 257–9).

[52] Gothic dynasties as parvenus: Heather (1991: 19–33); rise of Clovis: Gregory of Tours, *Hist.* 2.37–40. Hierarchy of posts: *Variae* esp. book 7.

There was also considerable continuity in the organisation of legal affairs. The picture seems clearest for the Burgundian and Visigothic kingdoms, where Roman legal structures survived in two distinct ways. First, both produced summaries of Roman law – the *Lex Romana Burgundionum* and the *Breviary of Alaric* (or *Lex Romana Visigothorum*) – drawing on the major sources of Roman legal authority as they were understood in the late fifth century: the Codes, especially the Theodosian Code, imperial novels issued since the latter's publication, and the writings of the jurisconsults.[53] Both texts stand in an unbroken Roman tradition, not only because of their contents, but more especially because they attempted to solve the most pressing contemporary problem in Roman law: how to turn disparate sources of law and the ever-increasing mass of new imperial rulings into a coherent system. Both were realisations, if on a much smaller scale,[54] of a project envisaged but not undertaken by the compilers of the Theodosian Code in the 430s, and only brought to fruition in the *Digest* of Justinian.[55]

Also very much in the tradition of written Roman law, Visigothic and Burgundian kings issued and collected written declarations, by which the law continued to be updated. This tradition put down strongest roots in the Visigothic kingdom, the results clearly visible in a second text, the Visigothic Code (or *Forum Iudicum*), a collection of royal rulings subsequent to the collection of the *Breviary*. Visigothic Kings explicitly demanded that cases not covered by previous edicts should be referred to them. They also laid down severe penalties should cases be decided without reference to their legal texts, and periodically reissued the Code with necessary revisions. When a revised text was compiled, old editions had to be destroyed. A direct continuation of Roman traditions thus allowed Gothic kings to place themselves in the emperor's old position, at the heart of dispute settlement.[56]

The independent kings of Burgundy acted in precisely the same way. A second text from this kingdom, often known as the *Lex Gundobada*, fulfilled the same function as the Visigothic Code. Its proper title, and a much better name for it, is the *Liber Constitutionum*, for that is precisely what it is: a collection of new royal decrees (not all with dates), dealing with new cases and revising established rulings. Its level of sophistication was not as great as among the Visigoths. The contents of the *Liber Constitutionum*

[53] *Lex Romana Burgundionum*, ed. de Salis; *Lex Romana Visigothorum*, ed. Hanel.
[54] Especially true of *Lex Romana Burgundionum*: a short text which may not have been royally sponsored; Wood (forthcoming).
[55] The second Theodosian project that never appeared is described at *C. Th.* 1.1.5; Justinian's project: Honoré (1978: ch. 5).
[56] *Forum Iudicum*, ed. Zeumer; cf. Wormald (1977: esp. 113, 117, 124); Collins (1983: 24ff., 1990: 117–18).

were not arranged by subject and title, for instance, as was the Visigothic Code. A subject will be dealt with, on occasion, at one place, a series of other topics will then be covered, only to be followed by a further ruling on the first subject. To take, however, the example of inheritance in marriages without children (met first at 14.2, returned to at 42.1, and again at 74.1), the second and third rulings explicitly refer back to the first and second, and are clearly modifications put forward on separate occasions. There is a principle of organisation here, then, but it is chronological not topical; broadly speaking, rulings seem to have been added to the end of the text as they were given. A fundamental Roman legal principle was that the latest ruling had most validity, so that such a pattern of organisation, if not matching the Visigothic ideal (where chronological order was maintained within separate topics), was far from irrational.[57]

In Ostrogothic Italy, no summary of Roman law was produced, but this was for ideological reasons. The Ostrogothic regime presented itself as marking no break with the past, and part of this conceit was an obsessive respect for imperial prerogative. Only emperors could tamper with fundamental law (*ius*). Other officials could, however, issue edicts (*edicta*), so Theoderic and his successors made their legal pronouncements in this form.[58] In practice, it is hard to see that this distinction hampered their ability to legislate. In both Gothic kingdoms and among the Burgundians, then, literate Roman legal traditions simply continued, considerably expanding the powers of the Germanic kings they now served.[59]

Further north, this was only partly the case. In Britain, legal literacy seems to have played no role whatsoever in the early Anglo-Saxon kingdoms. Their kings may well have had important legal functions, but made no use of charters or written law-codes before the reintroduction of Christianity in the seventh century. By contrast, the *Book of Llandaff* shows that the written grant was important in the British world, even if again no law-codes were issued at this early date.[60] The situation in Frankish Gaul is more difficult to read, but does seem to fall somewhere within the spectrum of possibilities encountered so far: strong continuity in Roman patterns close to the Mediterranean, becoming weaker as one moves north. Frankish kings issued no compendium of Roman law, but after 507 took

---

[57] Again (cf. n. 54) it is not clear whether the *Liber Constitutionum* in its entirety is a royal compilation, or, at least in part, the work – for instance – of a lawyer collecting new rulings as he could. See further Wood (forthcoming).

[58] *Edict of Theoderic*, ed. Baviera; *Edict of Athalaric: Variae* 9. 18; see further Heather (forthcoming b).

[59] See further Riché (1976: 71–8, an account again supplemented and modified by the material in nn. 53–8.

[60] Anglo-Saxons and Charters: John (1960: ch. 1). British: Davies (1982); cf. Nash-Williams (1950).

over lands where the *Breviary* had already been promulgated, and, after the conquest of Burgundy in the 530s, this role could also have been filled by the *Lex Romana Burgundionum.*[61] *Lex Salica* itself is also a puzzle. The text tradition includes two prologues (a longer and shorter) and one epilogue; the shorter prologue describes *Lex Salica* as the work of four wise law-givers, but the longer prologue and the epilogue credit royal initiative. The latter are certainly later additions (early Carolingian and later Merovingian respectively), but it is not certain either that the shorter Prologue was part of the original recension.[62] All one can say is that there is no sign whatsoever that *Lex Salica*, although probably originating in royal circles,[63] ever boasted a Preface extolling the virtues of a royal creator.

Its purpose and relation to any Roman law collections in circulation are equally mysterious. Although written in Latin, it came equipped with vernacular glosses, and its contents bore little relation to Roman law. Frankish kings did on occasion issue Roman -style edicts (some of which survive). This has led Ian Wood to suggest that *Lex Salica* may actually be similar to the *Liber Constitutionum* or the *Forum Iudicum*. Rather than a body of material issued on one occasion, it is possible (as with many of the Burgundian edicts) that dates have simply been omitted. If so, *Lex Salica* would be evidence for a living tradition of written royal law. The manuscript evidence does provide some indication, however, that an original 65-title text was composed as a single entity, and its contents (particularly the long lists of injuries and compensations) are perhaps more suggestive of fundamental codification than of a collection of updating edicts.[64] At this point, then, definite conclusions would be rash. It would be wrong to minimise either the role of documents (of various kinds) in the settlement of disputes,[65] or the importance of Frankish kings to the legal process.[66] None the less, it would seem that among the Franks royal power

[61] Sixth- and seventh-century evidence shows that Roman legal texts, mainly in the form of Alaric's *Breviary*, were known and used in secular as well as ecclesiastical contexts: Wood (forthcoming).

[62] *Pactus Legis Salicae*, ed. Eckhardt. On the competing prologues and epilogue, see Wood (forthcoming). I am grateful to Patrick Wormald (pers. comm.) for the observation that the shorter Prologue is never transmitted other than in association with the longer Prologue, and that the main evidence for its priority is its use by the author of the *Liber Historiae Francorum*.

[63] Wormald (1977: 108).

[64] Eckhart showed that the Malberg glosses were part of the original text. Royal edicts: most are incorporated into *Lex Salica: PLS* 66ff.; cf. also *Capitularia Merowingica* 1, ed. Boretius, and Gregory of Tours, *Hist*. 9.20; cf. Wood (forthcoming). Again I am grateful to Patrick Wormald (pers. comm.), for underlining the strong MS evidence suggesting that the 65-title 'A' text was originally self-contained, although its earliest MS is no earlier than 770 AD. See Eckhardt's introduction to his edition of A, esp. pp. xxviii–xlii; McKitterick (1989: 40ff.); Wormald (1977: 109–10), on contents.

[65] James (1983); Wood (1986); Fouracre (1986); Wood (1990).

[66] E.g. the importance of appealing to the king in the dispute at Tours recounted by Gregory:

was not enhanced by an alliance with Roman legal literacy to quite the same degree as among the Goths and Burgundians. Frankish kings do not seem to have issued codifications of Roman and subsequent legislation in their own names, nor regularly updated an established body of written law with their own edicts.

The difficulties of *Lex Salica* aside, in the medium term – say the mid-sixth century – literacy clearly continued to play a fundamental role in the business of government in most successor kingdoms. As such, it certainly empowered kings. Apart from taxation and law, the *Formulary of Marculf* (a seventh/eighth-century compilation, much of whose contents is sixth-century) presents a striking picture of Merovingian kings issuing written orders on a wide range of subjects: requisitioning food, making gifts, granting protection, responding to petitions, making episcopal appointments, and so forth. There is even a model letter for writing back to the king to say that his written command had arrived.[67] Literacy also continued to empower individuals who served in administrative capacities. At the top end, governmental service was still the path to very great success for individuals such as Cassiodorus, Parthenius and Asclepiodotus.[68] On a much more modest scale, local scribal or notarial traditions seem to have continued in some places unbroken from late antiquity.[69] Literacy thus remained a valuable skill in a wide variety of social contexts.

In the longer term

Taking the slightly longer term, however, there are important ways in which literacy – especially, but not simply, classical literary literacy – became increasingly marginal both to the winning of power by individuals, and to its public exercise by kings. There were significant regional variations; literate law-making traditions continued unbroken in Visigothic Spain throughout the seventh century.[70] But in the bulk of the old imperial territories of western Europe, literate royal administration shrank in importance.

The beginnings of decline can perhaps already be seen in the sixth century. The appearance of books of *formulae* may in itself suggest a loss of vitality, if we take their existence to mean that official letter-writers now needed models to follow. We have already met the *Formulary of Marculf*, and Cassiodorus explicitly prepared some of his *Variae* for the same

Hist. 7.47, 9.10.
[67] Marculf, *Formulae*, ed. Zeumer; cf. James (1988: 186–9); cf. Wood (1989: 64–6).
[68] A few from a much longer list; for discussion of such men, see Riché (1976) as below n. 88; Wood (1990 and forthcoming).
[69] McKitterick (1989: 81ff. esp. 85) on Raetia, with suggestive remarks about northern Italy.
[70] And beyond: Collins (1983: 129ff., 1985).

purpose.[71] Our ignorance of late imperial bureaucratic training methods, however, makes it dangerous simply to assume that such models had had no precedents.[72] A decline in classical literacy is unequivocally demonstrable, however, in the writings of laymen.

Ian Wood has recently drawn attention to a letter-writing tradition in Gaul, which started in late antiquity with Sidonius Apollinaris, stretched through the Burgundian period with Avitus of Vienne (the contemporary collection of Ferreolus of Uzes has unfortunately been lost), and continued long into the Merovingian period. The *Epistulae Austrasiacae* (itself possibly a formulary) bears witness to a sequence of letter-writers including Gogo, Parthenius, and Desiderius.[73] The contributors to this line were clearly conscious of continuity; all wrote in the full-blown highly rhetorical style – *stylum pingue atque floridum* – considered appropriate in the late imperial period. On another level, however, these writers also highlight a crucial change. For, while the later writers produced a decent imitation of the 'correct' style, their grammar and orthography were far from classical.[74] In late antiquity, absolutely 'correct' language was everything; any linguistic failing made it clear that a person had socially dubious origins. The non-classical Latin of these later writers thus tips us off that the link between a shared artificial language and élite status had already been broken (in Gaul at least) by the mid- to late-sixth century.[75]

On a different, and even more fundamental level, the land tax disappeared from western Europe as a major instrument of power, although it did continue to be levied in Byzantine southern Italy. In some cases, the disappearance would seem to have had straightforward causes; in northern Italy and Britain, the arrival of the Lombards and Anglo-Saxons seems to have been attended with too much disruption for complex tax structures to survive. But in Francia and Burgundy, Frankish kings gradually abandoned the land tax over time, as, seemingly, did Visigothic kings in Spain (although the evidence is not quite so clear).[76] This development is very perplexing; why did Frankish kings give away the single most potent lever of government which the Roman Empire had delivered into their hands?

---

[71] Books 6 and 7; cf. Barnish (1992: xv, xviiiff.).

[72] Cf. Noble (1990), the Papacy closely followed imperial bureaucratic practice and (esp. 95–6) used *formulae* for training, so this may have been standard Roman practice.

[73] Wood (1990: 67–71).   [74] Wood (ibid. 71–2).

[75] Cf. Wood (ibid. 71); the situation is complicated by the fact that Latin was gradually being ousted by Romance. As above p. 183, however, Roman upper-class classicism may have been holding Romance in check since the first century, and its spread among the educated may be effect rather than cause of the breaking of élite literary literacy. See further Wright (1982: ch. 2) for archaising written forms after *c.* AD 500.

[76] Wickham (1984); cf. Collins (1983: 109), Spain; Brown (1984: 113–16), Byzantine Italy. On Britain, see further below p. 196 and n. 87. The attempt of Durliat (1990) to argue for the survival of large-scale taxation is unconvincing.

Much of the answer to this question is tied up with the fate of the Roman landowning upper class in the post-Roman period. If there is an orthodox answer to this question, it is that these men turned their backs on secular politics, and sought refuge in their libraries and the Church. Sidonius Apollinaris' career move to become bishop of Clermont can be put alongside the world unlocked by Gregory of Tours a century later to illustrate the rise of great episcopal dynasties of Roman aristocratic descent.[77] Such a transformation is certainly part of the story, and the period which concerns us did see important developments in the tripartite relationship of Church, literacy and power.

The triumph of Christianity is sometimes seen as the root cause of the disappearance of Roman classical literacy. One easily identifiable line of Christian thinking overtly hostile to classical letters can be found in works by men such as Caesarius of Arles who were strongly influenced by ascetic traditions.[78] A second, and more dominant strand of thinking, however, preferred to this total rejection of classical authors the kind of compromise evolved separately in the fourth century by Basil of Caesarea and Augustine. Both cheerfully identified aspects of the traditional pagan education useful to such Christian activities as Biblical interpretation, and exploited them to the full.[79] Thus Oberhelman and Hall have recently demonstrated that Jerome, Ambrose and Augustine were conscious stylists who made traditional kinds of choices between different modes of discourse according to the particular audience they envisaged for any individual piece of work. All assumed that the devices of classical rhetoric were entirely appropriate for Christian use, and, at the same time, created a new Christian literary form by combining this classical heritage with a homiletic style modelled on the Bible.[80] Fifth-century Gallic writers continued and developed this accommodation in a variety of forms, and the mantle was picked up in the sixth century by Cassiodorus, Gregory the Great and Isidore and Leander of Seville, as well as finding a reflection in the court culture of Merovingian Gaul.[81] Even Gregory of Tours stands partly in this tradition; although commending his own non-classical Latin for its accessibility, he was nevertheless sniffy about Chilperic's inability to make his verse scan properly.[82] Late and post-Roman Churchmen, then,

---

[77] See e.g. Heinzelmann (1976a and b); Van Dam (1985: ch. 7); Mathisen (1979); Kaster (1988: 92).   [78] See e.g. Riché (1976: ch. 3); cf. Harris (1989: 299ff. with refs.).

[79] E.g. Basil, *On Greek Literature*; Augustine, *De Doctrina Christiana*. The secondary literature on this subject is enormous; a brief selection: Marrou (1982); Riché (1976: ch. 3); Kaster (1988: 70–95), all with further refs.

[80] Oberhelman (1991); Oberhelman and Hall (1984, 1985a, 1985b, 1986a, 1986b); I am grateful to M. Vessey for these references.

[81] Gaul: Vessey (1988). Sixth century: Riché (1976: ch. 5 with refs.); Wood (1990).

[82] Gregory of Tours, *Hist.* 5.44; cf. Wood (1990: 67, 71–2). See also Goffart (1988: ch. 3) on Gregory as a literary stylist.

wrote with different purposes in mind from their forebears among the
imperial landowning élite, but were happy to accept a traditional
education, for as long as it was available, as a first step towards wisdom,
and did not cause its decline in any straightforward way.[83] Christianity may
be part of the answer via its promotion of new types of literary activity,[84]
but it is hard to believe that this alone would have altered the hold of
literary literacy upon the élite, had not it coincided with a profound
transformation in the socio-political structure of western Europe.

For the fate of the Roman landowning class in post-Roman Europe has
been only very incompletely told. The mass of Christian literature which
dominates our sources makes the aristocrat-turned-bishop a well-
documented figure, but he represents merely a part of the story. By the third
quarter of the sixth century, the same military obligations were being
imposed by the kings of successor states upon the descendants of their
Roman subjects as upon the descendants of their original followers. The
end of the Roman Empire saw a single unitary state being replaced by
several mutually hostile successors, and the fires of war were further
charged by the habit of dividing realms equally between a king's sons.
Faced with endemic insecurity, it is hardly surprising that monarchs
demanded military service above all from their populations. There is no
space here to do more than state this baldly, but it brought about a
sea-change, as battlefield rather than bishopric replaced the bureau for the
bulk of the post-Roman élite.[85]

For one thing, it changed the balance of the political relationships which
had underwritten the land tax. In the late Empire, the *quid pro quo* which
made the population (and especially the landowning élite) at all willing to
pay their taxes was the fact that the state's professional army defended
them. Once the general population was required to act physically in its own
defence, this relationship was undermined, especially since the 'barbarian'
followers of the same kings had probably never paid taxes. It thus became
increasingly common and expected for kings to grant tax immunities as a

[83] It is perhaps no accident, therefore, that many Christian educational initiatives broadly
coincide with the disappearance of grammarians in the sixth century at different points
depending upon geographical locale (earlier in Gaul and Spain, later in Italy, for instance).
The relevant material is surveyed in Riché (1976: chs. 4–5).

[84] Cf. Vessey (1992: 149–5, and esp. 159–60) for some opening remarks to this important line
of enquiry.

[85] Though sometimes noted (e.g. Van Dam 1985: 152), this crucial transformation requires a
separate study, and I will do no more than list some evidence. Francia: Gregory of Tours,
Hist. 4.30 shows that *civitas* levies were composed of Gallo-Romans as well as Franks (for
an introduction to these levies – and most known derive from areas not settled by Franks –
see Bachrach (1972: 66ff.). Visigothic Spain: *Forum Iudicum* 9.2 (laws 8–9 make clear the
obligations falling on Hispano-Romans). Even in Byzantine Italy, a military aristocracy
dominated: Brown (1984: esp. chs. 4–5).

mark of favour.[86] Other factors, of course, were also important. The dislocations associated with the prevalence of warfare within and between the successor states also meant that it was harder to maintain the administrative and economic structures – land and population registers, and a plentiful coinage – which made a land tax feasible to collect. In these circumstances, it was perhaps natural for tax dues to be transformed into an obligation to provide periodic hospitality for kings and their immediate retinues, the fundamental right around which itinerant early medieval kingship was built.[87] The change in élite life-styles thus undermined the land tax in a variety of ways and broke the link between literacy and state power. As Wickham articulated so clearly, the disappearance of the land tax also meant that early mediaeval states – unable to draw upon a large and annually renewable source of revenue – were fundamentally weaker than their Roman predecessor.[88]

The same sea-change also broke the link between classical literacy and high status. Classical literacy was an artificial standard, which could be maintained only by paying someone for the best part of ten years to beat it into one's children. Once this education was no longer the key to a whole range of highly rewarding careers, then, certain individuals aside, the average élite parent would not be so ready to pay for it. This, I would argue, is what underlay the end of classical literacy between the late fifth and subsequent centuries. Once the financial benefits of this kind of education disappeared as bureaucrats became warrior aristocrats, the grammarians lost most of their customers, prompting the collapse of a privately financed educational infrastructure.[89] The disappearance of bureaucratic careers thus pulled the rug out from underneath the whole edifice by which classically 'correct' Latin had been maintained. No one (and certainly not the Christians) wanted the grammarians to go out of business, nor did Goths go round assassinating them. Elite status now revolved around

---

[86] Again, some evidence. Late Roman Empire: Ammianus 20.11.5 for the complaint of Ursulus, Count of the Sacred Largesse, about idle soldiers wasting taxes; or Zosimus 3.33ff. on responses to the surrender of Nisibis to the Persians. Post-Roman world: Gregory of Tours, *Hist*. 3.36 on the lynching of Parthenius, financial officer of king Theudebert, because of the taxes he imposed. For this and other material suggestive of a world where granting tax immunities had become a more valuable act to kings than the levying of taxation, Wickham (1984: 21–2). A partial parallel is provided by close relationships between William I and his main henchmen which meant that so many tax immunities were granted to (or simply taken by) them after the conquest that the *heregeld* drastically declined as a source of revenue: Harvey (1987).

[87] The literature on itineration is enormous; a very important study is Charles-Edwards (1989), making a crucial distinction between honourable obligations to provide hospitality and dishonourable obligations to provide tribute.

[88] Wickham (1984).

[89] Kaster (1988: 216–30) on the limited role of state subventions.

military service and royal favour, and in this new context the grammarians and their wares became redundant.[90]

From the militarisation of the aristocracy, therefore, followed a shift in political relationships and in the means by which the social élite was defined. As we have seen, its effects were felt at different times in different places: in the fifth century in Britain, but considerably later closer to the Mediterranean. Everywhere, however, this transformation made redundant both taxation mechanisms and the role of classical Latin as a class marker. It did not, however, bring literacy to an end, nor break its link with power on every level. Ian Wood has recently argued convincingly for the existence of a Merovingian court culture shared by laymen and ecclesiastics, together with their womenfolk, who all had some education. It was, however, a different kind of literacy, which did not lead its lay participants to active classicising composition, or much composition at all. A pattern had been set which did not really change until after the twelfth-century renaissance, when active writing, as opposed to a more passive ability to read, regained a general importance among laymen which had been lost somewhere in the late fifth and sixth centuries.[91]

[90] Cf. above n. 75 on the possible link between this development and the long-delayed triumph of vernacular Romance. The change, of course, did not happen everywhere at once, and classical cultural distinction continued to be associated with high status for some time. Very quickly after 500, however, this link was being maintained by individual initiative and family traditions, rather than forming a structural part of upper-class life: Riché (1976: 184ff., 250ff.) has gathered the material for Gaul and Spain respectively, suggesting, as one might expect (cf. p. 189) that the link retained more vigour in Spain.

[91] Wood (1990). On active lay literacy in the later Middle Ages, and the important point that before this many could read even if unable to write: Clanchy (1979: ch. 7, esp. 182). (I was unable to consult the new and expanded edition of this work.)

13   Texts as weapons: polemic in the Byzantine dark ages

Averil Cameron

The so-called Byzantine 'dark ages', that is, the period which runs from the later seventh to the ninth century, are characterised both by profound social change and by a striking concern for texts and their authority. In the sixth century, Justinian was burning the books of suspected pagans and closing the Academy at Athens;[1] in AD 843, the so-called 'triumph of orthodoxy' marked the official ending of the Iconoclast controversy and released a considerable recovery of learning and a flowering of encyclo-paedism and codification. A parallel process took place in visual art, licensing the liturgical use of icons and permitting the development of the classic Middle Byzantine scheme of church decoration.[2] Historians remain divided as to the extent of urban breakdown or continuity during these centuries, which had seen the dramatic loss of two-thirds of the territories of the Empire, and the reasons behind the imperial policy of Iconoclasm which split Byzantium for more than a hundred years from the reign of Leo III, but the extent of the social, military and administrative change taking place in the Byzantine state is well recognised.[3] The military system, the mode of taxation and the constitution of the élite were all undergoing a process of transformation, even if the surviving evidence does not allow us to trace it in detail.[4] Out of this period of change emerged the 'Middle Byzantine state', different in many important ways from its early Byzantine predecessor. In part for that very reason, contemporaries liked to gloss over the unlovely record of the Macedonian dynasty itself and emphasise the alleged order and continuity of Byzantine institutions; just one of the literary productions of the tenth century which does so, while affirming the social and administrative hierarchy which had by now emerged, is the *Book of Ceremonies* of the Emperor Constantine VII Porphyrogenitus,

---

[1] Malalas, *Chronographia*, p. 491 Bonn; Lemerle (1986: 76).
[2] Schulz (1986: 55–6); Brubaker (1989a, 1989b).
[3] See Haldon (1990). Discussions of the social and economic transformation abound: see for example Kazhdan and Epstein (1985: ch. 1); Harvey (1989: ch. 1).
[4] The 'themes': Haldon (1990: ch. 6); tax system: Oikonomides (1987); administrative class: Winkelmann (1985, 1987a).

with its constant stress on the importance of *taxis* ('order') in the state.[5]

During the 'dark' centuries of Byzantium one thing that was at stake was the role – even the very existence – of the state. Catastrophic loss of revenue-bearing territory to the Arabs, the removal of the court to Sicily for a time during the seventh century, repeated and dangerous Arab sieges of Constantinople culminating in that of AD 717–18, all put the state's very survival in jeopardy. The population of the capital city shrank dramatically, reaching on one recent estimate a low of scarcely more than 40,000.[6] Against this background came the Iconoclast controversy, following soon after the last, and only narrowly averted, Arab siege. This long internal struggle (it did not end until AD 843) prominently displayed that tension between church and state which was to characterise much of the later history of Byzantium,[7] reflected potential or actual fissures between the army and their leaders and the rest of the population, and brought to the fore the monasteries from which some of the resistance to Iconoclasm was led. Questions of the location of power in society at large, and of the authority of church and state, were therefore contested during this period on a variety of different levels; this must be borne in mind throughout as forming the background to the texts and issues that form the subject of this chapter.

As traditionally defined by historians, 'dark ages' are usually those we don't know much about, and this is certainly true of the later seventh and eighth centuries in relation to traditional secular historiography. The sources for what we might call the political history of the period are exceptionally sparse. Recent work has made it clear once again how little there is of substance in either the *Short History* of the Patriarch Nicephorus or the *Chronicle* of Theophanes, our two main historical sources, and how little historical material was actually available in Constantinople for the period in question.[8] Virtually nothing was written in Constantinople itself up to the 780s.[9] The cost and rarity of books, especially outside a very limited number of centres, have also been emphasised, and the consequences for literacy in the period have received some discussion, with emphasis on the paucity of available information.[10] Yet the sheer volume of religious and ecclesiastical writing is simply enormous. Literally millions of words were pouring out. Some of the most important writers in Byzantine or orthodox theology belong to this period. Others less well-known but

---

[5] Cameron (1987).   [6] Mango (1985: 54).

[7] See Brown (1973) for Iconoclasm as an assertion of imperial authority.

[8] Mango (1978, 1990); see also Whitby (1992: 66–74).

[9] Mango (1992: 149); the *Parastaseis Syntomoi Chronikai* is put *c.* 800 by Berger (1988: 40–9), as 'ein typisches Werk der ersten Phase der byzantinischen Renaissance' (ibid.: 47).

[10] Mango (1975) is basic; on literacy see Mullett (1990), with earlier bibliography.

equally voluminous are becoming more accessible thanks to modern critical editions, among them Anastasius of Sinai, author of a wide range of polemical and catechetical writings in the late seventh century.[11] The beginnings of the Byzantine commentaries on the liturgy also lie in this period. So do several important collections of miracle stories attached to shrines of particular saints – which are, among other things, a prime source for the study of popular culture, 'rationality' and the survival of paganism, magic and other non-Christian elements. Naturally these are not at all necessarily the artless compilations they may appear: the stories attached to the Egyptian shrine of SS Cyrus and John, for instance, were edited by Sophronius, the future patriarch of Jerusalem and a highly learned man.[12] The *Miracles of St Demetrius*, to take another example, are an extremely important source for the history of early mediaeval Thessaloniki and exist in two parts, the first put together by an early seventh-century archbishop of the city and the second a later supplement.[13] The huge range and quantity of available material can also be seen within the large *œuvre* of individual writers; Maximus Confessor and John of Damascus are exceptional, perhaps, but others have also left very extensive writings.

These works are all to a greater or less extent ecclesiastical or religious in character, a fact which has tended to prevent them from receiving the full attention of historians. What we note in the present context, however, is that this literature and its exponents, and indeed, the whole religious history of the period, show an extraordinary awareness of the importance of texts, in particular in relation to the many bitter religious divisions. Texts not only carried authority; they could also be, and indeed were, used as weapons. The religious polemic of the period is worth studying in itself in terms of the attitudes displayed towards textual authority, and the techniques used – in terms, in fact, of its contribution to the sociology of knowledge; but it may also illumine a dark period of Byzantine history. At any rate, it deserves not to be marginalised because it is the wrong kind of literature.

A high proportion of the surviving works, as also of those known only indirectly, consists of material written with a polemical purpose. Iconoclasm itself, a policy initiated by the imperial court, and which objected to the veneration of religious images, was actively implemented, by physical force, by the whitewashing of church walls and the imprisonment of monks; but it was also hotly fought over in words, and inspired large quantities of 'hate' literature, of which most of that extant comes from the iconophile side, i.e. from the victorious party. Nowhere is this polemical tendency more clearly seen than in the surviving proceedings of the Second

---

[11] See Cameron (1992).   [12] Ed. N. Fernandez-Marcos (Madrid, 1975).
[13] Ed. Lemerle (1979–81); see Cormack (1985: ch. 2).

Council of Nicaea in AD 787, which temporarily vindicated images. But the eighth-century Iconoclast emperor Constantine V himself wrote a polemical attack on images in which he showed himself to be a considerable theologian,[14] and the Iconoclastic council of Hiereia, called by him in AD 754, argued out its side of the matter in detail. Typically, its records having been efficiently suppressed by the winning side, we know of it only through iconophile condemnation; the 'Horos' ('definition') of the Council of AD 754 was formally read out and as formally refuted at the Second Council of Nicaea in AD 787.[15] As will be seen, this and the other councils of the period placed a quite exceptional stress on textual proof and on the authenticity of the texts cited. Predictably, therefore, the Iconoclastic controversy led not only to the 'discovery' of hitherto unknown texts, but even to actual falsification. Once this was noticed, it was everywhere suspected, and measures introduced to guard against it, for Iconoclasm also acted as a stimulus to a certain kind of 'research'. Already the Sixth Ecumenical Council of AD 680–1, which had formally condemned the doctrine of Monothelitism supported by several seventh-century emperors, had been much concerned with the authentication of the citations adduced during its proceedings.[16] Books were brought out under seal, by imperial order, and so high did suspicion run that eventually the emperor decreed that no more written testimonies could be admitted, only oral evidence; the documents that were submitted were subjected to comparison with copies kept in the patriarchal library, only to be found wanting in completeness.[17] In AD 649, a meeting in Rome attended by many Easterners, which came to be known as the Lateran Synod, incorporated into its acts a whole range of quoted statements and documents attacking Monothelitism and attempting to anathematise its originators.[18] As the emperor Constans was a supporter of Monothelitism, Maximus Confessor, who was one of the leading spokesmen in Rome, and his supporters, were in practice setting themselves up as the true upholders of orthodoxy against the imperial church. Both Pope Martin and Maximus himself were eventually put on trial in Constantinople and both died in exile (AD 655 and 662). All these events, like the complicated narrative of the promulgation of and resistance to Monothelitism in the 630s and 640s, placed the status of certain texts at a premium, and gave rise to a deluge of writing, and especially of polemic.

[14] The so-called *Peuseis* ('Inquiries'), known through the *Antirrhetici* of Nicephorus. Text: Hennephof (1969) 52ff., with Mondzain-Baudinet (1989) 10, 301; see also Gero (1974, 1975). The *Peuseis* had an iconoclastic *florilegium* attached, also preserved by Nicephorus.
[15] G. Mansi, *Sacrorum Conciliorum Nova et Amplissima Collectio* (53 vols., Paris–Leipzig, 1901–27) XIII 202–364.   [16] On this see Herrin (1987: 277–9), and further below.
[17] Ed. Riedinger (1990: 179.2–3, 208.20–1, 232.11–12); the issue turned partly on the testimonies produced in a Monothelite *florilegium*, which was eventually ruled out of court (ibid.: 276).   [18] Ed. Riedinger (1984: 425–36) for the dyothelite *florilegium*; below, 209.

The proceedings of the trials themselves provide yet another example.[19] To take only one further example, we may turn to the public debate held in Carthage in AD 645, on the very eve of the defeat of the exarch Gregory by the Arabs, between the same Maximus Confessor and Pyrrhus, the controversial former patriarch of Constantinople. Though this was not to be the end of the story, on this occasion Pyrrhus acknowledged defeat and travelled to Rome with Maximus, where he asked forgiveness from the pope for his error. But the debate – in Greek – remains, another example of this zeal for the marshalling of theological argument in a polemical context.[20]

Even these few examples give some idea of the importance of debate and polemical argument in this context. They may also hint at a certain kind of scholasticism in regard to ecclesiastical texts, which is already becoming characteristic in the period.[21] Yet another process can be traced, that of the steady production of various kinds of didactic literature for the purpose of Christian instruction. Some of this material has been surveyed in an important article by J. Munitiz, which surveys Byzantine methods of religious instruction, and classifies some of it as 'catechetical', in particular the religious treatises, the sets of questions and answers on religious topics and the collections of edifying stories.[22] But my emphasis here is rather a different one. For behind the desire to instruct lay the insistence on orthodoxy and the appeal to authority, while correct belief was itself defined by attacking what was held to be incorrect. Very often, therefore, instruction itself proceeded by means of polemic. The recently edited *Hodegos*, or 'Guide', by Anastasius of Sinai (late seventh century) is a lengthy, and at times even impassioned, attack on Monophysites, cast, like many such works, in the form of a dialogue or debate.[23] And while they also belong in a long preceding tradition of such works, the treatises from this period listing and attacking heresies, such as the *De haeresibus et synodis* attributed to the patriarch Germanos I of Constantinople (resigned AD 730), and of course John of Damascus' *De Haeresibus*, fulfil a similar function.[24] Exiled as an iconophile by Leo V in the early ninth century, the Patriarch Nicephorus used his time in composing a series of violent attacks on the strain in Iconoclast thought represented by Constantine V, and in developing a whole language and typology of condemnation.[25]

[19] See Winkelmann (1987b) for the sources for the Monothelite controversy, fragmentary enough in their present state, but indicative of intense activity involving letters, treatises, meetings, debates and polemical tracts.

[20] *Patrologia Graeca* 91.287–354; see Haldon (1990: 306–8); Van Dieten (1972).

[21] Alexander (1957) traces this tendency during the second phase of Iconoclasm in the early ninth century, but it can be seen developing earlier: Cameron (1990).

[22] Munitiz (1988).

[23] Ed. K.-J. Uthemann, Corpus Christianorum series graeca 8 (1981).

[24] Germanos: *Patrologia Graeca* 98.40–88; John of Damascus, *De Haer,* ed. Kotter IV (1981).

[25] Mondzain-Baudinet (1989: 327–50) provides a lexicon of Nicephorus' polemical vocabulary.

Thus the Byzantine 'dark ages', I want to argue, were a period which saw an enormous amount of polemical argument, marshalling of proof texts, collecting of citations and refinement of the techniques of controversy. Now the collection of citations and polemical argument had admittedly been features of Christian writing since a very early stage. All the same, I would point in this period to two particular features: first, the very frequency, not to say dominance, of such material, which in the absence of secular alternatives comes to occupy the centre stage, and second, the strong tendency towards synthesis and codification that we find in many of these texts. In what follows I want to look first at the weapons themselves – the armoury of polemic – and then to raise some of the questions which they suggest.

I want to point first to some of the particular types of polemical writing employed by authors in the period; these are, in turn, disputations, *florilegia*, heresiologies, catecheseis, and syntheses. While we are not on the whole in the presence of new phenomena in Christian writing, their sheer frequency during this period does seem to mark out these forms for special attention, the more so since there is so little secular material against which to set them. It is worth asking what general conclusions if any can be drawn from the prevalence of such material.

The first phenomenon to be noted, then, is one to which I have drawn attention elsewhere, namely that of the very frequency of disputation or debate – argument set in dialectical, and often in polemical form. By 'disputation' I mean formal debate between real or imaginary interlocutors, either mentioned in the sources, or, as often, preserved in literary form. Such debates range from highly scholastic literary exercises to informal conversations mentioned but not written down, or at least, not preserved. Thus St Symeon the Younger (late sixth-century) is said to have debated with astrologers, and Anastasius of Sinai refers to 'debating' with Arabs (διαλέγεσθαι).[26] Maximus' debate with Pyrrhus in Carthage is an example of a public debate which does survive. The proceedings at the church councils also belong to this category, as in the sixth session of the Seventh Council of AD 787, when each clause of the Definition of the Iconoclast council of 754 was formally read out, followed by its iconophile refutation ('the refutation of the fabricated and falsely called "Definition" of the mob assembly of the accusers of the Christians', as its supporters called it).[27] Debates are recorded on many subjects, and on many levels. Clearly these were sometimes real, and indeed, major, confrontations; thus there were, from the sixth century onwards, several large-scale debates between

---

[26] On the latter, see Griffith (1987); Symeon the Stylite: *Vita Symeonis iun,* ed. P. Van den Ven (Brussels, 1962–70), 157, 138–9.   [27] Mansi 13.205a, transl. Sahas (1986: 49).

Chalcedonians and Monophysites. In addition we also have literary debates against Manichaeans and Nestorians, while a particular sub-category among the literary debates consists of those between Christians and Jews, or more properly, works purporting to be discussions but actually consisting of Christian polemic against the Jews.[28] Very many literary works written in the period on theological issues were themselves cast in the form of a dialogue. Thus the Patriarch Germanos' dialogue *On the Terms of Life*, dealing with the question of predestination,[29] and several disputations no longer surviving on the subject of Monothelitism, two ascribed to the emperor Heraclius.[30] It was both conventional and natural, therefore, to cast the major concerns of the day into the genre of a formal debate instead of a continuous argument; another example was the so-called *Nouthesia*, a disputation about religious images which allegedly took place in the reign of Constantine V between an Iconoclast bishop and an iconophile monk.[31] Now dialogue had already had a long history in Christian literature, and the Christian/Jewish disputations in particular reach back as far as the second century. What is impressive here is rather the very large number and wide range of known examples from the period. The works attributed to John of Damascus alone included a whole range of such disputes, among them his treatise against the Manichaeans, which consists of a mechanical dialogue, described as a λογικὴ συζήτησις (a 'theoretical', or 'philosophical' discussion),[32] and the genre continued to be practised by his successors at the monastery of Mar Saba near Jerusalem. It was to become the standard vehicle for the later Christian *apologiae* against Muslims, in the production of which Mar Saba played a vital role.[33]

Within the structure of the surviving dispute texts, a characteristic technique consisted in the marshalling of citations and the exegesis of proof texts. Again, *florilegia*, or collections of such texts designed to prove a particular point, had already emerged at an earlier stage in Christian controversy. In our present period many collections of such proof texts were in circulation, some overlapping in content, of which a number are incorporated into the texts of the disputes themselves. These polemical or doctrinal *florilegia* (as distinct from the spiritual *florilegia* which were also developing during this period)[34] tended to draw on Scriptural citations (in

[28] On debates and disputations in general, Cameron (1991); Christian/Jewish disputations: Déroche (1991).

[29] Garton and Westerink (1979); Speck (1986: 226) dates the work to the ninth century on stylistic grounds.

[30] See Winkelmann (1987b).   [31] For this see Herrin (1987: 366).

[32] Ed. Kotter (1969–88: IV 333–98); the fact that works on this theme might form part of the repertoire during a dialectical/rhetorical training (Lieu 1992: 216) does not preclude them from also having a wider contemporary significance.

[33] See e.g. Griffith (1990).   [34] Richard (1964); Chadwick (1966).

particular in the case of the Christian/Jewish disputes) or citations from the Fathers. In either case the aim was twofold: first, to appeal to authority and tradition, and second, in case of a challenge, to provide a correct exegesis. Thus the anti-Jewish disputes, among them the so-called *Trophies of Damascus*, probably of AD 681,[35] strive to show that Jesus was indeed the Messiah foretold in the Old Testament; the repertoire of available quotations was already traditional – it is the technique which is of interest. There were also ready collections of Scriptural texts with which to rebut Jewish objections to Christian belief, especially to the doctrine of the Trinity and the belief that Jesus was the Son of God. One of the main charges allegedly imputed by Jews against Christians in the seventh century was the accusation that they were idolaters through their worship of the Cross, and, later, icons; against these charges Christian controversialists collected passages from the Scriptures which showed Jews venerating material objects. Leontius of Neapolis is one author of an apology against the Jews who included a *florilegium* in his dialogue.[36] Monothelite *florilegia* also existed, as did Monophysite ones; at the Sixth Council in AD 680–1, Macarius of Antioch produced a Monothelite patristic *florilegium* whose status the Council discussed in much detail.[37] Anastasius of Sinai's *Hodegos*, already mentioned, incorporates a range of extracts from the Fathers directed against Monophysites, and his other works include a *florilegium* against the Monothelites;[38] lost doctrinal *florilegia* feature among the works attributed to Sophronius and Maximus. Hitherto unknown texts were introduced into the debate: the Iconoclasts produced a letter of Eusebius of Caesarea to the Empress Constantia and part of a letter attributed to Nilus of Ancyra.[39] In his treatise on the *trisagion*,[40] John of Damascus explicitly argues against a patristic *florilegium* compiled by an 'abbot Anastasius' in order to justify the opposing cause. It was therefore inevitable that iconophile and Iconoclast *florilegia* would also be developed. The *Horos* ('Definition') of the Iconoclastic council of 754 came together with its attached *florilegium* of extracts held to justify Iconoclasm, among them Eusebius' letter.[41] In contrast, and very deliberately, the Council of AD 787 did not itself make use of *florilegia*, but drew its citations only from complete books, precisely because the use of *florilegia* had been so discredited by misuse.[42] On the other hand, the brief to the committee

---

[35] Ed. Bardy, *Patrologia Orientalis* 15 (Paris, 1927) 169–292; see Déroche (1991: 280).
[36] See also Déroche (1986).   [37] Chadwick (1992: 631).
[38] Ed. K.-H. Uthemann, Corpus Christianorum series graeca 12 (1985) 87–96.
[39] Mansi 13.292B–324C; see Maraval (1987). Letter to Constantia: Mansi 13.313A; Gero (1981). The effect of the citation of Eusebius was to revive his Arianism as a live issue: Mansi 13.316A.   [40] Ed. Kotter (1969–88) IV 289–332.
[41] See Anastos (1955); Alexander (1958); Maraval (1987).
[42] See Van den Ven (1957), especially at 360, citing the account of the fourth session, where

charged by Leo V with the task of preparing the Iconoclastic council of AD 815 included yet again the task of putting together an Iconoclastic *florilegium*.[43] It was a long tradition: Theodoret's *Eranistes* provides a fifth-century model both for the dialogue form and for the use of *florilegia*, and *florilegia* were already in use at the councils of Constantinople (AD 381) and Chalcedon (AD 451). But in our period such works enjoyed a veritable boom.

Heresiologies, works which we may call 'catalogues' of wrong belief, also flourished. Again, the term serves to designate a range of works, one among which is the treatise *De Haeresibus et Synodis* attributed to Germanos I.[44] This is at first sight simply an unoriginal listing of heresies, with their refutations, following earlier works such as Epiphanius' *Panarion* (fourth-century), a work which by now was cited as a classic of the genre. Ironically, Epiphanius, included in the Iconoclastic *florilegium* of AD 754, was an author especially favoured by the Iconoclasts, who claimed him as an opponent of images – to which the iconophiles at II Nicaea retorted that the texts they attributed to Epiphanius were actually by someone else.[45] He had already been cited at the Sixth Council for his attack on Arianism.[46] But heresiologies are not innocent lists, and Germanos' treatise had a strongly contemporary purpose, in that it supports the claims of the Sixth Council in relation to conciliar tradition generally, which, assuming that part to be genuine, it then accuses the Iconoclasts of abandoning. There are difficulties about Germanos' authorship, and about his own position *vis-à-vis* Monothelitism. Munitiz has shown however that in addition to its denunciation of heresies, the argument of the work represents an important early stage in the development of the synopses of the councils, which later proliferated into a full-blown genre in their own right.[47] From a later perspective, it was essential that the Sixth Council be recognised as official, and similar issues were to arise over that of AD 787, whose status was challenged in turn in AD 815.[48] Finally, the victory of the iconophiles in AD 843 would authorise the evolution of an 'official' version of the first seven councils as constitutive of correct belief. As part of this development, the iconophile seventh council was now commemorated in religious art

this is made explicit. This article investigates in detail the citations used at the council of 787, and discusses the contribution of the Acts of the Council to the manuscript tradition of the works it cites; see also Mango (1975).   [43] Mondzain-Baudinet (1989: 16).
[44] *Patrologia Graeca* 98.40–88; Gouillard (1965: 306–7). On the question of authenticity of the chapters about images see Stein (1980: 262–8), dating them just before AD 754, and in general see also Munitiz (1988: 78), with the observation that the longer treatises, such as Epiphanius', must have been 'intended for professional theologians'.
[45] See Gouillard (1965). Epiphanius and images: Maraval (1987).
[46] Riedinger (1990: 328–9).   [47] Munitiz (1974).   [48] Alexander (1953, 1958).

along with the six earlier councils, of which it could now be presented as the culmination.[49] As for the *De Haeresibus et Synodis*, the argument leads logically to Iconoclasm as the greatest heresy of all, while icons are defended in turn by reference to the tradition of the Fathers and the councils: the human representation of Christ was ordained by the Sixth Council and is therefore itself part of that tradition.[50]

John of Damascus' *De Haeresibus*, in which he develops Epiphanius' *Panarion*, is another example of these listings of heresies and their refutations. The technique of counting Islam a 'heresy', assuming the final chapter on the Arabs to be genuine,[51] was already traditional in the case of Judaism and 'Hellenism', and is here yet another device designed to bring a problem under control, by demonstrating that Islam too was merely another departure from the tradition of the Scriptures and the Fathers. Other such works included a certain Timothy's *De Receptione Haereticorum* and Theodore of Raithu's *Praeparatio*.[52] Their polemical intent is obvious enough; we can also point to the *Synodical Letter* of Sophronius of Jerusalem (AD 634), presumably one of many such, in which the new patriarch announced his orthodoxy by long lists of anathemas, pronounced first against all individual heretics from Simon Magus to John Philoponus and those living in Sophronius' own day, and then against thirty-odd named sects.[53] Later in the seventh century, the anonymous author of the anti-Jewish disputation known as the *Trophies of Damascus* composed a companion piece, directed against Monophysites, in which he first lists and attacks all heresies, beginning with that of 'the famous Arius'.[54] By the ninth century, Nicephorus' works written in exile included a heresiological work known as the *Apologeticus Maior*.[55] These and similar texts engage in a crucially important activity in terms of the development of belief-systems, that is, classification, or the naming of parts;[56] in a context of intense argument over belief, their role becomes all the more significant.

Up to a point, the heresiological treatises also fall within the scope of catechetical literature, designed to inform the faithful, or to tell the clerical how to inform the faithful, about the constituents of correct belief. More obviously instructive at this level however are the several surviving sets of questions and answers, which might, like the so-called *Quaestiones* of

[49] Walter (1987).   [50] *Patrologia Graeca* 98.80A.
[51] See now Le Coz (1992). John's treatise reaches a total of one hundred heresies, whereas in the fourth century Epiphanius had managed to count eighty-seven.
[52] *Praeparatio*, ed. Diekamp (1938); Timothy: *Patrologia Graeca* 86.40–45.
[53] *Patrologia Graeca* 87.3189–92, 3193, also included in the documents of the Sixth Council; see Munitiz (1974: 152n.).
[54] Ed. Bonwetsch (1909); the prologue is published by Bardy, *Patrologia Orientalis* 15 (1927) 277ff.   [55] *Patrologia Graeca* 100.533–831.   [56] See e.g. Douglas (1987).

Pseudo-Athanasius,[57] themselves contain material from *florilegia*, and even passages of traditional disputation material. The types of 'questions' answered in these texts range from correct procedure in relation to the Eucharist, through moral and sexual matters, to beliefs about fate and paradise. Much of this material is pastoral in character, and the canons of the Quinisext Council of AD 691, which was mainly concerned with pastoral matters and questions of church discipline, certainly suggest that such material may have filled a gap. In contrast, some of Maximus Confessor's collections of questions and problems (*Quaestiones, Ambigua, Aporiai*), also containing many earlier extracts, are far more abstruse and scholastic, and belong probably in more monastic milieux.[58] All sorts of issues thus suggest themselves in relation to this material: what is popular and what scholastic, how did such writings circulate, what was the oral component and what connection is there if any between the sets of questions, the collections of miracle stories and the 'edifying tales', also being put together at this time? Any answers would be premature, as these works are for the most part only just beginning to receive critical editions. But in total this material too points in the same directions as the other kinds of works that we have already surveyed.

Catechesis shades easily into synthesis, another genre whose purpose is to provide the correct answers. Collections of material from conciliar canons fall into this category, but so does the compendium of John of Damascus, the *Fount of Knowledge*, and, earlier, Maximus' scholia on Pseudo-Dionysius the Areopagite and the commentaries on the liturgy by Maximus (*Mystagogia*) and Germanos (*Historia Ecclesiastica*).[59] The sheer volume of these works is overwhelming; but, again, they have a contemporary point to make, and here too it is ultimately a polemical one. This is not encyclopaedism simply for its own sake; it always has an argumentative object in view. It is there to prove a case.

Finally, some of these authors and controversialists resorted to outright forgery. So much depended on authoritative texts that the temptation to manufacture them was very great. So great in fact that although several scholars have recently written about the use of forgeries in this period, and about its corollary, the concern for verification, I think we are only just

[57] *Patrologia Graeca* 28.597–699.
[58] *Ambigua ad Iohannem iuxta Iohannis Scotti Eriugenae latinam interpretationem*, ed. E. Jeanneau, Corpus Christianorum series graeca 18 (Louvain, 1988); *Quaestiones et dubia*, ed. J. H. Declerck, Corpus Christianorum series graeca 10 (Louvain, 1982) (miscellaneous questions, many Scriptural, much cited in later collections); *Quaestiones and Thalassium* I–II, ed. C. Laga and C. Steel, Corpus Christianorum series graeca 7, 22 (Louvain, 1980, 1990) (similar).
[59] See Taft (1980–1), with Cameron (1992: 37–8); Schulz (1986: 43ff., 184ff.). Taft sees Maximus's work as directed at a monastic audience.

beginning to realise the full implications. Again, forgery and tampering with texts were already traditional in ecclesiastical conflicts; to take only one example, Rufinus' Latin translation of the controversial writer Origen's *De Principiis* was attacked by Jerome and others on these grounds, and their accusations accepted by modern scholars.[60] A main instrument for such tampering was precisely the *florilegium*, a type of composition whose frequency in our period has already been noted, and which offered an all too easy repository for bogus texts. By the sixth century the occurrence of this kind of forgery has even been described as 'a universal phenomenon'.[61] The accusation of forgery was also tactically useful; after a day of discussion, the Fifth Ecumenical Council of AD 553 resolved the troublesome question of the Letter of Ibas, for example, by simply declaring it to be a forgery.[62] It is now clear that the 'acts' of the so-called Lateran Synod held in Rome in AD 649 were originally composed in Greek, at the instigation of Maximus Confessor and his eastern supporters, whence the question arises how far if at all we can count on the authenticity of their record, especially as far as concerns their reporting of opinion in Rome and Italy.[63] At the Sixth Council of AD 680–1 the Roman delegation challenged the official version of the acts of the Fifth Council produced in Constantinople and found that it had been tampered with by the Monothelite side.[64] It was after this that all documents subsequently produced were checked from copies in the patriarchal library, and supporting documents brought by the various parties actually sealed until they were due to be officially discussed. The extent of falsification, if not of outright forgery in the later texts relating to Iconoclasm is well known, and has recently been emphasised yet again in a detailed consideration of the famous 'event' which traditionally began official Iconoclasm, namely the destruction of the icon of Christ on the Chalce gate of the imperial palace by Leo III.[65] It was a tactic which even extended to official inscriptions.[66]

The attention to texts already evident in the seventh century increased as time went on: the Iconoclastic council of AD 754 was preceded by days of library work, and at the Second Council of Nicaea in 787, some fifty books, on Mango's count, were produced for the Council's use by the 'organisers' and another twenty or so by various bishops and others attending.

[60] See Scott (1992: 169).
[61] Henry (1988); see also Bardy (1936); Wilson (1983: 61–2); Brubaker (1989a: 28–9). Works wrongly attributed, which are equally rife during this period, are in theory a different matter, though the categories often overlap.
[62] Henry (1988: 286).
[63] See Riedinger (1979: 9ff.); cf. 11 'Die Akten der Lateransynode sind also als Konzilsakten in mehrerer Hinsicht eine Fiktion.'
[64] Mansi 11.225Bff.; Herrin (1987: 276); Chadwick (1992).
[65] Auzépy (1990).   [66] Mango (1963), cited by Auzépy (1990: 445).

Incidentally, this gives precious information not only about the spread of libraries in the period, especially monastic ones, but also about their deficiencies, and in particular about the apparent scarcity even of some very important texts.[67] Some key works are known only through their citation in the course of these arguments, and it was not uncommon for more than one version to be produced of the same text. One curious question which arises is whether the Council of 787, which vindicated John of Damascus after his anathematisation in 754, actually had any of his writings before it. If it did not, as suggested by Van den Ven,[68] many further questions are raised about circulation of writings in general, and about contacts between Constantinople and the East, not to mention about the genesis of John's own writings on images, and it remains odd that John's works were not explicitly cited. Finally, it is worth repeating what has already been said by others, namely that the very reliance that had come to be placed on *florilegia*, that is on collections of extracts rather than on complete books, no doubt itself contributed to the loss of the original texts, and added markedly to the danger of wrong attribution, even if not to actual falsification.

We can now begin to draw together some of the threads and to address the issues posed by this material. These can be divided into the general and the particular, for there are cognitive issues at stake as well as problems of detail.

It is not a legitimate move for historians to relegate texts like these to the realms of theology, or to select from them merely those works which seem to have a directly historical bearing. The church councils of the period were undoubtedly political events of the first order. They were called by emperors, and attended by lay officials in prominent positions. An earlier meeting before the Second Council of Nicaea was broken up by an alliance of the church and the military, and the humiliation of patriarchs by emperors was a feature of the Iconoclast period; the marital plans of Constantine VI having played a major role in the relations between emperor and patriarch at the end of the eighth century, the patriarch Nicephorus, raised from lay status by imperial intervention and against ecclesiastical opposition, found himself exiled in turn by a later emperor.[69] The patriarchate itself stood to gain from the creation of a suitable official version of recent history, as also from its control of access to texts.[70] The role of the monks of Studios, more purist than some others in the church, was another major factor during this phase, and indeed, it was the monks and monasteries who did well out of Iconoclasm in terms of later influence and prosperity. Many no doubt remained untouched by the finer points of

[67] Mango (1975: 31–3); Herrin (1987: 421–2).   [68] Van den Ven (1957: 336–8).
[69] Auzépy (1990: 476ff.) emphasises the political context of the second phase of Iconoclasm.
[70] Auzépy (ibid.: 488–9).

controversy, or even unaware of the actual issues being contested – the *Life of Philaretos*, for instance, dating from AD 821–2, conspicuously fails to make Iconoclasm an issue. But Iconoclasm at any rate touched public life at many points, as with the public humiliation of monks under Constantine V. In broader terms, the main issue during this period was the nature of the Byzantine state, and specifically of the future location of power within it. To return to the point from which we began, the military, administrative and economic systems were all undergoing basic, though to us still often mysterious, processes of change. Even more fundamentally, the status of Byzantium as a world-empire (in ancient Mediterranean terms) had been put at risk. In the late seventh century it recognised for the first time the status of the caliphate as a legitimate power, with what implications for its own sense of self we can easily guess.[71] A new mental geography would be needed to match the changed political map.

Nor should we ignore how far the situation had changed by the early ninth century. The issues debated in the time of Germanus I, deposed under Leo III in AD 730, had moved on by the time of Nicephorus, exiled almost a century later, also for his iconophile views, and the case was argued on somewhat different terms. But the vocabulary of hatred and condemnation had meanwhile intensified. Nicephorus' *Antirrhetici*, the work of someone who became an ecclesiastic at a late stage in his life and was criticised by the more aggressive monastic element, demonologised iconoclasts as never before.

One way of looking at the polemics of the period is in terms of increased attempts by state and society to control deviance.[72] While hostile contemporaries saw Iconoclasm as the most recent and most dangerous heresy, it was in fact simply the most energetically pursued of several such moves. Though it was ultimately unsuccessful as an imperial strategy, the danger which this posed to imperial authority was averted in the late eighth century by the successful imperial expedient of changing to the winning side, and aided by the high turnover in occupants of the imperial throne which was characteristic of Byzantine history in general. Later, a lively rewriting of the history of the Iconoclast period assisted the authorities to turn it to their own advantage. On this deviance model, heretics – dualists, Monothelites, Monophysites – join pagans (Hellenes), Jews and Muslims, as far as the texts are concerned, as stereotypes of the 'bad guy'. It is no accident that during this period the construction of the stereotyped image of the Jew underwent a particularly flourishing development,[73] or that Constantine V, the most active Iconoclast emperor, received the blackest possible portrayal[74] (according to Theophanes, Constantine was an

---

[71] Chrysos (1992: 27).   [72] So Haldon (1990: esp. ch. 9).
[73] I propose to treat this separately elsewhere.
[74] By Nicephorus (see Mondzain-Baudinet 1989), and others (see Speck 1990).

accursed wretch, God's enemy, impious, arrogant, unholy, jealous, evilly-named, beastlike and savage, to take only some examples). In the case of heresy, as with other topics, the corollary of such image-making is that the historian is often unable on the basis of these sources to distinguish the real from the imaginary or the literary construct.[75] Setting up an authoritarian discourse is an important technique, and demonologising one's opponents, dealing with real or potential enemies by subsuming them into old familiar categories of abuse, or even setting up imaginary opponents, are all good ways of dealing with the perceived threat.

What then were these polemics about? I have argued elsewhere that it was one function of icons – to iconophiles at any rate – that they constituted a sign-system through which absolute truth could be perceived, and this is in fact the way in which they are presented by their defenders in the first stage of Iconoclasm, such as John of Damascus.[76] The Iconoclasts challenged the application, not the principle; they restricted the accepted 'signs' without attacking the conception of an absolute truth which could be known. It was an argument about detail, or about interpretation, not about principles. In the light of the material and institutional change characteristic of the period, I have also argued that this was – at least temporarily – a reformulation of the past in Christian rather than classical terms, at a time when the classical past had rather rapidly receded from view.[77] It is worth remembering that the ending of Iconoclasm brought with it not only legitimation for iconic church decoration, a new lease of life for figural art and increased influence for monasteries, but also a return of interest in recovering the classical past.

Clearly this material also raises many important questions about education, literacy and book production as such in the period of the Byzantine 'dark ages'. One such issue, recently emphasised by Cyril Mango, is the role played by the monasteries of Palestine, particularly Mar Saba near Jerusalem, home to John of Damascus and others, and a particularly active centre in the first half of the seventh century also. A related one, also stressed by Mango, is the impact of Greek-speaking emigrants from Palestine in Sicily and south Italy,[78] something which can also be seen in the Greek acts of the Lateran Synod. Individual 'wandering monks' like Maximus, Sophronius, John Moschus, Anastasius of Sinai, crossed political boundaries and carried culture with them, engaging in polemics as they did so. During the Monothelite controversy, Cyprus was a particularly favoured location for such meetings and discussions, and

---

[75] Gouillard (1965: 302–3); Haldon (1990: 341–2).   [76] Cameron (1992).
[77] See on this also Dagron (1984). The question of classical images in relation to Byzantine Iconoclasm would repay further investigation.   [78] Mango (1974, 1992).

many letters went to and fro in the interests of controversy and argument. But we are not here in the environment of the great Western monastic scriptoria. Ecclesiastical, monastic and lay culture were not discrete spheres, and it would be a mistake to regard these phenomena as devoid of direct effect on the lay world. It was not so surprising, given the 'dark age' context, if at this time it was primarily among ecclesiastics that texts and their preservation, recovery and verification, acquired such intense importance. But the interplay of lay and clerical is apparent at all levels – after all, both Nicephorus and Photius were patriarchs raised from lay status, and Constantine V was no mean theologian. The encyclopaedism and scholasticism of these theologians is different in scope, but not in type, from the secular encyclopaedism of the tenth-century world of Constantine Porphyrogenitus.

However, I have been concerned in this paper with broader cognitive issues. We surely have here a much wider phenomenon, not one that is concerned only with Iconoclasm. Debate, polemic, the systematisation and collection of authoritative texts, are employed in a wide variety of contexts; when Iconoclasm came it merely intensified an existing development. The arguments over Monothelitism in the seventh century provided a stimulus and a pattern for many of these techniques, so that the weaponry was already prepared when Iconoclasm did become a major issue in the eighth century. In particular, orthodoxy was a matter of imperial policy as well as something for church councils; emperors too would issue documents (*Ekthesis*, *Typos*), to which writing was also the appropriate counter-move. However, this is not the whole story. I would like to consider together the whole range of systematising and polemical productions in the period, and to see in them a degree of scholasticism and even encyclopaedism, such as did indeed flourish after the final ending of Iconoclasm.

An alternative way of looking at the same developments is in terms of their cognitive function. Sharper definition of opposites, together with a clearly defined linear (and orthodox) view of history enabled contemporaries to make sense of their own world and especially of its fluidity. They were in other words busy creating for themselves an imagined world of certainty and strong boundaries.

The ending of Iconoclasm and the formal dedication of an apse mosaic of the Virgin and Child in St Sophia, praised in a famous homily of the Patriarch Photius delivered on 29 March AD 867, were followed in the same year by the establishment of a new dynasty, that of the Macedonians, in particularly bloody circumstances, and by the deposition of the same Photius. The Emperor Basil I, who had obtained the throne for himself by murdering his colleague, was spectacularly whitewashed at the instigation of his descendant Constantine Porphyrogenitus, the same emperor whose

Book of Ceremonies claimed to glorify the 'order' and appointed rhythm of the imperial court. Contemporary lists of officials according to their elaborately graded order of precedence[79] testify to the extent of the administrative and institutional change which had taken place in the preceding period; bishops, and even metropolitans, are listed together with the lay officials, and rank below military commanders. The same Patriarch Photius produced works including a *Lexikon* and the *Bibliotheca*,[80] in which the encyclopaedic tendency visible in much of our material was extended to classical texts. Already in the ninth century other figures, such as the deacon Ignatius and John the grammarian, were demonstrating the beginnings of the scholarly and academic side of what was to turn into a real revival of learning.[81] I would argue that rather than positing a sharp break in continuity, as has often been the case, the textual polemics of the dark ages should be read in this developing historical context.

If texts can be weapons, so can pictures. Basil I was a church builder and restorer who also had himself and his large family depicted in the palace in contentious style, for a murderer married to the mistress of the man he had murdered, in juxtaposition with the Cross.[82] A question often raised during the Iconoclast arguments was that of the respective claims of writing and pictures in relation to their capacity for expressing the truth.[83] John of Damascus cited St Basil on the equivalence of words and pictures. Both could be, and often were in this period, deeply tendentious. But a deeper issue was also that of exegesis, how to attain knowledge: written versus unwritten tradition, literalism versus symbolism, pictures versus words, the 'Old and New Testaments and the words of the holy and elect Fathers' versus 'the foul, loathsome and unclean writings of the accursed Manichaeans, Gnostics and the rest of the heretics'.[84] No one doubted that the proper way to attain knowledge was by collection, preservation and synthesis. After the victory of the iconophiles and the formal ending of Iconoclasm in AD 843, a statement known as the Synodikon of Orthodoxy came to be read each year on the first Sunday of Lent, the Feast of Orthodoxy; among its later anathemas was one directed at 'those who believe in Plato, and those who cling to τὰ ἑλληνικά, and do not read them only for instruction' (διὰ παίδευσιν μόνον).[85]

Possibly very soon after AD 843, the *Bibliotheca* of Photius was put together, and preserved for us the knowledge of a not inconsiderable

---

[79] Oikonomides (1972).
[80] Often dated, though without certainty, to the period before his first patriarchate.
[81] Wilson (1983); Lemerle (1986).
[82] Texts in translation: Mango (1972: 102–202).
[83] Brubaker (1989a: 70–1, 1989b: 28–9); Dagron (1991).
[84] Joh. Dam. *Or.* 2.10, trans. D. Anderson (Crestwood, New York, 1980) 57.
[85] Ed. Gouillard (1967: lines 214–24).

amount of otherwise lost works of classical literature. The polemics of the 'dark ages' were a way of defining new groups or defending existing ones during a period of change and upheaval on many fronts. But they also represent a way of reformulating knowledge, at a time when the old norms had been disrupted. While their subject matter differed in range and content, they can fairly be linked with the broader encyclopaedism of the ninth and tenth centuries, by which time grammar, mathematics, philosophy and classical literature were all back on the agenda. Their polemical technique enabled the arguments to be sharpened and the supporting material collected and marshalled. But it too can be linked to a broader context, that of the combativeness and rivalry that was never far below the surface emphasis in Byzantine culture on 'order' and 'harmony'. The calm, dignity and order of imperial Byzantium are the outward signs which Constantine VII Porphyrogenitus most wanted to demonstrate through works such as the *Book of Ceremonies* and the *De Administrando Imperio*. As his own life showed, the reality was different. The dark-age polemics show us just that underside which Constantine knew so well and which he most wanted to conceal.

Works cited

Journal titles are abbreviated according to the conventions of *L'Année Philologique*, or else are cited in full.

1. LITERACY AND POWER IN THE ANCIENT WORLD

Adams, J. N. (1977) *The Vulgar Latin of the Letters of Claudius Terentianus.* Manchester.
   (1992) 'British Latin: the text, interpretation and language of the Bath Curse Tablets', *Britannia* 23: 1–26.
Austin, M. M. (1981) *The Hellenistic World from Alexander to the Roman Conquest.* Cambridge.
Baumann, G. (ed.) (1986) *The Written Word. Literacy in Transition.* Oxford.
Beard, W. M. (1985) 'Writing and ritual: a study of diversity and expansion in the Arval Acta', *PBSR* 53: 114–62.
   (1991) '*Ancient Literacy* and the function of the written word in Roman religion', in Humphrey (1991) 35–58.
Blanchard, A. (ed.) (1989) *Les Débuts du codex.* Brepols.
Bloch, M. (1989) 'Literacy and enlightenment', in Schousboe and Larsen (1989) 15–38.
Boak, A. E. R. and Youtie, H. C. (1960) *The Archive of Aurelius Isidorus.* Ann Arbor, MI.
Boswinkel, E. and Pestman, P. (eds.) (1978) *Textes grecs démotiques et bilingues* (Papyrologica Lugduno-Batava 19). Leiden.
Bowie, E. L. (1970) 'The Greeks and their past in the Second Sophistic', *Past and Present* 46: 3–41, repr. in M. I. Finley (ed.) *Studies in Ancient Society* (London 1974) 166–209.
Brown, P. R. L. (1968) 'Christianity and local culture in late antique Roman Africa', *JRS* 58: 85–95.
Cameron, Averil (1991) *Christianity and the Rhetoric of Empire. The Development of Christian Discourse* (Sather Classical Lectures 55). Berkeley.
Clanchy, M. T. (1979) *From Memory to Written Record: England 1066–1307.* London.
   (1983) 'Looking back from the invention of printing', in Resnick (1983) 7–22.
Cotton, H. M. and Geiger, J. (1989) *Masada II, The Yigael Yadin Excavations 1963–5, Final Reports, The Latin and Greek Documents.* Jerusalem.
Cressy, D. (1980) *Literacy and the Social Order. Reading and Writing in Tudor and Stuart England.* Cambridge.
Day, J. W. (1989) 'Rituals in stone: early Greek epigrams and monuments', *JHS* 109: 16–28.

Desbordes, F. (1990) *Idées romaines sur l'écriture*. Lille.

Detienne, M. (ed.) (1988) *Les Savoirs de l'écriture en Grèce ancienne*. Lille.

Elsner, J. (1992) 'Pausanias: a Greek pilgrim in the Roman world', *Past and Present* 135: 3–29.

Fink, R. O. (1971) *Roman Military Records on Papyrus*. Cleveland, OH.

Finnegan, R. (1988) *Literacy and Orality. Studies in the Technology of Communication*. Oxford.

Franklin, J. R.,‑Jr (1991) 'Literacy and the parietal inscriptions of Pompeii', in Humphrey (1991) 77–98.

Franklin, S. (1985) 'Literacy and documentation in early mediaeval Russia', *Speculum* 60/1: 1–38.

Furet, F. and Ozouf, J. (1982) *Reading and Writing. Literacy in France from Calvin to Jules Ferry*. Cambridge.

Gledhill, J., Bender, B. and Larsen, M. T. (eds.) (1988) *State and Society: The Emergence and Development of Social Hierarchy and Political Centralisation* (One World Archaeology 4). London.

Goody, J. R. (ed.) (1968) *Literacy in Traditional Societies*, Cambridge.

(1977) *The Domestication of the Savage Mind*. Cambridge.

(1986) *The Logic of Writing and the Organisation of Society*. Cambridge.

(1989) *The Interface between the Oral and the Written*. Cambridge.

Goody, J. R. and Watt, I. (1963) 'The consequences of literacy', *CSSH* 5: 304–45, reprinted in Goody (1968) 27–68.

Gough, K. (1968) 'Implications of literacy in traditional China and India', in Goody (1968) 69–84.

Graff, H. J. (1979) *The Literacy Myth. Literacy and Social Structure in the Nineteenth Century City*. New York.

(ed.) (1981) *Literacy and Social Development in the West. A Reader*. Cambridge.

(1987) *The Legacies of Literacy. Continuities and Contradictions in Western Culture and Society*. Bloomington, IN.

Harbsmeier, M. (1988) 'Inventions of writing', in Gledhill et al. (1988) 173–91.

(1989) 'Writing and the Other: travellers' literacy or towards an archaeology of orality', in Schousboe and Larsen (1989) 197–228.

Harris, W. V. (1989) *Ancient Literacy*. Cambridge, MA.

Havelock, E. A. (1982) *The Literate Revolution in Greece and its Consequences*. Princeton.

Hopkins, K. (1991) 'Conquest by book', in Humphrey (1991) 133–58.

Howgego, C. J. (1992) 'The supply and use of money in the Roman world 200 B.C. to A.D. 300', *JRS* 82: 1–31.

Humphrey, J. (ed.) (1991) *Literacy in the Roman World* (*JRA* supplement 3). Ann Arbor, MI.

Koenen, L. (1983) 'Ägyptische Königsideologie am Ptolemäerhof', *Egypt and the Hellenistic World* (Studia Hellenistica 27) 143–8. Leiden.

(1985) 'The dream of Nectanebos', *BASP* 22: 171–94.

Larsen, M. T. (1988) 'Introduction: literacy and social complexity', in Gledhill et al. (1988) 173–91.

Lévi-Strauss, C. (1955) *Tristes Tropiques*. Paris.

Lewis, N. (1989) *The Documents from the Bar Kokhba Period in the Cave of Letters, Greek Papyri*. Jerusalem.

McKitterick, R. (1989) *The Carolingians and the Written Word*. Cambridge.
(ed.) (1990) *The Uses of Literacy in Early Mediaeval Europe*. Cambridge.
MacMullen, R. (1990) *Changes in the Roman Empire. Essays in the Ordinary*. Princeton.
Matthews, J. F. (1974) 'The letters of Symmachus', in J. W. Binns (ed.) *Latin Literature of the Fourth Century* 58–99. London.
Millar, F. G. B. (1968) 'Local cultures in the Roman empire: Libyan, Punic and Latin in Roman Africa', *JRS* 58: 126–34.
Musurillo, H. A. (1954) *The Acts of the Pagan Martyrs. Acta Alexandrinorum*. Oxford.
Ong, W. J. (1982) *Orality and Literacy. The Technologising of the Word*. London.
(1986) 'Writing is a technology that restructures thought', in Baumann (1986) 23–50.
Pagels, E. H. (1979) *The Gnostic Gospels*. New York.
Pattison, R. (1982) *On Literacy. The Politics of the Word from Homer to the Age of Rock*. Oxford.
Rea, J. R. (1977) 'A new version of P. Yale inv. 199', *ZPE* 27: 151–6.
Resnick, D. P. (ed.) (1983) *Literacy in Historical Perspective*. Washington, DC.
Roberts, C. H. and Skeat, T. C. (1983) *The Birth of the Codex*. London.
Robinson, J. M. (ed.) (1977) *The Nag Hammadi Library in English Translation*. Leiden.
Schousboe, K. and Larsen, M. T. (eds.) (1989) *Literacy and Society*. Copenhagen.
Scribner, S. and Cole, M. (1981) *The Psychology of Literacy*. Cambridge, MA.
Stock, B. (1983) *The Implications of Literacy: Written Language and Models of Interpretation in the Eleventh and Twelfth centuries*. New Jersey.
Street, B. V. (1984) *Literacy in Theory and Practice*. Cambridge.
Thomas, K. (1986) 'The meaning of literacy in early modern England', in Baumann (1986) 97–131.
Thomas, R. (1989) *Oral Tradition and Written Record in Classical Athens*. Cambridge.
(1992) *Literacy and Orality in Ancient Greece*. Cambridge.
Tomlin, R. S. O. (1988) 'The Curse Tablets', in B. Cunliffe (ed.) *The Temple of Sulis Minerva at Bath. Volume 2: The Finds from the Sacred Spring* (Oxford Committee for Archaeology monograph 16) 14–277. Oxford.
Veyne, P. (1983) '"Titulus Praelatus": offrande, solemnisation et publicité dans les ex-voto gréco-romains', *RA* 281–300.
Ward, B. (1975) *The Sayings of the Desert Fathers*. London.
Ward, B. and Russell, N. (1980) *The Lives of the Desert Fathers*. London.
Williamson, C. (1987) 'Monuments of bronze; Roman legal documents on bronze tablets', *Classical Antiquity* 6: 160–83.

2. THE PERSEPOLIS TABLETS: SPEECH, SEAL AND SCRIPT

Balkan, K. (1959) 'Inscribed Bullae from Daskyleion-Ergili', *Anatolia* 4: 123–8.
Bowman, R. A. (1970) *Aramaic Ritual Texts from Persepolis* (Oriental Institute Publications 91). Chicago.
Brosius, M. (1991) 'Royal and non-royal women in Achaemenid Persia (559–331 B.C.)', D.Phil. thesis, Univ. of Oxford.
Cameron, G. G. (1948) *Persepolis Treasury Texts* (Oriental Institute Publications 65). Chicago.
(1973), 'The Persian satrapies and related matters', *JNES* 32: 47–56.
Cowley, A. (1923) *Aramaic Papyri of the Fifth Century B.C.* Oxford.

Dalley, S. and Postgate, J. N. (1984) *The Tablets from Fort Shalmaneser* (Cuneiform Texts from Nimrud 3). London.

Dandamayev, M. A. (1967) 'Egyptians in Babylonia', in *Drevnij Egipet i drevnaja Africa* 15–26. Moscow.

(1983) *Babilonskie Pistsi (Babylonian Scribes in the First Millennium B.C.).* Moscow. (References in square brackets are to the English summary.)

Dandamayev, M. A. and Lukonin, V. G. (1989) *The Culture and Social Institutions of Ancient Iran.* Cambridge.

Driver, G. R. (1957) *Aramaic Documents of the Fifth Century B.C.* Oxford.

Garrison, M. B. (1992) 'Seals and the élite at Persepolis; some observations on Early Achaemenid Art', *Ars Orientalis* 21: 1–29.

Gershevitch, I. (1969a) 'Amber at Persepolis', in *Studia Classica et Orientalia Antonino Pagliaro Oblata* II 167–251. Rome.

(1969b) 'Iranian nouns and names in Elamite garb', *TPhS* (1969) 167–200.

(1970) 'Island-Bay and the Lion', *Bulletin of the School of Oriental and African Studies* 33: 82–91.

(1971) 'Editor's preface' to R. T. Hallock 'The evidence of the Persepolis Tablets'. Cambridge. (This is a pre-printed version of Hallock (1985) below; the 'Editor's preface' does not appear in the published book.)

(1979) 'The alloglottography of Old Persian', *TPhS* (1979) 114–90.

Greenfield, J. C. and Porten, B. (1982) *The Bisitun Inscription of Darius the Great. Aramaic Version* (Corpus Inscriptionum Iranicarum I.V.I). London.

Grillot-Susini, F. (1987) *Eléments du grammaire élamite.* Paris.

Hallock, R. T. (1960) 'A new look at the Persepolis Treasury tablets', *JNES* 19: 90–100.

(1969) *Persepolis Fortification Tablets* (Oriental Institute Publications 92). Chicago.

(1977) 'The use of seals in the Persepolis Fortification texts', in M. Gibson and R. D. Biggs (eds.) *Seals and Sealings in the Ancient Near East* (Bibliotheca Mesopotamiaca 6) 127–33. Malibu.

(1978) 'Selected fortification texts', *Cahiers de la Délégation archéologique française en Iran* 8: 109–36.

(1985) 'The evidence of the Persepolis tablets', in *Cambridge History of Iran* II 588–609. Cambridge.

Harper, R. F. (1892–1914) *Assyrian and Babylonian Letters Belonging to the Kouyunjik Collection of the British Museum* I–XIV. London.

Hinz, W. (1967) 'Zu den Zeughaustäfelchen aus Susa', in *Festschrift für Wilhelm Eilers* 85–98. Wiesbaden.

(1968) 'Zur Entstehung der altpersischen Keilschrift', *Arch. Mitt. Iran* n.s. 1: 95–8.

(1971) 'Achämenidische Hofverwaltung', *Zeitschrift für Assyriologie* 61: 260–311.

(1973) *Neue Wege im Altpersischen.* Wiesbaden.

(1975) 'Zu den Mörsern und Stösseln aus Persepolis', *Acta Iranica* series 2, *Monumentum H. S. Nyberg* I 371–85. Leiden.

Hinz, W. and Koch, H. (1987) *Elamisches Wörterbuch.* Berlin.

Kinnier Wilson, J. V. (1972) *The Nimrud Wine Lists* (Cuneiform Texts from Nimrud 1). London.

Koch, H. (1981) '"Hofschaftswarte" und "Schatzhäuser" in der Persis', *Zeitschrift für Assyriologie* 71: 232–47.

(1986) 'Die Achämenidische Poststrasse von Persepolis nach Susa', *Arch. Mitt. Iran* n.s. 19: 133–47.

(1990) *Verwaltung und Wirtschaft im persischen Kernland zur Zeit der Achämeniden* (Beihefte zum Tübinger Atlas des vorderen Orients B 89). Wiesbaden.

Lewis, D. M. (1977) *Sparta and Persia* (Cincinnati Classical Studies n.s. 1). Leiden.

(1985) 'Persians in Herodotus', in *The Greek Historians, Literature and History. Papers Presented to A. E. Raubitschek.* Stanford, CA.

Lipiński, E. (1975) *Studies in Aramaic Inscriptions and Onomastics* I. Louvain.

Luckenbill, D. D. (1927) *Ancient Records of Babylonia and Assyria* II. Chicago.

Luschey, H. (1968) 'Studien zu dem Darius-Relief von Bisitun', *Arch. Mitt. Iran* n.s. 1: 63–94.

Metzger, H., Laroche, E., Dupont-Sommer, A. and Mayrhofer, M. (1979) *La Stèle trilingue du Létôon* (Fouilles de Xanthos 6). Paris.

Millard, A. R. (1983) 'Assyrians and Arameans', *Iraq* 45: 101–8.

Naveh, J. and Shaked, S. (1973) 'Ritual texts or Treasury documents?', *Orientalia* 42: 445–57.

Piepkorn, A. C. (1933) *Historical Prism Inscriptions of Ashurbanipal I.* Chicago.

Porten, B. and Yardeni, A. (1986–   ) *Textbook of Aramaic Documents from Ancient Egypt*, 3 vols. Jerusalem.

Root, M. C. (1988) 'Evidence from Persepolis for the dating of Persian and Archaic Greek coinage', *NC* 148: 1–12.

Schaeder, H. H. (1930) *Esra der Schreiber.* Tübingen.

Scheil, V. (1907 and 1911) *Textes élamites-anzanites, troisième série* and *quatrième série* (Mémoires de la délégation en Perse 9 and 11). Paris.

Schlumberger, D., Robert, L., Dupont-Sommer, A. and Beneveniste, E. (1958) 'Une bilingue gréco-araméenne d'Aśoka', *JA* 246: 1–48.

Schmidt, E. F. (1957) *Persepolis II. Contents of the Treasury and Other Discoveries* (Oriental Institute Publications 69). Chicago.

Starr, C. G. (1976) 'A sixth-century Athenian tetradrachm used to seal a clay tablet from Persepolis', *NC* 136: 219–22.

Stolper, M. W. (1984) 'The Neo-Babylonian text from the Persepolis fortification', *JNES* 43: 299–310.

(1985) *Entrepreneurs and Empire.* Leiden.

Trümpelmann, L. (1967) 'Zur Enstehungsgeschichte des Monumentes Dareios' I. von Bisutun und zur Datierung der Einführung des altpersischen schrift', *Archäologischer Anzeiger* 3: 281–98.

Vattioni, F. (1970) 'Epigrafia aramaica', *Augustinianum* 10: 493–532.

Vickers, M. J. (1985) 'Early Greek coinage, a reassessment', *NC* 145: 1–44.

Williamson, H. G. M. (1985) *Ezra, Nehemiah* (Word Biblical Commentary 16). Waco, TX.

3. LITERACY AND THE CITY-STATE IN ARCHAIC AND CLASSICAL GREECE

Boegehold, A. L. (1990) 'Andocides and the decree of Patrokleides', *Historia* 39: 149–62.

Boring, T. A. (1979) *Literacy in Ancient Sparta.* Leiden.

Burford, A. (1971) 'The purpose of inscribed building accounts', in *Acta of the Vth*

International Congress of Greek and Latin Epigraphy (Cambridge 1967) 71–6. Oxford.

Cartledge, P. (1978) 'Literacy in the Spartan oligarchy', *JHS* 98: 25–37.

Clanchy, M. T. (1979) *From Memory to Written Record*. London.

Cramer, F. H. (1945) 'Bookburning and censorship in ancient Rome', *JHI* 6: 157–96.

Dover, K. (1975) 'Freedom of the intellectual in Greek society', *Talanta* 7: 24–54; repr. in *Collected Papers* II. *The Greeks and Their Legacy* (Oxford 1988) 135–58.

Goody, J. (1986) *The Logic of Writing and the Organization of Society*. Cambridge.

Harris, W. V. (1989) *Ancient Literacy*. Cambridge, MA.

Herrmann, P. (1981) 'Teos und Abdera im 5. Jahrhundert v. Chr.', *Chiron* 11: 1–30.

Knoepfler, D. (ed.) (1988) *Comptes et Inventaires dans la cité grecque. Actes du colloq. internat. d'épigraphie. Neuchâtel 1986*. Neuchâtel and Geneva.

Kroll, J. H. (1977) 'An archive of the Athenian cavalry', *Hesperia* 46: 83–140.

Lambinudakis, W. and M. Wörrle (1983) 'Ein hellenistisches Reformgesetz über das öffentliche Urkundenwesen von Paros', *Chiron* 13: 283–368.

Larsen, M. T. (1988) 'Introduction: literacy and social complexity', in J. Gledhill, B. Bender and M. T. Larsen (eds.) *State and Society: The Emergence and Development of Social Hierarchy and Political Centralization* 173–91. London.

Lévi-Strauss, C. (1976) *Tristes Tropiques*. London. French original first published 1955. Paris.

Lewis, D. M. (1973) 'The Athenian rationes centesimarum', in M. I. Finley (ed.) *Problèmes de la terre en Grèce ancienne* 187–212. Paris.

    (1984) 'Democratic institutions and their diffusion', in ΠΡΑΚΤΙΚΑ ΤΟΥ Η΄ΔΙΕΘΝΟΥΣ ΣΥΝΕΔΡΙΟΥ ΕΛΛΕΝΙΚΗΣ ΚΑΙ ΛΑΤΙΝΙΚΗΣ ΕΠΙΓΡΑΦΙΚΗΣ (Eighth International Epigraphical Congress, Athens, Oct. 1982) 55–61. Athens.

Lewis, D. M. (1987) 'The Athenian Coinage Decree', in I. Carradice (ed.) *Coinage and Administration in the Athenian and Persian Empires* 53–63 (*BAR IS* 343). Oxford.

Linders, T. (1975) *The Treasurers of the Other Gods in Athens and Their Functions*. Meisenheim am Glan.

Meiggs, R. (1972) *The Athenian Empire*. Oxford.

Mitsos, M. T. (1983) 'Une inscription d'Argos', *BCH* 107: 243–9.

Ostwald, M. (1973) 'Was there a concept ἄγραφος νόμος in classical Greece?', in E. N. Lee, A. P. D. Mourelatos and R. M. Rorty (eds.) *Exegesis and Argument: Studies in Greek Philosophy Presented to G. Vlastos* (*Phronesis* suppl. vol. I) 70–104. Assen.

Posner, E. (1972) *Archives in the Ancient World*. Cambridge, MA.

Ruzé, F. (1988) 'Aux débuts de l'écriture politique: le pouvoir de l'écrit dans la cité', in M. Detienne (ed.) *Les Savoirs de l'écriture en Grèce ancienne* 82–94. Lille.

Stupperich, R. (1977) *Staatsbegräbnis und Privatgrabmal im klassischen Athens*, diss., Münster.

Thomas, K. (1986) 'The meaning of literacy in early modern England', in G. Baumann (ed.) *The Written Word* 97–131. Oxford.

Thomas, R. (1989) *Oral Tradition and Written Record in Classical Athens*. Cambridge.

    (1992) *Literacy and Orality in Ancient Greece*. Cambridge.

(forthcoming) 'Written in stone? Liberty, equality, orality and the codification of law', in L. Foxhall and A. Lewis (eds.) *Papers on Greek Law*. Oxford.
Vallois, R. (1914) 'APAI', *BCH* 38: 250–71.
West, W. C. (1989) 'The public archives in fourth-century Athens', *GRBS* 30: 529–43.
Whitehead, D. (1977) *The Ideology of the Athenian Metic* (*PCPS* suppl. 4). Cambridge.
    (1986) *The Demes of Attica, 508/7 – ca. 250 B.C.* Princeton, NJ.

4. LITERACY AND LANGUAGE IN EGYPT IN THE LATE AND PERSIAN
PERIODS

Austin, M. M. (1970) *Greece and Egypt in the Archaic Age* (*PCPS* suppl. 2). Cambridge.
Baines, J. R. (1983) 'Literacy and ancient Egyptian society', *Man* n.s. 18: 572–99.
Baines, J. R. and Eyre, C. J. (1983) 'Four notes on literacy', *Göttinger Miszellen* 61: 65–96.
Bresciani, E., Pernigotti, S. and Betro, M. C. (1983) *Ostraka demotici da Narmuti I* (Quaderni de Medinet Madi 1). Pisa.
Brunner, H. (1965) *Hieroglyphische Chrestomathie*. Wiesbaden.
Černý, J. (1976) *Coptic Etymological Dictionary*. Cambridge.
Clarysse, W. (1987) 'Greek loan words in Demotic', in *Aspects of Demotic Lexicography* (Studia Demotica 1, ed. S. P. Vleeming, Leuven) 9–33.
Devauchelle, D. (1984) 'Remarques sur les méthodes d'enseignement du démotique', in H.-J. Thissen and K.-Th. Zauzich (eds.) *Grammata Demotika. Festschrift für E. Lüddeckens* 47–59. Würzburg.
Donadoni, S. (1955) 'Il greco di un sacerdote di Narmuthis', *Acme* 8: 73–83.
Grelot, P. (1972) *Documents araméens d'Egypte*. Paris.
Griffith, F. Ll. (1909) *Catalogue of the Demotic Papyri in the John Rylands Library* III. Manchester.
Helck, W. and Otto, E. (1982) *Lexikon der Ägyptologie* IV. Wiesbaden.
Johnson, J. H. (1975) 'The demotic magical spells of Leiden I 384', *Oudheidkundige Medelingen vit het Rijksmuseum van Oudheden te Leiden* 56: 29–64.
    (1977) 'The dialect of the demotic Magical Papyrus of London and Leiden' in J. H. Johnson and E. F. Wente (eds.) *Studies in Honor of G. R. Hughes* (Studies in Ancient Oriental Civilizations 39) 105–32. Chicago.
    (1986) 'The Egyptian priesthood in Ptolemaic Egypt' in L. H. Lesko (ed.) *Egyptological Essays in Honor of Richard A. Parker* 70–84. Providence, RI.
Kaplony-Heckel, U. (1974) 'Schüler und Schulwesen in der ägyptischen Spätzeit', *Studien zur altägyptischen Kultur* 1: 227–46.
Kienitz, F. K. (1953) *Die politische Geschichte Ägyptens vom 7. bis zum 4. Jahrhundert vor der Zeitwende*. Berlin.
Kornfeld, W. (1973) 'Jüdisch-aramäische Grabinschriften aus Edfu', *Anz. AW Wien* phil.-hist. Kl. 110: 123–37.
Leclant, J. (1991) 'Les Phéniciens et l'Egypte', in *Atti del II Congresso di studi fenici e punici* 6–17. Rome.
Lichtheim, M. (1980) *Ancient Egyptian Literature* III. California.
Lloyd, A. B. (1975) *A Commentary on Herodotus Book II: Introduction*. Leiden.
    (1988) *A Commentary on Herodotus Book II: Chapters 99–182*. Leiden.
Masson, O. (1978) *Carian Inscriptions from North Saqqâra and Buhen*. London.

Masson, O. and Yoyotte, J. (1988) 'Une inscription ionienne mentionnant Psammétique Ier', *Epigraphica Anatolica* 11: 171–80.
Parkinson, R. B. (1991) *Voices from Ancient Egypt*. London.
Posener, G. (1985) *Le Papyrus Vandier*. Cairo.
Ray, J. D. (1976) *The Archive of Hor*. London.
   (1988) 'Egypt, 575–404 BC', in *CAH²* IV.1 254–86. Cambridge.
   (1990) 'The names Psammetichus and Takheta', *JEA* 76: 197–201.
Redford, D. B. (1970) *A Study of the Biblical Story of Joseph (Genesis 37–50) (VT* Suppl. 20). Leiden.
Sancisi-Weerdenburg, H. (ed.) (1987) *Achaemenid History* I (= *Proceedings of the Groningen 1983 Achaemenid Workshop*). Leiden.
Sasson, J. M. (ed.) (forthcoming) *Civilizations of the Ancient Near East*. New York.
Satzinger, H. (1985) 'On the prehistory of the Coptic dialects', in T. Orlandi and F. Wisse (eds.) *Acts of the Second International Congress of Coptic Studies* 307–12. Rome.
Sauneron, S. (1967) *Les Prêtres dans l'ancienne Égypte*. Paris.
   (1989) *Un traité égyptien d'Ophiologie*. Cairo.
Schousboe, K. and Larsen, M. T. (eds.) (1989) *Literacy and Society*. Copenhagen.
Schulman, A. R. (1975) 'On the Egyptian name of Joseph', *Studien zur Altägyptischen Kultur* 2: 235–43.
Shisha-Halévy, A. (1989) 'Papyrus Vandier *Recto*: an early demotic literary text?', *JAOS* 109: 421–35.
Thompson, D. J. (1988) *Memphis under the Ptolemies*. Princeton, NJ.
Trigger, B. G., Kemp, B. J., O'Connor, D. and Lloyd, A. B. (1983) *Ancient Egypt: A Social History*. Cambridge.
Vernus, P. (1990) 'Entre néo-égyptien et démotique (Étude sur la diglossie I)', *Revue d'Egyptologie* 41: 153–208.
Vleeming, S. P. and Wesselius, J. W. (1985) *Studies in Papyrus Amherst 63*. Amsterdam.
Wilcken, U. (1927) *Urkunden der Ptolemäerzeit I*. Berlin and Leipzig.

5. LITERACY AND POWER IN PTOLEMAIC EGYPT

Andrews, C. A. R. (1990) *Catalogue of Demotic Papyri in the British Museum* IV. *Ptolemaic Legal Texts from the Theban Area*. London.
Bagnall, R. S. (1984) 'The origin of Ptolemaic cleruchs', *BASP* 21: 7–20.
Baines, J. (1983) 'Literacy and ancient Egyptian society', *Man* n.s. 18: 572–99.
   (1988) 'Literacy, social organization, and the archaeological record: the case of early Egypt', in J. Gledhill, B. Bender and M. T. Larsen (eds.) *State and Society: The Emergence and Development of Social Hierarchy and Political Centralisation* 192–214. London.
Baines, J. and Eyre, C. J. (1983) 'Four notes on literacy', *Göttinger Miszellen* 61: 65–96.
Bevan, E. R. (1927) *A History of Egypt under the Ptolemaic Dynasty*. London.
Bresciani, E. (1978) 'La spedizione di Tolomeo II in Siria in un ostrakon demotico inedito da Karnak', in Maehler and Strocka (1978) 31–7.
   (1983) 'Registrazione catastale e ideologia politica nell' Egitto tolemaico', *Egitto e Vicino Oriente* 6: 15–31.
   (1984) 'Testi lessicali demotici inediti da Tebtuni presso Istituto G. Vitelli di Firenze', in Thissen and Zauzich (1984) 1–9.

Burstein, S. M. (1985) *The Hellenistic Age from the Battle of Ipsos to the Death of Kleopatra VII* (Translated Documents of Greece and Rome 3). Cambridge.

Canfora, L. (1989) *The Vanished Library. A Wonder of the Ancient World*. Transl. M. Ryle. London.

Clanchy, M. T. (1979) *From Memory to Written Record: England 1066–1307*. London.

Clarysse, W. (1978) 'Notes on some Graeco-demotic surety contracts', *Enchoria* 8: 5–8.

(1983) 'Literary papyri in documentary "archives"', in Van 't Dack, Van Dessel and Van Gucht (1983) 43–61.

(1987) 'Greek loan-words in demotic', in Vleeming (1987) 9–33.

Crawford, D. J. (1974) '*Skepe* in Soknopaiou Nesos', *JJP* 18: 169–74.

Criscuolo, L. and Geraci, G. (1989) *Egitto e storia antica dall' ellenismo all' età araba. Bilancio di un confronto. Atti del colloquio internazionale Bologna, 31 agosto – 2 settembre 1987*. Bologna.

de Cenival, Fr. (1973) *Cautionnements démotiques*. Paris.

Devauchelle, D. (1984) 'Remarques sur les méthodes d'enseignement du démotique', in Thissen and Zauzich (1984) 47–59.

el-Abbadi, M. (1990) *The Life and Fate of the Ancient Library of Alexandria*. Paris.

Fraser, P. M. (1972) *Ptolemaic Alexandria*. 3 vols. Oxford.

Guéraud, O. and Jouguet, P. (1938) *Un livre d'écolier du III* siècle avant J.-C.* (Publications de la Société Royale Egyptienne de Papyrologie. Textes et Documents 2). Cairo.

Hammond, N. G. L. (1990) 'Royal pages, personal pages, and boys trained in the Macedonian manner during the period of the Temenid monarchy', *Historia* 39: 261–90.

Hanson, A. E. (1991) 'Ancient illiteracy', in J. Humphrey (ed.) *Literacy in the Roman World* (*JRA* Supplementary Series 3) 159–98. Ann Arbor, MI.

Hopkins, K. (1991) 'Conquest by book', in J. Humphrey (ed.) *Literacy in the Roman World* (*JRA* Supplementary Series 3) 133–58. Ann Arbor, MI.

Kaplony-Heckel, U. (1974) 'Schüler und Schulwesen in der ägyptischen Spätzeit', *Studien zur altägyptischen Kultur* 1: 227–46.

Lichtheim, M. (1973) *Ancient Egyptian Literature: A Book of Readings* I. *The Old and Middle Kingdoms*. Berkeley, CA.

(1976) *Ancient Egyptian Literature: A Book of Readings* II. *The New Kingdom*. Berkeley, CA.

Maehler, H. and Strocka, V. M. (1978) *Das ptolemäische Ägypten. Akten des internationalen Symposions 27.–29. September 1976 in Berlin*. Mainz am Rhein.

McKitterick, R. (1989) *The Carolingians and the Written Word*. Cambridge.

Most, G. W. (1990) 'Canon fathers: literacy, mortality, power', *Arion* (Ser. 3) 1.1: 35–60.

Pestman, P. W. (1978) 'L'agoranomie: un avant-poste de l'administration grecque enlevé par les Egyptiens?', in Maehler and Strocka (1978) 203–10.

(1983) 'Some aspects of Egyptian law in Graeco-Roman Egypt', in Van 't Dack, Van Dessel and Van Gucht (1983) 281–302.

(1989) 'Egizi sotto dominazione straniere', in Criscuolo and Geraci (1989) 137–58.

Petrie, W. M. F. (1907) *Gizeh and Rifeh*. London.

Ray, J. D. (1986) 'The emergence of writing in Egypt', *World Archaeology* 17.3: 307–16.

Sethe, K. (1904) *Hieroglyphische Urkunden der griechisch-römischen Zeit*. Leipzig.

Silverman, D. P. (1990) *Language and Writing in Ancient Egypt*. Pittsburgh, PA.

Smith, H. S. (1958) 'Another witness-copy document from the Fayyum', *JEA* 44: 86–96.

Street, B. V. (1984) *Literacy in Theory and Practice* (Cambridge Studies in Oral and Literate Culture 9). Cambridge.

Tait, W. J. (1988) 'Rush and reed: the pens of Egyptian and Greek scribes', in *Proceedings of the XVIII International Congress of Papyrology, Athens 25–31 May 1986* II 477–81. Athens.

Thissen, H.-J. (1980) 'Chronologie der frühdemotischen Papyri', *Enchoria* 10: 105–25.

Thissen, H.-J. and Zauzich, K.-Th. (eds.) (1984) *Grammata Demotika. Festschrift für E. Lüddeckens zum 15. Juni 1983*. Würzburg.

Thompson, D. J. (1987) 'Ptolemaios and "The Lighthouse": Greek culture in the Memphite Serapeum', *PCPS* 213 (n.s. 33): 105–21.

(1988) *Memphis under the Ptolemies*. Princeton, NJ.

(1992a) 'Literacy in early Ptolemaic Egypt', in A. H. S. Mosalamy (ed.) *Proceedings of the XIXth International Congress of Papyrology, Cairo 2–9 September 1989* II 77–90. Cairo.

(1992b) 'Literacy and the administration in early Ptolemaic Egypt', in J. H. Johnson (ed.) *Life in a Multi-cultural Society: Egypt from Cambyses to Constantine and Beyond* (Studies in Ancient Oriental Civilization 51) 335–8. Chicago.

(1992c) 'Language and literacy in early Hellenistic Egypt', in Per Bilde, Troels Engberg-Pedersen, Lise Hannestad and Jan Zahle (eds.) *Ethnicity in Hellenistic Egypt* (Studies in Hellenistic Civilization 3) 39–52. Aarhus.

(forthcoming) 'Conquest and literacy: the case of Ptolemaic Egypt', in D. Keller-Cohen (ed.) *Literacy: Interdisciplinary Conversations*. Cresskill, NJ.

Turner, E. G. (1974) 'A commander-in-chief's order from Saqqara', *JEA* 60: 239–42.

Van 't Dack, E., Van Dessel, P. and Van Gucht, W. (1983) *Egypt and the Hellenistic World. Proceedings of the International Colloquium Leuven – 24–26 May 1982* (Studia Hellenistica 17). Leuven.

Vleeming, S. P. (1987) *Aspects of Demotic Lexicography*. Leuven.

Wilcken, U. (1927) *Urkunden der Ptolemäerzeit (ältere Funde)*. I. *Papyri aus Unterägypten*. Berlin and Leipzig.

Williams, R. J. (1972) 'Scribal training in ancient Egypt', *JAOS* 92: 214–21.

Youtie, H. C. (1970) 'Callimachus in the tax-rolls', *Proceedings of the XIIth International Congress of Papyrology* (American Studies in Papyrology 7) 545–55. Toronto. (Republished in *Scriptiunculae* II 1035–41, Amsterdam, 1970.)

6. POWER AND THE SPREAD OF WRITING IN THE WEST

Allen, D. F. (1980) *The Coins of the Ancient Celts*. Edinburgh.

Bats, M. (1988) 'La logique de l'écriture d'une société à l'autre en Gaule méridionale protohistorique', *RAN* 21: 121–48.

Bintliff, J. (1984) 'Iron age Europe in the context of social evolution from the Bronze age through to historic times', in J. Bintliff (ed.) *European Social Evolution* 157–225. Sheffield.

Bloch, M. (1989) 'Literacy and Enlightenment', in Schousboe and Larsen (1989) 15–38.

Burley, E. (1955–6) 'A catalogue and survey of the metalwork from Traprain Law', *Proc. Soc. Ant. Scot.* 89: 118–221.

Champion, T. C. (1985) 'Written sources and the study of the European iron age', in Champion and Megaw (1985) 9–22.

Champion, T. C. and Megaw, J. V. S. (eds.) (1985) *Settlement and Society. Aspects of West European Prehistory in the First Century B.C.* Leicester.

Clifford, E. M. (1961) *Bagendon. A Belgic Oppidum.* Cambridge.

Cunliffe, B. W. (1988) *Greeks, Romans and Barbarians. Spheres of Interaction.* London.

Dauge, Y. A. (1981) *Le Barbare. Recherches sur la conception romaine de la barbarie et de lā civilisation* (Collection Latomus 176). Brussels.

Desbordes, F. (1990) *Idées romaines sur l'écriture.* Lille.

Duval, A., Morel, J. P. and Roman, Y. (eds.) (1990) *Gaule Interne et Gaule Méditerranéenne aux IIᵉ et Iᵉʳ siècles avant J.C. Confrontations Chronologiques* (*RAN* supplement 21). Paris.

Egger, R. (1961) *Die Stadt auf dem Magdalensberg: ein Grosshandelsplatz.* Vienna.

Fitzpatrick, A. P. (1989) 'The uses of Roman imperialism by the Celtic barbarians in the later Republic', in J. C. Barrett, A. P. Fitzpatrick and L. Macinnes (eds.) *Barbarians and Romans in North-West Europe from the Later Republic to Late Antiquity* (BAR IS 471) 27–54. Oxford.

Furger-Gunti, A. (1979) *Die Ausgraben im Basel-Münster I. Die spätkeltische und augusteische Zeit* (Basler Beiträge zur Ur- und Frühgeschichte 6). Basel.

Gledhill, J., Bender, B. and Larsen, M. T. (eds.) (1988) *State and Society: The Emergence and Development of Social Hierarchy and Political Centralisation* (One World Archaeology 4). London.

Goody, J. R. (1977) *The Domestication of the Savage Mind.* Cambridge.

(1986) *The Logic of Writing and the Organisation of Society.* Cambridge.

Goudineau, C. (1989) 'L'apparition de l'écriture en Gaule', in J. P. Mohen (ed.) *Le Temps de la préhistoire* I 236–8. Paris.

Graff, H. J. (1979) *The Literacy Myth. Literacy and Social Structure in the Nineteenth Century City.* New York.

Gruel, K. and Brunaux, J. L. (eds.) (1987) *Monnaies gauloises découvertes en fouilles* (Dossiers de Protohistoire 1). Paris.

Harbsmeier, M. (1988) 'Inventions of writing', in Gledhill et al. (1988) 173–91.

(1989) 'Writing and the Other: travellers' literacy or towards an archaeology of orality', in Schousboe and Larsen (1981) 197–228.

Harris, W. V. (1989) *Ancient Literacy.* Cambridge, MA.

Hartog, F. (1988) *The Mirror of Herodotus. The Representation of the Other in the Writing of History.* Berkeley, CA.

Haselgrove, C. C. (1987) *Iron Age Coinage in South-East England. The Archaeological Context* (BAR BS 174). Oxford.

(1988) 'Coinage and complexity: archaeological analysis of socio-political change in Britain and non-Mediterranean Gaul during the later Iron Age', in D. B. Gibson and M. N. Geselowitz (eds.) *Tribe and Polity in late Prehistoric Europe* 69–96. New York.

Hawkes, C. F. C. and Hall, M. R. (1947) *Camulodunum. The First Report on the Excavations at Colchester 1930–9.* London.

Jacobi, G. (1974) 'Zum Schriftgebrauch in keltischen Oppida nördlich der Alpen', *Hamburger Beiträge zur Archäologie* 4: 171–81.

Krämer, W. (1982) 'Graffiti auf spätlatènekeramik aus Manching', *Germania* 60: 489–99.

Larsen, M. T. (1988) 'Introduction: literacy and social complexity', in Gledhill et al. (1988) 173–91.

Laubenheimer, F. (1990) *Le Temps des amphores en Gaule*. Paris.

Lejeune, M. (1973) 'La grande inscription celtibère de Botorrita', *CRAI* 622–47.

(1983) 'Rencontres de l'alphabet grec avec les langues barbares au cours du Ier millénaire avant J.C.', in *Modes de Contacts et Processus de transformation dans les sociétés anciennes. Actes du colloque de Cortone 1981* (Collection de l'Ecole Française à Rome 67) 731–53.

(1985) 'Textes gaulois et gallo-romains en cursive latine: II. Le plomb de Larzac', *Etudes Celtiques* 22: 95–177.

Lejeune, M. and Marichal, R. (1976–7) 'Textes Gauloises et Gallo-romaines en cursive Latine I', *Etudes Celtiques* 15: 151–7.

Lévi-Strauss, C. (1955) *Tristes Tropiques*. Paris.

MacMullen, R. (1965) 'The Celtic renaissance', *Historia* 14: 93–104; repr. in idem (1990) *Changes in the Roman Empire, Essays in the Ordinary* ch. 5. Princeton.

(1966) 'Provincial languages in the Roman empire', *AJPh* 87: 1–17; repr. in idem (1990) *Changes in the Roman Empire, Essays in the Ordinary* ch. 4. Princeton.

Maluquer de Motes, J. (1968) *Epigrafía prelatina de la peninsula ibérica*. Barcelona.

Marichal, R. (1988) *Les Graffites de la Graufesenque* (*Gallia* supplement 47). Paris.

Megaw, J. V. S. (1985) 'Meditations on a Celtic hobby-horse: notes towards a social archaeology of iron age art', in Champion and Megaw (1985) 161–91.

Meid, W. (1983) 'Gallisch oder Lateinisch? Soziolinguistische und andere Bemerkungen zu populären gallo-lateinischen Inschriften', *ANRW* 2.29.2: 1019–44.

Millar, F. G. B. (1968) 'Local cultures in the Roman empire: Libyan, Punic and Latin in North Africa', *JRS* 58: 126–34.

Moberg, C.-A. (1987) 'Quand l'archéologie rencontre les rencontres d'alphabets (quelques reflexions sur des monnaies épigraphes celtiques)', in *Mélanges offerts au Docteur J.-B. Colbert de Beaulieu* 639–49. Paris.

Mooseleitner, F. and Zellner, K. (1982) 'Beschriftete Tontafel aus keltischer Zeit am Dürrnberg', *Salzburger Museumsblätter* 43.3.

Nash, D. (1978a) *Settlement and Coinage in Central Gaul c. 200–50 B.C.* (BAR IS 39). Oxford.

(1978b) 'Territory and state formation in central Gaul', in D. Green et al. (eds.) *Social Organisation and Settlement* (BAR IS 47) 455–75. Oxford.

Nash, D. and Collis, J. R. (1983) 'Les monnaies du chantier IV d'Aulnat', in J. R. Collis, A. Duval and R. Périchon (eds.) *Le deuxième âge du fer en Auvergne et en Forez* 57–66. Sheffield.

Neumann, G. and Untermann, J. (1980) *Die Sprachen im römischen Reich der Kaizerseit* (*Bonner Jahrbücher* Beiheft 40). Bonn.

Obermayer, A. (1971) *Kelten und Römer am Magdalensberg*. Vienna.

Ong, W. J. (1982) *Orality and Literacy. The Technologising of the Word*. London.

Partridge, C. (1982) *Skeleton Green. A Late Iron Age and Romano-British Site* (*Britannia* monograph 2). London.

Píč, J. L. (1906) *Le Hradischt de Stradonitz en Bohême*. Leipzig.

Ralston, I. B. M. (1988) 'Central Gaul at the Roman conquest: conceptions and misconceptions', *Antiquity* 62: 786–94.

Schousboe, K. and Larsen, M. T. (eds.) (1989) *Literacy and Society*. Copenhagen.

Street, B. V. (1984) *Literacy in Theory and Practice*. Cambridge.

Thomas, R. (1992) *Literacy and Orality in Ancient Greece*. Cambridge.

Tomlin, R. S. O. (1987) 'Was ancient British Celtic ever a written language? Two texts from Bath', *Bulletin of the Board of Celtic Studies* 34: 18–25.

Tovar, A. (1961) *The Ancient Languages of Spain and Portugal*. New York.

Untermann, J. (1969) 'Lengua gala y lengua ibérica en la Gala Narbonensis', *Archivo de Prehistoria Levantina* 12: 99–163.

(1975) *Monumenta Linguarum Hispanicorum*. I. *Die Münzlegenden*. Wiesbaden.

(1980) *Monumenta Linguarum Hispanicorum*. II. *Die Inschriften in iberischer Schrift aus Südfrankreich*. Wiesbaden.

Vaginay, M. and Guichard, V. (1988) *L'Habitat gaulois de Feurs (Loire) (DAF* 14). Paris.

Van Arsdell, R. (1986) 'An industrial engineer (but no papyrus) in Celtic Britain', *Oxford Journal of Archaeology* 5: 205–21.

Wells, C. M. (1972) *The German Policy of Augustus*. Oxford.

Wiedemann, T. E. J. (1986) 'Between men and beasts: barbarians in Ammianus Marcellinus', in I. Moxon, J. D. Smart and A. J. Woodman (eds.) *Past Perspectives: Studies in Greek and Roman Historical Writing* 189–201. Cambridge.

Wild, J. P. (1966) 'Papyrus in pre-Roman Britain?', *Antiquity* 40: 139–42.

Woolf, G. D. (1993) 'Rethinking the Oppida', *Oxford Journal of Archaeology* 12.2: 223–4.

(forthcoming a) 'The social significance of trade in late iron age Europe', in C. Scarre (ed.) *Trade and Exchange in Prehistoric Europe, Acts of the Prehistoric Society Conference, Bristol 1992*.

(forthcoming b) 'European social development and Roman imperialism', in P. Brun et al. (eds.) *Les Frontières de l'empire romain, Actes du colloque internationale de Nemours, 1992*.

7. TEXTS, SCRIBES AND POWER IN ROMAN JUDAEA

Archer, L. J. (1990) *Her Price is above Rubies: The Jewish Woman in Graeco-Roman Palestine*. Sheffield.

Barr, J. (1983) *Holy Scripture: Canon, Authority, Criticism*. Oxford.

Barton, J. (1986) *Oracles of God: Perceptions of Ancient Prophecy in Israel after the Exile*. London.

Beckwith, R. (1985) *The Old Testament Canon of the New Testament Church and its Background in Early Judaism*. London.

Benoit, P., Milik, J. T. and De Vaux, R. (1960–1) *Les Grottes de Murabba'at* (Discoveries in the Judaean Desert 2). Oxford.

Bickermann, E. J. (1988) *The Jews in the Greek Age*. New York.

Cook, M. J. (1978) *Mark's Treatment of the Jewish Leaders* (*Novum Testamentum* Supplementary Volume 51). Leiden.

Davis, E. F. (1989) *Swallowing the Scroll: Textuality and the Dynamics of Discourse in Ezekiel's Prophecy*. Sheffield.

Golb, N. (1989) 'The Dead Sea scrolls: a new perspective', *The American Scholar* 58.2: 177–207.

Goodman, M. D. (1983) *State and Society in Roman Galilee, A.D. 132–212.* Otowa, NJ.
   (1990) 'Sacred scripture and "defiling the hands"', *JThS* 41: 99–107.
Higger, M. (1937) *Masseket Soferim.* New York.
Jeremias, J. (1964) 'Grammateus', in Kittel (1964).
   (1969) *Jerusalem in the Time of Jesus.* London.
Kittel, G. (1964–74) *Theological Dictionary of the New Testament,* 9 vols. Grand
   Rapids, MI.
Leiman, S. Z. (1976) *The Canonization of Hebrew Scripture: The Talmudic and
   Midrashic Evidence.* Hamden, CT.
Leon, H. J. (1960) *The Jews of Rome.* Philadelphia, PA.
Lieberman, S. (1962) *Hellenism in Jewish Palestine: Studies in the Literary
   Transmission, Beliefs and Manners of Palestine in the I century B.C.E. – IV
   Century C.E.,* 2nd edn. New York.
Reif, S. C. (1988) *Published Material from the Cambridge Genizah Collection: A
   Bibliography.* Cambridge.
Saldarini, A. J. (1989) *Pharisees, Scribes and Sadducees in Palestinian Society.*
   Edinburgh.
Sanders, E. P. (1990) *Jewish Law from Jesus to the Mishnah: Five Studies.* London.
   (1992) *Judaism: Practice and Belief, 63 BCE – 66 CE.* London.
Sanders, J. A. (1965) *The Psalms Scroll of Qumran Cave 11 (11QPsa)* (Discoveries
   in the Judaean Desert 4). Oxford.
Schams, C. (1992) 'The attitude towards sacred and secular written documents in
   first-century Judaism', M. Phil. thesis, Univ. of Oxford.
Schraeder, H. H. (1930) *Esra der Schreiber.* Tübingen.
Schürer, E. (1973–87) *The History of the Jewish People in the Age of Jesus Christ,* 3
   vols., rev. edn. Edinburgh.
Schwartz, D. R. (1985) '"Scribes and Pharisees, hypocrites". Who were the
   Scribes?', *Zion* 50: 121–32 [in Hebrew].
Skehan, P. W. and Di Lella, A. A. (1987) *The Wisdom of Ben Sira, Anchor Bible*
   vol. XXXIX. New York.
Strack, H. L. and Stemberger, G. (1991) *Introduction to the Talmud and Midrash.*
   Edinburgh.
Tov, E. (1990) *The Seiyal Collection* I: *The Greek Minor Prophets Scroll from Nahal
   Hever (8 Hev XII gr)* (Discoveries in the Judaean Desert 8). Oxford.
Vermes, G. (1970) 'Bible and midrash', in *The Cambridge History of the Bible* I
   199–231. Cambridge.
   (1973) *Scripture and Tradition in Judaism: Haggadic Studies,* 2nd edn. Leiden.
   (1977) *The Dead Sea Scrolls: Qumran in Perspective.* London.
Yadin, Y. (1971) *Bar-Kokhba: The Rediscovery of the Legendary Hero of the Last
   Jewish Revolt against Imperial Rome.* London.
   (1989) *The Documents from the Bar-Kokhba Period in the Cave of Letters: Greek
   Papyri,* ed. N. Lewis. Jerusalem.

8. THE ROMAN IMPERIAL ARMY: LETTERS AND LITERACY ON THE
NORTHERN FRONTIER

Adams, J. N. (1977) *The Vulgar Latin of the Letters of Claudius Terentianus.*
   Manchester.

Bagnall, R. S. (1976) *The Florida Ostraca: Documents from the Roman Army in Upper Egypt* (Greek, Roman and Byzantine Monographs 7). Durham, NC.

Bammesberger, A. and Wollmann, A. (1990) *Britain 400–600, Language and History.* Heidelberg.

Beard, W. M. (1985) 'Writing and ritual. A study of diversity and expansion in the Arval Acta', *PBSR* 53: 114–62.

Birley, E. (1988) *The Roman Army, Papers 1929–86.* Amsterdam.

Birley, R. E. (1977) *Vindolanda. A Roman Frontier Post on Hadrian's Wall.* London.

Bischoff, B. (1990) *Latin Palaeography, Antiquity and the Middle Ages.* Cambridge.

Bowman, A. K. (1975) 'The Vindolanda writing-tablets and the development of the Roman book form', *ZPE* 18: 237–52.

(1991) 'Literacy in the Roman empire: mass and mode', in Humphrey (1991) 119–31.

(1994) *Life and Letters on the Roman Frontier. Vindolanda and its People.* London.

Bowman, A. K. and Thomas, J. D. (1983) *Vindolanda, the Latin Writing-tablets* (*Britannia* Monograph 4).

(1987) 'New texts from Vindolanda', *Britannia* 17: 125–42.

(1991) 'A military strength report from Vindolanda', *JRS* 81: 62–73.

(1994) *The Vindolanda writing-tablets (Tabulae Vindolandenses II).* London.

Bowman, A. K., Thomas, J. D. and Adams, J. N. (1990) 'Two letters from Vindolanda', *Britannia* 20: 33–52.

Brandt, R. and Slofstra, J. (eds.) (1983) *Roman and Native in the Low Countries* (BAR IS 184). Oxford.

Breeze, D. J. (1974) 'The organisation of the career structure of the immunes and principales of the Roman army', *Bonner Jahrbücher* 174: 245–92.

Caruana, I. (1987) 'A wooden ansate panel from Carlisle', *Britannia* 18: 274–7.

Cotton, H. M. and Geiger, J. (1989) *Masada II, The Yigael Yadin Excavations 1963–1965. Final reports: The Latin and Greek Documents.* Jerusalem.

Cugusi, P. (1972–3) 'Le più antiche lettere papiracee latine', *Atti della Accademia delle Scienze di Torino* 107: 641–87.

(1981) 'Gli ostraca latini dello Wâdi Fawâkhir', *Letterature comparate, problemi e metodo. Studi in onore di E. Paratore* II 719–53. Bologna.

(1983) *Evoluzione e forme dell'epistolografia latina nella tarda repubblica e nei primi due secoli dell'impero.* Rome.

(1992) *Corpus Epistularum Latinarum.* Florence.

Cunliffe, B. W. (1988) *The Temple of Sulis Minerva at Bath* II. *The Finds from the Sacred Spring.* (Oxford University Committee for Archaeology, Monograph 16). Oxford.

Evans, D. E. (1990) 'Insular Celtic and the emergence of the Welsh language', in Bammesberger and Wollmann (1990) 149–77.

Fink, R. O. (1971) *Roman Military Records on Papyrus.* Cleveland, OH.

Ganz, P. (1990) *Tironische Noten.* Wiesbaden.

Gilliam, J. F. (1986) *Roman Army Papers.* Amsterdam.

Goody, J. (1986) *The Logic of Writing and the Organisation of Society.* Cambridge.

(1987) *The Interface between the Written and the Oral.* Cambridge.

Harris, W. V. (1989) *Ancient Literacy.* Cambridge, MA.

Hopkins, K. (1991) 'Conquest by book', in Humphrey (1991) 133–58.

Humphrey, J. H. (ed.) (1991) *Literacy in the Roman World (JRA* supplement 3). Ann Arbor, MI.

Isaac, B. (1992) *The Limits of Empire: The Roman Army in the East*, 2nd edn. Oxford.

Jones, G. D. B. (1990) 'The emergence of the Tyne–Solway frontier', in Maxfield and Dobson (1990) 98–107.

Kramer, J. (1991) 'Die Verwendung des Apex und P. Vindob. L 1 c', *ZPE* 88: 141–50.

Lanham, C. D. (1975) *Salutatio Formulas in Latin letters to 1200: Syntax, Style and Theory* (Münchener Beiträge zur Mediävistik und Renaissance-Forschung 22). Munich.

McKitterick, R. (ed.) (1990) *The Uses of Literacy in Early Medieval Europe*. Cambridge.

Maxfield, V. A. and Dobson, M. J. (eds.) (1990) *Roman Frontier Studies 1989, Proceedings of the XVth International Congress of Roman Frontier Studies*. Exeter.

Nicolet, C. (1988) *L'Inventaire du monde, géographie et politique aux origines de l'empire romain*. Paris.

Parkes, M. B. (1991) *Scribes, Scripts and Readers*. London.

Parsons, P. J. (1980) 'The papyrus letter', *Didactica Classica Gandensia* 20: 3–19.

Reynolds, J. M. and Volk, T. R. (1990) Review of Tomlin (1988), *Britannia* 21: 379–91.

Richmond, I. A. (1953) 'Three Roman writing-tablets from London', *Antiquaries Journal* 33: 206–8.

Stevenson, J. (1990) 'Literacy in Ireland: the evidence of the Patrick dossier in the Book of Armagh', in McKitterick (1990) 11–35.

Teitler, H. C. (1985) *Notarii and Exceptores*. Amsterdam.

Temporini, H. and Haase, W. (1974) *Aufstieg und Niedergang der römischen Welt* II.1. Berlin.

Thomas, R. (1991) Review of Harris (1989), *JRS* 81: 182–3.

Tjäder, J.-O. (1986) Review of Bowman and Thomas (1983), *Scriptorium* 50: 297–301.

Tomlin, R. S. O. (1986) 'Roman Britain in 1985', *Britannia* 17: 450–2.

(1988) 'The curse tablets', in Cunliffe (1988) 4–277.

(1992) 'The Twentieth legion at Wroxeter and Carlisle in the first century: the epigraphic evidence', *Britannia* 23: 141–58.

Turner, E. G. (1978) 'The terms Recto and Verso, the anatomy of the papyrus roll', in J. Bingen and G. Nachtergael (1978) *Actes du XVe congrès internationale de papyrologie*, 1e partie (Papyrologica Bruxellensia 16) 1–71. Brussels.

(1987) *Greek Manuscripts of the Ancient World*, 2nd edn revised by P. J. Parsons. London.

Watson, G. R. (1974) 'Documentation in the Roman army', in Temporini and Haase (1974) 493–507.

Welles, C. B., Fink, R. O. and Gilliam, J. F. (1959) *The Excavations at Dura-Europus, Final Report V, Part I: The Parchments and Papyri*. New Haven, CT.

Wierschowski, L. (1974) *Heer und Wirtschaft, das römische Heer als Wirtschaftfaktor*. Bonn.

Wingo, E. O. (1972) *Latin Punctuation in the Classical Age*. The Hague.

9. LITERACY AND POWER IN EARLY CHRISTIANITY

Bacht, H. (1972) *Das Vermächtnis des Ursprungs*. Würzburg.

Barns, J. W. B. (1978) *Egyptians and Greeks* (Papyrologica Bruxellensia 14). Brussels.

Barr, J. (1966) *Old and New in Interpretation*. London.

Beard, W. M. (1991) '*Ancient Literacy* and the function of the written word in

Roman religion', in J. H. Humphrey (ed.) *Literacy in the Roman World* (*JRA* supplement 3) 35–58. Ann Arbor, MI.

Blanchard, A. J. (1989a) 'Les Origines du Codex', in Blanchard (1989b) 13–35.

(1989b) *Les Débuts du Codex*. Brepols – Turnhout.

la Bonnardière, A.-M. (1986) *Saint Augustin et la Bible*. Paris.

Brown, P. R. L. (1968) 'Christianity and local culture in Late Roman Africa', *JRS* 58: 85–95.

Brox, N. (1991) *Der Hirt des Hermas*. Göttingen.

Brunt, P. A. (1979) 'Divine elements in the imperial office', *JRS* 69: 174–5.

Burkert, W. (1987) *Ancient Mystery Cults*. Cambridge, MA.

Clarke, G. W. (1984) 'An illiterate lector', *ZPE* 57: 103–4.

(1984–7) *The Letters of St Cyprian*, 4 vols. New York.

Davis, E. F. (1989) *Swallowing the Scroll*. Sheffield.

Deleani, S. (1985) 'L'utilisation des modèles bibliques de martyre par les écrivains du IIIème siècle', in Fontaine and Pietri (1985) 315–39.

Den Boeft, J. and Bremmer, J. (1991) 'Notiunculae Martyrologicae IV', *VChr* 45: 105–22.

Dolbeau, R. (1983) 'La passion des Saints Lucius et Montanus', *REAug* 29: 39–82.

Elm, S. (1991) 'Evagrius Ponticus's *Sententiae ad Virginem*', *DOP* 45: 97–120.

Eyice, S. and Noret, J. (1973) 'S. Lucien, disciple de S. Lucien d'Antioche: à propos d'une inscription de Kirsehir (Turquie)', *AB* 91: 363–77.

Fahey, M. A. (1971) *Cyprian and the Bible in Third Century Exegesis*. Tübingen.

Feissel, D. (1984) 'La Bible dans les inscriptions grecques', in Mondésert (1984) 223–32.

Fontaine, J. and Pietri, C. (1985) *Le Monde latin antique et la Bible*. Paris.

Fowden, G. (1986) *Egyptian Hermes: A Historical Approach to the Late Pagan Mind*. Cambridge.

Friedrichsen, G. W. (1926) *The Gothic Version of the Gospels*. London.

(1939) *The Gothic Version of the Epistles*. Oxford.

(1961) *Gothic Studies*. Oxford.

Gaudemet, J. (1985) 'La Bible dans les conciles', in Fontaine and Pietri (1985) 289–314.

Graff, H. J. (ed.) (1981) *Literacy and Social Development in the West*. Cambridge.

Greenslade, S. L. (1943) 'Scripture and other doctrinal norms in early theories of the Ministry', *JThS* 44: 162–76.

Harnack, A. (1912) *Bible Reading in the Early Church*, English edn. London.

Harris, W. V. (1989) *Ancient Literacy*. Cambridge, MA.

Hefele, J. (1907) *Histoire des Conciles*, 4 vols. Paris.

Herbig, R. (1958) *Neue Beobachtungen am Fries der Mysterienvilla im Pompeii*. Baden-Baden.

Hunt, A. S. and Edgar, C. C. (1934) *Select Papyri*, 2 vols. Cambridge, MA.

Johansson, E. (1981) 'The history of literacy in Sweden', in Graff (1981) 160.

Koenen, L. (1974) 'Ein Mönch als Berufschreiber', in *Festschrift zum 150 jahrigen Bestehen des Berliner Ägyptischen Museums*. Berlin.

Koep, L. (1952) *Das Himmlische Buch in Antike und Christentum*. Bonn.

Lane Fox, R. J. (1986) *Pagans and Christians*. London.

(1991) *The Unauthorized Version*. London.

Leclercq, H. (1899) *Notes sur la légende de la lettre du Christ tombée du ciel*. Paris.

Le Roy Ladurie, E. (1982) *Montaillou, Village Occitan*, 2nd edn. Paris.

Lewis, N. (1989) *Papyrus in Classical Antiquity: A Supplement* (Papyrologica Bruxellensia 23). Brussels.

Liepoldt, J. and Morenz, S. (1953) *Heilige Schriften*. Leipzig.

Lieu, S. N. C. (1983) 'An early Byzantine formula for the renunciation of Manichaeism', *JbAC* 26: 152–218.

(1985) *Manichaeism in the later Roman Empire and medieval China*. Manchester.

Luttikhuizen, G. P. (1985) *The Revelation of Elchesai*. Tübingen.

MacCormick, M. (1989) 'The birth of the Codex and the Apostolic life style', *Scriptorium* 39: 150–8.

McKitterick, R. (ed.) (1990a) *The Uses of Literacy In Early Medieval Europe*. Cambridge.

(1990b) 'Text and image in the Carolingian world', in McKitterick (1990a) 297–318.

Marin, M. (1989) 'Le Sententiae LXXXVII Episcoporum: in Margine al Problema del Rapporto fra Sacra Scrittura e Concili', *Invigilata Lucernis* (Rivista dell'Istituto di Latina, Universita di Bari 11) 329–59. Bari.

Merkelbach, R. (1980) 'Analphabetische Klostervorsteher in Konstantinopel und Chalkedon', *ZPE* 39: 211–14.

Metzger, B. M. (1977) *The Early Versions of the New Testament, their Origins, Transmission, and Limitations*. Oxford.

Mondésert, C. (1984) *Le Monde grec ancien et la Bible*. Paris.

Monfrin, F. (1985) 'La Bible dans l'iconographie chrétienne d'Occident', in Fontaine and Pietri (1985) 207–42.

Morin, G. (1939–40) 'The homilies of St Caesarius of Arles', *Orate Fratres* 14: 481–6.

Nock, A. D. (1972) *Essays on Religion and the Ancient World*, 2 vols. Oxford.

Paoli-Lafaye, E. (1986) 'Les "Lecteurs" des textes liturgiques', in La Bonnardière (1986) 59–74.

Parker, G. (1992) 'Success and failure during the first century of the Reformation', *Past and Present* 136: 43–82.

Peterson, E. (1934) 'Das jugendliche Alter der Lectoren', *Ephemerides Liturgicae* 48: 437–42.

Pietri, C. (1985) 'La Bible dans l'épigraphie de l'Occident latin', in Fontaine and Pietri (1985) 189–206.

Roberts, C. H. (1963) *Buried Books In Antiquity*. London.

(1979) *Manuscript, Society and Belief*. London.

Roberts, C. H. and Skeat, T. C. (1983) *The Birth of the Codex*. London.

Robinson, J. M. (1988) *The Nag Hammadi Library in English*, 3rd edn. New York.

Rossi, F. (1887) *Papiri Copti del Museo Egizio di Torino*. Torino.

de Sainte Croix, G. E. M. (1954) 'Aspects of the "Great" persecution', *HThR* 47: 75–113.

Saxer, V. (1986) *Bible et hagiographie: textes et thèmes bibliques dans les actes des martyres authentiques des premières siècles*. Berne.

Segal, J. B. (1970) *Edessa*. Oxford.

Skeat, T. C. (1982) 'The length of the standard papyrus roll and the cost advantage of the Codex', *ZPE* 45: 169–75.

Smout, T. C. (1982) 'Born again at Cambuslang: new evidence on popular religion and literacy in 18th century England', *Past and Present* 97: 114–27.

von Soden, H. (1909) 'Sententiae LXXXVII Episcoporum. Das Protokoll der

Synode von Karthago am 1 September 256', *Nachrichten von der Königl. Gesell. der Wiss. zu Göttingen* Phil. hist. Klasse 247–307.

Speyer, W. (1970) 'Büchervernichtung', *JbAC* 13: 123–52.

Thraede, K. (1969) 'Exorzismus', *Reallexikon für Antike u. Christentum* Band VII, Cols. 65–105. Stuttgart.

Turner, E. G. (1977) *The Typology of the Early Codex.* Pennsylvania.

van der Meer, F. (1961) *Augustine the Bishop.* London.

van Haelst,˜ J. (1989) 'Les origines du Codex', in Blanchard (1989b) 13–35.

van Unnik, W. C. (1949) 'De la règle μήτε προσθεῖναι μήτε ἀφελεῖν dans l'histoire du canon', *VChr* 3: 1–36.

Veilleux, A. (1968) *La Liturgie dans le Cénobitisme Pachomien au IVème Siècle* (Studia Anselmiana 57). Rome.

Vessey, J. M. (1988) 'Ideas of Christian writing in late Roman Gaul', D. Phil. thesis, Univ. of Oxford.

de Vogué, A. (1977) *La Règle de S. Benoît*, 7 vols. Paris.

West, M. L. (1983) *The Orphic Poems.* Oxford.

Wiles, M. F. (1963) 'The theological legacy of St Cyprian', *JEH* 14: 139–49.

Wilken, R. L. (1983) *John Chrysostom and the Jews.* California.

Williams, R. D. (1987) *Arius: Heresy and Tradition.* London.

Wipszycka, E. (1983) 'Un lecteur qui ne sait pas écrire', *ZPE* 50: 117–21.

   (1984) 'Le degré d'alphabétisation en Egypte Byzantine', *REAug* 30: 279–96.

10. GREEK AND SYRIAC IN LATE ANTIQUE SYRIA

Bardy, G. (1948) *La Question des langues dans l'église ancienne.* Paris.

Bellinger, A. R. and Welles, C. B. (1935) 'A third-century contract of sale from Edessa in Osrhoene', *YCIS* 5: 95–154.

Bowersock, G. W. (1990) *Hellenism in Late Antiquity.* Cambridge.

Brock, S. P. (1982) 'From antagonism to assimilation: Syriac attitudes to Greek learning', in Garsoian, Mathews and Thomson (1982) 17–34.

   (1985) 'Syriac and Greek hymnography: problems of origin', *Studia Patristica* 16: 77–81.

   (1989) 'From Ephrem to Romanos', *Studia Patristica* 20: 139–51.

   (1991 [1993]) 'Some new Syriac documents from the third century AD', *Aram* 3: 259–67.

Contini, R. (1987) 'Il Hawran preislamico: ipotesi di storia linguistica', *Felix Ravenna* 4.1–2: 25–79.

Dagron, G. (1969) 'Aux origines de la civilisation byzantine: langue de culture et langue d'état', *Revue historique* 241: 23–56.

Drijvers, H. J. W. (1970) 'Bardaisan of Edessa and the Hermetica. The Aramaic philosopher and the philosophy of his time', *Jaarbericht Ex Oriente Lux* 21: 190–210; repr. in Drijvers (1984) ch. 11.

   (1984) *East of Antioch. Studies in Early Syriac Christianity.* London.

Feissel, D. and Gascou, J. (1989) 'Documents d'archives romains inédits du Moyen Euphrate', *Académie des Inscriptions et Belles-Lettres, Comptes Rendus* 535–61.

Fiaccadori, G. (1990) *Autori classici in lingue del vicino e medio oriente.* Rome.

Garsoian, N., Mathews, T. and Thomson, R. (eds.) (1982) *East of Byzantium: Syria and Armenia in the Formative Period.* Washington, DC.

Hendriks, O. (1958) 'Les premiers monastères internationaux syriens', *L'Orient Syrien* 3: 165–84.

Hugonnard Roche, H. (1989) 'Aux origines de l'exégèse orientale de la logique d'Aristote: Sergius de Reš'aina', *Journal Asiatique* 277: 1–17.

Jones, A. H. M. (1959) 'Were ancient heresies national or social movements in disguise?', *JThS* n.s. 11: 280–98.

Kennedy, H. and Liebeschuetz, J. H. W. G. (1988) 'Antioch and the villages of Northern Syria in the fifth and sixth centuries A.D. Trends and problems', *Nottingham Medieval Studies* 32: 65–90.

Laga, C., Munitiz, J. A. and Van Rompay, L. (1985) *After Chalcedon: Studies in Theology and Church History offered to Professor A. Van Roey* (Orientalia Lovaniensia Analecta 18). Leuven.

Lavenant, R. (1984) *Jean d'Apamée. Dialogues et traités* (Sources chrétiennes 311). Paris.

Macomber, W. (1973) 'A theory of the origins of the Syrian, Maronite and Chaldean rites', *Orientalia Christiana Periodica* 39: 235–42.

MacMullen, R. (1966) 'Provincial languages in the Roman Empire', *AJPh* 87: 1–17.

Millar, F. G. B. (1971) 'Paul of Samosata, Zenobia and Aurelian: the church, local culture and political allegiance in third-century Syria', *JRS* 61: 1–17.

(1987) 'Empire, community and culture in the Roman Near East: Greeks, Syrians, Jews and Arabs', *Journal of Jewish Studies* 38: 143–64.

Neumann, G. and Untermann, J. (1980) *Die Sprachen im römischen Reich der Kaiserzeit* (Beihefte der Bonner Jahrbücher 40). Cologne/Bonn.

Peeters, P. (1950) *Le Tréfonds oriental de l'hagiographie byzantine* (Subsidia Hagiographica 26). Brussels.

Petersen, W. L. (1986) 'New evidence for the question of the original language of the Diatessaron', in Schrage (1986) 325–43.

Poggi, V. (1990) 'Situazione linguistica dell'Oriente bizantino nel secolo V', in Fiaccadori (1990) 105–24.

Sauget, J.-M. (1985) 'Vestiges d'une célébration gréco-syriaque de l'Anaphore de Saint Jacques', in Laga, Munitiz and Van Rompay (1985) 309–45.

Schmitt, R. (1980) 'Die Ostgrenze von Armenien über Mesopotamien, Syrien bis Arabien', in Neumann and Untermann (1980) 187–214.

Schrage, W. (1986) *Studien zum Text und zur Ethik des Neuen Testament.* Berlin.

Teixidor, J. (1990) 'Deux documents syriaques du IIIe siècle après J.-C. provenant du Moyen Euphrate', *Académie des Inscriptions et Belles-Lettres, Comptes Rendus* 146–66.

Van Rompay, L. (1990) 'Palmyra, Emesa en Edessa', *Phoenix* [Leiden] 36: 73–84.

Vööbus, A. (1965) *History of the School of Nisibis* (Corpus Scriptorum Christianorum Orientalium, Subsidia 26). Louvain.

11. LATE ROMAN BUREAUCRACY: GOING THROUGH THE FILES

Archi, G. G. (1976) *Teodosio II e la sua codificazione* (Storia del pensiero giuridico 4). Naples.

Bowman, A. K. (1985) 'Landholding in the Hermopolite Nome in the fourth century A.D.' *JRS* 75: 137–63.

Caimi, J. (1984) *Burocrazia e diritto nel de Magistratibus di Giovanni Lido* (Univ. di Genova Fondazione Nobile Agostino Poggi 16). Milan.

Casson, S., Talbot Rice, D., Hudson, G. F. and Jones, A. H. M. (1928) *Preliminary Report upon the Excavations Carried out in the Hippodrome of Constantinople in 1927 on Behalf of the British Academy*. London.

Chastagnol, A. (1960) *La Préfecture Urbaine à Rome sous le Bas-Empire* (Publications de la Faculté des Lettres et Sciences Humaines d'Alger 34). Paris.

Dagron, G. (1974) *Naissance d'une capitale Constantinople et ses institutions de 330 à 451* (Bibliothèque Byzantine Etudes 7). Paris.

Duncan-Jones, R. P. (1981) review of Sijpesteijn and Worp (1978), *JRS* 71: 198–9.

Ebersolt, J. (1910) *Le Grand Palais de Constantinople et le Livre des Cérémonies* (Bibliothèque de la Fondation Thiers 21). Paris.

Gaudemet, J. (1954) 'L'Empereur, interprète du droit', in W. Kunkel and H. J. Wolff (eds.) *Festschrift für Ernst Rabel II Geschichte der antiken Rechte und allgemeine Rechtslehre* 169–203. Tübingen.

(1957) *La Formation du droit séculier et du droit de l'église aux IVe et Ve siècles* (Institut de Droit Romain de l'Univ. de Paris XV). Paris.

(1979) *'Indulgentia Principis': Etudes de droit romain II. Institutions et doctrines politiques*, eds. L. Labruna, B. Buti and F. Salerno, 235–79. (Pubblicazioni della Facoltà di Giurisprudenza della Univ. di Camerino 4/2, Univ. di Camerino.)

Guilland, R. (1969) *Etudes de topographie de Constantinople Byzantine* (Deutsche Akademie der Wissenschaften zu Berlin Institut für griechisch-römische Altertumskunde Berliner byzantinistische Arbeiten 37). Berlin and Amsterdam.

(1970) 'Etudes sur l'Hippodrome de Byzance XI: Les dimensions de l'Hippodrome', *Byzantine Studies* 31.1: 1–11.

Honoré, T. (1986) 'The making of the *Theodosian Code*', *ZRG* 103: 133–222.

Janin, R. (1950) *Constantinople Byzantine développement urbain et répertoire topographique* (Archives de l'Orient Chrétien 4, Institut Français d'Etudes Byzantines). Paris.

Jones, A. H. M. (1964) *The Later Roman Empire 284–602. A Social, Economic and Administrative Survey*, 3 vols. Oxford.

MacMullen, R. (1962) 'Roman bureaucratese', *Traditio* 18: 364–78.

Mamboury, E. (1936) 'Les fouilles Byzantines à Istanbul et dans sa banlieue immédiate aux XIXe et XXe siècles', *Byzantion* 11: 229–83.

Mamboury, E. and Wiegand, T. (1934) *Die Kaiserpaläste von Konstantinopel zwischen Hippodrom und Marmara-Meer*. Archäologisches Institut des deutschen Reiches Abteilung Istanbul, Berlin.

Mommsen, T. (1900) 'Das theodosische Gesetzbuch', *ZRG* 21: 149–90.

Müller-Wiener, W. (1977) *Bildlexicon zur Topographie Istanbuls*. Deutsches Archäologisches Institut, Tübingen.

Noethlichs, K. L. (1981) *Beamtentum und Dienstvergehen: Zur Staatsverwaltung in der Spätantike*. Wiesbaden.

Posner, E. (1972) *Archives in the Ancient World*. Harvard.

Piganiol, A. (1936) 'La loge impériale de l'Hippodrome de Byzance et le problème de l'Hippodrome couvert', *Byzantion* 11: 383–90.

Rees, B. R. (1952) 'The *Defensor Civitatis* in Egypt', *JJP* 6: 73–102.

Seeck, O. (1919) *Regesten der Kaiser und Päpste für die Jahre 311 bis 476 n. Chr. Vorarbeit zu einer Prosopographie der Christlichen Kaiserzeit.* Stuttgart.

Sijpesteijn, P. J. and Worp, K. A. (1978) *Zwei Landlisten aus dem Hermupolites (P. Landlisten)* (Studia Amstelodamensia ad Epigraphicam, Ius Antiquum et Papyrologicam Pertinentia 7). Amsterdam.

Stein, E. (1922) *Untersuchungen über das Officium der Prätorianerpräfektur seit Diokletian.* Vienna.

Steinwenter, A. (1915) *Beiträge zum öffentlichen Urkundenwesen der Römer.* Graz.

Tassi, A. M. (1967) 'Costanzo II e la difesa della maestà imperiale nell'opera di Ammiano Marcellino', *CS* 6.2: 157–80.

Turpin, W. N. (1982) 'The late Roman law codes: forms and procedures for legislation from the classical age to Justinian', unpubl. Ph.D. dissertation, Univ. of Cambridge, 2 Feb. 1982 (no. 12174).

Valensi, L. (1957) 'Quelques réflexions sur le pouvoir impérial d'après Ammien Marcellin', *BAGB* 16.4: 62–107.

Vera, D. (1981) *Commento storico alle Relationes di Quinto Aurelio Simmaco introduzione, commento, testo, traduzione, appendice sul libro X, 1–2, indici* (Biblioteca di Studi Antichi 29). Pisa.

Vogt, A. (1935) 'L'Hippodrome de Constantinople', *Byzantion* 10 (1935) 471–88.

Volterra, E. (1980) 'Intorno alla formazione del *Codice Teodosiano*', *BIDR* 83: 109–45.

　(1981) 'Sul contenuto del *Codice Teodosiano*', *BIDR* 84: 85–124.

　(1983) 'Sulla legge delle citazioni', *Atti Acc. Lincei* (ser. 8) 27.4: 185–267.

Weber, M. (1985) *Wirtschaft und Gesellschaft: Grundriss der verstehenden Soziologie*, 5th rev. edn, ed. J. Winckelmann. Tübingen.

Wenger, L. (1953) *Die Quellen des römischen Rechts* (Österreichische Akademie der Wissenschaften Denkschriften der Gesamtakademie 2). Vienna.

12. LITERACY AND POWER IN THE MIGRATION PERIOD

Bachrach, B. S. (1972) *Merovingian Military Organisation 481–751.* Minneapolis.

Barnish, S. J. B. (1992) *Cassiodorus: Variae* (transl. with notes). Liverpool.

Barrett, J. C., Fitzpatrick, A. P. and Macinnes, L. (eds.) (1989) *Barbarians and Romans in North-west Europe from the Later Republic to Late Antiquity* (BAR IS 471). Oxford.

Bloemers, J. H. F. (1989) 'Acculturation in the Rhine/Meuse Basin in the Roman period: demographic considerations', in Barrett et al. (1989) 175–97.

Brown, P. R. L. (1967) *Augustine of Hippo: A Biography.* London.

Brown, T. S. (1984) *Gentlemen and Officers: Imperial Administration and Aristocratic Power in Byzantine Italy A.D. 554–800.* Rome.

Campbell, J., John, E. and Wormald, P. (1982) *The Anglo-Saxons.* Oxford.

Charles-Edwards, T. (1989) 'Early medieval kingships in the British Isles', in S. Bassett (ed.) *The Origins of the Anglo-Saxon Kingdoms* 28–39. Leicester.

Clanchy, M. T. (1979) *From Memory to Written Record: England 1066–1307.* London.

Collins, R. (1983) *Early Medieval Spain: Unity in Diversity, 400–1000.* London.

　(1985) '*Sicut Lex Gothorum continet*: law and charters in ninth- and tenth-century Leon and Catalonia', *EHR* 100: 489–512.

　(1990) 'Literacy and the laity in early mediaeval Spain', in McKitterick (1990) 109–33.

Dauge, Y. A. (1981) *Le Barbare: recherches sur la conception romaine de la barbarie et de la civilisation* (Coll. Latomus 176). Brussels.

Davies, W. (1982) *Wales in the Early Middle Ages*. Leicester.

Davies, W. and Fouracre, P. (eds.) (1986) *The Settlement of Disputes in Early Medieval Europe*. Cambridge.

Desbordes, F. (1990) *Idées romaines sur l'écriture*. Lille.

Dionisotti, C. (1982) 'From Ausonius' Schooldays?: a Schoolbook and its relatives', *JRS* 72: 83–125.

Durliat, J. (1990) *Les Finances publiques de Dioclétien aux Carolingiens (284–889)*. Sigmaringen.

Fontaine, J. (1980) 'King Sisebut's *Vita Desiderii* and the political function of Visigothic hagiography', in E. James (ed.), *Visigothic Spain: New Approaches* 93–129. Oxford.

Fouracre, P. (1986) '*Placita* and the settlement of disputes in later Merovingian Francia', in Davies and Fouracre (1986) 23–43.

Friedrichsen, G. W. S. (1926) *The Gothic Version of the Gospels: A Study of its Style and Textual History*. Oxford.

(1939) *The Gothic Version of the Epistles*. Oxford.

Fulford, M. G. (1985) 'Roman material in barbarian society c. 200 B.C. to c. A.D. 400', in T. C. Champion and J. V. S. Megaw (eds.) *Settlement and Society: Aspects of West European Prehistory in the first Millennium B.C.* 91–108. Leicester.

George, J. W. (1992) *Venantius Fortunatus: A Poet in Merovingian Gaul*. Oxford.

Gledhill, J., Bender, B. and Larsen, M. T. (eds.) (1988) *State and Society: The Emergence and Development of Social Hierarchy and Political Centralisation*. London.

Goffart, W. (1988) *The Narrators of Barbarian History (AD 550–800): Jordanes, Gregory of Tours, Bede, and Paul the Deacon*. Princeton, NJ.

Goody, J. (1977) *The Domestication of the Savage Mind*. Cambridge.

(1986) *The Logic of Writing and the Organization of Society*. Cambridge.

Goody, J. and Watt, I. P. (1963) 'The consequences of literacy', *CSSH* 5: 304–45.

Harris, W. V. (1989) *Ancient Literacy*. Cambridge, MA.

Harvey, S. (1987) 'Taxation and the economy', in J. C. Holt (ed.) *Domesday Studies* 249–64. Bury St Edmunds.

Heather, P. J. (1986) 'The crossing of the Danube and the Gothic conversion', *GRBS* 27: 289–318.

(1991) *Goths and Romans*. Oxford.

(forthcoming a) 'New Men for New Constantines: creating an imperial elite in the eastern Mediterranean', in P. Magdalino (ed.) *New Constantines: The Theme of Imperial Renewal in Byzantine History*.

(forthcoming b) 'The historical culture of Ostrogothic Italy', *Atti di XIII congresso internazionale di studi sull'alto medioevo*. Milan.

Heather, P. J. and Matthews, J. F. (1991) *The Goths in the Fourth Century*. Liverpool.

Hedeager, L. (1988) 'The evolution of Germanic society 1–400 AD', in R. F. J. Jones, J. H. F. Bloemers, S. C. Dyson and M. Biddle (eds.) *First Millennium Papers: Western Europe in the First Millennium* 129–44 (BAR IS 401). Oxford.

Heinzelmann, M. (1976a) *Bischofsheerschaft in Gallien: Zur Kontinuität römischer Führungsschichten vom 4. bis zum 7. Jahrhundert: Soziale, prosopographische und bildungsgeschichtliche Aspekte*. Munich.

(1976b) 'L'aristocratie et les évêches entre Loire et Rhin jusqu'à la fin du VIIᵉ siècle', *Revue d'Histoire de l'Eglise de France* 62: 75–90.

Honoré, T. (1978) *Tribonian*. London.

Hopkins, M. K. (1961) 'Social mobility in the later Roman Empire: the evidence of Ausonius', *CQ* n.s. 11: 239–49.

(1965) 'Elite mobility in the Roman Empire', *P&P* 32: 12–26.

James, E. (1983) '*Beati Pacifici*: Bishops and the law in sixth-century Gaul', in J. Bossy (ed.) *Disputes and Settlements: Law and Human Relations in the West* 25–46. Cambridge.

(1988) *The Franks*. Oxford.

John, E. (1960) *Land Tenure in Early England*. Leicester.

Jones, A. H. M. (1964) *The Later Roman Empire: A Social, Economic and Administrative Survey*. Oxford.

Kaster, R. A. (1988) *Guardians of the Language: The Grammarians and Society in Late Antiquity*. Berkeley, CA.

Kelly, S. (1990) 'Anglo-Saxon lay literacy and the written word', in McKitterick (1990) 36–62.

Lapidge, M. and Dumville, D. (1984) *Gildas: New Approaches*. London.

McKitterick, R. (1989) *The Carolingians and the Written Word*. Cambridge.

(1990) (ed.) *The Uses of Literacy in Early Medieval Europe*. Cambridge.

MacMullen, R. (1962) 'Roman bureaucratese', *Traditio* 18: 364–78.

(1976) *Roman Government's Response to Crisis A.D. 235–337*. New Haven, CT.

Marrou, H. I. (1982) *History of Education in Antiquity*, transl. G. Lamb. Wisconsin.

Mathisen, R. W. (1979) 'Hilarius, Germanus, and Lupus: the aristocratic background of the Chelidonius Affair', *Phoenix* 33: 160–9.

Moorhead, J. (1992) *Victor of Vita: History of the Vandal Persecution*, transl. with notes. Liverpool.

Myhre, B. (1978) 'Agrarian development, settlement history and social organisation in Southwest Norway in the Iron Age', in K. Kristiansen and C. Paludan-Muller (eds.) *New Directions in Scandinavian Archaeology* 224–35, 253–65. Copenhagen.

Nash-Williams, V. E. (1950) *The Early Christian Monuments of Wales*. Cardiff.

Nellen, D. (1981) *Viri Litterati: Gebildetes Beamtentum und spätrömisches Reich im Westen zwischen 284 und 395 nach Christus*, 2nd edn. Bochum.

Nixon, C. E. V. (1992) 'Relations between Visigoths and Romans in fifth century Gaul', in J. Drinkwater and H. Elton (eds.) *Fifth Century Gaul: A Crisis of Identity?* 64–74. Cambridge.

Noble, T. F. X. (1990) 'Literacy and the papal government in late antiquity and the early middle ages', in McKitterick (1990) 82–108.

Norberg, D. (1954) *La Poésie latine rythmique du haut Moyen Age*. Stockholm.

Oberhelman, S. M. (1991) *Rhetoric and Homiletics in Fourth-Century Christian Literature*. Atlanta, GA.

Oberhelman, S. M. and Hall, R. G. (1984) 'A new statistical analysis of accentual prose rhythms in imperial Latin prose', *CPh* 79: 114–30.

(1985a) 'Rhythmical clausulae in the *Codex Theodosianus* and the *Leges novellae ad Theodosianum pertinentes*', *CQ* n.s. 35: 201–14.

(1985b) 'Metre in accentual clausulae of Late Empire Latin', *CPh* 80: 214–27.

(1986a) 'Internal clausulae in late Latin prose as evidence for the displacement of metre by word-stress', *CQ* n.s. 36: 208–24.

(1986b) 'Internal clausulae in the letters of Augustine as a reflection of rhetorical and cultural goals', *Augustiniana* 37: 258–78.

Page, R. I. (1987) *Runes*. London.

Pearson, M. P. (1989) 'Beyond the pale: barbarian social dynamics in Western Europe', in Barrett et al. (1989) 198–226.

Riché, P. (1976) *Education and Culture in the Barbarian West*, transl. J. J. Contreni. South Carolina.

Rosenblum, M. (1961) *Luxorius: A Latin Poet among the Vandals*. New York.

Schaferdiek, K. (1970) 'Der germanische Arianismus: Erwägungen zum geschichtliche Verständnis', *Miscellanea Historiae Ecclesiasticae* 3: 71–83.

Stock, B. (1983) *The Implications of Literacy: Written Language and Models of Interpretation in the Eleventh and Twelfth Centuries*. Princeton, NJ.

Teillet, S. (1984) *Des Goths à la nation gothique: les origines de l'idée de nation en Occident du V.ᵉ au VII.ᵉ siècle*. Paris.

Teitler, H. C. (1985) *Notarii and Exceptores*. Amsterdam.

Van Dam, R. (1985) *Leadership and Community in Late Antique Gaul*. Berkeley, CA.

Vessey, M. (1988) 'Ideas of Christian writing in late Roman Gaul', unpubl. D. Phil. thesis, Univ. of Oxford.

(1992) 'Literacy and *Litteratura*, A.D. 200–800', *Studies in Medieval and Renaissance History* n.s. 15: 139–60.

Wickham, C. (1984) 'The other transition: from the ancient world to feudalism', *P&P* 103: 3–36.

Wolfram, H. (1988) *History of the Goths*. Berkeley, CA.

Wood, I. N. (1986) 'Disputes in late fifth- and early sixth-century Gaul: some problems', in Davies and Fouracre (1986) 7–22.

(1990) 'Administration, law and culture in Merovingian Gaul', in McKitterick (1990) 63–81.

(forthcoming) 'The *Codex Theodosianus* in Merovingian Gaul', in J. Harries (ed.) *Proceedings of the Theodosian Code Conference, St Andrews 1990*.

Wormald, P. (1977) '*Lex Scripta* and *Verbum Regis*: legislation and Germanic kingship from Euric to Cnut', in P. H. Sawyer and I. N. Wood (eds.) *Early Medieval Kingship* 105–38. Leeds.

Wright, R. (1982) *Late Latin and Early Romance in Spain and Carolingian France*. Liverpool.

13. TEXTS AS WEAPONS: POLEMIC IN THE BYZANTINE DARK AGES

Alexander, P. J. (1953) 'The iconoclastic council of St Sophia (815) and its definition', *DOP* 7: 37–66.

(1957) *The Patriarch Nicephorus of Constantinople*. Oxford.

(1958) 'Church councils and patristic authority: the iconoclastic councils of Hiereia (754) and St Sophia (815)', *HSPh* 63: 493–505.

Anastos, M. V (1955) 'The argument for iconoclasm as presented by the iconoclastic council of 754', in Weitzmann (1955) 177–88.

Auzépy, M.-F. (1990) 'La destruction de l'icone du Christ de la Chalcé par Léon III: propaganda ou réalité?', *Byzantion* 60: 445–92.

Bardy, G. (1936) 'Faux et fraudes littéraires dans l'antiquité chrétienne', *RHR* 32: 290–2.

Boespflug, F. and Lossky, N. (eds.) (1987) *Nicée II, 787–1987. Douze siècles d'images religieuses.* Paris.

Bonwetsch, N. (1909) 'Ein antimonophysitischer Dialog', *Nachr. der kgl. gesellschaft der Wiss. Göttingen* 123–59.

Brown, Peter (1973) 'A Dark-Age crisis: aspects of the Iconoclastic controversy', *EHR* 346: 1–34.

Brubaker, L. (1989a) 'Byzantine art in the ninth century: theory, practice and culture', *Byzantine and Modern Greek Studies* 13: 23–93.

(1989b) 'Perception and conception: art, theory and culture in ninth-century Byzantium', *Word and Image* 5: 19–32.

Byzantine Books and Bookmen (1975). Washington, DC.

Cameron, Averil (1987) 'The construction of court ritual: the Byzantine *Book of Ceremonies*', in Cannadine and Price (1987) 106–36.

(1990) 'Models of the past in the late sixth century: the *Life* of the Patriarch Eutychius', in Clarke (1990) 205–23.

(1991) 'Disputations, polemical literature and the formation of opinion in the early Byzantine period', in Reinink and Vanstiphout (1991) 91–108.

(1992) 'The language of images. The rise of icons and Christian representation', in Wood (1992) 1–42.

Cameron, Averil and Conrad, Lawrence, I. (eds.) (1992) *The Byzantine and Early Islamic Near East I: Problems in the Literary Source Material.* Princeton, NJ.

Cannadine, D. and Price, S. (eds.) (1987) *Rituals of Royalty. Power and Ceremonial in Traditional Societies.* Cambridge.

Cavallo, G., de Gregorio, G. and Maniaci, M. (eds.) (1992) *Scritture, libri e testi nelle aree provinciali di Bisanzio, Atti del Seminario di Erice (18–25 sett. 1988).* Spoleto.

Chadwick, H. (1969) Art. s.v. Florilegium, in *Reallexicon für Antike und Christentum* VII 1131–60.

(1992) Review of Riedinger (1990) and of Riedinger, *Der Codex Vindobonensis 418. Seine Vorlage und seine Schreiber* (Instrumenta Patristica 17, Bruges, 1989), *JEH* 42: 630–5.

Chrysos, E. (1992) 'Byzantine diplomacy, AD 300–800', in Shepard and Franklin (1992) 25–39.

Chrysostomides, J. (ed.) (1988) *Kathegetria. Essays Presented to Joan Hussey.* Camberley.

Clarke, G. W., Croke, B., Mortley, R. and Nobbs, A. E. (eds.) (1990) *Reading the Past in Late Antiquity.* Canberra.

Cormack, R. (1985) *Writing in Gold.* London.

Dagron, G. (1984) 'Le culte des images dans le monde byzantin', in idem. *La Romanité chrétienne en Orient.* London.

(1991) 'Holy images and likeness', *DOP* 45: 23–33.

Déroche, V. (1986) 'L'authenticité de l'*Apologie contre les Juifs* de Léontios de Néapolis', *BCH* 110: 655–69.

(1991) 'La polémique anti-judaïque au VIᵉ et au VIIᵉ siècle.-Un mémento inédit, les *Kephalaia*', *T&MByz* 11: 275–311.

Diekamp, F. (ed.) (1938) *Timothy of Rhaithu, Praeparatio* (Orientalia Christiana Analecta 117). Rome.

Douglas, Mary (1987) *How Institutions Think.* London.

Garton, C. and Westerink, L. G. (1979) *Germanos. On Predestined Terms of Life.* Buffalo, NY.

Gero, S. (1974) 'Notes on Byzantine Iconoclasm in the eighth century', *Byzantion* 44: 23–42.

(1975) 'The Eucharistic doctrine of the Byzantine iconoclasts and its sources', *ByzZ* 68: 4–22.

(1981) 'The true image of Christ: Eusebius's Letter to Constantia reconsidered', *JThS* 32: 460–79.

Gouillard, J. (1965) 'L'hérésie dans l'empire byzantin des origines au XII siècle', *T&MByz* 1: 301–24.

(1967) 'Le Synodikon de l'Orthodoxie. Edition et commentaire', *T&MByz* 2: 1–316.

Griffith, S. (1987) 'Anastasius of Sinai, the *Hodegos* and the Muslims', *Greek Orthodox Theological Review* 32: 341–58.

(1990) 'Islam and the Summa Theologiae Arabica; Rabi' I, 264 A.H.', *Jerusalem Studies in Arabic and Islam* 13: 225–64.

Haldon, J. (1990) *Byzantium in the Seventh Century. The Transformation of a Culture.* Cambridge.

Harvey, Alan. (1989) *Economic Expansion and Recovery in the Byzantine Empire 900–1200.* Cambridge.

Hennephof, H. (1969) *Textus Byzantinos ad Iconomachiam Pertinentes.* Leiden.

Henry, P. (1988) 'Forgery as an instrument of progress: reconstructing the theological tradition in the sixth century', *ByzZ* 81: 284–9.

Herrin, J. (1987) *The Formation of Christendom.* Oxford.

Kazhdan, A. and Epstein, A. Wharton (1985) *Change in Byzantine Culture in the Eleventh and Twelfth Centuries.* Berkeley and Los Angeles, CA.

Kotter, B. (ed.) (1969–88) *Die Schriften des Johannes von Damaskos,* 7 vols. Berlin–New York.

Le Coz, R. (ed.) (1992) *Jean Damascène. Écrits sur l'Islam* (Sources Chrétiennes 383). Paris.

Lemerle, P. (1979–81) *Les plus anciens recueils des miracles de saint Demetrius* I–II. Paris.

(1986) *Byzantine Humanism: The First Phase. Notes and Remarks on Education and Culture in Byzantium from its Origins to the Tenth Century* (Byzantina Australiensia 3). Canberra. Transl. by H. Lindsay and A. Moffat of *Le Premier Humanisme byzantin: notes et remarques sur enseignement et culture à Byzance des origines au Xe siècle* (Bibliothèque byzantine, études, 6). Paris 1971.

Lieu, S. C. (1992) *Manichaeism in the Later Roman Empire and Medieval China,* 2nd rev. edn. Tübingen.

McKitterick, R. (ed.) (1990) *The Uses of Literacy in Early Medieval Europe.* Cambridge.

Mango, Cyril (1963) 'A forged inscription of the year 781', *Zbornik Radova Vizantološkog Instituta* 8: 201–7.

(1972) *The Art of the Byzantine Empire 312–1453.* Englewood Cliffs, NJ.

(1974) 'La culture grecque et l'Occident au VIIIe siècle', in *I problemi dell'Occidente nel secolo VIII* (Settimane di Spoleto 20) 683–70. Spoleto.

(1975) 'The availability of books in the Byzantine empire, AD 750–850' in *Byzantine Books and Bookmen* (1975) 29–45.

(1978) 'Who wrote the Chronicle of Theophanes?', *Zbornik Radova Vizantološkog Instituta* 18: 9–17.

(1985) *Le Développement urbain de Constantinople (IVe–VIIe siècles)*. Paris.

(1990) *Nikephoros, Patriarch of Constantinople: A Short History*. Washington, DC.

(1992) 'Greek culture in Palestine after the Arab conquest', in Cavallo, de Gregorio and Maniaci (1992) 149–60.

Maraval, P. (1987) 'Epiphane, "docteur des iconoclastes"', in Boespflug and Lossky (1987) 51–62.

Mondzain-Baudinet, M.-J. (1989) *Nicéphore. Discours contre les iconoclastes. Traduction, présentation, et notes*. Paris.

Mullett, M. (1990) 'Writing in early medieval Byzantium', in McKitterick (1990) 156–85.

Munitiz, J. (1974) 'Synoptic Greek accounts of the seventh council', *REByz* 32: 147–86.

(1988) 'Catechetical teaching-aids in Byzantium', in Chrysostomides (1988) 69–83.

ODB (1991) *Oxford Dictionary of Byzantium* I–III. New York / Oxford.

Oikonomides, N. (1972) *Les Listes de préséance byzantines des IXe et Xe siècles*. Paris.

(1987) 'De l'impot de distribution à l'impot de quotité à propos des premiers cadastres byzantins (7e–9e siècles)', *Zbornik Radova Vizantološkog Instituta* 26: 9–19.

Reinink, G. J. and Vanstiphout, H. L. J. (eds.) (1991) *Dispute Poems and Dialogues in the Ancient and Mediaeval Near East*. Leuven.

Richard, M. (1964) 'Florilèges spirituels grecs', *Dictionnaire de Spiritualité* V, s.v. Paris.

Riedinger, R. (ed.) (1979) *Lateinische Übersetzungen griechischer Häretikertexte des siebenten Jahrhunderts* (Sitz. österr. Akad. der Wiss. 352). Vienna.

(1984) *Concilium Lateranense a. 649 celebratum* (Acta Conciliorum Oecumenicorum II.1). Berlin.

(1990) *Concilium Universale Constantinopolitanum. Actiones I–XI* (Acta Conciliorum Oecumenicorum II.2.1). Berlin.

Sahas, D. (1986) *Icon and Logos. Sources in Eighth-century Iconoclasm*. Toronto.

Scott, Alan (1992) *Origen and the Life of the Stars. A History of an Idea*. Oxford.

Schulz, H.-J. (1986) *The Byzantine Liturgy*, Eng. transl. New York.

Shepard, J. and Franklin, S. (eds.) (1992) *Byzantine Diplomacy*. Aldershot.

Speck, P. (1986) 'Klassizismus im achten Jahrhundert. Die homelie [*sic*] des Patriarchen Germanos über die Rettung Konstantinopels', *REByz* 44: 209–27.

(1990) *Ich bin's nicht. Kaiser Konstantin ist es gewesen* (Poikila Byzantina 10). Bonn.

Stein, D. (1980) *Der Beginn des byzantinischen Bilderstreites und seine Entwicklung bis in die 40e Jahre des 8. Jahrhunderts* (Miscellanea Byzantina Monacensia 25). Munich.

Taft, R. (1980–1) 'The liturgy of the Great Church: an initial synthesis of structure and interpretation on the eve of Iconoclasm', *DOP* 34–5: 45–76.

Uthemann, K.-H. (1985) *Anastasius Sinaites. Sermones duo in constitutionem hominis secundum imaginem Dei, necnon opuscula adversus monothelitas* (Corpus Christianorum series graeca 12). Louvain.

Van den Ven, P. (1957) 'La patristique et l'hagiographie au concile de Nicée de 787', *Byzantion* 25–7: 325–62.

Van Dieten, J.-L. (1972) *Geschichte der Patriarchen von Sergios I bis zum Johannes VI (610–715)* Amsterdam.

Walter, C. (1987) 'Le souvenir du IIᵉ Concile de Nicée dans l'iconographie byzantine', in Boespflug and Lossky (1987) 167–83.

Weitzmann, K. (ed.) (1955) *Late Classical and Medieval Studies in Honor of A. M. Friend, Jr.* Princeton, NJ.

Whitby, Michael (1992) 'Greek historical writing after Procopius: variety and vitality', in Cameron and Conrad (1992) 25–80.

Wilson, N. G. (1983) *Scholars of Byzantium.* London.

Winkelmann, F. (1985) *Byzantinische Rang- und Ämterstruktur im 8. und 9. Jahrhundert* (Berliner byzantinische Arbeiten 53). Berlin.

(1987a) *Quellenstudien zur herrschenden Klasse von Byzanz im 8. und 9. Jahrhundert* (Berliner byzantinische Arbeiten 54). Berlin.

(1987b) 'Die Quellen zur Erforschung des monoergetisch-monotheletischen Streites', *Klio* 69: 515–59.

Wood, D. (ed.) (1992) *The Church and the Arts* (Studies in Church History 28). Oxford.

Index

abbreviation, 115–16
Abydos, 56
Achaemenid empire, 10, 15; *see also* Persia
Achaemenids, 57, 61
addresses, 113, 114
Aeschines, 35
Alamanni, 180
Alexander the Great, 69, 72
Alexandria, 67, 73, 76; Library of, 67; Martyrs of, 8
Amasis, 51, 55
Ambrose, 194
Ammianus Marcellinus, 168, 170
Anastasius of Sinai, 200, 202, 203, 205, 212
Antioch, 140
Apologeticus Maior, 207
Apries, 51
archives, 35, 36, 45, 110, 162, 163, 164, 167
Arianism, 206
Aristophanes, 44
Aristotle, 35
army, Roman, ch. 8 passim
Artemidorus, 131
Arval Brethren, 13
Assyrian empire, 19, 26
Athens, 15, 34, 38, 40–50 passim; assembly of, 1, 41, 42, 43, 48, 50; empire, of, 43
Attila, 186
Augustine, 139, 145, 183, 194

Babatha, 102
Babylonia, 25–6, 52
barbarians, 84, 89, 90, 94–7, 177
Bardaisan, 152, 155
Basil of Caesarea, 194
Batavians, 111, 124
Bede, 133
Behistun inscription, 2, 8, 19, 20, 22, 28, 32; *see also* Darius
Ben Sira, Treatise of, 105–6
Bible, 99, 154, 178–9; *see also* New Testament, Gospels, Pentateuch, Septuagint

bilingualism, 11, 12, 28, 73, 78, 153, 155, 159
bishops, 128, 134, 135, 136, 137, 138, 194, 195
Book of Ceremonies, 163, 194, 214, 215
Book of the Dead, 57
Book of Llandaff, 190
book-burning, 36–7
books, 199, 212
Breviary, 191
Britain, ch. 8 passim
Bu-Njem, 119
bureaucracy, 9, 10, 15, 18, 34, 35, 36, 49, 50, 70, 72, 73, 74, 77, 78, 79, 94 ch. 11 passim, 182, 184, 185, 188
Burgundy, 180, 189
Byzantium, ch. 13 passim

Caesar, Julius, 90, 93, 115
Canopus Decree, 6
Carians, 55
Carthage, 136; Council of, 139
Carthaginians, 86–7
Cartonnage, see writing-materials (papyrus)
Cassiodorus, 192, 194
catacheseis, 203
Catullus, 117
Celts, 85, 112, 125
censorship, 7, 8, 36–7, 53
census, 74, 75, 90
Cerialis, Flavius, 111, 114, 117, 122, 124
Chalcedon, council of, 206
Chalcedonians, 204
chancery, 116
children, 24, 25
Chnodomarius, 181
Christianity, 9, ch. 9 passim, 155, 158, 179, 194, ch. 13 passim
Christians, 6, 8, 12, 13, 99, ch. 9 passim, ch. 13 passim
Church, 12, 104, ch. 9 passim, ch. 13 passim; *see also* Councils
Cicero, 182, 183
Cleisthenes, 38

245